Y0-BDO-090

Physics Careers, Employment and Education

(Penn State, 1977)

AIP Conference Proceedings
Series Editor: Hugh C. Wolfe
No. 39

Physics Careers, Employment and Education

(Penn State, 1977)

Editor
Martin L. Perl
Stanford Linear Accelerator Center

American Institute of Physics
New York 1978

L.C. Catalog Card No. 77-94053
ISBN 0-88318-138-X
DOE CONF-770861

ACKNOWLEDGEMENT

The Conference Steering Committee is very grateful for the financial support of the Conference by the following organizations:

The Bell Telephone Laboratories

The Committee on Education of the American Physical Society

The Committee on Professional Concerns of the American Physical Society

E.I. du Pont de Nemours and Company

The Ford Motor Company

The Forum on Physics and Society of the American Physical Society

The General Electric Company

The International Business Machines Corporation

PREFACE

A Conference on Changing Career Opportunities for Physicists was held at The Pennsylvania State University on 1-3 August 1977. The Conference was sponsored by the Forum on Physics and Society, the Committee on Education, and the Committee on Professional Concerns of the American Physical Society and by the American Association of Physics Teachers.

The purpose of this Conference was to study present and future manpower problems in the physics profession. What changes in traditional employment patterns have taken place and will take place? What nontraditional employment possibilities have developed? How should the physics community act to broaden the opportunities open to its new members? Should the universities further revise their programs and attitudes?

This conference was a sequel to that on Tradition and Change in Physics Graduate Education, held in the summer of 1974 at The Pennsylvania State University. The first conference provided a valuable interchange among physicists in government, industries, and universities. There, the central question was: "Does the traditional training in physics serve the best interest of society, of the physics community, and of the individual physicist?" There have been changes in the physics profession, especially in attitudes, in recent years, and this Conference took a new, realistic look at these problems.

The breadth and depth of the Conference is demonstrated by these Proceedings. All aspects of physics employment and physics careers were discussed by speakers from government, from industry — both traditional and non-traditional, and from the academic world. In addition, many areas of physics education relevant to careers in physics were examined. The speakers and participants included undergraduate students, graduate students, physicists doing applied research, physicists doing basic research, managers, administrators, employment and manpower experts, self-employed physicists, and physics teachers at all levels from the junior college thru the university. We hope that the readers of these Proceedings not only find the Proceedings useful and interesting, but that they can also feel some of the excitement that was generated at the Conference by having participants from so many different parts of physics.

The Steering Committee of the Conference consisted of Roland H. Good, Jr. (co-chairman), Martin L. Perl (co-chairman), Ralph A. Alpher, Barry M. Casper, W. Dale Compton, Frederick J. Darnell, Lee Grodzins, David W. Hafemeister, Roger M. Herman, Allan Hoffman, E. Leonard Jossem, William H. Kelly, Thomas L. Neff, Brian Schwartz, Thomas P. Sheahen, Stanley J. Shepherd, Mary L. Shoaf, and Vigdor L. Teplitz.

We wish to gratefully acknowledge the work of the production editor of these Proceedings, Karen Goldsmith.

Martin L. Perl
Stanford Linear Accelerator Center
Stanford, California
October, 1977

TABLE OF CONTENTS

A: Facts, Myths, and Projections. Chmn. M. L. Perl

THE WORK OF THE PHYSICS MANPOWER PANEL

Milan D. Fiske
General Electric Corporate Research and Development
Schenectady, N.Y. 12301

ABSTRACT

The Physics Manpower Panel is an ad hoc committee of the American Physical Society charged with describing long-term trends in the supply and demand for doctoral physicists, discerning potential improvements which should be made in their training, and recommending appropriate actions to the APS Council. This paper introduces the studies being performed concerning career paths and supply and demand, which are detailed in the following four papers. It also describes briefly the current status of work on regional academia-industry conferences, quality indicators for graduate physics programs, and a proposed study of possible futures of graduate physics education.

The Physics Manpower Panel* was established by the Council of the American Physical Society in February, 1976 on the recommendation of the Panel on Public Affairs and charged with two tasks. The first was to "identify and quantify long-term trends in the supply and demand for physicists" and "to develop a system for periodic updating of these appraisals and for communicating them to appropriate bodies." It is this first task which will be reported upon in some detail in the following four presentations at this session. It is my purpose in this opening remark to give some background for these reports, and then to sketch briefly the content and status of the second of the two tasks of our charge.

The manpower field is characterized more by questions than by good hard data and answers, and it was these unanswered questions that prompted the formation of our Panel. As examples:

What are the employment potentials for physicists now and in the near future in "traditional" physics research and teaching? In "non-traditional" physics, whatever that is? If one leaves traditional physics what is one likely to face; how useful will various

* PANEL MEMBERS

Ralph A. Alpher
Richard H. Bolt
B. S. Chandrasekhar
A. M. Clogston
Conyers Herring
Lee Grodzins
Mary L. Shoaf
Dale T. Teaney
Rolf W. Landauer ('76 only)
G. King Walters ('76 only

SUB-PANEL MEMBERS - TASK I

David Breneman
Richard Hartman

TASK II

Elizabeth Y. Baranger
Donald N. Langenberg

AIP Liaison

Beverly F. Porter

ISSN:0094-243X/78/001/$1.50

parts of one's training have been? How applicable are the skills and attitudes acquired in graduate education in physics to work in a different field, in a different discipline? And so on, no end to them. These questions face particularly the graduate student and the new Ph.D. whose main options may be in unconventional fields, in directions not very well-known in the traditional physics communities.

To attempt to answer some of these questions and related ones, the Manpower Panel proposed a series of studies, subsequently funded by Council. Several of these were addressed via questionnaires, following the employment paths of the new Ph.D. as he/she takes a post-doc, moves into a junior faculty position, leaves that position for another, moves out of academia into conventional physics employment in industry or government, or disappears from traditional physics employment altogether -- or any combination of these courses.

The first of these studies, done jointly with the Professional Concerns Committee, traced the careers of some 280 junior faculty members at 18 universities who did not get tenure appointments during the period 1962-3 to 1975-6. The aim here was to find out where they went, how they got there, what they have been doing and how they feel about their present career and future options. Returns from this pilot study were then used in the design of questionnaires in the succeeding three studies.

In the next, faculty members who had left academia in 1975-76 were queried, seeking where they went and why, what they are doing now and how they regard it, their attitudes toward their graduate physics training, etc. In the third, those who held post-docs in 1973 were questioned in a similar vein. And in a fourth, some 3400 questionnaires were sent to physics Ph.D.'s in industry, seeking information about career paths and attitudes concerning their present careers and their graduate preparation for them.

All of these questionnaires have been designed by Panel members and by the staff in the Manpower Statistics Division of the American Institute of Physics under the general supervision of Beverly Porter. She and Dan Harrison will be discussing this morning what has been learned from the returns, not all of which are in as yet.

The fifth of the studies funded in Task I is one which is certain to attract some of the keenest interest: the projection of supply and demand for Ph.D. physicists. Lee Grodzins has been responsible for this work done largely at M.I.T., and will be telling you about it in the last talk this morning.

All of the foregoing have concentrated almost exclusively on the physics Ph.D. Ted Senator, working with Grodzins, became interested in the non-Ph.D. physicist and has used data in the 1973 Register to produce a profile of that genus. His report will follow these remarks.

Let me now review briefly what the Panel has undertaken under its second major task, namely "to discern those changes which may be needed in the training of physicists to prepare them better for future occupational demands" and "to recommend to Council selected actions the American Physical Society can take in improving the training of physicists." The focus here again is at the doctoral level. This task is, of course, a pretty tall order. Some 176 Ph.D. granting institutions in the United States are actively concerned about the first of these charges, and a standing committee of APS (the Education Committee) about both of them. What an ad hoc committee such as our Panel may hope to contribute is at least fresh point of view and perhaps some specific suggestions. Three new programs are being pursued.

The first is addressed to the improvement of understanding between the academic and the industrial communities concerning the contributions physicists do and can make in industry. Since this was an objective shared also by the APS Committee on the Applications of Physics (C.A.P.) it was fortunate that B. S. Chandrasekhar is a member of both bodies. He proposed and organized the first of what we hope will be a continuing series of regional 2-day conferences, this one on "The Physics of Tires", held at the University of Akron this past April 21 and 22. It drew some 35 professors from 12 graduate departments within a few hundred miles of Akron, plus 15 scientists from 5 rubber companies, plus several others as well. Presentations were made by the participants from industry, and there was ample opportunity for discussion. Quoting from the report by Chandrasekhar and A. N. Gent, "The idea behind the Symposium was to bring together physics professors and scientists from an industry in which physicists are relatively rare, in order to stimulate interaction between the two groups.... We conclude that the Symposium was very successful. The unanimous view was expressed that other such symposia should be organized in the future." There are doubtless other industrial groupings such as textiles in the southeast, or small industry in the northeast, where physicists are little known, for which a regional conference akin to the Akron symposium would also be both instructive and germinal to new relations. What is needed is some local leadership akin to that provided by Chandrasekhar, plus some stimulation and organizational and perhaps financial help from APS. The Panel will make some recommendations to Council on these latter institutional points.

The second of the programs under Task II has been initiated by Mary Shoaf with a subpanel comprising herself, Elizabeth Baranger and Donald Langenberg. They are developing a system of quality indicators for graduate physics programs which a department may apply to itself without outside surveillance. The APS Council has repeatedly opposed any appraisal system exposing departments to the outside world without their concurrence, such as does the accreditation system of the American Chemical Society. Nevertheless there have been recurrent requests from overview bodies to APS or AIP for systematic appraisals of the quality of the graduate physics programs under their purview. For instance, New York State a few years ago reviewed the doctoral programs in several disciplines in all the Ph.D.-granting institutions within the state. Neither APS nor AIP had anything systematic to offer the physics review, but APS was able to suggest an eminently qualified review committee chaired by

Herman Feshbach, which then did the job. The system being developed by the Shoaf subpanel (in cooperation with the Educational Testing Service at Princeton) will enable a department to compare itself with a profile of indicators synthesized from all departments cooperating with the project. Initially to include a sample 25, it would expand to include all departments wishing to cooperate. The Executive Committee of APS has asked the Shoaf subpanel to develop a proposal for NSF funding of the system test with 25 departments, and that program is moving ahead.

The third of the programs under Task II calls for a comphrehensive study on "the best of current thinking and experimentation on graduate physics education" leading to "a report which would present such consensus as was found on what graduate education in physics should become in the next decade or two. The consensus might involve only a common core; beyond that the report would present a representative variety of futures seen by thoughtful educators and physicists." The work on this would be done by a small group of distinguished physicists/physics educators supported by a full-time study director of national stature. The report, perhaps entitled "Futures of Graduate Physics Education," would be of great value to departmental chairmen, deans and others charged with the responsibility for developing curricula for a discipline which faces great uncertainties over the next few decades: What is physics, should it be expected to grow, or will it shrink to a more and more esoteric core? How can it stay alive and vital if it does not grow? How can it attract the very best of young minds? Should graduate education be largely decoupled from university research programs? Should the future physics Ph.D. be more of a generalist? More classically trained? Educated in whatever academic physics is at the moment, or trained for occupational expectations? And so forth. There will be no single answers to these questions and others like them, but it would be useful to those who must plan, to have collections of the best of contemporary thinking about them. This program has been approved in principle by the APS Council, subject to being able to recruit a study director and committee of the calibre required. That search is under way now.

These three programs represent positive contributions to the charge of Task II, I believe, if they can be brought off. But improving the training of doctoral physicists is an open-ended challenge, and we need more good ideas.

I look forward to some of them appearing at this Conference.

PROFILE OF NON-PhD PHYSICISTS

Ted E. Senator
Massachusetts Institute of Technology, Cambridge, MA 02139

ABSTRACT

Data about non-PhD physicists from the NSF-sponsored 1974 National Survey of Scientists and Engineers were analyzed. Use of this survey partially resolves the difficulties of defining non-PhD physicists and of finding an unbiased population group to sample, which were present in earlier studies such as the 1973 AIP-APS Register of Physicists and Related Scientists and the National Register Surveys.

Only 13% of the 16,000 who hold only a baccalaureate degree in physics are employed in physics, 61% are in engineering and 9% in other sciences. These numbers are 28%, 39% and 13% for master's degree holders. Almost everyone employed as a physicist has earned his highest degree in physics, regardless of the level of his degree.

Non-PhDs are employed predominantly by business and industry and, to a lesser extent, research institutes. Less than 2% of baccalaureates teach, and 50% of masters who teach are not employed by four-year colleges and universities.

Non-PhDs are heavily involved in administration, design and development, and other primary work activities.

The salaries of non-PhD physicists are roughly comparable to those of PhDs, probably because the types of jobs held by non-PhDs tend to be higher paying (at a fixed degree level) than those held by PhDs.

The foreign-born component is 3% for bachelor's degree holders, 10% for master's and 23% for PhDs.

INTRODUCTION

A great deal of information is known about PhD physicists* from sources such as the now-discontinued National Register Surveys[1,2] and the 1973 APS-AIP Register of Physicists and Related Scientists.[3] Data about non-PhDs were also obtained in these surveys; however, their validity is uncertain for two major reasons.

---

* The term "physicist" in this report includes astronomers and astrophysicists.

ISSN:0094-243X/78/005/$1.50

The method of population selection and the application of an arbitrary, though not inappropriate, definition of a physicist create questions about the meaningfulness of conclusions that can be drawn from such sources. These problems were partially resolved by the 1974 National Sample of Scientists and Engineers (NSSE),[4] conducted for the NSF by the Bureau of the Census. In this paper, data derived from the NSSE about non-PhD physicists are presented. Data about PhD physicists are also given for purposes of comparison. Different definitional groups are studied, and comparisons with other surveys are made, in order to determine the errors introduced by the population selection and the definition of a physicist.

Analyses of the 1974 NSSE presented here were performed using extracts containing the relevant groups from the 1974 Public Use File, available from the Census Bureau. Data from other surveys are taken from published reports based on them. Only a small fraction of the analyses that were performed are included here; the complete set of tables is available as an appendix.*

The patterns that emerged from the NSSE analysis can be explained by realizing that the non-PhD is less "strongly bound" to physics than the PhD. This causes him to be less involved in traditional work activities such as research and teaching and more likely to be employed in business and industry than his more highly educated colleagues. Because the salaries for researchers are, on the average, lower than those for administrators, the salary difference between non-PhDs and PhDs is smaller than one would guess -- only $3,000/year between bachelor's and PhDs. This is true for all definitional groups, but the salary for those employed as physicists is $1,000/year less than for those whose highest degree is in physics, again because the latter group contains people who have "advanced" out of physics into administrative-type jobs. Master's degree holders are the only group that is employed to a major extent at junior colleges and technical institutes. Four-year colleges and universities employ about 18% of non-PhDs whose occupation is physics, but only 3% of bachelor's degree holders and 11% of master's with physics degrees, an example of the fact that the differences caused by level of degree are more significant in the less restrictive definitional groups. Of the physics degree holders, 95% of the full-time employed non-PhDs are in a science or engineering position, while 98% of the PhDs are. The sex and racial breakdowns exhibit slight degree variations. Only 1% of bachelor's degree physicists are female, while 3% of master's and PhDs are, a fairly insignificant difference. Almost all bachelor's degree physicists are white, while 3% of master's and 6% of PhDs are Chinese, Japanese or Korean.

---

* Due to a programming error which has now been corrected, there are some differences between the numbers presented here and those given at the Penn State Conference. Very slight discrepancies with the values tabulated in reference 4 are due to an uncorrectable computer error.

The foreign-born component is only 3% for bachelor's degree physicists, but it rises to 10% for master's and 23% for PhDs. Regarding the government's relation to physics, almost 65% of bachelor's and PhD physicists receive some federal support, while only 55% of master's degree holders are subsidized by public funds. The areas of national interest in which physicists work, however, do not depend highly on degree.

PRELIMINARIES

The population selection for the 1974 NSSE occurred in two stages. First, the sample for the 1972 Professional, Technical and Scientific Manpower Survey was chosen from those people who, according to the 1970 U.S. Census of Population 20% Sample were in the 1970 experienced civilian labor force and either were employed in scientific, engineering, technical or related occupations, or were employed in other occupations and had completed a minimum of four years of college. The first group, designated as the "target" segment, consisted of 150,358 people and the second, the "residual" population, contained 5,758 respondents. The second stage was the selection from the target segment of the 1974 National Sample. Respondents were classified according to their field of science or engineering in 1972, which was determined by applying a complex set of criteria established by the NSF. The 50,093 people comprising the 1974 NSSE are those who were determined to be "in-scope", i.e., in a field of science or engineering in 1972. Note that no people who entered the labor force between 1970 and 1974 are included in the NSSE. (See references 4 and 5 for more information about the sample selection.)

The Census computed a "weight" for each 1972 respondent to correct for sex, race, age, occupation (in 1970) and non-response (in 1972), and to normalize the results to U.S. totals. The weights vary between about eight and one hundred. All estimates derived from the 1974 NSSE are the sums of these weights. No adjustment for non-response in 1974 was made and, since the 1974 response rate was about 90% for those in the physical sciences, the actual totals are approximately 11% higher than the data presented here. The NSF estimates that the number of scientists and engineers represented by the NSSE is 60% of the total in the United States in 1974. (References 4 and 5 contain detailed explanations of the weighting procedure, which include estimated standard errors.)

The Scientific-Technical Field classification is but one of many possible definitions of a physicist. The actual criteria that were used are quite complex and will not be stated here, but, in general, to be classified as a physicist, a person had to have two of the following three characteristics: (1) employment in physics or a related field, (2) attainment of at least a bachelor's degree in physics or a related field and (3) self-identification as a physicist. (See reference 4 for a complete description of these criteria.)

In addition to the group consisting of those whose 1974 Scientific-Technical Field was physics (designated as STF), two other definitional groups were analyzed. They are OCC, those whose occupation in 1974 was physics (including college and university professors) and MFHD, those whose major field of highest degree as of 1974 was physics. The smallest group, OCC, contains 20,801 people, the next most restrictive one is STF, with 27,482 members, and the largest, MFHD, is comprised of 49,316 persons.

The errors introduced by biases in the sampling procedure are believed to be quite small for both the OCC and STF groups, since the criteria for inclusion in the 1974 NSSE are so similar to the criteria for membership in these subsamples. This is not true for the MFHD group; someone whose highest degree is in physics but has followed a career far removed from science and engineering would not be represented.

The problem of definition becomes more significant when the groups are analyzed according to highest degree. Figure 1 shows the percentage degree distributions for the three groups that were studied, as well as the total number in each group. The percentage of bachelor's degree holders increases as the definition becomes less restrictive, and the opposite is true of PhDs. If the actual numbers are determined (see Table 1, lines 1, 3 and 7), it is seen that the totals also decrease at each degree level as the definition becomes more strict. The difference is most important for bachelor's degree holders, and almost insignificant for PhDs. The ratio of degree-holding physicists to employed physicists is 6.4 at the bachelor's level, 2.5 at the master's level, and only 1.5 for PhDs. Similar effects are obtained for the ratios of MFHD to STF and STF to OCC. Thus, the choice of definition has a much greater impact on the conclusions drawn about non-PhDs than on PhDs.

OTHER SURVEYS

We now compare the 1974 NSSE to the 1973 APS-AIP Register of Physicists and Related Scientists (APS/AIP) and the 1968 and 1970 American Science Manpower (ASM) reports based on the National Register Surveys. Some data from the 1972 Professional, Technical and Scientific Post-Censal Manpower Study (PMS)[5] are also examined. In Table 1 we present degree distributions for various definitions from the above studies.

The STF definition used in 1968, 1970 and 1973 is "an individual with a doctorate, master's or bachelor's degree in physics, plus two years of additional training or the equivalent. Continued involvement in physics or a related field is assumed." The difference between the STF groups in 1973 and in 1968 and 1970 is due to the ability to apply the same definition more rigorously in 1973

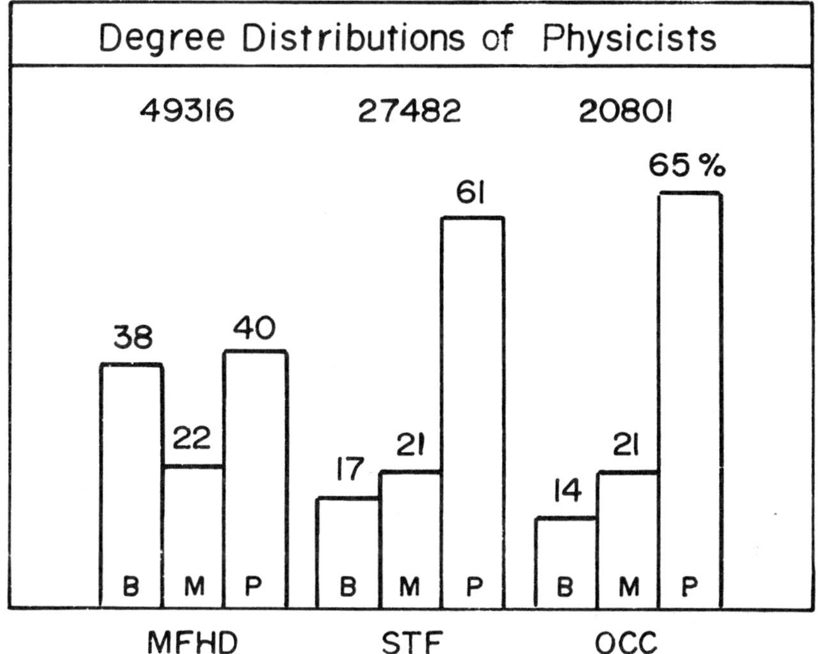

B Bachelor's
M Master's
P Ph D

Figure 1

TABLE 1

Effect of Definition and Survey

Definition	Survey	Year	Bachelor's No.	%	Master's No.	%	PhD No.	%	Total No.
OCC	NSSE	1974	2,877	14	4,440	21	13,484	65	20,801
OCC	PMS	1970	7,904	25	9,636	30	14,725	46	32,269
STF	NSSE	1974	4,785	17	5,846	21	16,851	61	27,482
STF	APS/AIP	1973	4,498	13	10,380	30	19,722	57	34,600
STF	ASM	1970	7,342	20	12,215	34	16,631	46	36,238
STF	ASM	1968	7,239	22	10,776	33	14,311	44	32,326
MFHD	NSSE	1974	18,508	38	11,054	22	19,754	40	49,316
MFHD	PMS	1972	21,941	47	10,772	23	14,017	30	46,730
MFHD	ASM	1970	7,044	23	9,864	32	13,531	44	30,439
MFHD	ASM	1968	5,760	22	8,148	32	11,800	46	25,708

Summary of Terminology (see text)

OCC Occupation
STF Scientific-Technical Field
MFHD Major Field of Highest Degree
NSSE National Sample of Scientists and Engineers
PMS Post-Censal Manpower Study
APS/AIP APS/AIP Register
ASM National Register

because of additional information available in the APS/AIP questionnaire. It was not possible to determine a person's work experience in physics from the ASM; it was assumed to be the same as his total professional work experience. This accounts for two apparent anomolies in the data -- the lower number of non-PhDs in 1973 than in 1970 and the larger number of STF physicists than MFHD physicists at all degree levels in both the 1968 and 1970 ASM reports. In 1968 and 1970, both people who had earned physics degrees and were no longer working in physics and people who had not earned physics degrees but were working in physics were included in the STF group; since only the former were also in MFHD, it appears to contain fewer respondents. Some measure of consistency was restored in 1973 as individuals who had moved out of physics were excluded. This partially accounts for the lower number of non-PhD physicists in 1973 than in 1970. The only difference between the 1968 and 1970 ASM groups is the total, the degree distributions remain the same. The effect of definition on this survey is similar -- a reflection of the effective similarity of the two different criteria.

Other differences between studies were caused by the sampling procedure. The methodologies for the 1968, 1970 and 1973 surveys were very much alike. Mailing lists were developed by the AIP, and questionnaires were sent to everyone. This, of course, introduces a bias against inclusion of people who are further removed from physics, i.e., people who would be in the MFHD group but not in STF or OCC. The 1972 PMS is the most comprehensive survey since it was based on the 1970 Census, and it includes everyone in a scientific, engineering, technical or related occupation. The reason for the large number of non-PhDs (17,540) employed in physics is not well understood; a guess would be that the definition "employed in physics" had a different meaning to those responding to the 1970 Census than to the NSF and other survey-sponsoring organizations.

RESULTS

1. Overlap Between Definitional Groups

The different definitional groups overlap to a considerable extent. Figure 2 shows the occupations of physics degree holders. Most notable is the decrease in the proportion of engineers by a factor of six and the corresponding increase in the proportion of physicists between bachelor's and PhDs. The chances of being employed as a physicist are only 13%* for someone who stops at the bachelor's degree level. The converse, however, is not true. Of those employed as physicists, 87% of the bachelor's, 78% of the

---

* The 16% number given earlier included 3% who reported their occupations as "other physical science". We absorb this group into the "other natural science" category.

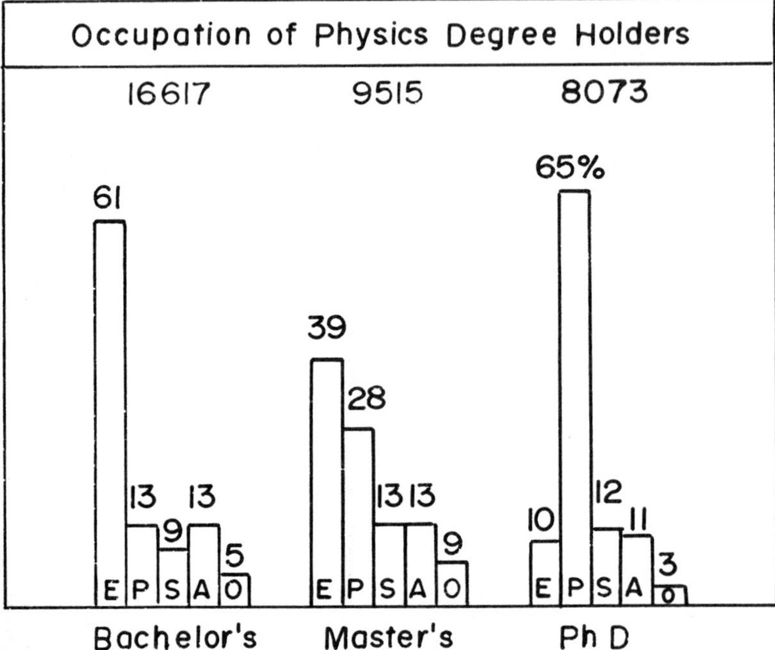

E - Engineer
P - Physicist
S - Other Natural Scientist
A - Administrator
O - Other

Figure 2

master's and 92% of the PhDs hold their highest degree in physics. The remainder were educated in engineering, other physical sciences, and the mathematical sciences. Philosophy is also represented at the bachelor's level, and education becomes significant at the master's level. These numbers increase to 92%, 87% and 95% when the STF group is analyzed. Almost all employed physicists satisfy the NSF criteria for being in the physics category, while only 27% of the bachelor's, 52% of the master's and 83% of the PhDs who majored in physics are considered by the NSF to be in physics. Engineering and other physical sciences are the two fields comprising most of the remainder, with a significant proportion (9%) of bachelor's degree holders in computer specialties. Of those whose STF is physics, 61% of the bachelor's, 73% of the master's and 81% of the PhDs are employed as physicists. About 3% are employed in engineering, with the remainder mostly in administration.

2. Employment Status

The employment status data are somewhat misleading, and they illustrate the major sources of errors that are made by use of the NSSE. We present the data in Table 2. The major categories are full-time employed, part-time employed, unemployed and not in labor force. The full-time employed group is divided into those in scientific or engineering positions and those who are not, with the latter subdivided by reason for leaving science or engineering. Clearly, everyone in OCC is in a scientific position, and almost everyone in that group is employed. (It is not clear how someone's occupation in 1974 could have been physicist if he was not employed in 1974.) The "not in labor force" category is inflated due to retirements that occurred after the original sample selection in 1970. Similarly, the "not in science or engineering position category" would be decreased because the population selection depended very heavily on employment in science or engineering. Non-PhDs in OCC and STF are more likely to be unemployed than PhDs in the same groups; however, this does not apply to members of MFHD. Perhaps this means that non-PhDs hurt their employment prospects by a desire to remain in physics. Part-time employment is fairly high for non-PhDs, while it is no more than 3% for PhDs. This is most true for the two more restrictive definitions. Because of the small numbers involved, few meaningful conclusions can be drawn from the reason for leaving science or engineering data.

3. Work Description

Analyses of employment sectors and primary work activities were performed for all three definitional groups. Only full-time employed respondents were included. Non-PhDs exhibited a dependence on definition, while PhDs did not. The employment sectors are as follows: (1) four-year colleges and universities (AC), including medical schools, (2) other academia (AO), including junior colleges, technical institutes, secondary schools and other educational institutions, (3) research institutes (RI), (4) business and

TABLE 2

Employment Status

Definition	Employment Status	Bachelor's No.	Bachelor's %	Master's No.	Master's %	PhD No.	PhD %
Occupation	Full Time	2,466	86	3,605	81	12,873	95
	Part Time	296	10	588	13	334	2
	Full/Part Time Unknown			86	2	25	
	Unemployed	12		12		74	1
	Not in Labor Force	103	4	149	3	178	1
	TOTAL	2,877	100	4,440	100	13,484	100
Scientific-Technical Field	Full Time	4,029	84	4.723	81	15,602	93
	In Sci/Eng Position	3,762	79	4,469	76	15,404	91
	Not in Sci/Eng Position	254	5	242	4	187	1
	Preferred Non-Sci/Eng	133	3	119	2	33	
	Promoted Out of Sci/Eng	27	1	52	1	17	
	Pay Better in Non-Sci/Eng			12			
	Locational Preference						
	Sci/Eng Not Available	43	1	59	1	125	1
	Other	51	1			12	
	Part Time	308	6	662	11	448	3
	Full/Part Unknown			125	2	25	
	Unemployed	199	4	52	1	74	
	Not in Labor Force	249	5	284	5	702	4
	TOTAL	4,785	100	5,946	100	16,851	100
Major Field of Highest Degree	Full Time	16,774	91	9,527	86	18,098	92
	In Sci/Eng Position	15,898	86	9,034	82	17,765	90
	Not in Sci/Eng Position	823	4	481	4	298	2
	Preferred Non-Sci/Eng	328	2	257	2	106	1
	Promoted Out of Sci/Eng	211	1	52		17	
	Pay Better in Non-Sci/Eng	55		24		12	
	Locational Preference			14		12	
	Sci/Eng Not Available	90		134	1	125	1
	Other	139	1			26	
	Part Time	650	4	803	7	619	3
	Full-Part Unknown	90		139	1	41	
	Unemployed	277	1	192	2	138	1
	Not in Labor Force	717	4	393	4	858	4
	TOTAL	18,508	100	11,054	100	19,754	100

industry (BI), (5) government (GV) and (6) other (OT). Primary work activities are (1) research (R), (2) teaching (T), (3) administration (A), (4) design and development (D) and (5) other (O), including consulting, report and technical writing, quality control, operations, distribution, statistical work and computer work. Table 3 displays employment sector information and Table 4, primary work activity data. Table 5 is a breakdown by both employment sector and primary work activity of STF. Figures 3 and 4 present the employment sector and primary work activity distributions, also for STF.

The major distinguishing characteristic of non-PhDs is their not being employed in four-year colleges and universities. Even among those who are still doing physics, less than 20% are employed in this category. Bachelor's degree holders are employed mainly in business and industry, except for those who are working as physicists, who are employed mainly in research institutes. Government directly employs about 10% of non-PhDs, compared with only 4% of PhDs. Master's degree holders are the only group that is employed to a significant extent in other academia. The absolute number of non-PhDs in academia does not vary much with definition; it is the number in business and industry and in government that accounts for the major portion of the difference between non-PhDs in the two less restrictive groups and in MFHD. What this means is that if a non-PhD wishes to be employed in physics, he must stay in academia, and his chances are still much smaller than if he has a PhD.

A similar pattern is present in the primary work activity data. Non-PhDs are more amply represented in the administration, design and development, and other categories. The greatest number of non-PhD degree holders are employed in these three areas. The largest increment in administration occurs between the OCC and STF groups, but for the other non-researchers or teachers it occurs between STF and MFHD. This is most likely due to the particular criteria that were established for the STF definition; an administrator with a physics background was considered to be a physicist while an engineer with a physics background was regarded as an engineer. The traditional, i.e., research and teaching, categories are quite interesting. Combined, the percentage is greater for both the higher degree holders and the more restrictive definitional groups, just as would be expected. The same effect occurs for the teaching category alone. A surprisingly large fraction of bachelor's degree holders in OCC and STF is employed doing research. It is believed that this reflects the fact that in order for a bachelor's degree holder to be employed as a physicist, he must actually be working in physics; a graduate degree holder can move further away from physics while still considering himself employed in physics.

The correlations between employment sector and primary work activity are interesting, though not surprising. No bachelor's degree physicists teach in four-year colleges and universities; almost all are researchers (83%) or administrators (14%). Holders of graduate degrees divide up similarly; about 30% are researchers,

TABLE 3

Employment Sector

Definition	Employment Sector	Bachelor's No.	Bachelor's %	Master's No.	Master's %	PhD No.	PhD %
OCC (Full Time Employed)	4-Year Colleges & Universities	431	17	702	19	6,691	52
	Other Academia	48	2	564	16	270	2
	Research Institutes	1,041	42	1,200	33	3,687	29
	Business & Industry	607	25	704	20	1,765	14
	Government	263	11	321	9	266	2
	Other	76	3	114	3	182	1
	TOTAL	2,466	100	3,605	100	12,861	100
STF (Full Time Employed)	4-Year Colleges & Universities	444	11	769	16	7,151	46
	Other Academia	48	1	600	13	282	2
	Research Institutes	1,152	29	1,299	28	4,399	28
	Business & Industry	1,981	49	1,549	33	2,774	18
	Government	314	8	346	7	620	4
	Other	90	2	160	3	352	2
	TOTAL	4,029	100	4,723	100	15,578	100
MFHD (Full Time Employed)	4-Year Colleges & Universities	555	3	1,077	11	8,090	45
	Other Academia	97	1	643	7	291	2
	Research Institutes	2,833	17	1,894	20	4,850	27
	Business & Industry	10,244	61	4,583	48	3,570	20
	Government	2,339	14	930	10	785	4
	Other	666	4	362	4	488	3
	TOTAL	16,734	100	9,489	100	18,074	100

TABLE 4

Primary Work Activity

Definition	Primary Work Activity	Bachelor's No.	Bachelor's %	Master's No.	Master's %	PhD No.	PhD %
OCC	Research	1,214	50	1,281	36	6,050	48
(Full Time	Teaching	48	2	1,001	28	4,313	34
Employed)	Administration	432	18	515	14	864	7
	Design/Development	318	13	375	11	856	7
	Other	438	18	394	11	494	4
	TOTAL	2,450	100	3,566	100	12,577	100
STF	Research	1,226	31	1,297	28	6,452	42
(Full Time	Teaching	48	1	1,047	22	4,369	29
Employed)	Administration	1,547	39	1,200	26	2,511	16
	Design-Development	539	13	428	9	914	6
	Other	640	16	687	15	1,049	7
	TOTAL	4,000	100	4,659	100	15,295	100
MFHD	Research	1,894	11	1,903	20	7,253	41
(Full Time	Teaching	109	1	1,244	23	4,808	27
Employed)	Administration	4,497	27	2,497	27	2,888	16
	Design/Development	3,880	23	1,873	20	1,406	8
	Other	6,133	37	1,805	19	1,362	8
	TOTAL	16,513	100	9,322	100	17,717	100

TABLE 5

Employment Sector and Primary Work Activity
of Full Time Employed STF Physicists

Type of Employer & Primary Work Activity	Bachelor's No.	Bachelor's %	Master's No.	Master's %	PhD No.	PhD %
All Employers						
Research	1,226	31	1,297	28	6,452	42
Teaching	48	1	1,047	22	4,369	29
Administration	1,547	39	1,200	26	2,511	16
Design/Development	539	13	428	9	914	6
Other	640	16	687	15	1,049	7
SUBTOTAL	4,000	100	4,659	100	15,295	100
Unknown	29		64		307	
TOTAL	4,029		4,723		15,602	
4-Year Colleges & Universities						
Research	368	83	220	29	2,255	32
Teaching			441	58	4,141	59
Administration	63	14	61	8	491	7
Design/Development			12	2	30	
Other	13	3	24	3	106	2
SUBTOTAL	444	100	758	100	7,023	100
Unknown			11		128	
TOTAL	444		769		7,151	

Table 5 con't.

Other Academia						
Research					54	20
Teaching	48	100	541	92	216	80
Administration			35	6		
Design/Development						
Other			11	2		
SUBTOTAL	48	100	587	100	270	100
Unknown			13		12	
TOTAL	48		600		282	
Research Institutes						
Research	573	50	622	49	3,032	71
Teaching					12	
Administration	345	30	260	20	765	18
Design/Development	127	11	172	13	200	5
Other	107	9	221	17	283	7
SUBTOTAL	1,152	100	1,275	100	4,292	100
Unknown			24		107	
TOTAL	1,152		1,299		4,399	
Business & Industry						
Research	164	8	303	20	839	31
Teaching						
Administration	1,035	53	677	44	793	29
Design/Development	350	18	208	14	684	25
Other ——	419	21	345	23	422	15
SUBTOTAL	1,968	100	1,533	100	2,738	100
Unknown	13		16		36	
TOTAL	1,981		1,549		2,774	

Table 5 con't.

Government						
Research	73	23	87	25	150	25
Teaching			65	19		
Administration	90	29	109	32	350	58
Design/Development	62	20	36	10		
Other	89	28	49	14	108	18
SUBTOTAL	314	100	346	100	608	100
Unknown					12	
TOTAL	314		346		620	
Other						
Research	48	65	65	41	122	35
Teaching						
Administration	14	19	58	36	112	32
Design/Development						
Other	12	16	37	23	118	34
SUBTOTAL	74	100	160	100	352	100
Unknown	16					
TOTAL	90		160		352	

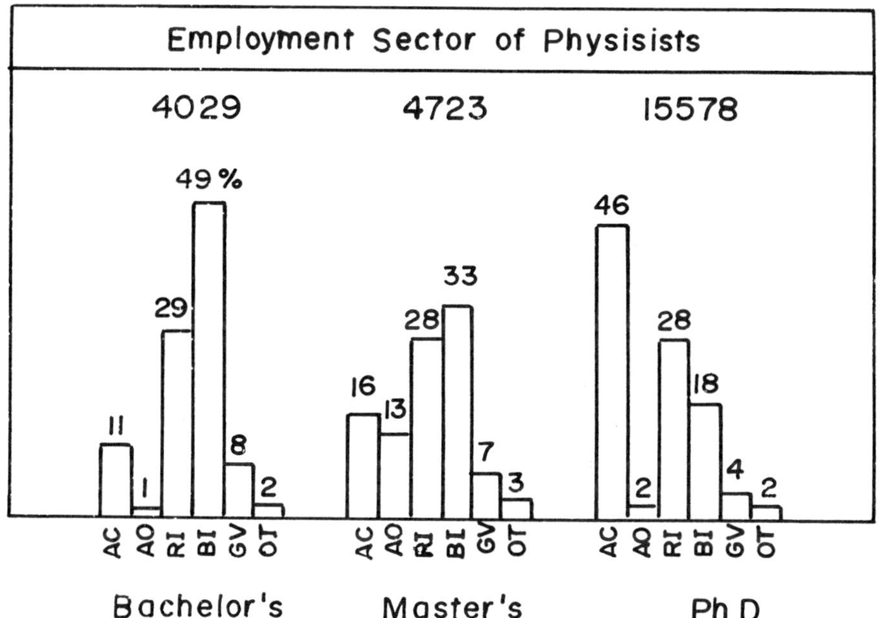

Employment Sector of Physisists
4029
4723
15578
49 %
29
11
1
8
2
33
28
16
13
7
3
46
28
18
2
4
2
AC AO RI BI GV OT
AC AO RI BI GV OT
AC AO RI BI GV OT
Bachelor's
Master's
Ph D

Figure 3

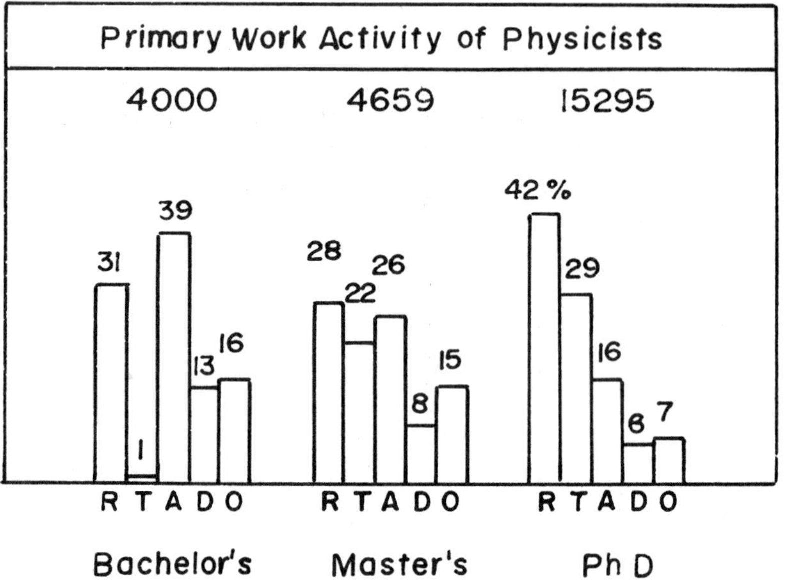
Primary Work Activity of Physicists
4000
4659
15295
31
1
39
13
16
28
22
26
8
15
42 %
29
16
6
7
R T A D O
R T A D O
R T A D O
Bachelor's
Master's
Ph D

Figure 4

60% teachers, and 10% administrators. Although there is no significant difference in this distribution between master's and PhDs, the absolute numbers differ by nearly a factor of 10. Almost everyone employed in other academia teaches, regardless of the level of his highest degree. Only 50% of non-PhDs employed by research institutes are primarily engaged in research; this contrasts with 70% of PhDs. The remainder are administrators, engineers and others. A major degree dependence is exhibited by employees of business and industry. The fraction of people in research increases 23% between bachelor's and PhDs, while the proportion in administration exhibits a decline of almost the same percent. The number in design and development and other is not highly dependent on degree. The number of physicists employed in government is too small to permit any significant generalizations. (It is believed that a large number of people actually employed by government are absorbed into the research institute category.)

4. Salaries

Annual salary rates for 1974 were analyzed for all three groups as a function of employment sector, primary work activity and age. The median was determined, using an estimation process that grouped respondents into $1,000 intervals and assumed a uniform distribution within each interval. Medians were determined only for groups containing more than 200 people (in the weighted sum). The data are presented in Table 6.

A person's salary is slightly higher if he earns a higher degree, regardless of employment sector, primary work activity and age. The apparent counter-examples to this statement are all from groups containing relatively few respondents, except for PhDs under the age of 40. It is believed that their lower salary than master's degree holders is due to their having less employment experience; they enter the labor force at a later age because of the time necessary to earn a PhD. The same effect is not observed for bachelor's and master's degree holders because the time difference here is much smaller. Using years since highest degree instead of age should cause this effect to disappear.

Major differences in salary are not caused by level of highest degree; they depend much more heavily on employment sector, primary work activity and age. These differences in salary due to degree are lessened because non-PhDs are more likely to be employed in sectors and activities that have higher salaries; i.e., business and industry and administration.

The total amount of money earned over the course of a career is about the same, regardless of degree. The incremental median salary between holders of bachelor's and PhD degrees in physics is $2,890/year. Assuming that it takes 5 years (beyond the baccalaureate) to earn a PhD, and it costs $15,190/year in unearned salary, it would take 26 years to break even. Of course, earning

Table 6

Median Annual Salary by Employment Sector,
Primary Work Activity and Age

	OCC			STF			MFHD		
	Bachelor's	Master's	PhD	Bachelor's	Master's	PhD	Bachelor's	Master's	PhD
Employment Sector									
4-Year Colleges & Universities	10,450	15,860	19,140	10,450	16,610	19,120	10,780	17,290	19,290
Other Academia		18,040	16,210		17,710	19,620		14,910	16,200
Research Institutes	19,700	20,720	22,790	19,900	21,980	23,150	19,980	21,730	22,930
Business & Industry	17,350	21,550	23,380	19,670	23,810	24,930	18,830	21,480	24,110
Government	20,030	19,720	25,790	20,750	19,770	30,960	20,770	19,710	28,900
Other						24,360	20,440	22,940	23,790
Primary Work Activity									
Research	17,330	20,560	22,320	17,430	20,600	22,060	19,070	20,330	22,130
Teaching		17,350	19,330		17,170	19,240		16,290	19,330
Administration	24,040	24,380	26,860	22,290	25,550	31,440	22,010	24,740	31,000
Design/Development	18,540	19,850	22,260	19,120	19,960	21,970	18,470	20,120	22,050
Other	16,030	14,890	19,850	17,290	21,310	19,810	18,020	19,960	19,580
Age									
25 - 29	14,410	16,140	13,000	13,970	16,350	10,870	15,190	16,270	13,990
30 - 34	17,080	18,770	17,300	18,090	19,150	17,310	17,410	18,720	17,120
35 - 39	19,890	20,110	20,050	20,320	22,250	20,570	18,920	21,790	20,600
40 - 44	22,070	21,900	23,660	22,080	22,290	23,880	20,900	22,350	23,900
45 - 49			27,760	20,380	24,200	29,110	21,530	22,810	29,700
50 - 54	23,500	22,550	26,310	25,880	22,940	30,160	23,220	23,740	30,130
55 - 59			28,090			35,130	20,360	24,600	31,190
60 - 64						34,250			
TOTAL	18,390	20,270	21,520	19,440	21,110	22,110	19,220	20,590	22,110

the doctorate would cause a person to work different sectors and be engaged in different activities than a non-PhD.

5. Demography and Geography

Data on age, sex, marital status, race, place of birth, father's educational level and place of employment were also analyzed. Figure 5 is the age distribution of STF physicists and Table 7 contains sex and marital status information.

Only 1% of non-PhD physicists are women, while 3% of PhDs are. Further breakdowns of the female physicists are meaningless because of the small numbers involved. Of the men, 82% of the non-PhDs and 91% of the PhDs are married, while 5% of the non-PhDs and only 1% of PhDs are divorced. Almost all bachelor's degree physicists are white, while only 95% of master's and 93% of PhDs are. The remainder are mostly Chinese, Japanese or Korean, with some blacks represented at the master's degree level. The distribution of place of birth is fairly independent of degree for U.S. born physicists. Foreign-born physicists account for 3% of the bachelor's, 10% of the master's and 23% of the PhDs. The educational level of a physicist's father is related to the degree his son will eventually earn. The fathers of 33% of baccalaureate physicists, 47% of master's and 25% of PhDs did not complete high school; 30% of the bachelor's, only 26% of the master's and 41% of the PhDs' fathers graduated from college. Most physicists (80%) are employed in metropolitan areas, in all parts of the country

SUMMARY AND CONCLUSIONS

The employment profile for non-PhD physicists is quite unlike that for PhDs, although the difference tends to be obscured by frequent use of a selection or definition that favors people who follow traditional career paths. People with non-PhD degrees in physics do not, as a rule, do physics. Instead, they branch out into other areas, including engineering and administration. Non-PhDs are not employed in the same type of environments as their more highly educated colleagues; they work primarily for business and industry and, to a lesser extent, research institutes. Almost no physics baccalaureates teach, and of the 13% of master's degree holders who do, one half do so in junior colleges, technical institutes and secondary schools. Despite these differences, and maybe even because of them, the salaries of non-PhDs are nearly the same as those of PhDs. A non-PhD physicist does different things than a PhD, but gets paid almost the same amount because of this.

Some questions about the non-PhD physicist still remain unanswered. Why do non-PhDs leave physics? Are they forced out, do they prefer to leave, or did they earn physics degrees with no intention of continuing in physics? These could be answered by a more comprehensive survey, conducted through either the Census

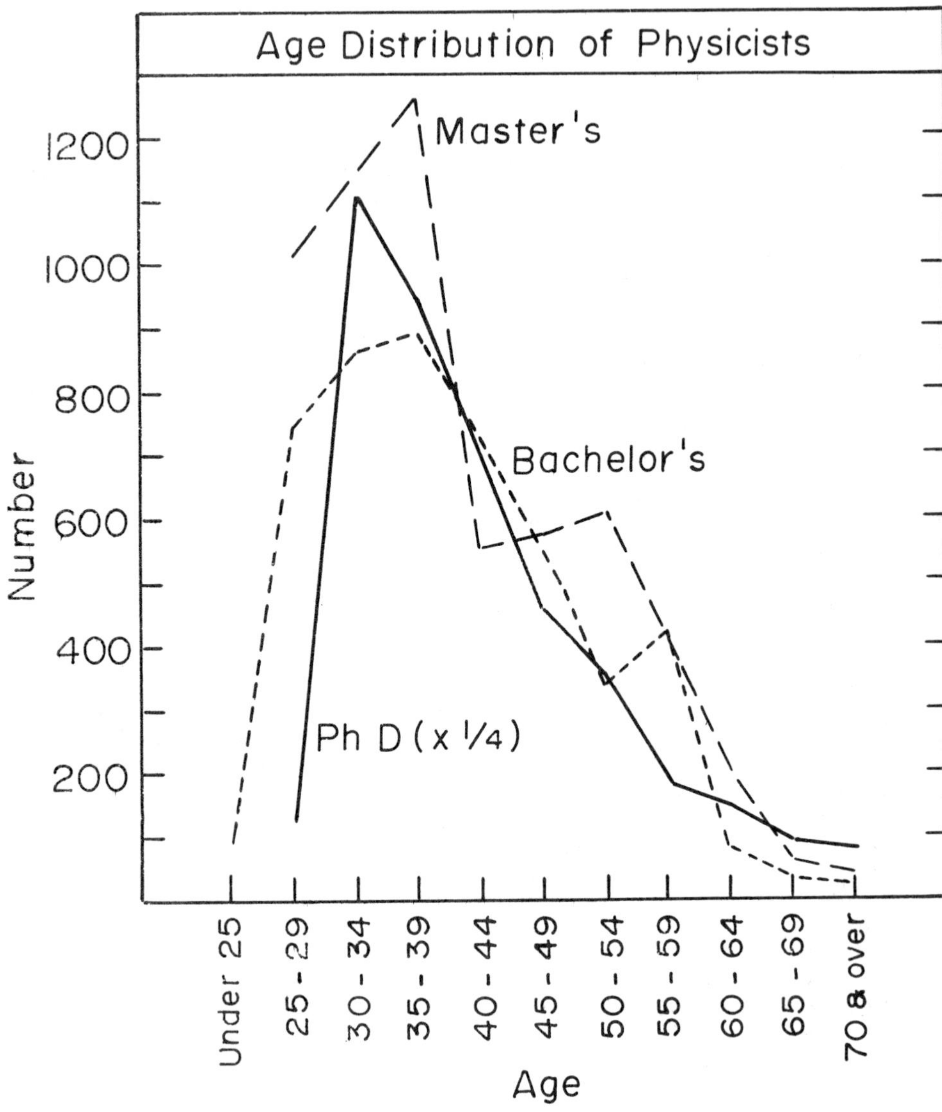
Age Distribution of Physicists
1200
1000
800
600
400
200
Number
Master's
Bachelor's
Ph D (x 1/4)
Under 25
25 - 29
30 - 34
35 - 39
40 - 44
45 - 49
50 - 54
55 - 59
60 - 64
65 - 69
70 & over
Age

Figure 5

TABLE 7

Sex and Marital Status of Physicists

Sex and Marital Status		Bachelor's No.	Bachelor's %	Master's No.	Master's %	PhD No.	PhD %
Married	M	2,090	81	2,742	82	9,039	91
	F	47	100	89	66	268	73
	T	2,137	82	2,831	82	9,307	91
Separated or Divorced	M	132	5	155	5	116	1
	F					31	8
	T	132	5	155	4	147	1
Widowed	M	105	4	12		38	
	F						
	T	105	4	12		38	
Never Married	M	239	9	426	13	695	7
	F			46	34	69	19
	T	239	9	472	14	764	7
SUBTOTAL	M	2,566	100	3,335	100	9,888	100
	F	47	100	135	100	368	100
	T	2,613	100	3,470	100	10,256	100
Unknown	M	2,155		2,314		6,489	
	F	17		62		106	
	T	2,172		2,376		6,595	
TOTAL	M	4,721	99	5,649	97	16,377	97
	F	64	1	197	3	474	3
	T	4,785	100	5,846	100	16,851	100

Bureau or university alumni offices. First, though, it would be useful to determine the size of the errors introduced by basing the sample on occupation and scientific technical field.

We close this paper by posing a more crucial question, one that cannot be so easily answered. Will training in physics continue to be valuable to people who will not, in all likelihood, work in traditional areas of physics after graduation?

I would like to thank Mary K. Friday of the Census Bureau for her help in working with the data, and Doug Gilmore of the University of Illinois for providing the extracts from the 1974 Public Use File. But most of all, I wish to thank Lee Grodzins, who has been a constant source of guidance and assistance, who originally interested me in physics manpower problems, and who suggested the topic for this paper.

REFERENCES

1. American Science Manpower 1970: A Report of the National Register of Scientific and Technical Personnel, National Science Foundation, NSF 71-45.

2. American Science Manpower 1968: A Report of the National Register of Scientific and Technical Personnel, National Science Foundation, NSF 69-38.

3. 1973 American Physical Society - American Institute of Physics Register of Physicists and Related Scientists, several reports by B. Porter, et al., including Physics Today (April 1977).

4. Surveys of Science Resources Series, "Characteristics of the National Sample of Scientists and Engineers 1974", National Science Foundation, Parts 1, 2 and 3, NSF 75-333, NSF 76-323 and NSF 76-330.

5. U.S. Bureau of the Census (Characteristics of Persons in Engineering and Scientific Occupations: 1972), Technical Paper No. 33, U.S. Government Printing Office, Washington, D.C., 1974.

NONACADEMIC PHYSICS EMPLOYMENT: A CHALLENGE TO TRADITIONAL VALUES

Dan Harrison*
American Institute of Physics, New York, N.Y. 10017

ABSTRACT

Our studies indicate that many physicists employed outside academe are reporting just as favorable attitudes toward professional challenge, research facilities, congruence between career goals and nonacademic work, time for research, research funding, and other dimensions of the work situation as they reported for prior academic employment. On most of these dimensions they reported more favorable evaluations of their nonacademic employment than they reported for prior academic employment. To some respondents in our studies this realization came as a surprise. Despite this,however, respondents overwhelmingly indicated at the time they left their faculty position that they preferred academic employment over other types of employment and many never even considered a nonacademic job option when looking for a position to follow their academic employment. This paper analyzes this apparently incongruous result. Evidence suggests that inappropriate stereotyping of nonacademic employment and professional norms concerning "acceptable" forms of employment play a key role in determining whether a physicist will even consider nonacademic employment. In a time of current and projected increases in retrenchment in higher education, these stereotypes and values will become increasingly self-defeating and maladaptive for those who are serious about doing physics.

INTRODUCTION

The tight job market for physicists over the last several years is one of the factors which led the sponsors of this conference and other physicists to investigate more fully the employment opportunities for physicists in a variety of areas,particularly the nonacademic ones. This paper,in a slight departure from this theme, examines some of the professional norms of the physics community concerning "acceptable" physics employment--i.e., that kind of employment which will enhance or at least not diminish the professional status of a physicist who engages in it. The question is, do the norms held by many physicists promote or inhibit the investigation of new avenues of employment for physicists? Based on the preliminary investigations to be reported in this paper, the answer would be that many of the currently held norms appear to serve to inhibit the seeking of varied modes of employment. This is a factor, then, to be taken into consideration by this conference on changing career opportunities for physicists; part of the employment difficulty facing many physicists might be resolved by devising ways to moderate existing norms concern-

*The author wishes to thank his wife, Nancy, and colleague Beverly Fearn Porter for reviewing this paper in some detail. They have contributed much to its strength and appropriately protested its weaknesses.

ISSN:0094-243X/78/029/$1.50

ing "acceptable" physics employment. As the participants consider new modes of employment for physicists they might also ask if physicists themselves are doing all they can to alleviate their employment difficulties by dropping counterproductive notions of employment possibilities.

The data upon which the analysis of this study is based is drawn from one completed American Physical Society study called the Pilot Study and three other APS studies which are now in process--the Industrial Study, the Postdoc Study, and the Follow-Up Study. The Pilot Study is based on the responses of 273 junior faculty who left 17 top-rated U.S. graduate physics departments sometime over the period 1962-1975. The Follow-Up Study is based on the responses of physics faculty who left any U.S. institution of higher education during the 1975/76 academic year and took a nonacademic next position. The Postdoc Study is based on the responses of physicists identified in the 1973 APS-AIP Register of Physicists and Related Scientists as holding a Postdoc in 1973. The Industrial Study is based on the responses of individuals with Ph.D.'s in physics who were identified in the 1973 APS-AIP Register as being employed in industry; for the present paper the responses of the subgroup of industrial physicists who received their physics Ph.D.'s 1969 or later were selected for study. The Follow-Up, Industrial, and Postdoc results reported here are based on the returns from the first wave of mailed questionnaires.

The analysis presented here first looks at respondent evaluations of academic and nonacademic physics employment to determine if physicists are satisfied with nonacademic employment and to determine how it compares with academic employment. Of particular interest is evidence of attitude shifts which occurred after the transition to nonacademic employment. This evidence is used to establish whether respondent stereotypes of nonacademic employment are accurate or not. The analysis then presents evidence on the job options considered by our respondents and the means they used to find employment to see, in a tight job market, just how broadly they have conducted their job search. On the basis of responses to a number of questionnaire items and on the basis of what is known about the professional socialization process, it is then argued that the job search pattern of our respondents is influenced by employment stereotypes and professional norms concerning "acceptable" physics employment and that the character of this influence is to discourage the search for many kinds of nonacademic employment.

RESPONDENT EVALUATIONS OF ACADEMIC AND NONACADEMIC EMPLOYMENT

Eighty-six percent of the Pilot Study respondents now holding nonacademic physics employment reported professional challenge to be satisfactory; this is about the same as the other Pilot Study respondents now holding academic appointments. This is true even though 44% of the academic respondents now hold their appointments in Roose-Andersen-rated physics Ph.D.-granting institutions.[1] In several other key categories the nonacademic employers were a minimum of 18 percentage points more favored than the academic employers; these categories include available research funding, research facilities, number of assistants, salary, and department strength. (Department strength reflects a heavy FFR&DC influence.) Time for research and fringe benefits were found to be more satisfactory for nonacademic employers by 11 percentage points or more. Advancement opportunity was essentially the same for both groups. Academic employment, on the other hand, had a 12 percentage point advantage in use of physics training, a 15 percentage point advantage in autonomy and independence, and a 22 percentage point advantage in job security.* Thus, looking at the results for these two groups of respondents, the currently academically and nonacademically employed, the nonacademic employment compares very favorably with academic employment satisfaction ratings on a variety of significant dimensions.

Initial results from the Follow-Up Study suggest that most of these respondents appear to be either satisfied or very satisfied** with their nonacademic employment in terms of use of physics training, professional challenge, and job security. More than two-thirds are satisfied or very satisfied with their job security; evidently the broader sampling of physicists in the Follow-Up Study reveals a somewhat greater sense of security but a somewhat lesser use of physics training than that experienced by their nonacademically employed counterparts from the 17 top physics departments in the Pilot Study.

There is more direct evidence available from the Pilot Study on the relative satisfactoriness of academic versus nonacademic employment. Respondents were requested to make a direct comparison between their top rated physics departments and their next position on almost all of the dimensions mentioned above. If these respondents are divided into two groups-- those who took academic next positions and those who took nonacademic next positions--the following

---

*Job security ratings are substantially the same for recent Ph.D.'s (defined here as Ph.D.'s obtained 1967 or later) as for the overall distribution of respondents. The higher rating on job security by academic respondents is interesting in light of the present and anticipated difficulties forecast for U.S. institutions of higher education. For an interesting study of this problem touching on such topics as expected institutional closings, revision of tenure rules, dropped programs, etc. see the staff report of the Carnegie Foundation for the Advancement of Teaching, More Than Survival: Prospects for Higher Education in a Period of Survival (Jossey-Bass, San Francisco,1975).

**This finding on professional challenge from the Follow-Up Study and the finding on professional challenge from the Pilot Study does not say anything about the importance to physics of the problems being worked on for the various types of employers but it does suggest,if linked with the finding from both studies that most respondents report satisfactory use of physics training in nonacademic employment, the favorable possibilities for doing physics for nonacademic employers and, thus, should be of interest to this conference as it considers nonacademic physics employment.

results are obtained:

Those who took nonacademic next employment reported substantially higher ratings on research facilities, funds for research, and time for research. Professional challenge, congruence with career goals, autonomy and independence, and number of assistants were rated about the same as for their former top-rated academic position. Other variables such as salary,chance for advancement, job security, and less competition and internal politics were also more highly rated in their nonacademic position. In fact, use of physics training was the only variable not as favored in nonacademic employment as in the former academic position. This is a rather substantial endorsement for nonacademic employment vis a vis academic employment.

On the other hand, those respondents who took academic next employment experienced a substantial decline on several key dimensions--strength of department, research facilities, time for research, and experienced a substantial increase in administrative responsibilities. (For this group, professional challenge, congruence between positions and career goals, use of physics training, and number of assistants declined slightly between five and ten percent.)Evidently, those who went into academic next employment did not fare as well, overall, as those who went into nonacademic next employment.

The Follow-Up Study does not have a question asking respondents to make item-by-item comparisons between their former 1975/76 academic and current nonacademic positions, but respondents were asked to state whether, in general, they preferred their academic position over their current nonacademic position. Almost half indicated they were more satisfied with their nonacademic position, in contrast with just a small percentage who indicated that they were less satisfied with it. One-third preferred some aspects of the academic position and other aspects of the nonacademic position. Another question in the Follow-Up Study asks respondents to indicate the relative professional challenge of academic and nonacademic employment. The vast majority of respondents indicated that physics is just as challenging in a nonacademic setting as in an academic setting. This is additional evidence supporting nonacademic physics employment.

It is also possible to examine these job satisfaction results in terms of more detailed type-of-next-employer breakdowns than just the academic/nonacademic dichotomy. Table I contains data from the Pilot Study for a four-way breakdown of this kind--academic, university-related research centers, Federally Funded Research and Development Centers (FFR&DC's), and industry. A fifth breakdown, U.S. Other types of employers, has been omitted because of the small number of Pilot Study respondents falling in this category.

Consider the case of industry. From Table I it can be seen that those who went into industry feel their position has improved on 14 of 16 dimensions surveyed; the two exceptions are a decline in the use of physics training (down 17 percentage points for these respondents) and a decline in autonomy and independence (down 20 percentage points). The areas of greatest improvement for the industrially employed are research facilities, funds for research, congruence with career goals, time for research, salary, chance for advancement, job security, reduced competition and internal politics, and reduced pressure to publish. Improvements in these categories ranged between 42 and 86 percentage points. Administrative responsibilities increased

Table I. Job Satisfaction Comparisons*
by Type of Next Employer

	Academic	Univ. Res. Centers	FFR&DC	Industry	Government & Gov't. Labs
Stronger Department	-61		-24	45	
More Research Facilities	-29		53	67	
More Funds for Research	-9		59	79	
Greater Prof. Challenge	-1	-40	31	30	
More in Line With Career Goals	-5	20	10	42	
More Time for Research	-25	70	63	65	
Greater Use of Physics Training	-7		-19	-17	
More Autonomy & Independence	48		13	-20	
Higher Salary	56	20	90	86	100
More Chance for Advancement	66	-33	75	85	
More Job Security	70		75	67	63
More Assistants	-10		-4	18	
Less Competition & Internal Pol.	25		45	43	
Less Pressure to Publish	20		41	63	
Greater Range of Activities	27		35	26	38
More Admin. Responsibilities	49		52	47	38
Range in Number of Respondents	40 to 107	5 to 9	8 to 27	6 to 20	5 to 8

*For this Pilot Study data a negative sign indicates a decline from

49 percentage points.

FFR&DC respondents reported very much the same distribution of job satisfaction as the industrial respondents; ratings improved for every comparison with the exception of two items which evidenced decline: department strength declined by 19 percentage points and administrative responsibilities increased by 52 percentage points. Three other dimensions evidenced very little change for FFR&DC respondents: congruence with career goals, autonomy and independence, and number of assistants.

University related research centers and government plus government laboratory respondents were too few to permit meaningful job satisfaction comparisons across all 16 dimensions surveyed. For the university related research centers those items which did have at least a minimal number of responses with which to make comparisons evidenced a mixed employment satisfaction experience: there is an improvement in career congruency, salary, and time for research, and a decline in chance for advancement and professional challenge. Government and government laboratory respondents were sufficiently numerous to permit only four comparisons to be made: in three of these--salary, job security, and range of activities--they registered an improvement over their former academic employment. However they experienced an increase in administrative responsibilities. Increases ranged between 38 and 100 percentage points for this government plus government laboratory group. U.S. Other employer respondents were too few to permit analysis of comparisons.

Academic next position respondents experienced a decline in several professional criteria, while experiencing an improvement in their salary, fringe benefits, and employment setting. Principal professional declines were in department strength, research facilities, time for research, and quality of students, while increasing administrative responsibilities and course loads. The range of decline or increased burden in these categories was 21 to 61 percentage points. Principal gains were in autonomy and independence, salary, chance for advancement, job security, range of activities engaged in, reduced competition and internal politics, and less pressure to publish. Gains in these categories ranged from 20 to 70 percentage points. The remaining categories--all professional items--remained about the same or declined slightly, with a range of decline of 1 to 10 percentage points.

The conclusion, then, of this job satisfaction comparison by type of next employer is as follows: for the FFR&DC and industrially next employed respondents there is little doubt that their employment situation improved after they left academe.* The academically next employed did not appear to fare as well as the FFR&DC or industrially employed respondents: professional criteria declined in many cases while eco-

---

the former top-rated department percentage to the percentage accorded the next position; data are expressed as differences in percentage points. For example, for use of physics training, those who took industry as the next position experienced a decline in physics useage relative to their former academic positions of 17 percentage points. Table entries with fewer than seven respondents are left blank.

*Judging from the commentary added by a number of respondents, this finding came as a surprise to many.

nomic and working conditions benefits improved; FFR&DC and industrially employed respondents, on the other hand, generally experienced increases in both. For the two remaining types of nonacademic employers for which there is sufficient data to make comparisons across a limited number of questionnaire items the government plus government laboratory respondents experienced an improvement in three areas related to pay and working conditions, while experiencing an increase in administrative responsibilities; the other employer type, university related research centers, the employment experience is only partly satisfactory. The U.S. Other employer category has too few respondents to make a comment.

The Follow-Up Study responses to the general comparison between academic and nonacademic employment can also be analyzed in terms of types of employers. Again, because these are first wave results only general tendencies will be noted per employer type. Industrial respondents evidenced an overwhelming proportion favoring their current position over their former academic positon. FFR&DC respondents were fairly split between their former academic and current nonacademic positions. Government plus government laboratory, nonprofits (including university related research centers), and U.S. Other employees had too few responses to permit meaningful comparisons to be made, although it can be noted that nonprofit employees were mostly ambiguous about their present employment; the great majority favored some aspects of their former position and other aspects of their current position. From the preliminary Follow-Up Study data it would appear that there is at least as much satisfaction with nonacademic employment as with academic employment--at least in the case of industry and the FFR&DC's where there is sufficient data to make a comparison.

The net conclusion of the analysis thus far is that there is substantial evidence from the Pilot and Follow-Up Studies that the nonacademic working environment compares quite favorably with, and in most cases, more favorably than, academic employment across a number of significant dimensions. Those that stayed in academe after leaving top-rated physics departments experienced decline in their condition in terms of a number of professional criteria and also experienced a decline relative to their nonacademically employed cohorts on a number of significant dimensions,professional and otherwise.

EVIDENCE ON INCORRECT STEREOTYPING

The preceding analysis presents evidence that physicists have found nonacademic physics employment to be desirable,both in terms of professional criteria and as a way of earning a living. If this is true, the next question is, do physicists perceive that this is the case? Do the images they hold of the nature of nonacademic physics employment accord with reality?

There is some evidence on this point from the Industrial Study in the form of pre-employment versus during-employment attitudes toward industrial employment--a specific form of nonacademic employment. The Industrial Study asks respondents to state their attitudes toward industrial employment while in graduate school (and prior to applying for or accepting an industrial position) and then to state their attitudes toward industrial employment at the present time. These attitudes are to be stated in terms of Likert* evaluations of 11 statements presented in the questionnaire.(This assessment calls for comparisons with academic employment in 7 of the 11 instances.)This comparison is of particular interest because it elicits attitudes from a respondent for a period of time at which he or she usually had no prior contact with professional employment other than academic employment--the period of graduate study--and thus would be selecting career paths in terms of perceived stereotypes of desirable professional physics employment.(These stereotypes, it is later argued, are conditioned by the graduate experience.) In what follows the pre-employment evaluations are compared with respondent evaluations of their current industrial employment to see if a shift has occurred, and if so, what the character of this shift is. The greater the amount of shift, the greater the inaccuracy of the original stereotype of industrial employment. Since the sample of industrial respondents selected for study here received their Ph.D.'s 1969 or later this view is for a fairly recent period of time and during a tight physics job market. Again, since the results reported here are from the first wave of mailings specific percentages are not indicated.

Industrial Study responses for these comparisons indicate that a substantial shift has occurred for several items: perceived physics job opportunity in industry, the competence and accessibility of people in the respondents' area of interest, and control of R&D findings by employers. Some shift also occurs for professional challenge, perceived stress in the work environment, perceived job security, and the visibility of the results of one's work. A slight shift occurs in salary and fringe benefits, freedom in problem selection, and employer interest in sponsoring basic research in physics. A shift of varying amounts occurs, then, for all 11 categories; eight of these shifts occur in a direction favorable to industrial employment.**

Because so much shifting has occurred it does seem from this preliminary data that inaccurate stereotypes of industrial employment _vis a vis_ academic employment did exist in graduate school and because the overwhelming character of these shifts is in a direction favorable to industry, it follows that respondents held prejudicially inaccurate stereotypes of industrial employment while in graduate school. These

---

*A Likert-scaled questionnaire item is one which asks the respondent to select one of 5 possible responses in terms of some symmetric ordinal evaluation criterion such as degree of agreement/disagreement with a given questionnaire item. A typical Likert scale also offers the respondent additional opportunity to forego an evaluational response on such grounds as a failure to recall, lack of information, inability to decide, etc.

**Two of the three shifts that are unfavorable to industry concern academic freedom issues--freedom to publish or communicate the results of one's own research and freedom to select the problems one works on.

data probably come from the most favorably disposed graduate respondents as far as industrial employment is concerned, because all of these respondents eventually took industrial positions. If respondents who took academic rather than nonacademic employment were to be polled on the same questions, it is quite possible that this evidence for inappropriate stereotyping of industrial employment would be even more prominent. It remains to be seen if inappropriate and prejudicial stereotyping also applies to other forms of nonacademic employment.

EVIDENCE ON RESPONDENT JOB-SEEKING BEHAVIOR

Three APS studies--the Pilot, the Follow-Up, and the Postdoc--provide information on the kinds of employers these respondents considered in a tight physics job market. Table II indicates the types of employers these respondents considered in the Pilot Study:

Table II. Employment Options Considered* (Pilot Study)

General Breakdowns	(percentages)	Specific Breakdowns (selected)	(percentages)
University	86	University, Tenure Line	84
Other Academic	35	University, Temporary	29
Industry	32	Four Year Colleges	23
FFR&DC	34	Junior Colleges	4
Government & Government Labs	18	Industrial Research	29
U.S. Other (incl. nonprofits, other science, engineering, miscellaneous)	13	Industrial Development	14
		Industrial Administration	5
		FFR&DC Research	34
		FFR&DC Development	8
		FFR&DC Administration	3
		Government Research	16
		Government Development	5
		Government Administration	5
		Other U.S. Employer Types	7 to 9 (range)

*Respondents may select multiple categories so percentages are not additive across categories.

A university(faculty) position is the one most sought after (86%). The search for other types of employment beyond this drops, however. Thus, industry had a 32% selection rate; FFR&DC's had a 34% selection rate.As the table indicates, the most favored specific types of employment are university (tenure line), university (temporary), industrial research, and FFR&DC research positions. (The selection rate for the university positions was 84%; the selection rates for the remaining three positions were 29%, 29%, and 34%, respectively.)

The Follow-Up Study respondents likewise seek university positions very extensively, but this broader sample of physicists (i.e., from more varied academic positions) seek industrial employment just as extensively. FFR&DC's are also very popular. The remaining modes of employment are much less frequently sought after, particularly the U.S. Other employers. Compared with the physicists from the 17 top-rated physics departments in the Pilot Study, the Follow-Up Study respondents are engaged in a substantially broader job search pattern. Even so, the Follow-Up Study respondents could have given greater consideration to additional types of employers.

The Postdoc Study questionnaire employer categories are roughly comparable to those of the Pilot and Follow-Up Studies. As for the Pilot Study, Postdoc Study respondent interest in university positions dominates the employer types considered. For the Postdoc respondents Industry and FFR&DC positions are much less considered than the university positions; Postdoc and Pilot Study consideration levels for these two employer types are quite similar. The remaining employer types are given only minimal consideration by the Postdoc respondents.

The pattern of respondent search roughly parallels the Roose-Andersen ratings of their former institutions of academic employment. The higher the Roose-Andersen rating of their former academic employer at the time they undertook their job search the greater the tendency to look for university positions and the less other types of employers are considered. The exception to this is the search for Other Academic positions,which draws greater interest from the Pilot Study respondents than the respondents of the other two studies.

The net conclusion concerning breadth of job search, based on the preceding findings, is that for most respondents the types of employers considered could be considerably expanded; even for the most broadly interested group--the Follow-Up Study respondents, there are substantial numbers of respondents who could have expanded their job option repertoire.

If, as the results of the 1973 APS-AIP Register of Physicists and related Scientists indicated,[2] the principal employers of Ph.D. physicists (including postdocs)* are academe, industry, FFR&DC's, and government (including government laboratories) the following evidence indicates that the search pattern within this group is surprisingly limited. Thus, when asked how difficult they thought it would be to find a position when they knew they were going to be leaving their top-rated physics department positions, the Pilot Study respondents who left 1969 or later indicated that they expected to find a tight job market in academe (mean Likert=4.2 on a range of 1 to 5, with 5 indicating a very tight job market) and a somewhat tight job market for the other three categories of employer (mean Likert range 3.4 to 3.5). Despite this, FFR&DC, government, and industrial positions were

*In the 1973 study these four types of employers employed 96% of physics Ph.D.'s.

not even <u>considered</u>, as far as job market conditions are concerned, by 20%, 40%, and 60% of the Pilot Study respondents, respectively. Still, a large number of Pilot Study respondents complained that they experienced substantial difficulty in finding new physics employment after leaving their 17 top-rated physics departments.

Whether the job options considered by the respondents in the Pilot, Postdoc, and Follow-Up Studies reflect the actual division of employment opportunity for physicists remains to be seen, but the fact is that the types of employers they <u>considered</u> for employment could be broader. Except for those who got unsolicited job offers or were able to find positions right away, even the types of employers that <u>are</u> considered are not approached by anywhere near as many of the respondents in the three studies as could have done so.

If attention is drawn to the <u>number of inquiries</u> made to find particular types of positions as an indicator of the amount of effort respondents made to find positions, the effort exerted does not appear to be as extensive as might have been expected, given the tight physics job market. Thus, in the Postdoc study, of the types of employers considered, those by far the most considered by these respondents (university tenure line positions, other university positions, FFR&DC's, and industry) are found to have received only one to five inquiries from the majority of respondents. The most popular choice, university tenure line positions, received only one to five inquiries from most respondents. The remaining three types of employers received only one to three inquiries from the majority of respondents. If an arbitrary criterion of 15 inquiries is used as an indicator of a more strenuous job search then it can be noted that there is a small minority of Postdoc respondents that indicated such an effort was made to find university and industrial positions.

In addition to limited job options being considered and limited search effort being made, there are also few means being employed to locate positions. In the Pilot Study, respondents relied principally on informal colleague contacts to find positions (76% relied on colleagues to act as informal intermediaries to find positions and 46% relied on information from colleagues on job openings).* Forty-four percent of respondents reported they relied on queries <u>from</u> employers and 42% indicated they made direct queries <u>to</u> employers. The remaining kinds of job location means used by these respondents never exceeded 16% (mean useage=8%).**

The Follow-Up Study suggests that the principal means used

---

*Multiple responses are permitted so percentages are not additive across categories. Nonrespondents inflate these percentages by 1%.

**The effectiveness of the principal reliance on the collegial network in finding positions of course requires that there be substantial linkages with nonacademic employers if physics jobs are to be found there by these means. However, it remains to be seen whether contacts in the physics profession are fully extended into the nonacademic sector. Judging from the comments volunteered in the Pilot Study, it seems questionable that this is the case. This is one area where expanded professional communication could improve the job locating strategies of physicists.

to find positions for this broader institutional sampling of physicists are somewhat more extensive than for the elite Pilot Study group, but still quite limited. A substantial group of Follow-Up respondents tries informal or formal direct contacts with potential employers. A smaller, but still substantial, group relies on unsolicited queries from employers, information or contacts of colleagues, and responses to advertisements in professional journals or newsletters. A much smaller percentage of respondents relies on a variety of other means. It does appear that the Follow-Up Study respondents used a much more varied pattern of means to find employment than the Pilot Study respondents did. It is possible that the broader options pattern considered by the Follow-Up respondents, when linked with a broader pattern of means used to locate positions, may account for the broader distribution of subsequent employer types observed for this group, relative to that observed for the Pilot and Postdoc respondents.

THEORY AND EVIDENCE ON THE IMPACT OF PROFESSIONAL NORMS ON JOB-SEEKING BEHAVIOR

In the preceding sections of this paper evidence has been presented indicating, on the one hand, that physicists give active consideration to only a limited number of types of employers (and vary among themselves in the extent to which this limited group of employers is given consideration) and appear to use only a modestly energetic and thorough job location strategy; on the other hand, evidence has been presented that, at least in the case of industrial employment, physicists had acquired inappropriately negative stereotypes of nonacademic employment <u>prior</u> to applying or accepting such positions while in graduate school. Other evidence at the outset of this paper indicates that nonacademic physics employment is in many professionally significant ways just as satisfactory (and in some ways more satisfactory) than academic physics employment; this assessment is even more true for "bread-and-butter" issues such as salary and fringe benefits and for working conditions. In this concluding substantive section of this paper evidence on the "acceptability" of nonacademic physics employment by physics professionals will be presented and utilized in a professional socialization theory explanation for the apparently counterproductive job-seeking orientation and inappropriate stereotyping of nonacademic physics reported above.

Consider, first, evidence from these surveys on the existence of norms concerning nonacademic physics employment. The Follow-Up Study asked respondents to state their degree of agreement or disagreement with the following statement:

> "In terms of professional status, it is preferable for a physicist to select academic rather than nonacademic employment"

About half of the industrial respondents agree with this statement, one-third disagree with it, and one-fifth are neutral on the matter. In this first wave of results there are as yet too few respondents in the other categories of employment to report their responses individually. If the other employer types are treated as an aggregate, one-fifth agree with the statement, about half disagree with it, and one-third are neutral. On the basis of this preliminary data, then, it is not possible to discern a definite trend one way or the other with respect to this questionnaire item from the Follow-Up Study. It is interesting that these physics professionals--all of whom have accepted nonacademic employment--should find it so difficult to arrive at a consensus on this question. While it would not be particularly surprising if the academic "stayers" cohort of the Follow-Up nonacademic "leavers" should indicate a considerable amount of agreement with the above statement, it is a little surprising that the industrial respondents should agree with it and the other employer type respondents cannot arrive at a consensus with respect to it--unless a professional norm is influencing attitudes toward the statement, even among the non-academically employed.

The Follow-Up Study asks an additional question which may throw more light on nature of professional norms concerning nonacademic employment. The Follow-Up respondents were asked to state their degree of agreement or disagreement with the following question:

"My graduate school advisors tended to disparage nonacademic physics employment"

In this study the industrial and FFR&DC respondents are rather evenly divided on this question. Nonprofit employees (including consultants) and government respondents mostly agree with the statement. Government laboratory respondents and U.S. Other employer respondents mostly disagree with the statement. Again, there is a problem of limited numbers to work with in this first wave of Follow-Up results, but early responses, in the aggregate, tend to agree with this statement. From this preliminary evidence it would appear that, at the very least, faculty supposedly in close contact with graduate students--their graduate advisors--presented an ambiguous image about the professional acceptability of nonacademic employment. At worst, they may have actively discouraged it.

The Industrial Study investigated the perceived attitudes of those in the respondent's graduate school milieu in greater detail. Industrial respondents were asked the following question:

"While you were a graduate student what was your perception of the typical attitudes of the following toward the desirability of employment in industry?"

a) thesis advisor
b) other faculty
c) other graduate students and recent graduates
d) other physicists you knew but were not on the faculty of your graduate school

To get a fairly recent picture of the responses to this question only those Industrial Study respondents who obtained their Ph.D.'s 1969 or later were included for analysis. Also, to obtain a greater insight into the graduate physics department milieu influencing these respondents the data was trichotomized in terms of the Roose-Andersen rating of the respondents' graduate institutions (faculty): Upper Roose-Andersen (the 30 leading institutions), Lower Roose-Andersen (the 23 lower-ranked institutions), and the Other U.S. Universities (unranked in the Roose-Andersen study). "Other faculty" at the Upper Roose-Andersen and Lower Roose-Andersen institutions were judged by these

Industrial Study respondents to have conveyed the impression that industrial employment is undesirable. The data is less clear regarding faculty at Other Ph.D. institutions, since most faculty were seen as neutral on the matter. Thesis advisors, student peers and recent graduates, and other physicist acquaintances all tend to be perceived as being neutral on the matter, although there is a tendency to be more supportive of nonacademic employment as one moves from the Upper Roose-Andersen institutions to the Other Ph.D.-granting institutions.

It is the "other faculty" and "thesis advisor" results which are of particular interest since graduate students are not the ones, in general, that set the professional standards which graduate students aspire to and since many graduate students may not have non-faculty physicist acquaintances. Faculty attitudes are of particular importance because it is this group which serves as the prime vehicle for the professional socialization of the graduate student--it is a prime model for professional values and behavior. In a variety of ways it is the faculty that convey to the student what physics is all about--what problems are important, what it is that physicists do, and how they do it. This is conveyed in lectures, seminars, publications, informal conversations, research projects, colleague relations, and other ways. A substantial and growing body of literature on the subject of professional socialization provides empirical evidence and theory suggesting that such a faculty role exists in a variety of graduate and professional fields.* The relative importance of the thesis advisor versus other faculty in this socialization process is less well known, however.

It is interesting that no group identified in the questionnaire item turned out, in the aggregate, to be <u>supportive</u> of nonacademic physics employment, even in the job crunch. Not all respondents felt that this was true of their faculty, associates, or peers, but the majority did. This is more true of the Roose-Andersen rated physics departments than the Other Ph.D.-granting departments, as noted.**

---

*See, for example, studies by Kendall and Selvin[3], Huntington,[4] and Becker, et. al.[5] Moore [6] draws attention to the role of significant others (respected and esteemed advanced graduate students and faculty) in internalizing professional norms in the graduate and professional schools. Jencks and Riesman[7], in a study of arts and sciences Ph.D. departments and five types of professional schools concludes that a key role of these entities is to socialize students into professional norms.

**For an extended discussion of the disinterested posture of graduate arts and sciences departments toward nonacademic research and employment see Chapter V in Jencks and Riesman (<u>ibid</u>.). These authors suggest that the dominant norm of the Ph.D. department, scientific and otherwise, is that the worthwhile problems are those defined as important by the discipline and that academic professionals should work on such problems. Nonacademic employers, in this view, are not considered to be addressing such problems. In the Pilot Study 25% of respondents indicated they wish they had had more useful career counselling. A substantial number of respondents volunteered comments indicating their faculty counsellors knew little about nonacademic physics employment. If the Jencks and

It is also interesting that the thesis advisor was judged by most Industrial Study respondents to be neutral about the desirability of industrial employment. The thesis advisor usually has a closer contact with the graduate student than other faculty; as a consequence, there is greater opportunity for interpersonal and professional judgemental variables to influence the communication or acceptance of professional norms concerning employment. It is therefore difficult, without further study, to know how to interpret what a neutral thesis advisor attitude toward industrial employment really means.

What is less ambiguous, however, is the perceived hostility of "other faculty" toward industrial employment (it remains to be seen whether this perceived hostility would also apply to other types of nonacademic employment). It is highly probable,therefore--given the key role that the faculty play in the professional socialization of the graduate student--that this attitude of hostility to nonacademic employment is passed along by the faculty to the graduate student as a norm to be internalized in the professional socialization process. If this is the case, then one place to begin to modify professional norms concerning nonacademic physics employment is with the graduate school faculty. Wider dissemination of information on the relative satisfactoriness of nonacademic physics employment vis a vis academic employment on a number of key dimensions of professionalism may encourage greater acceptance of nonacademic employment by the graduate faculty.*

CONCLUSION

The Follow-Up Study results indicate that almost half the respondents took nonacademic positions not because they wanted to but, partly or solely, because there was no academic position available. Indeed, a third of the Follow-Up respondents took nonacademic employment not because they wanted to but because they were forced out of their academic positions. A substantial number of Postdoc respondents reported they dropped out of physics not because they wanted to but because they could not find a satisfactory position. What this paper has attempted to do is to present evidence from the Pilot Study and preliminary evidence from several other studies on the relative satisfactoriness of academic and nonacademic physics employment on a number of professional and other dimensions; what this evidence has tentatively shown is that, as far as professional criteria are concerned, it was not necessary for these Follow-Up and Postdoc respondents (or other physicists) to have such a negative opinion of nonacademic physics employment. This study has not addressed the issue of the availability of nonacademic physics positions (although it has found evidence that physicists are

---

Riesman analysis of prevailing norms in academic graduate departments concerning the centrality of academic versus nonacademic concerns is correct, then the preceding findings might well be expected.

*Conferences such as that organized this year by Prof.B.S.Chandrasekhar on the physics of tires attempt to deal with the issue of problem importance by introducing physicists directly to the research of their industrial colleagues; the aim is to identify the physics problems that can be found there and to improve communication between the two groups.

rather inefficient in the way they go about job searching), but it does present evidence that physicists who hold to incorrect stereotypes about nonacademic physics employment and internalize inappropriate norms concerning "acceptable" physics employment will find this to be increasingly self-defeating and maladaptive in a time of current and projected increases in retrenchment in higher education.

REFERENCES

1. Roose-Andersen ratings are taken from the 1969 American Council on Education study prepared by Kenneth D. Roose and Charles J. Andersen, A Rating of Graduate Programs (Washington, D.C.,1970).

2. Data from the 1973 Register appear in several AIP publications. See, for example, Beverly Fearn Porter, Nuclear Physics Manpower (AIP Physics Manpower Report R-268, N.Y., June, 1975),p.5.

3. Patricia Kendall and Hanan Selvin, "Tendencies Toward Specialization in Medical Training", in Robert K. Merton, et.al., eds.,The Student Physician: Introductory Studies in the Socialization of Medical Education (Harvard University Press, Cambridge, Mass.,1957),pp.153-174.

4. Mary Jean Huntington, "The Development of a Professional Self-Image," in Robert K. Merton, et.al.,eds. ibid.,pp.179-187

5. Howard S. Becker, et. al., Boys in White: Student Culture in Medical School (University of Chicago Press, Chicago, 1961).

6. Wilbert E. Moore, "Occupational Socialization" in David Goslin, ed., Handbook of Socialization Research (Rand McNally & Co.,Chicago,1969). A fuller version of the same paper is found in Wilbert E. Moore, Professions: Roles and Rules (Russell Sage, N.Y.,1970).

   A useful additional reference is John A. Jackson, ed.,Professions and Professionalization (Cambridge University Press, N.Y.,1970).

AFTER OLYMPUS WHAT?
VARIED CAREER PATTERNS OF TODAY'S YOUNG PHYSICIST

Beverly Fearn Porter
American Institute of Physics, New York New York 10017

ABSTRACT

In the past several years many young physicists have held and then left academic positions at top U.S. research universities. These physicists of the 1970's have been thrust into quite a different world than their colleagues in the halycon days of the 1960's. Facing limited opportunities for stable academic research careers, they have followed a broad variety of career paths ranging from small colleges to industrial corporations. Some paths have led out of physics completely. A series of APS studies conducted in 1976-1977 delved into the experiences of many of these physicists, examining both the difficulties encountered and the new avenues they have explored. The studies indicate that the search for stable positions has frequently proven hard and misdirected, leaving for some a lingering bitterness. Yet the same studies show that most of these physicists have found or created exciting and stimulating new roles and positions for themselves.

INTRODUCTION

During the late 1960's and early 1970's more than 13,000 physics Ph.D.'s were produced. They have encountered quite a different employment scene than their predecessors. Academic positions particularly tenure line ones, have become extremely tight; federal funding has declined and there has been no sign of major growth in the industrial sector. While many, after sometimes extensive searching, found potentially permanent academic or non-academic physics positions, others hung on taking a series of temporary positions. Some went abroad; some left physics altogether.

This is an all too familiar picture to most of you here. Less familiar, except through often conflicting anecdotes, is what later happened to these individuals and what their attitudes towards the field and their career have become. Have we produced a disaffected, alienated 'elite'? Will the experience of the past decade turn off a generation of potential physicists and scientists? Are their alternative career paths which have proven rewarding? And finally how can and/or should graduate physics training be changed?

These are certainly among some of the major concerns in the physics community today. The studies which we in the AIP Manpower Division are conducting for APS have tried to address such concerns. Underlying these studies is the basic assunption that we can not only learn something about but also learn something <u>from</u> the experiences of these physicists, something of aid both to those coming through the educational pipeline--diminished, but still over 1000 physicists a year-- and to those already launched into employment.

ISSN:0094-243X/78/045/$1.50

By aid I mean not 'crystal ball' solutions. They do not exist. However, we should be able to obtain a clearer picture of the alternatives.

Any firm statistics cited here are derived from the completed APS Pilot Study conducted in the fall of 1976. As outlined in earlier papers in this session, this study traced nearly 300 physicists who, between 1962 and 1975, left leading U.S. physics departments without receiving tenure. However, the first wave of responses from the other APS studies have also been received and some reflections based on these returns will also be made. For reference the APS studies carried out in 1976-77 are referred to here as 1) The Pilot, 2) The Postdoctoral follow-up, 3) Academic to Non-Academic Employment - 1975, 4) Physics Ph.D.'s in Industry, and 5) Projections-Industrial Demand.

AN ALIENATED ELITE?

Has the physics community produced an alienated elite? This concern certainly played a part in the design of the pilot study. Here were physicists who had spent from one to six years at top research physics departments and then left before attaining tenure. Nearly two-thirds of these departing physicists were clearly denied tenure; others did not have contracts renewed or were dissatisfied with academic politics and their chances for advancement. Although some left because they had received better employment offers or wanted to try something new, this represented but a small minority of those leaving. The 'push' factor was clearly more predominant than the 'pull'factor in explaining the mobility of this young faculty group.

What happened to this group? Did they become dissatisfied, embittered, alienated from the field of physics? The results of the pilot study present little support for such a thesis. Eighty-eight percent of them are still employed in physics. Only twelve percent have left the field of physics primarily going into the biosciences, engineering, computer science and business. In examining where they are employed, the figures indicate that seventy percent of them have moved on to other academic employment, although less than half to physics departments as highly ranked as the ones they had left.[1] The remaining thirty percent have gone into non-academic employment, most heavily into Federally Funded Research and Development Centers such as Brookhaven, Argonne, Los Alamos, and Fermi Laboratories.

Many of these individuals spent a considerable period of time looking for a position and, according to their comments, felt the job search was difficult. How satisfied are they now with their current positions? Tabe I lists the various job satisfaction dimensions which were examined and the percentage which found their current positions satisfactory or unsatisfactory on each dimension.

TABLE I CURRENT JOB SATISFACTION - PILOT STUDY

Job Satisfaction Dimension [a]	Percentage Satisfied [b]	Percentage Unsatisfied [b]
Professional Challenge	85%	4%
Autonomy & Independence	84%	5%
Use of Physics Training	82%	5%
Congenial Work Relations	77%	7%
Job Security	75%	10%
Research Facilities	73%	9%
Range of Activities	72%	6%
Advancement	61%	17%
Fringe Benefits	61%	14%
Research Funding	60%	22%
Deaprtment Strength	59%	14%
Salary	59%	15%
Research Time	58%	18%
Pressure to Publish	56%	6%
Teaching Load	50%	19%
Competition & Int. Pol.	45%	22%
Admin. Respons.	44%	16%
No. of Assistants	42%	13%
Student Quality	37%	29%

a) Items are ordered by percentage satisfied.
Percentages are based on toal known relevant responses. This number varies for each item. Response rates for each item were high, from 96 to 98 percent of the 273 respondents, but some of these items, e.g. student quality, were relevant only to those now academically employed.

b) Satisfactory includes very satisfactory and satisfactory; unsatisfactory includes very unsatisfactory and unsatisfactory. The extent to which the two percentages shown do not sum to 100 percent reflects those individuals with a neutral response.

Over 80 percent of the group are finding satisfaction on the crucial dimensions of professional challenge, autonomy and independence, and use of physics training. There were some areas where satisfaction was rather low, and dissatisfaction somewhat high: quality of students, number of assistants, internal politics. One suspects that these are dimensions which frequently are a source of irritation no matter where one works; they appear to be the core of 'common complaints' both in varied questionnaire responses and general discussion.

There was, however, some variation in current job satisfaction depending on where the individual was currently employed. As might be expected those who took positions at other 'top'[2.] university physics departments were the most satisfied with their current positions; followed closely, however, by those employed in Federally Funded Research & Development Centers and Industry. The physicists who appeared to be the least satisfied were those who had taken 'other' academic positions i.e. at four year colleges or lower ranked university departments. Most were heavily involved in teaching. For those physicists whose basic interests had originally stressed teaching, there were few problems; however, for those physicists whose interest had been primarily centered on research, such employment was frequently not fully satisfactory. Many of them appeared to be holding on, waiting for research offers which were not coming. In the waiting process they were growing bitter. They felt they had been led into dead end positions. They had expected more, but it hadn't occurred. From this relatively small group there was some anger, but mainly disappointment and resignation.

Does any evidence of an alienated elite appear to be rising from the returns of the other APS studies? Certainly not, so far, from the study of physics Ph.D.'s employed in Industry. Some of those who had originally planned academic careers and are now employed in industry, exhibit a resigned attitude; however, many more appear to have found a new and exciting direction- one in which the opportunity to see ones result used, and to work on relevant practical problems has become important.

Evidence from the follow-up study of Ph.D's who held postdoctoral positions in 1973 is less clear.[3.] The results, so far, show a mixed group. There is a delight and excitement in past postdoctoral research projects which emanate from many of these returns. Some Ph.D.'s were involved in fore front areas of basis physics research; others used it to explore different physics and related science areas. However, from a number of them, there is simply an expression of relief that they were at least able to find a position which enabled them to have something to live on. While most of them generally perceived their postdoctoral experience as an asset, they tended to consider it either a a liability or irrelevant in terms of attaining job security or advancement. As several commented on their questionnaires, "I seem to have fallen behind many of my colleagues." Clearly they are the least settled of the various groups being studied. More than half, so far, have held multiple postdocs; some as many as four or five. Many appear still to be in temporary positions, holding on. While some of these temporary positions will turn into more permanent faculty or nonfaculty research position - the latter certainly being a new and expanding role - others will not. Many of these physicists are now in their mid-thirties; their future is not at all clear. One wonders, was the question of an alenated elite asked too soon? Clearly this group needs the continued attention of the physics community.

TURNING OFF A GENERATION OF SCIENTISTS?

Recent experiences of physicists have, in many cases, been difficult. Is this likely to result in turning off a generation of scientists? Clearly the number of new physics Ph.D.'s produced annually has diminished from a peak of 1,545 in 1970 to 1,111 in 1976, although this production decline appears now to be leveling off.[4].

In the pilot study, physicists were asked if they would recommend physics to a bright young person? Despite the difficulties many of them had faced 60% stated they would recommend physics, although quite a few noted 'only for a very, very bright young person'; only 18% stated they would not recommend physics; one-fifth of the group remained unsure.

Results now coming in from the other studies regarding recommending physics, appear to indicate a greater degree of hesitancy than evidenced in the pilot study. The reasons for the hesitancy are very heavily concentrated on the tight employment prospects which most of our respondents see to be continuing in the coming years. They appear not to be 'turning off' potential physicists as much as proceeding with caution. Studying physics, they agree, is an exciting and useful pursuit, no matter what one does in the future; however, students who are planning careers in physics research particularly academic based research, should realize that the path ahead may well be difficult, and they would recommend it only to the most determined. It sounds not as if a generation is being turned off, but rather given a glimpse of reality.

ALTERNATIVE CAREER PATHS

In the various APS studies cited earlier, attention was paid to the alternative career paths which different physicists followed. Some of them indicated that if they had the chance to do it over again they would have selected another career path rather than physics; In the pilot study 23% said they would have chosen an area other than physics; returns from the other studies seem to suggest a similar pattern of response. The areas most frequently cited appear to be medicine and electrical engineering. However, very few actually made such switches, particularly into medicine. As one respondent who had made the move noted, "It is extremely hard, time consuming work!". More switches were made into medical physics, biomedical science areas, computer science, business and engineering; some have even dealt with problems in the softer social sciences. In many of these fields they were applying physics principles and a physicist's analytic approach to a new area. Evidence so far suggests that those individuals who have made such moves are usually quite pleased with their new careers.

An area frequently overlooked in the discussion of alternative career paths for physicists, is that of the independent entrepreneur one who runs his own business or service bureau. Although this can be a path frought with mishaps, as several of our respondents pointed out, those who had followed this route, appeared to be one of the most excited and involved of the different groups surveyed. As one respondent pointed out there is a basic excitement in watching a business grow. And several added, 'Making money can also be fun!'

Some physicists have been particularly ingenious in developing varied career opportunities, as many of the papers at this conference detail. One, which was outlined in a questionnaire response, concerned a physicist who had held a series of temporary research positions. He was involved and fascinated with the research he was doing and he was relatively unconcerned with the temporary nature of his employment. He explained that he enjoyed doing many things; one of these was physics, another was building houses. His summer work on the latter, probably brought in more money than his physics research during the year, but both were clearly very satisfying career options for him.

Most of the physicists surveyed, have not made such unique accomodations; however, a number of them are finding that they can best develop a satisfying career by leaving their options open, continuing to explore new paths, and combining their physics background and abilities with a broad variety of other skills and interests.

RECOMMENDATIONS FOR PHYSICS GRADUATE STUDY

In the pilot study, few respondents indicated the need for any major changes in physics graduate study, although some felt that a bit more emphasis on experimental, applied, and classical physics would have been useful. More important, they felt, were the perspective and analytical skills which a physicist developed; he can excel anywhere, <u>if he wants to</u>. It is this latter attitude which is central. However, physicists' attitudes have not always been positive toward nor open to the various employment opportunities available. Many of the respondents felt that they would have benefited during graduate school, if they had had both more extensive information on the nature of applied physics work and direct contact with individuals who were involved in such work. In the same way, many wished they had developed a better grasp of what was going on in other sub-fields of physics and in other fields of science. Certainly such information would have eased mobility; it may well have also encouraged a greater flexibility in the self-definition of what constitutes a physics career.

The returns from the other APS studies are providing us with further feedback on the ways in which the graduate education experience might be altered. The first wave of returns from the study of physics Ph.D.'s currently employed in industry has come in. Some preliminary reflections, based on some of these early returns, may be in order. Respondents were asked on thirteen different items - ranging from course work to particular skills - how necessary they felt each was in their current positions, and then how adequate they felt their training had been in that area. Most necessary they felt was clearly 'the ability to proceed independently' and they felt that their training had prepared them quite well to fill that need. For the second and third most necessary items, they ranked 'skill in oral presentation' and 'skill in writing'. And yet in these areas they did not feel that they had been at all well prepared. Some of these men are now managers responsible for hiring, and they see the same lack in many of the new physics Ph.D.'s. While a strong basic expertise in physics is of course, a necessity in industrial physics work, these other skills are also important and may be crucial in terms of employment and advancement.

CONCLUSION

Despite the employment difficulties many young physicists have had to encounter in the past several years, including a few true horror stories, the results from the current APS studies - at least so far - have been generally encouraging. Most of the physicists appear to have found meaningful and frequently exciting positions for themselves both within and beyond the traditional bounds of physics. Completion of the remaining APS studies should provide us with fuller insights.

Certainly, one point stands out. The new generations of physicists will have their eyes much more widely open than the last. They may still decide to select the riskiest of options, but they will do so more knowingly.

REFERENCES

1. Any reference to rankings of physics departments made here are based on the now somewhat outdated, Roose-Andersen rankings. K.D. Roose and C.J. Andersen, A Rating of Graduate Programs (American Council on Education, Washington DC 1970) p. 98.

2. Ibid

3. An outline of the background characteristics of this group of Ph.D.'s can be found in B.F. Porter, "Postdoctoral Positions in Physics and Astronomy", (American Institute of Physics, New York 1975) R-270

4. S.D. Ellis, "Enrollment and Degrees," (American Institute of Physics, New York 1977,) R-151.14

SUPPLY AND DEMAND FOR PhD PHYSICISTS, 1975 TO 1986

L. Grodzins
Massachusetts Institute of Technology, Cambridge, MA 02139

ABSTRACT

An extrapolation of trends in doctoral supply leads to the conclusion that the number of new entrants into the physics/astronomy labor force (estimated to be 19,000 in 1975) will drop slowly from its present value of about 950 to about 750 in 1986. The components of demand are estimated separately: The number of positions resulting from death and retirement in the labor force is now about 1% of the total (180 positions); the percentage will increase to 1.6% (320 positions) by 1986.* The number of openings resulting from mobility out of the field by those in secure positions being attracted to other fields is estimated to be not less than 150 per year. The number of positions in traditional physics vacated by non-PhDs and filled by PhDs is expected to decline slowly from an estimated 200-300 in 1976 to 150-200 in 1986. The growth of the field is estimated to have been 1 to 1.5% per year in recent years and a continued growth of 1% per year is projected.

We conclude that the demand in traditional physics and astronomy will about match the supply of new entrants into the labor force by the mid-1980s. However, throughout the coming decade there will continue to be imbalances between supply and demand in specific sub-fields and employment sectors. And the physics community will continue to age. In particular:

The number of tenure openings per year in the 200 PhD-granting physics/astronomy departments is expected to be no greater than 100 in 1986; thus only about 15% of the new entrants into the physics labor force in the early 1980s are expected to attain permanent positions in doctoral-granting departments.

The demand for those who work in theoretical physics is expected to remain well below the supply of new entrants trained as theorists.

The average age of the physics community is now increasing at from 0.35 to 0.5 year/year. The rate is expected to decline slowly to 0.1 to 0.2 year/year by 1985.

The yearly output of experimental nuclear and particle physicists is dropping so sharply that the yearly demand may exceed

---

* This figure, which is considerably lower than the 2.5% value given at the Penn State Conference, results from the use of TIAA-CREF data instead of the previously used actuary data for white males.

ISSN:0094-243X/78/052/$1.50

the number of new entrants by the early 1980s.

INTRODUCTION

This is my first attempt at a long-range projection of the supply and demand for physicists.* A thankless job; damned if you do and damned if you don't. Indeed, it is triply damned: a projection will surely be incorrect if everyone acts as if it will be correct. (Alas, the converse is not necessarily true.)

Long-range projections of the supply and demand for scientists have been too global, too simplistic, to be of much value for either career or policy decisions in specific fields. Included in this charge are the projections made for broad areas of science by the National Science Foundation,[1] the Bureau of Labor Statistics,[2] the National Center for Educational Statistics,[3] as well as those made for physics in the past few years by Allan Cartter,[4] Nathan Dean,[5] and Richard Freeman.[6] (A summary of the art of projecting, as of 1973, is given in Reference 7.) The important early work of Cartter,[8,9] which inspired derivative studies of physics by Gruner[10] and Grodzins,[11] heralded the dimensions of the difficult times of the 1970s, though all the studies were wrong in their details. In any case, the physical sciences are so interconnected that long-range projections for physics alone are of limited value for counseling or policy decisions. So why bother.

First, projections up to five years forward can be accurate. There is so much inertia in the system that the near future is predicated on the near past: we believe that the present projections, based on data up to 1975-76, forecast supply as well as replacement components of demand through 1980-81, with less than 25% uncertainty. It is, therefore, my view that short-range projections should be made annually and that policy decisions can rely on their general integrity.

There is a need to expose the gross uncertainties which increase rapidly as we project forward in time. Career guidance for doctoral employment requires long-range forecasts and we cannot yet make such forecasts reliably. But we should be able to determine the upper and lower bounds of supply and demand a decade hence, which may help to define the options available to those making career choices or policy decisions.

Since the uncertainties in the projections arise in part from uncertainties in the facts which presage those projections, the effort may lead to the gathering of more appropriate data or the appropriate analysis of existing data; in particular, we must improve our understanding of the mobility and upgrading components of demand.

---

* The word "physicist" includes astronomers and astrophysicists, unless specifically excluded.

And, as we all agree, the methodology of projection must be improved; which will only happen through refinement of attempts such as this one.

While this is my first attempt to make detailed long-range projections of supply and demand, I did make some projections in a 1970 study of physics.[11] The projections of PhD output, through 1975, turned out to be accurate to within about 15%. The pessimistic projections for demand turned out to be optimistic. We stated that "unless new opportunities are found soon, there seems no escaping the conclusion that from 1969 through 1974 we will produce from 3500 to 5000 PhD physicists beyond the demand." In fact, during that period at least 6000 physicists left the employment of physics. We also conjectured that "the demand for physicists in traditional sectors will be from 800 to 1200 per year from 1972 through 1980." A portion of the results are now in and the best estimates are that between 1972 and 1975, only 400 to 600 PhDs in physics entered the field of employment of physics each year, i.e., about half our estimate, and only 1 in 3 of the graduating classes. It may not be unfair to generalize that soothsayers, especially those in the "establishment", tend to be optimistic about the future.

By almost every measure that we can find, the health of physics has been poorer than that of any other scientific field. The growth of employment has been less, the mobility out of physics has been greater, the number of young people entering into the physics community has been comparatively smaller, the physics community has been aging more rapidly. The reasons seem clear enough: more than in any other field, with the possible exception of the basic medical sciences, we concentrate our effort in basic research and in teaching. To a far greater degree than is the case in any other field, our efforts are carried out by doctorates, not by lesser degree holders. The support for physics research has been stagnant during the time when physics faculties ceased to grow and when the outpouring of new doctorate physicists has been unprecedented. The inevitable surplus of physicists had few niches in physics to fill. Thousands dispersed out of the field, staying, however, as close as possible to their physics heritage.[12]

OUTLINE OF METHODOLOGY

Projections should be disaggregated by employment sector, by major subfield, by activity. But the information we expected to be available for these purposes will not be for many months, so we concentrate in this paper on an overview of the supply and demand for all physicists.

Our model is simple: the extrapolation of separately identified components of supply and demand. No feedback loops are included for it is our view that such models are now of limited predictive value. One reason is that the time delays in the feedback loop involving the supply side of the equation are considerably longer than the time span between unpredictable changes in government funding of science. Another reason is that the imbalances between supply and demand not only influence future supply[5,6,8] but also have a direct influence on the mobility and up-grading components of demand, neither of which are well enough understood for such refinements.

The number of doctorates employed in physics in year, T, may be factored as:

$$N(T) = N(T-1) - N_D - N_R - N_O - N_E + N_I + N_{IM} + N_N$$

N(T) is the number of full-time employed doctoral scientists (regardless of the field in which they received their PhD) employed in a traditional physics or astronomy specialty such as atomic, molecular, thermal, optical, nuclear, etc.

The other parameters refer to those entering or leaving traditional employment between the year, T-1, and the year, T.

N_D is the number of N(T-1) who die

N_R is the number of N(T-1) who retire

N_O is the number of N(T-1) who are attracted (not pushed) out of traditional physics employment leaving a vacancy to be filled by a doctorate with physics qualifications

N_E is the number of N(T-1) who leave the country

N_N is the number of new entrants from the fresh PhD ranks

N_{MI} is the number pulled into physics from other fields

N_I is the number who enter from other countries

The demand for physicists is the sum of the replacement needs for those who die, retire, move out of the field or emigrate -- N_D, N_R, N_O, N_E, respectively -- plus the change due to the growth or reduction in the size of the field itself, plus the upgrading component in which PhDs are utilized in positions which hitherto were filled with non-PhDs. The last component can be large for example, the size of the faculties of the physics departments in colleges has been nearly constant from year to year (Figure 4), yet the number of PhDs on those faculties has been increasing as faculty without PhDs retire or leave and their replacements are predominantly PhDs. Upgrading is largely decoupled from funding changes. Upgrading can create demand; the greater the percentage of PhDs in a given sector, the more likely the new hires will have PhDs.

The supply component consists of those new PhDs who expect to enter the physics labor force plus those who are attracted in from other countries or from other fields. The last two components are non-trivial; even in the difficult times of the past 8 years there has been a significant in-mobility from other fields into physics. Moreover, if the physics job market improves, the mobility into the field will grow and can exceed the mobility out, as was the case throughout most of the 1950s and early 1960s.

When supply exceeds demand, then the experience of the past 8 years tells us that the surplus of trained physicists will move to other areas of science, if necessary into positions which were previously held by non-PhDs; neither the unemployment rate nor the out-mobility to the non-sciences will significantly exceed corresponding percentages in other fields. If demand exceeds the supply from fresh PhDs, then the demand will be filled by in-mobility from those previously employed outside of physics and be lesser degree holders. Demand will not wait on the PhD pipeline. (One caveat to this observation is that the demand for lower-paying transient jobs, i.e., postdoctoral or part-time staff in colleges, may well exceed the supply of those willing to accept such positions.)

We are concerned with the utilization in traditional physics. By the phrase "traditional physics" we mean those areas in which graduate schools of physics concentrate. Operationally, the labor force in traditional physics is determined by the number of PhDs who select one of the traditional sub-fields of physics when surveyed as to their principal specialty of employment. We use the phrase "non-traditional physics" to encompass those areas with substantial overlap with physics but which are not identified by those surveyed as being primarily physics. Non-traditional physics fields include growth areas such as nuclear medicine, as well as some sub-fields of mathematics, earth sciences, the bio-sciences and engineering which spun off from physics in decades past.

We will use recent trends to estimate each of the components of supply and demand. Upper and lower bounds will be projected for the supply. But we are principally concerned with the lower bound for the demand for "permanent" positions in traditional physics. We will be pessimistic in our counting of job openings. Yet we do not project a contraction of the physics labor force and we must be forewarned that economic, educational and government pressures may conspire to do just that and thus reduce the demand lower bound.

PRELUDES

The enrollments and degrees in physics astronomy during the past 20 or so years are given in Table 1; the sources are the American Institute of Physics (AIP)[13] and the National Research Council (NRC).[14] (Throughout this report we will make use of the NRC figures for doctoral production since they include astronomy

TABLE 1

PHYSICS PLUS ASTRONOMY ENROLLMENTS AND DEGREES

Academic Year	Juniors (AIP)	Seniors (AIP)	B.S.[1,2] (AIP)	First Yr. Graduate Enrollment (AIP)	M.S.[1] (AIP)	PhD[1] (AIP)	PhD[3] (DRF)
1950							422
1951							501
1952							520
1953							522
1954			2439		798	515	524
1955			2420		784	504	511
1956			2883		796	490	485
1957			3293		883	446	464
1958			3891		882	472	504
1959			4669		958	501	523
1960			5042		1156	533	574
1961	8264		5293		1321	615	601
1962	7934	6633	5622		1431	699	767
1963	7873	6386	5452		1850	858	829
1964	7520	6676	5611	4061	1907	792	936
1965	7132	6514	5517	4167	2045	983	1065
1966	7014	6296	5037	4358	2050	948	1187
1967	7345	5992	5236	4162	2193	1233	1360
1968	7822	6704	5520	4010	2077	1325	1447
1969	7587	7019	5975	3669	2223	1355	1575
1970	7480	6700	5782	3918	2268	1545	1715
1971	6884	6663	5755	3494	2300	1530	1740
1972	6593	6162	5282	3336	2143	1438	1635
1973	6012	5108	4923 (5054)	2904	1961	1445	1590
1974	5858	4909	4652 (4801)	2680	1772	1236	1334
1975	5660	4922	4571 (4707)	2668	1650	1167	1293
1976	5888	4930	4487 (4621)	2646	1543	1111	1235
1977	5711			2626			

1) Physics degrees only

2) Physics plus Astronomy are given in parentheses for 1973-1976.

3) From NRC Data on Doctorate Recipients

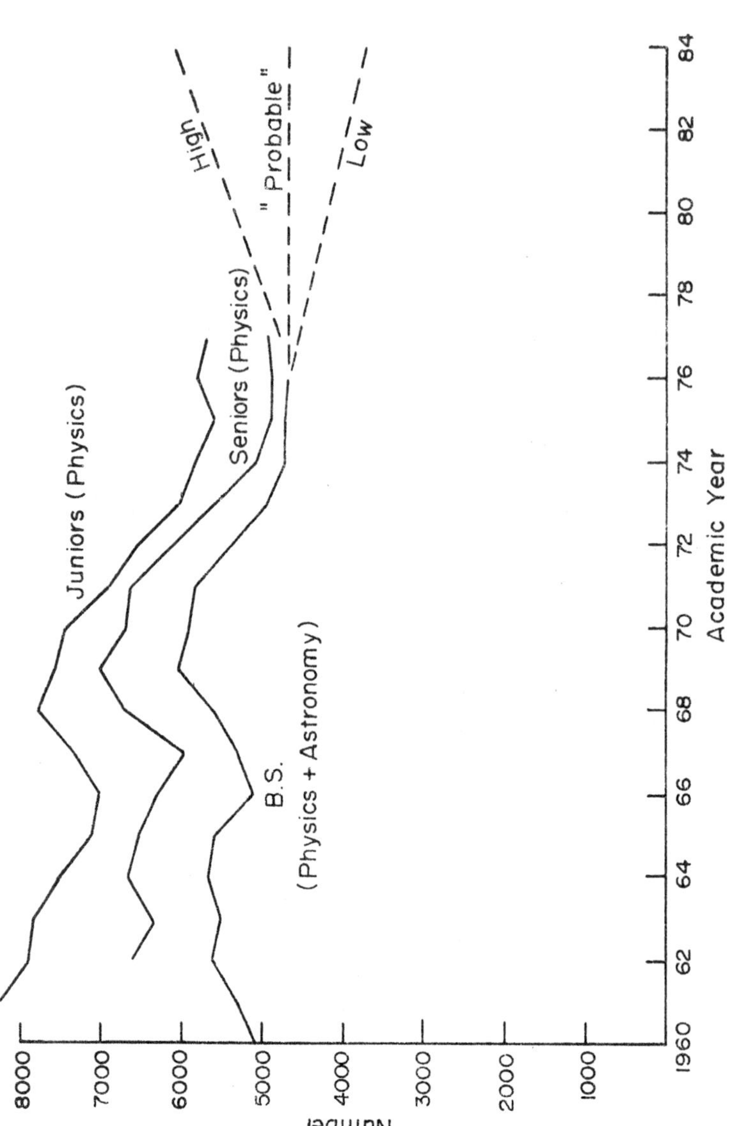
Juniors (Physics)
Seniors (Physics)
B.S.
(Physics + Astronomy)
High
" Probable "
Low
Number
8000
7000
6000
5000
4000
3000
2000
1000
1960
62
64
66
68
70
72
74
76
78
80
82
84
Academic Year

FIG. 1

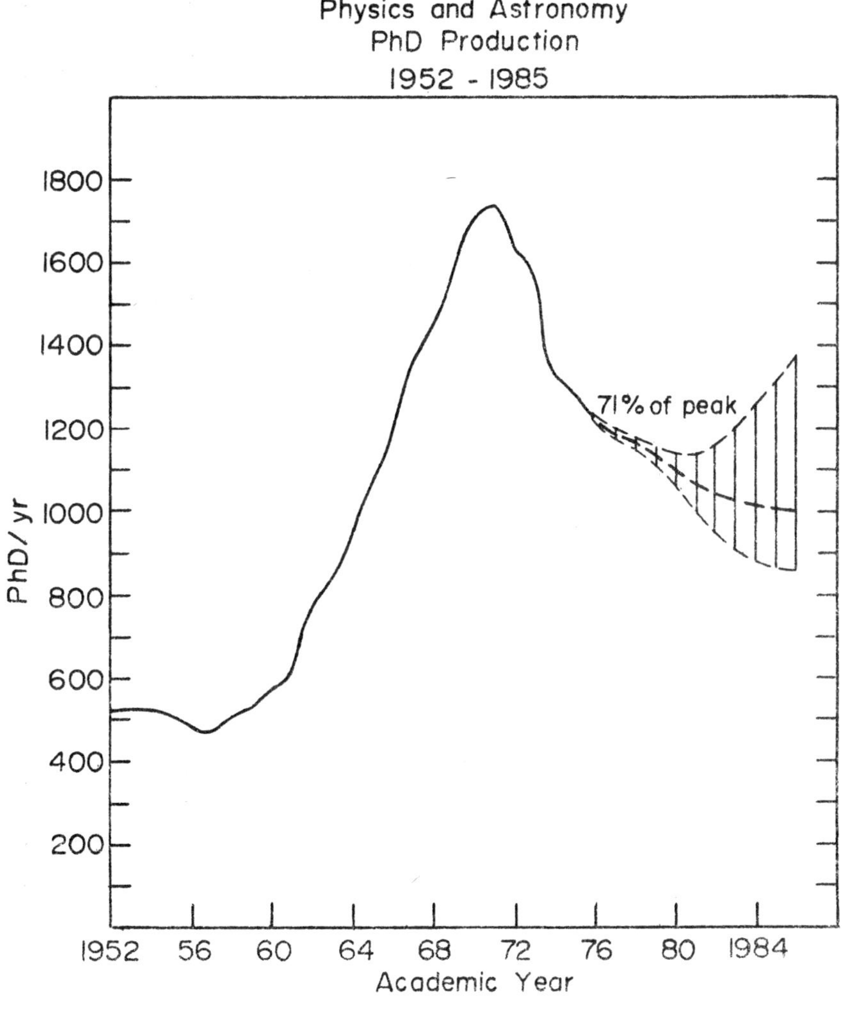

Physics and Astronomy
PhD Production
1952 - 1985
1800
1600
1400
1200
1000
800
600
400
200
PhD/yr
71% of peak
1952
56
60
64
68
72
76
80
1984
Academic Year

FIG. 2

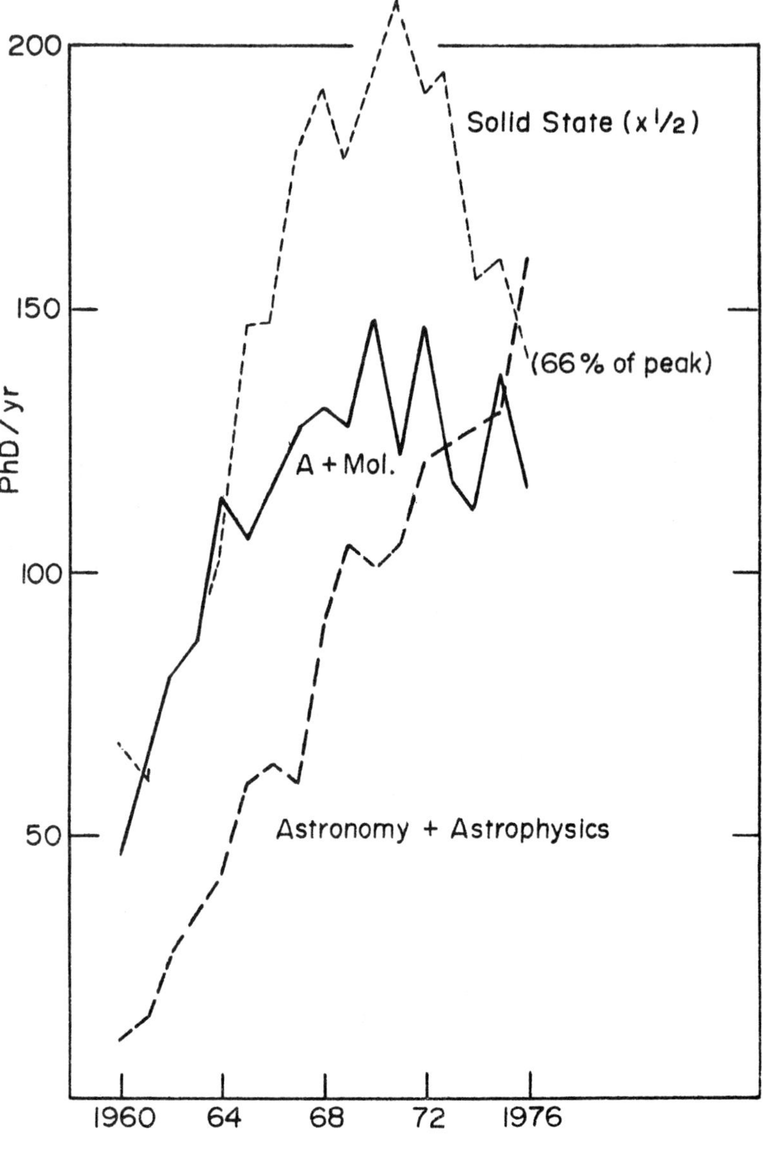
200
150
100
50
PhD / yr
Solid State (x 1/2)
(66% of peak)
A + Mol.
Astronomy + Astrophysics
1960
64
68
72
1976

FIG. 3a

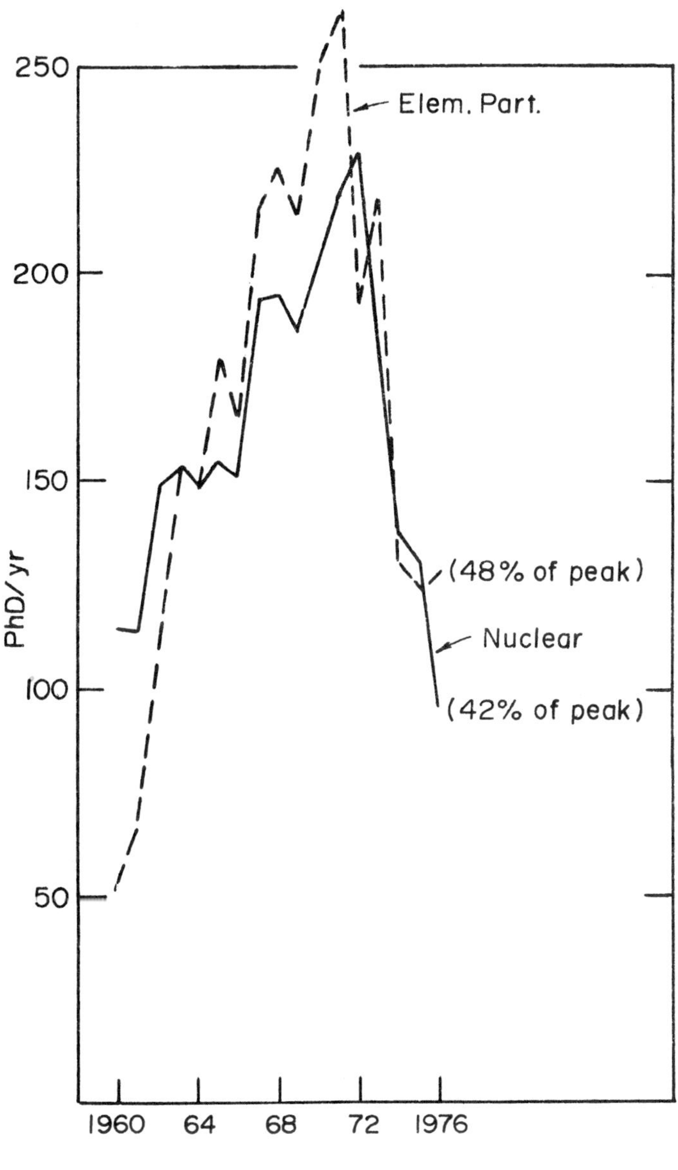
250
200
150
100
50
PhD/yr
1960
64
68
72
1976
Elem. Part.
(48% of peak)
Nuclear
(42% of peak)

FIG. 3b

TABLE 2

PhDs in Physics Subfields from 1960 to 1976

	1960	1961	1962	1963	1964	1965	1966	1967	1968	1969	1970	1971	1972	1973	1974	1975	1976
Physics/Astronomy	530	597	710	818	866	1046	1051	1311	1432	1454	1655	1737	1624	1588	1327	1293	1235
Astronomy										36	48	59	63	64	56	60	78
Astrophysics	11	16	28	34	45	64	66	69	98	67	63	54	66	67	77	71	72
Atom & Mol	49	68	81	90	114	112	117	130	135	131	152	124	150	122	116	138	116
Electromag	7	20	20	23	36	31	36	32	14	13	18	18	11	13	7	10	12
Mechanics	1	5	5	7	5	8	5	12	5	10	7	6	7	6	4	3	4
Acoustics	11	8	7	14	7	7	10	9	10	11	23	19	20	15	11	12	9
Fluids	4	19	30	22	14	33	33	54	44	24	21	21	28	28	20	22	20
Plasma								1		62	85	86	93	73	54	53	75
Optics	8	7	7	7	8	13	9	13	11	20	30	25	31	33	23	33	50
Thermal	3	2	4	12	10	21	21	20	12	18	17	17	18	16	16	9	4
Elem Parts	51	68	115	154	147	184	164	222	232	224	256	277	198	222	141	124	128
Nucl Struct	115	113	151	155	148	157	157	199	197	190	212	226	234	182	139	130	96
Solid State	136	123	161	175	212	299	303	369	390	362	403	442	393	400	331	319	282
Theoretical	88	114	55	3													
Phys, General	8	7	24	45	53	36	38	64	134	180	160	163	154	205	212	172	175
Phys, Other	36	25	22	77	67	81	102	122	150	97	160	200	168	142	120	137	114

degrees.)

The baccalaureate production figures and the PhD production figures are plotted in Figures 1 and 2; the S.B. production figures contain an estimate of the number of astronomy degrees awarded each year prior to 1972. The exponential growth of physics, which averaged about 7% per year for many decades, has now ceased. There may well be continued expansion of the physics community, but it will not be fueled by the need to teach an ever-growing percentage of the population desiring higher education in physics.

In Table 2 and Figures 3a and 3b, we present the PhD production of the physics fine fields since 1960.[14] The categories "general" and "other" are not well understood.

The PhD production in solid state physics fell in parallel with the total PhD physics production; the production in some sub-fields, i.e., nuclear and particle physics, have declined much more than the average; in other sub-fields, such as astrophysics and optics, production continues to rise.

The mobility in and out of the broad fields of science is shown in section E of Table 3.[16] More than 30% of all the physics PhDs are no longer employed in physics.

Table 4 gives some recent data on employment by sector of PhD physicists from 1972 through 1975; these data derive from the National Research Council's Surveys of Doctoral Scientists and Engineers carried out biennially under the sponsorship of the NSF. Table 4a shows the trends in employment for those with doctorates in physics; 4b gives the employment trends for PhDs (regardless of field) who are employed as physicists. From 1972 through 1975 the only substantial growth in physics employment was in positions in academia which were neither faculty not postdoctoral. There was no growth in physics employment in industry or government. Though the NRC data indicates a growth in PhD faculty, a head count (Figures 4 and 5) shows that the total size has been declining; the discrepancy is accounted for by up-grading. The consequences of a constant faculty size, together with a pressure to promote those who are on the faculty, results in a rapid reduction of opportunities for new hires. The number of assistant professors in the PhD-granting departments is now below the level of 1959 (Figure 5).

The physics community has been going through an extremely trying period. With so many negative signs for the health of physics, it hardly takes Cassandra to predict more of the same. But as we shall see, the PhD production is now so low that even a modest growth, such as appears to be taking place in the permanent staff positions of academia, can ameliorate the situation. If, however, such growth does not occur, then we must wait til at least the late 1980s before demand catches up with supply. And we will have lost a

TABLE 3

Mobility In and Out of Phyiscs -- from NRC Surveys of 1973 and 1975

	Math	Chem	Earth Sci	Eng	Biosci	Psych	Soc Sci	Non-Sci	Total	% of Total Employed
A) From employment in 1972 to employment in 1973										
Left Physics/Astronomy	71	81	137	398	81			97	865	4.8
Entered Physics/Astronomy	36	48	43	125				20	272	1.5
									Net =	-3.3
B) From employment in 1974 to employment in 1975										
Left Physics/Astronomy	102	121	149	417	73			57	919	5.0
Entered Physics/Astronomy	42	96	55	189	42				424	2.3
									Net =	-2.7
C) From 1972 PhD class to employment in 1973										
Left Physics/Astronomy	53	21	40	119	37			38	308	21.7
Entered Physics/Astronomy		12	23	110	8				153	10.8
									Net =	-10.9
D) From 1974 PhD class to employment in 1975										
Left Physics/Astronomy	73	29	52	103	44	16	3	19	339	29.3
Entered Physics/Astronomy		7		35	3				45	3.9
									Net =	-25.4

E) Total Doctoral Manpower Flow by PhD Field, as of 1975	Math	Physics	Chem	Earth Sci	Eng	Biosci	Psych	Soc Sci
Total number, by field of PhD	15989	25085	43248	8813	41228	70577	29435	39273
Number left field	1837	7889	9813	938	6004	6575	2573	6820
Number entered field	3613	2404	3360	4720	7839	6786	3586	2004

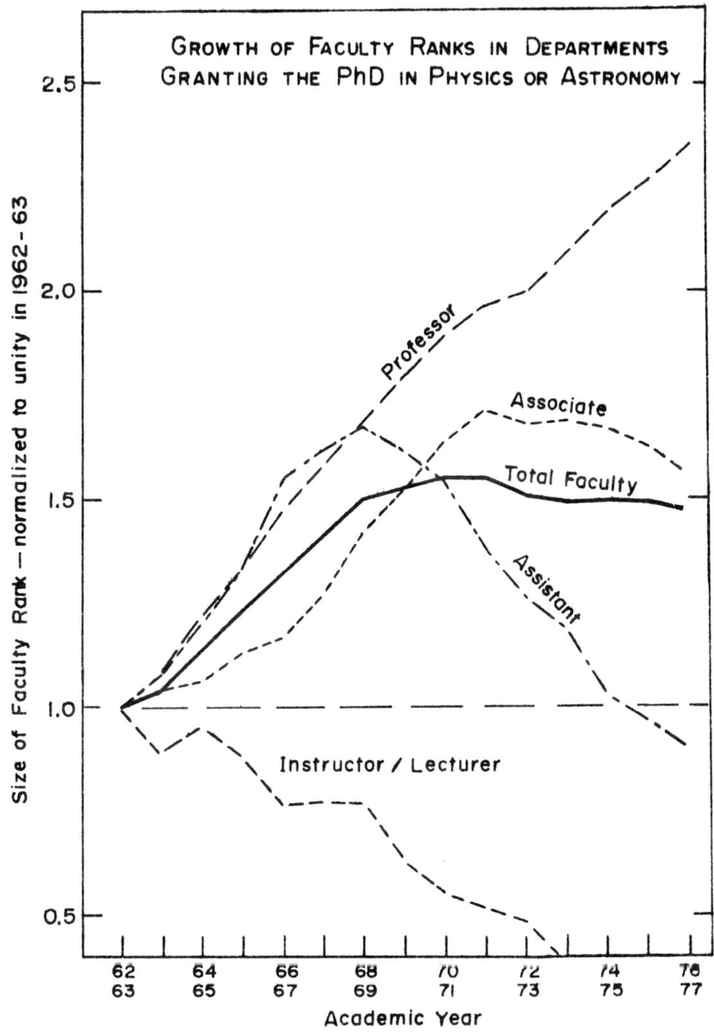
Growth of Faculty Ranks in Departments
Granting the PhD in Physics or Astronomy
Size of Faculty Rank — normalized to unity in 1962-63
2.5
2.0
1.5
1.0
0.5
Professor
Associate
Total Faculty
Assistant
Instructor / Lecturer
62 63
64 65
66 67
68 69
70 71
72 73
74 75
76 77
Academic Year

FIG. 4

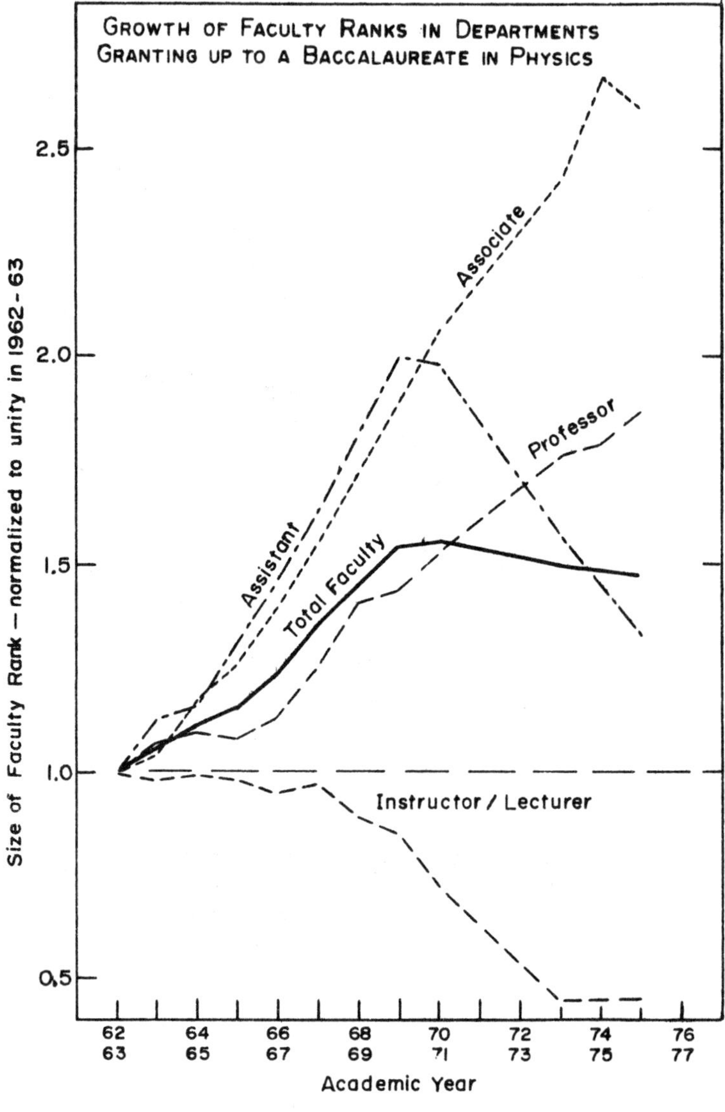
GROWTH OF FACULTY RANKS IN DEPARTMENTS
GRANTING UP TO A BACCALAUREATE IN PHYSICS
Associate
Professor
Assistant
Total Faculty
Instructor / Lecturer
2.5
2.0
1.5
1.0
0.5
Size of Faculty Rank — normalized to unity in 1962-63
62 63
64 65
66 67
68 69
70 71
72 73
74 75
76 77
Academic Year

FIG. 5

generation of physicists.

SUPPLY

1. Doctoral Labor Force

Surprisingly, there are several different definitions in use for the doctoral labor force: the NSF defines this group as the number who have PhDs in physics regardless of the field in which they are presently employed.[1] The American Institute of Physics generally defines the labor force[17] in terms of the number of those who identify themselves as physicists regardless of the field they work in. We will use a third definition: the doctoral labor force is the number who say they are employed in the field of physics, regardless of field of PhD. The best estimate for the labor force in 1975 is that given by the NRC in Table 4.

2. New Entrants into the Labor Force

The number of PhDs in physics per year in projected. We then subtract the number expected to leave the country immediately (mainly foreign citizens returning home) plus the number who leave physics on getting their PhD in order to work in other fields; consideration is given to the number of fresh PhDs from other fields who enter employment in physics, and to immigration.

To project the number of PhDs in physics per year one may adopt several different algorithms: one may, for example, determine the ratio of PhDs in a given year to baccalaureate production in physics some years earlier and, using the trends in that ratio, extrapolate the PhD production from the known baccalaureate production. The AIP uses such a transfer function with reasonable predictive accuracy.[13] Another simple procedure is to consider separately the transfer functions of junior to senior physics majors, of baccalaureates to first-year enrollment in physics and of first-year enrollments to PhD production; each transfer ratio having the appropriate time delay. This method was used by Grodzins in 1970[11] to make reasonably accurate projections through 1975. We can improve on these procedures -- and carry the projections several years further -- by using the distributions in the time lapse between the baccalaureate and the PhD in terms of the percent of a given B.S. class who obtain a PhD, N years later; these distributions, obtained from NRC data,[20] are given in Figure 6. These and other data show that the PhD pipeline is porous. Students leave and enter at various points along the training path, not just at the baccalaureate and master's degree levels. Using these completion distributions we have extrapolated the PhD production in physics to 1986. (First order corrections were made for PhDs who received their baccalaureates abroad or from fields other than physics, see Table 5 and Reference 14. The central (most probable) curve was obtained by assuming that we have reached a steady state in both the baccalaureate

TABLE 4a

Number of PhD Physicists Employed by Sector

	1972	1973	1974	1975	1972-75 Annual Growth Rate (%)
	20491	21782	23342	24310	5.9
Academia	10876	11387	13288	13547	7.6
Faculty	8267	8700	9142	9585	5.1
Postdocs	1159	1256	1124	1158	0.0
Other Staff	1450	1431	3022	2804	24.6
Business	5065	5463	5890	6443	8.4
Government	2936	3232	2721	2917	- 0.2
Other Sectors	1414	1522	1378	1373	- 1.0
Unknown	200	178	65	30	

TABLE 4b

Number of Doctorates Employed in Physics by Physics Sector

	1972	1973	1974	1975	1972-75 Annual Growth Rate (%)
	17421	18065	18346	18789	
Academia	9872	10188	11343	11569	5.4
Faculty	7551	7811	7837	8217	2.9
Postdocs	1077	1185	1058	1008	- 2.2
Other Staff	1244	1192	2448	2344	23.5
Business	3709	3836	3658	3800	0.8
Government	2549	2719	2275	2364	- 2.5
Other Sectors	1114	1155	1004	1026	- 2.7
Unknown	177	167	66	30	

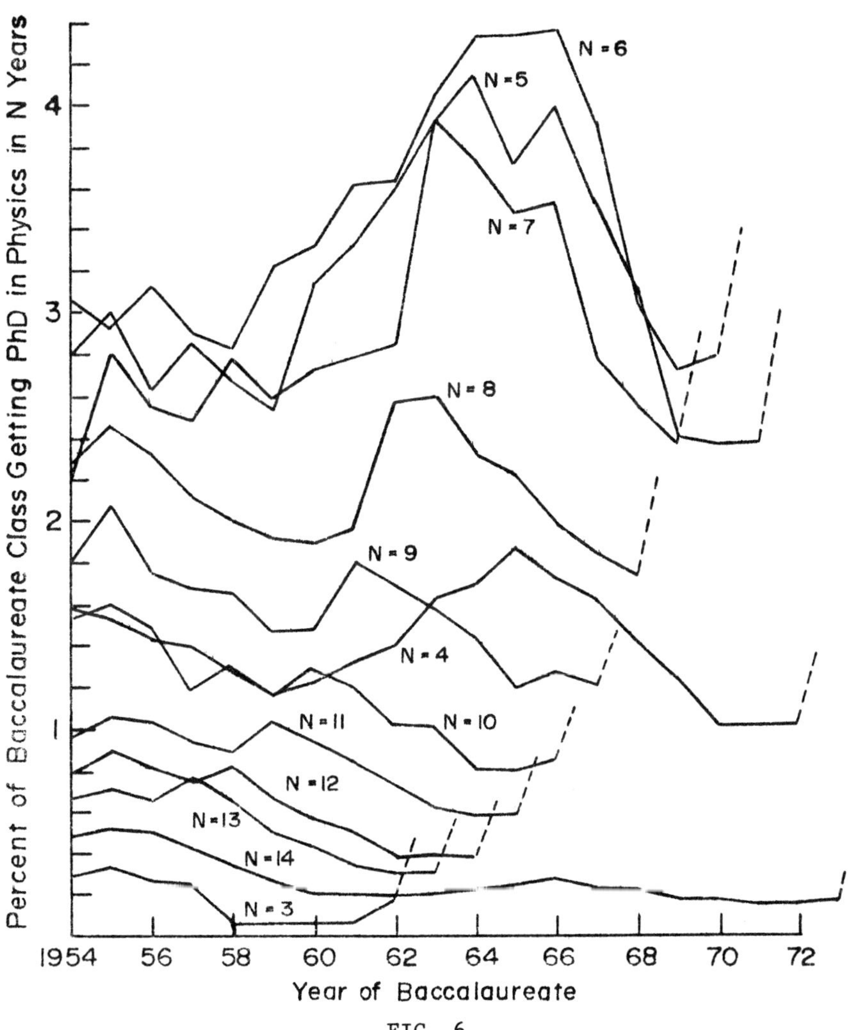
Percent of Baccalaureate Class Getting PhD in Physics in N Years
4
3
2
1
1954
56
58
60
62
64
66
68
70
72
Year of Baccalaureate
N = 6
N = 5
N = 7
N = 8
N = 9
N = 4
N = 11
N = 10
N = 12
N = 13
N = 14
N = 3

FIG. 6

production (middle curve of Figure 1) and in the baccalaureate to PhD completion factors (Figure 6). The lower PhD production curve assumes the same completion factors (no change from the recent percentages) but uses the lower projections for baccalaureate production, Figure 1. The upper curve assumes the upper projections for baccalaureate productions in Figure 1 and that completion factors increase about 6% per year; the magnitude of the extrapolations are indicated by the dashed upswing at the end of the graphs of Figure 6.

The most probable projection of PhD production, Figure 2, is similar to that obtained with simple algorithms discussed above. The lower projected values of Figure 2 are hardly a lower bound; greater leakage out of the pipeline could result in PhD outputs of 500 to 600 per year by 1985. On the other hand, it is hard to see how PhD production can rise above the upper projection of Figure 2 unless there are headlines announcing dramatic rises in the number of jobs for physicists in the next few years.

Our general conclusion is that the population in the educational pipeline fixes the PhD production for about the next 5 years and that extrapolation beyond that time have substantial and growing uncertainties reaching about 30% of the most probable value by 1986.

To obtain the number of new entrants into the physics labor force from the total number of U.S. PhDs awarded per year, we must estimate the prompt exodus abroad and to other fields and we must correct for in-mobility and immigration. To make these estimates we use NRC data on the characteristics of new PhDs, Table 5. The percentage of the doctoral classes that are foreign citizens has risen to the 25% level and there has been a corresponding rise in the number of new doctorates who leave the U.S. (Table 5). There has also been an increase in the percentage of the new doctorates that leave physics immediately. In the late 1960s about 7% of the physics PhDs expected to be employed outside physics after getting their degree; by 1975 the figure was close to 15% (Table 5). But these data, obtained at the time the doctorate was awarded, appear to underestimate the exodus out of the field. The 1973 and 1975 surveys[15,16] show a much greater out-mobility. In the spring of 1975 (the time when the 1975 survey was taken) only about 70% of the physics PhDs from the 1974 class, who stayed in the U.S., were employed in physics; the corresponding percentage from the 1972 class employed in physics as of the spring of 1973, was 76%. In 1973, the out-mobility was accompanied by a substantial amount of in-mobility; 308 left versus 153 entering (Table 3). But in 1975 only 45 PhDs from the 1974 PhD class entered physics from other fields while 339 physics PhDs left physics (Table 3).

The immigration component cannot be assessed at this time. We are aware of no data useful for our purposes, though studies have been made.[21] We, therefore, subsume this group into our estimate of net number of physicists who leave the labor force to work outside

TABLE 5

Profile of New PhDs in Physics/Astronomy

from N.R.C. Data

	1968	1969	1970	1971	1972	1973	1974	1975	1976
Total	1422	1452	1657	1740	1635	1590	1334	1293	1235
% Foreign Citizens	15.1	15.2	17.2	18.3	20.2	23.4	25.2	27.0	24.5
% with Baccalaureate in same field as PhD	75.7	76.7	76.7	77.0	78.5	78.5	81.5	81.0	80.2
Median Time Lapse Baccalaureate to PhD									
Total Time	6.3	6.3	6.4	6.7	6.8	7.0	7.1	7.2	7.0
Registered Time	5.6	5.8	5.8	6.0	6.0	6.1	6.1	6.2	6.1
% of class leaving U.S. after Doctorate	6.5	4.7	4.9	8.7	10.3	6.6	12.9	12.7	10.6
% of class staying in U.S., staying in physics		83.9	84.6	77.4	76.1	74.8	76.2	62.1	73.4
% of class staying in U.S., no report of field		9.0	3.8	8.1	9.4	11.2	11.4	19.1	13.4
% of class staying in U.S., expected to leave physics to take positions in:		7.1	11.6	14.5	14.5	14.0	12.4	18.8	13.2
Math		1.1	2.3	2.7	3.3	2.3	1.7	2.2	0.9
Chemistry		0.4	0.3	0.4	0.5	0.7	0.6	0.7	2.1
Earth Sciences		1.4	1.6	2.8	1.6	0.8	1.5	1.6	2.9
Engineering		2.7	3.2	3.7	2.8	3.3	3.7	7.7	4.3
Biosciences		0.9	1.8	2.1	3.5	4.0	2.2	3.8	3.3
Non-Science		0.7	2.4	2.7	2.9	2.7	2.6	2.7	1.6

the country.

For the purposes of extrapolation, we assume that 10% of a given graduating class will find employment outside the U.S. (Foreign citizens continue to make up 25% of the first-year graduate enrollments in physics.[24]) Thus an exodus of 10% is equivalent to assuming that the total immigration per year from those with PhDs abroad or from foreign citizens with U.S. PhDs, will be about 15% of a given PhD class.

We further assume that 15% of those who stay in the United States will seek employment outside of physics and will not be part of the physics labor force after the first-year. This is about two-thirds the out-mobility during the first year following the PhD. (We are, in effect, acknowleding that about one-third of the new PhDs who leave physics for other fields do so becuase they cannot find suitable employment in physics.)

To project the net new entrants into the labor force we, therefore, multiply the projected number of PhDs by 0.9 x 0.85 = 0.765. We anticipate that this percentage will not be greater than 0.81 nor less than 0.72.

Overall, then, from 1976 through 1986, the yearly entrants into the physics labor force should decline monotonically from about 900 to about 750 per year.

We thus anticipate a total of 13,300 new PhDs in physics/astronomy from 1975 through 1986, with an upper bound of 14,600 and a lower bound of 12,500. The total number of new entrants into the physics/astronomy labor force from 1975 through 1986 is expected to be 10,200; with a minimum of 9,000 and a maximum of 11,800.

The total number of new entrants into the doctorate labor force of physics, during the decade from 1975 to 1984, is expected to be less than 70% of that of the previous decade.

DEMAND

The total demand is subdivided into components for replacement -- death, retirement or migration out of traditional employment -- and for growth (or contraction) of the field. The growth component in unpredictable so long as long-range science planning is absent. According to the NRC surveys, there was a 2.6% growth per year in the positions of employment for PhD physicists between 1972 and 1975 (Table 4). We estimate that half of that growth was the result of upgrading which we treat separately below. An increase of 1.3% per year in new positions yields 250 jobs per year from a base of 19,000. Such an increase did not greatly alleviate the job difficulties during the early 1970s when PhD production was greater than 1500 per year, but when the new entrants into the field drop below 900, even a low growth rate of 1.3% per year can be decisive.

The demand for PhD physicists per year is defined as the number of openings per year in the traditional fields of physics employment. There are, of course, other demands for those with physics backgrounds. There is a need for some to work in the traditional fields of engineering, life sciences, earth sciences, etc., especially in sub-fields which were spawned from physics. And there is a demand for physicists in emerging areas which border physics and which make use of physics training, but which are not generally specific sub-fields which students are trained for in graduate school. The existence of a surplus of physicists can itself create the demand in these peripheral areas. But the demand is generally not long-lived, for if the peripheral field grows it will develop programs to train its own and new entrants will come predominantly from the more narrowly trained. A good example from the past is the field of nuclear engineering. Over 75% of the full professors of nuclear engineering received their degrees in other fields; but more than 75% of the assistant professors have their degrees in nuclear engineering. Medical physics appears to be a growing area for PhD physicists, most of whom are not trained specifically in that sub-field; but there are already schools which expect to train people for this cross discipline and we may anticipate that, in 10 years, production from these departments will restrict the flow from physics.

1. Replacement of Those who Die or Retire

To compute the death rate we use the mortality tables for males from TIAA-CREF, the main insurers of academia. These rates are about a factor of two smaller than those for the general population of white males (Figure 7). For the age distribution at retirement (Table 6) we use the distribution of ages at which people take their annuities from th TIAA-CREF Retirement Fund. The most recent age distribution for full-time employed physicists is given by the 1973 AIP survey of the physics community,[18] and we use that data to extrapolate death and retirement rates through 1986. Figure 8 shows the age distribution of faculty in PhD physics/astronomy departments in 1973; experimentalists and theorists are plotted separately.

The results for the death, retirement and combined rates as a function of year are given in Table 7.

Since the age distributions for the different sectors of physics, i.e., academia, government, industry, are not substantially different, one can use percentages of Table 7 to determine the replacement needs for the different sectors.

We see that the combined death and retirement rate is now about 1%; it will increase to only 1.6% by 1985.

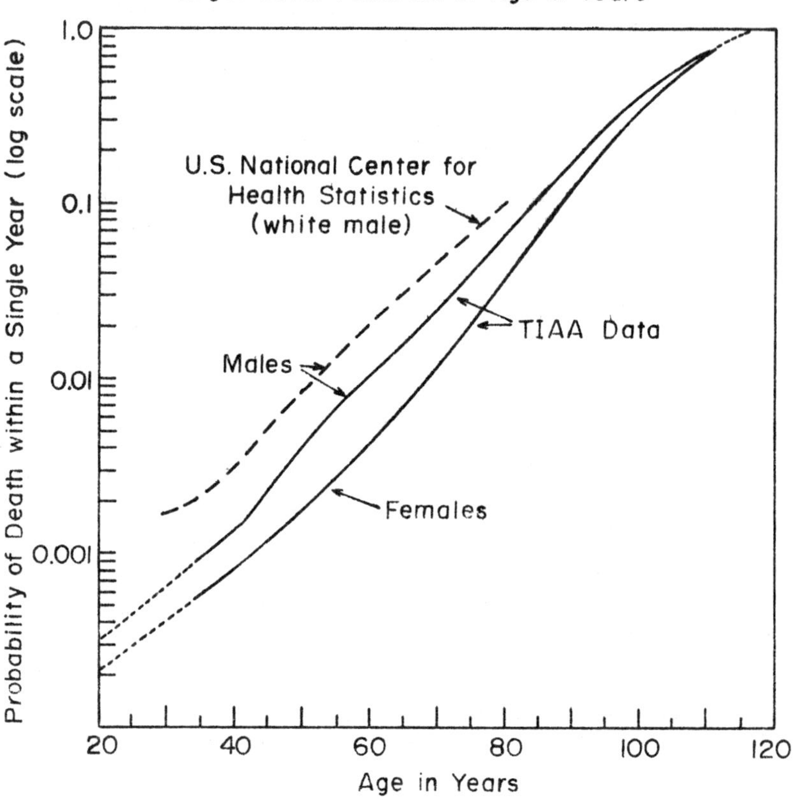
Probability of Death within One Year as a Logarithmic Function of Age in Years
Probability of Death within a Single Year (log scale)
1.0
0.1
0.01
0.001
U.S. National Center for Health Statistics (white male)
TIAA Data
Males
Females
20
40
60
80
100
120
Age in Years

FIG. 7

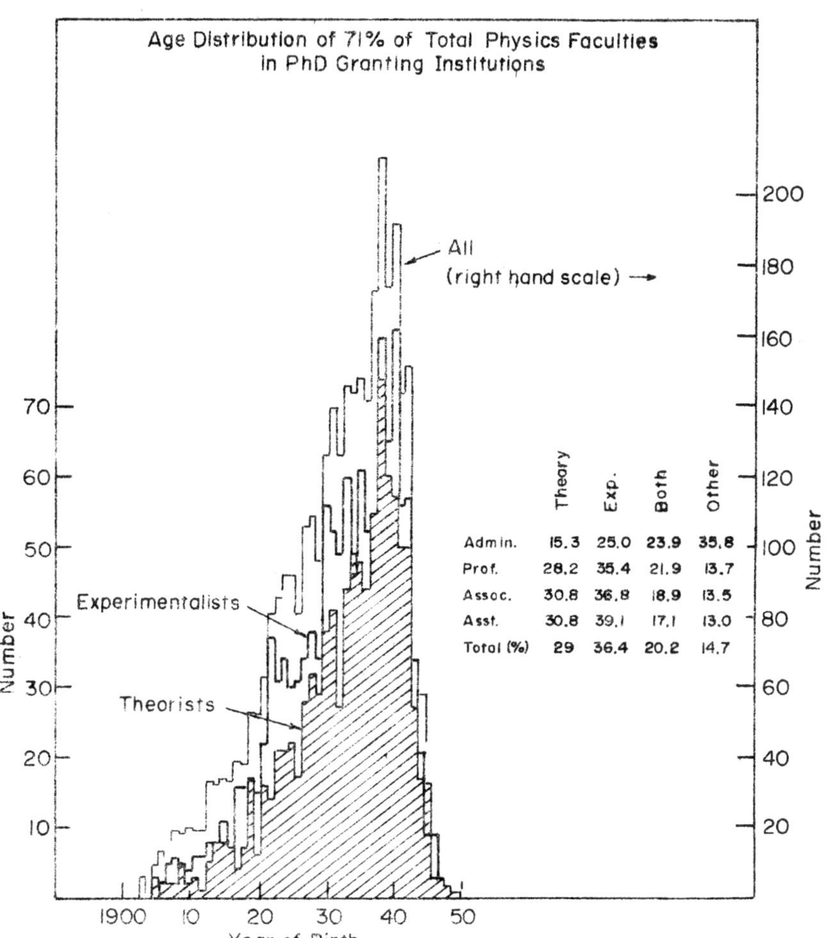

Age Distribution of 71% of Total Physics Faculties
in PhD Granting Institutions
All
(right hand scale)
Experimentalists
Theorists
Number
Year of Birth
1900
10
20
30
40
50
70
60
50
40
30
20
10
200
180
160
140
120
100
80
60
40
20
Theory
Exp.
Both
Other
Admin. 15.3 25.0 23.9 35.8
Prof. 28.2 35.4 21.9 13.7
Assoc. 30.8 36.8 18.9 13.5
Asst. 30.8 39.1 17.1 13.0
Total (%) 29 36.4 20.2 14.7

FIG. 8

TABLE 6

The Percent of a Given Age Group

Expected to Retire; Based on TIAA Distribution

of Starting Ages for Retirement Annuities

Age	60	61	62	63	64	65	66	67	68	69	70
Percent who retire	1	2	6	7	20	50	30	30	30	30	All

TABLE 7

Death and Retirement for Physics Doctoral Population

(Based on TIAA-CREF Actuary and Retirement Data for Males)

Year	Expected Mortality Per Thousand*	Expected Retirement Per Thousand*	Expected Death Plus Retirement In Percent*	Number Expected to Die or Retire**
1975	2.4	6.5	0.89	167
76	2.5	7.0	0.95	179
77	2.7	7.6	1.04	195
78	2.8	7.5	1.04	195
79	2.9	8.0	1.09	205
1980	3.1	8.5	1.16	218
81	3.2	8.9	1.21	228
82	3.5	9.6	1.31	246
83	3.6	9.9	1.35	254
84	3.8	10.5	1.42	268
1985	4.0	11.9	1.59	299
86	4.2	12.8	1.70	319
87	4.3	14.2	1.85	348
88	4.5	15.9	2.04	384
89	4.7	17.2	2.19	411
1990	4.8	18.6	2.34	441

* Based on AIP age distributions from 1973 Survey.

** Based on a 1974 labor force of 18,800.

2. Replacement of Those who Leave Traditional Physics Employment

There are two components which should be considered: those who change fields and at least some who change activities. We will only consider the former, but we note that when, for example, a professor of physics takes a position in the administration of the university (e.g., Dean, Provost, President), he leaves a vacancy which will generally be filled by hiring another physicist. Similarly, when a physicist in industry takes a managerial position whose compass is broader than physics, he does not usually fill a physicist's shoes, but he leaves behind a position which will be filled by a physicist. These are non-negligible components of demand, but we know of no data which give their measure.

The considerable overlap in the subject matter and the methodology of the various scientific disciplines leads to a natural flow of manpower between them. We are interested in the voluntary component of field mobility; positions which become open because someone who has a secure future in physics is attracted to another field. This component is partially off-set by the in-mobility from other fields; the present job shortages for physicists almost guarantees that any in-mobility is a pull into physics. During the last seven years, out-mobility has been more than three times in-mobility (Table 8); during the early 1960s, in-mobility was greater than out-mobility.

The mobility within physics need not be considered in this overview of physics but it should be understood that mobility between subfields, between activities and between employment sectors becomes increasingly important the more we disaggregate the projections.

We define a fungibility factor,[22] F_{IJ}, between fields I and J,

$$F_{IJ} = A_{IJ}/E_{IJ} = \frac{\text{Number actually transferring from I to J}}{\text{Number expected to transfer from I to J}}$$

We make the natural assumption that if there are not correlations between fields, the expected number transferring from I to J is given by simple proportions. Thus

$$E_{IJ} = \frac{\text{(Total number transferring into J)(total number transferring from I)}}{\text{(Total transferring into all fields, omitting those from field I)}}$$

so that the fungibility factor from I to J becomes

$$F_{IJ} = \frac{N_{IJ}}{\sum\limits_{i \neq j} N_{ij} \sum\limits_{j \neq i} N_{ij}} \sum_{i \neq I} \sum_{j} N_{ij}$$

If all fields are equally correlated, $F_{IJ} = 1$. Fungibility factors much greater than unity indicate a strong overlap; those less than unity very little overlap. The definition is hardly the only

TABLE 8

In- and Out-Mobility as a Function of PhD Class
Data Obtained by NRC in 1975 Survey

	Academic Year of PhD								
	1966	1967	1968	1969	1970	1971	1972	1973	1974
Total in Survey with Physics PhDs	1190	1460	1057	1399	1565	1610	1460	1426	1230
% of Actual No. of PhDs Graduated in Physics	1.12	1.11	0.74	0.96	0.95	0.93	0.89	0.92	0.93
Total PhDs Employed in Physics	810	1204	659	1091	1110	1203	1155	1030	858
Total with PhD in Physics Who are Employed in Physics	690	1065	583	913	955	988	942	865	793
Percentage of Row 1	58.0	72.9	55.2	65.3	61.0	61.4	64.5	60.7	64.7
Total Who Left Physics Row 1 minus Row 4	500	395	474	486	610	622	518	561	438
Total Who Entered Physics Row 3 minus Row 4	120	139	76	88	155	215	213	165	45
Ratio of Out-Flow to In-Flow:Rows 6:4	4.2	2.8	6.2	5.5	3.9	2.9	2.4	3.4	9.7

Table 9

FUNGIBILITY FACTORS BETWEEN BROAD FIELDS

(DATA FROM 1973 SURVEY OF DOCTORAL SCIENTISTS AND ENGINEERS)

Employment Field / PhD Field	Math	Physics	Chem	Earth Sci	Eng	Bio-Sci	Psych	Soc Sci	Non-Sci
Math		1.1	0.03	0.6	2.7	1.0	0.1	0.6	0.8
Physics	1.3		0.9	1.2	2.9	0.6	0.03	0.2	0.6
Chemistry	0.3	1.4		0.9	1.4	2.2	0.01	0.02	0.9
Earth Science	0.6	1.8	1.4		2.0	1.2	0.03	0.3	0.8
Engineering	2.3	3.3	1.7	1.2		0.3	0.06	0.4	0.8
Bio-Science	0.2	0.3	3.7	2.2	0.4		0.2	1.0	1.2
Psychology	0.8	0.2	0.01	0.05	0.2	1.1		2.2	1.9
Social Science	0.6	0.01	0.03	0.5	0.2	1.3	0.4		2.3
Non-Science	1.1	0.3	0.3	0.1	0.2	0.2	3.8	2.6	

one which might be invented, nor is it entirely satisfactory.

The fungibility factors between broad fields, from the 1973 Survey of Doctoral Scientists and Engineers, are given in Table 9. (The number are assumed to have 25% uncertainties due to difficulties in measuring mobility.) The generalities gleaned from the table are not surprising: there is considerable overlap between some fields, e.g., chemistry and bio-sciences, physics and engineering; very little overlap between others, e.g., physics and psychology; and the fungibility from I to J need not be the same as J to I, e.g., chemistry majors are more often employed as mathematicians than mathematicians are employed as chemists.

We define the demand component of field mobility as $D_{IJ} = F_{IJ} - 1$, and do not consider negative values of D. The net demand is then,

$$D_{physics,J} \; N_{physics,J} - {}_{I} \; D_{I,physics} \; N_{I,physics} \, ,$$

where $N_{physics,J}$ and $N_{I,physics}$ are the actual number of people in a given year who leave or enter physics from J and I each year, respectively.

The recent mobility between employment fields is known from the 1973 and 1975 NRC surveys, Tables 3 and 8. Assuming that fungibility factors and employment mobility will not change, we conclude that 150 net positions are opened up each year because physicists are pulled out of secure positions. This estimate -- determined by a well-defined, quantitative procedure -- is only about 50% of the net out-mobility of recent years. It would appear to be a conservative estimate.

3. <u>Upgrading</u>

The increased use of PhDs in positions formerly filled by non-PhD holders continues to be a significant source of positions in most scientific fields. Physics, however, is already dominated by its PhD component: two-thirds of the jobs in physics are carried out by PhDs; in the early 1960s two-thirds was done by non-PhDs. There is considerable evidence to support the thesis that, in physics, an open position, previously held by a non-PhD, is filled more often than not by the PhDs so available on the job market today. To estimate this component, we take the number of physics positions occupied by non-PhDs,[23] 5900, multiply by the job turnover rate, estimated to be 8% per year, and assume that 50% of these openings are filled by PhDs. We assume further that there is no growth in the non-PhD labor force; thus, the number of upgraded positions diminishes by about 4% per year.

The above algorithm predicts an upgrading component of demand of about 230 positions per year; but there are obviously large

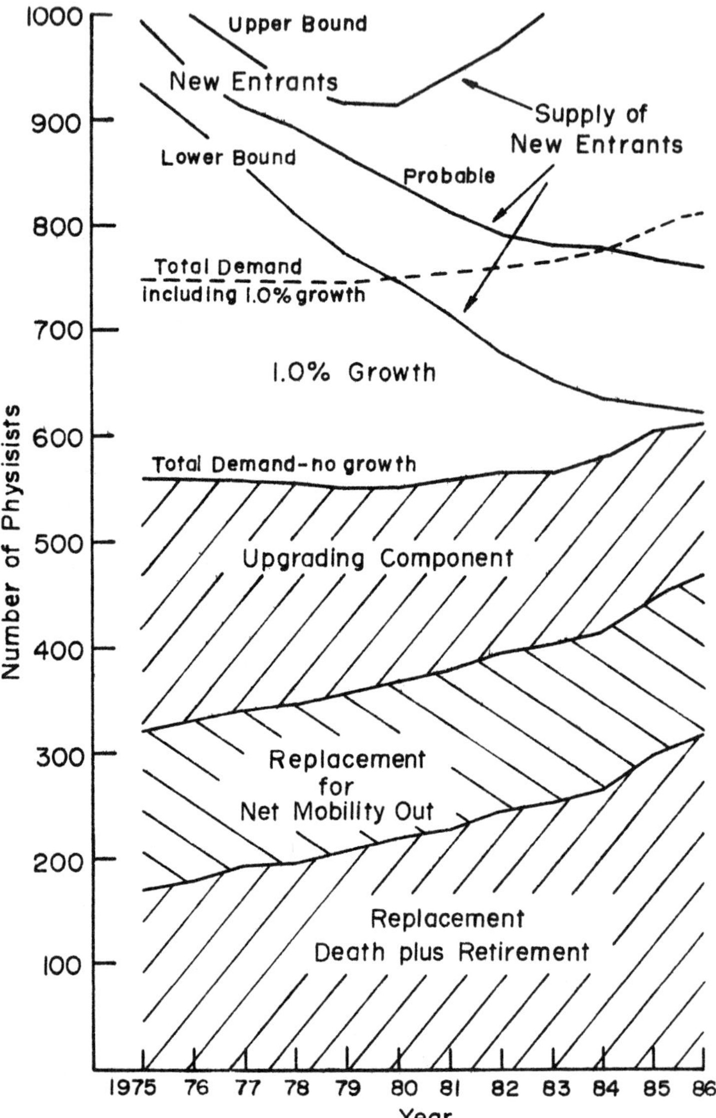
1000
900
800
700
600
500
400
300
200
100
Number of Physisists
Upper Bound
New Entrants
Lower Bound
Supply of
New Entrants
Probable
Total Demand
including 1.0% growth
1.0% Growth
Total Demand-no growth
Upgrading Component
Replacement
for
Net Mobility Out
Replacement
Death plus Retirement
1975 76 77 78 79 80 81 82 83 84 85 86
Year

FIG. 9

Table 10

SUMMARY OF SUPPLY-DEMAND PROJECTIONS FOR PhD PHYSICISTS

Year	SUPPLY PhDs/Yr.	SUPPLY New Entrants	DEMAND Death	DEMAND Retirement	DEMAND Mobility	DEMAND Upgrading	Total Replacement Demand	1% Growth	Total Yearly Demand
1975	1,293	990	45	122	150	230	547	188	735
1976	1,235	940	47	132	150	221	550	190	740
1977	1,190	910	51	143	150	212	556	192	749
1978	1,170	890	55	141	150	204	550	194	744
1979	1,140	870	58	150	150	195	553	196	749
1980	1,100	840	60	160	150	188	588	198	756
1981	1,070	820	66	167	150	180	563	200	763
1982	1,050	800	68	180	150	173	571	202	773
1983	1,030	790	71	186	150	166	573	204	777
1984	1,020	780	75	197	150	159	581	206	787
1985	1,010	770	79	224	150	153	606	208	814
1986	1,000	760	81	241	150	147	619	210	829
Sum 1975 through 1986:									
upper	14,600	11,800			2,400	4,000	9,200		11,600
	13,300	10,100	750	2,050	1,800	2,200	6,800	2,400	9,200
lower	12,500	9,000			1,500	1,400	5,700		8,100

uncertainties. We could well be low by 200 or more, or high by 80; a lower bound of 150 positions is given by the close estimate we can make of the upgrading demand in the 700 or so departments of physics which do not award the PhD and whose faculty are at least 20% non-PhD.

4. Total Demand

There will be a slow increase in the demand component resulting from death and retirement. If the average age at retirement rises by two years by 1985, the death and retirement component will decrease to 1.3%; a reduction of two years will increase this component to 1.9%.

There will be a minimum of 150 positions per year opened up because some in physics positions will be pulled to other fields; the upper bound is probably 350 positions per year.

The number of positions per year resulting from upgrading is estimated to be 230 this year, declining to about 150 positions by 1986. We estimate that the 230 per year figure has a lower bound of 150 and an upper bound of 400.

The growth component of demand is unknown. The doctoral physics labor force which grew at a rate of 7%/year in the 1960s, ceased to grow -- indeed contracted -- in the early 1970s but now seems to be growing at a rate of 2 - 2.5%/year. It does not seem unreasonable to project a modest growth of 1%/year; that is not to imply that such a projection is reasonable.

SUMMARY, COMMENTS, RECOMMENDATIONS ON DATA COLLECTION

The various components of supply and demand are summarized in Table 10 and Figure 9.

The physics community, taken as a whole, appears to have passed through its gravest hour. The job market is beginning to look healthier for new entrants into the field primarily because there are so few of them. By the middle 1980s, the number of positions in traditional physics should be about equal to the number of new entrants in the field.

This general conclusion must be treated cautiously since we have a poor understanding of field mobility and up-grading and no crystal ball for government policy. It is more prudent to remember the more limited conclusions

1. Through 1990, neither death nor retirement will be a significant factor in providing opportunities for young physicists.

2. Physics faculties are not as a whole expected to expand

in the next two decades. The slow decline of recent years (Figures 4 and 5) may even accelerate because the total population of college age students will begin to decline in 1979. But it is not clear that a decline in total enrollments in higher education will have a significant effect on the enrollment in the PhD-granting schools. Nor is it clear whether the total enrollment figures in the PhD-granting schools has very much relevance to the enrollment in physics courses which determine the need for physics faculty. If we assume that the present number of physics faculties in the PhD schools (5000 with the rank of Instructor or higher) remains constant, we can estimate the need for physics faculties. The only demand components are death, retirement and out-mobility. Death and retirement, now around 1%, will rise to only 1.6% by 1985. Out-mobility is expected to continue to be about 1%. If these positions are filled from the 1981 PhD class, we estimate that 12% of that class will find permanent positions in doctoral-granting departments. We consider this to be an optimistic projection since it is not unlikely that faculty sizes will shrink further. But even if the odds worsten, we expect that the situation will be less severe than it has been in recent years, when the odds that a PhD would get a permanent position in a PhD department were about 8%. Table 11 presents these probabilities for a number of years; the figures for the classes of 1963, 1966 and 1969 were derived from a detailed cohort study to be published.

Table 11

PERCENTAGE OF A PHYSICS/ASTRONOMY PhD CLASS

ATTAINING TENURE (ASSOCIATE PROFESSOR RANK)

PhD Yr.	Number of PhDs	Number Entering Job Market	Number Entering Faculty 4 Yrs. Later	Percent That Stick	Percentage of PhDs Who Enter Physics Labor Market Who Attain Tenure
1959-60	574	520 (90%)	350	70%	47%
1963-64	792	713 (90%)	350	70%	34%
1966-67	1233	1085 (85%)	260	57%	14%
1969-70	1545	1236 (80%)	200	50%	8%
1974-75	[illegible]	[illegible] (77%)	200	40%	[illegible]
1978-79	1100	850 (77%)	200	50%	12%

N.B. 1. A fixed interval of 4 years is assumed between PhD date and first entrance into faculty ranks.

2. Underlined values are estimates (see text).

3. We have only a poor measure of the number of theorists who get their PhDs per year; the only data are from the 1973 survey of the AIP.[18] From that survey we conclude that about 30% of all PhDs get their degrees as theorists (roughly 1/3 of all physics faculties in PhD schools are theorists). But in the employment fields outside of the PhD departments, theorists occupy only 15% of all physics positions; in industry, the fraction is 12% (more are hired, but not to do physics theory.) It thus appears that we are training 2/3 of the PhDs for about 85% of the available positions and 1/3 of the physicists for about 15% of the positions.

Unless the supply of theorists drops substantially (we do not know the trends at all), we expect the job market for theorists to remain very difficult.

4. The average age of the physics community is estimated to be increasing at a rate of about one-third of a year each year; that of physics faculties has been increasing at about one-half a year each year. The average age will continue to increase throughout the 1980s unless there is a real growth in the labor force of at least 3%/year. We are developing a generation gap in our community; there are far too few young physicists. The consequences for the health of our research and for the vitality of our teaching are profoundly disturbing.

5. The number of PhDs per year in nuclear particle physics has dropped so substantially, Figure 3, that supply and demand for experimentalists in these fields will probably cross in the next few years. Already, there are not enough nuclear and particle physicists for the one hundred or so postdoctoral positions available per year in each of these sub-fields. We expect that in these fields, post-doctoral positions will be converted to more permanent staff positions at a rate of about 25 to 40 positions per year and in consequence there will be an influx into these fields from those trained abroad or in other fields, as well as from those who have left nuclear and particle physics in recent years.

I am pleased to acknowledge the financial support of the American Physical Society during the early phases of this study.

REFERENCES

1. Projections of Science and Engineering Doctorate Supply and Utilization, 1980 and 1985, National Science Foundation, NSF 75-301.

2. Ph.D. Manpower: Employment Demand and Supply, 1972-1985, U.S. Department of Labor, Bureau of Labor Statistics, 1975, Bulletin 1860.

3. Projections of Education Statistics to 1985-86, M. Frankel and F. Harrison, National Center for Education Statistics, 1977, NCES 77-402.

4. A.M. Cartter, Ph.D.'s and the Academic Labor Market, McGraw-Hill, 1976.

5. N. Dean, Physics Today, p. 10, May 1973.

6. R. Freeman, American Economic Review 65, 27 (1975).

7. Scientific and Technical Manpower Projections, Report of the Ad Hoc Committee on Manpower, National Science Board, 1974, NSB 74-286 & 287.

8. A.M. Cartter, The Supply and Demand for College Teachers, Journal of Human Resources, 1 (1966).

9. A.M. Cartter, Scientific Manpower for 1970-1985, Science 172 (April 9, 1971).

10. W. Gruner, Physics Today (June 21, 1970).

11. L. Grodzins, The Manpower Crisis in Physics, B.A.P.S. (July 1971).

12. L. Grodzins, Where Have All the Physicists Gone, Tradition and Change in Physics Education, 1974.

13. American Institute of Physics Reports on Degrees and Enrollments.

14. Reports on Doctorate Recipients from United States Universities, National Research Council.

15. Doctoral Scientists and Engineers in the United States, 1973 Profile, National Academy of Sciences.

16. Doctoral Scientists and Engineers in the United States, 1975 Profile, National Academy of Sciences.

17. L. Grodzins, Physics Faculties 1959 to 1976, to be published.

18. American Institute of Physics, 1973 Survey, several reports by B. Porter et al. including Physics Today (April 1974).

19. Private communication.

20. A Century of Doctorates, L. Harmon, National Research Council, to be published.

21. See, for example, Immigrant Scientists and Engineers in the U.S., NSF 73-302 and Scientists, Engineers and Physicians from Abroad, NSF 72-312.

22. L. Grodzins and P. Coggeshall, The Fungibility of Scientists, to be published.

23. T. Senator, Profile of Non-Ph.D. Physicists. (The NSF estimates that the 5900 figure for non-PhDs in physics positions in 1975 may be low by 60%. We deliberately chose the lower figure for projections.)

24. Graduate Science Education, Student Support and Postdoctorals, National Science Foundation Series, issued annually.

MANPOWER STUDIES RELATING TO COLLEGE PHYSICS TEACHING IN THE MIDWEST

U. J. Hansen
Indiana State University, Terre Haute, IN 47809

ABSTRACT

A series of surveys conducted at Indiana State University in 71-73, results of which were reported at the Aug. 74 Tradition and Change in Graduate Physics Education Conference, had been designed to assess physics manpower needs in non Ph.D. granting institutions in the midwest with particular interest in preparation for college physics instruction. Following these, three additional surveys were conducted in 1975 covering the same geographical area. One survey was designed as an update, the other two were sent to Ph.D. granting institutions and their placement bureaus respectively, to obtain Ph.D. placement information. The update survey confirms the overwhelming (2:1) preference for teaching experience and preparation over research interests expressed in earlier surveys. Placement statistics are somewhat more puzzling - 31 of 46 institutions responded indicating that with 6002 students enrolled 304 Ph.D's were awarded in 1975 of which 249 were placed in industry, education or as post doctoral fellows, with 20 not employed in physics related areas nor expecting to be. Only 21 of 46 placement bureaus responded indicating 50 out of 189 registrants placed in employment.

TEXT

A series of surveys were taken in Indiana, Indiana's neighbors and in states bordering Indiana's neighbors. Questionnaires were sent to institutions without Ph.D. programs in physics in order to assess needs for faculty in smaller schools from a standpoint of number of staff members to be hired, potential faculty members' training and interest. A supporting questionnaire was sent to Ph.D. granting physics departments in the same states to get a feeling for graduate placement. Questionnaires were color coded in order to identify schools according to the following AIP categories:

MP - Master's degree offered in physics
BP - Bachelor's degree offered in physics
CP - Combined program (or minor) offered including physics
AP - Associate's degree offered in physics
GP - General science program requiring physics courses offered
IP - Only introductory physics courses offered

The 1971 survey was designed to investigate desired qualifications of potential faculty. Of 592 institutions contacted 388 responded. The 1973 survey directly evaluated response to a possible Doctor of Arts (D.A.) degree designed to give formal teacher preparation on the doctoral level. From 643 sent 312 answered with 267 positive and 45 negative responses, where 140 would hire a Ph.D. as first choice, 111 a D.A. and 48 someone with a Master's degree.

ISSN:0094-243X/78/087/$1.50

The 1975 survey was directed at Ph.D. granting universities with 31 out of 46 departments and 21 of 46 placement bureaus responding. The departments indicated that of 6002 students enrolled in Physics Ph.D. programs 304 degrees were awarded with 78 placed in industry or government laboratories, 50 in educational institutions, 121 as postdoctoral fellows and 20 not placed in physics nor expecting to be. Placement bureau statistics do not appear helpful; those responding indicate 189 registered and 50 placed. The 1975/6 survey was designed as an update of the earlier surveys on faculty qualifications. The 1975/6 instrument is reproduced below with total responses inserted in the blanks. The numbers associated with questions 2 and 3 represent the total cumulative number of responses listing these alternatives as 1st, 2nd or 3rd choices.

Questionnaire sent Winter 1975; returned & evaluated 1976

1) Department faculty need

_25_ a) We are currently seeking new or replacement faculty members.
____ b) We expect to have _185_ openings during the next 5 years.

2) Experience of potential candidate

Please rank candidates for hypothetical or real current faculty positions in your department (1-high, 5-low) with the following qualifications:

_194_ a) D.A. as described in the accompanying letter.
_102_ b) Ph.D. with several years of research experience.
_245_ c) Ph.D. with several years of teaching experience.
_177_ d) recent Ph.D.
_91_ e) person with a master's degree.

3) Interest and background of potential candidate

Please rank the following responses in order 1 (high) to 6 (low) as they reflect the situation in your department.

"_If_ we were recruiting _NOW_, we would be seriously interested in a ."

_190_ a) person with strong formal training and experience in exploring teaching techniques.
_272_ b) person with strong interest and experience in undergraduate teaching.
_123_ c) person with background in curriculum development.
_154_ d) experimentalist with interest in interdisciplinary problems.
_84_ e) experimentalist (please specify area ________________).
_34_ f) theoretician (please specify area ________________).

Table 1 summarizes faculty openings and projections by school category and survey year. Tables 2 and 3 give the raw data for questions 2 and 3 of the 1975/6 survey respectively.

CONCLUSION

It is clear from these responses that teaching experience and teacher preparation is valued highly. In fact a 2:1 preference is indicated when the sum of the 1st three choices of teaching related interests is compared to the first three choices of research related interests.

Table I Faculty Openings

	Spring 1976							1971	1973
	MP	BP	CP	AP	GP	IP	TOTAL	TOTAL	TOTAL
Current	4	11	1	1	3	5	25	40	25
5 year projection	40	61	10	30	8	30	185	310	197

Table II Response to question 2 of 1976 survey

Experience of potential candidate

	MP	BP	CP	AP	GP	IP	Total
a) D.A.							
1st	1	14	5	14	12	20	66
2nd	6	26	3	19	4	22	80
3rd	7	28	1	1	2	9	48
4th	14	22	2	1	3	8	50
5th	2	3	0	1	0	2	8
b) Ph.D., res. exp.							
1st	9	7	0	1	0	4	21
2nd	7	12	3	0	2	5	29
3rd	8	28	4	3	1	8	52
4th	6	22	2	9	5	14	58
5th	0	3	3	21	13	28	68
c) Ph.D., tc'g exp.							
1st	16	57	7	8	6	22	116
2nd	9	28	3	8	6	19	73
3rd	4	15	1	15	7	14	56
4th	0	0	0	4	3	8	15
5th	1	1	1	1	1	0	5
d) recent Ph.D.							
1st	13	31	1	0	2	3	50
2nd	7	27	3	5	2	11	55
3rd	8	23	5	8	9	19	72
4th	3	15	3	16	3	20	60
5th	1	5	0	6	6	6	24
e) Master's							
1st	0	3	0	14	4	23	44
2nd	0	4	0	10	8	3	25
3rd	1	6	1	5	2	8	22
4th	1	16	3	3	4	12	39
5th	26	67	7	3	4	14	121

Table III Response to question 3 of 1976 survey

Interest and background of potential candidate

	MP	BP	CP	AP	GP	IP	Total
a) formal tch. trg.							
1	1	13	2	9	3	23	51
2	3	23	5	14	11	33	89
3	5	21	1	9	4	10	50
4	7	21	2	0	1	10	41
5	9	11	2	1	3	0	26
6	4	2	0	0	0	1	7
b) undergr. tchg.							
1	13	72	8	26	17	61	197
2	9	16	1	8	6	14	54
3	3	7	3	1	4	3	21
4	3	6	0	0	0	1	10
5	0	1	0	0	0	0	1
6	4	0	0	0	0	0	4
c) curric. dev.							
1	1	8	1	2	1	6	19
2	3	14	1	6	3	9	36
3	3	14	5	15	5	26	68
4	4	21	3	6	8	14	56
5	8	20	0	1	0	7	36
6	9	16	2	1	2	2	32
d) interdisc. exp.							
1	8	19	0	2	1	4	34
2	6	30	2	3	3	10	54
3	12	21	2	3	8	20	66
4	5	23	7	17	6	26	84
5	0	4	1	4	3	1	13
6	0	1	0	1	1	2	5
e) exp.							
1	13	10	2	0	0	5	30
2	5	19	1	3	0	1	29
3	2	17	0	1	0	5	25
4	4	7	0	5	4	4	24
5	5	31	4	16	11	32	99
6	0	7	2	4	3	11	27
f) theor.							
1	0	3	0	0	0	1	4
2	5	2	2	0	0	3	12
3	4	8	1	1	2	2	18
4	2	8	1	0	1	0	12
5	4	15	2	5	2	11	39
6	14	52	4	26	13	38	147

ON ADVISING WOULD-BE PHYSICISTS

Bruce Rosenblum
University of California, Santa Cruz, CA. 95064

ABSTRACT

The demographic and technological reasons for the recent job shortage for Ph.D. physicists are reviewed. These factors are considered as they apply to students now starting or considering a physics education. It is concluded that there is <u>no valid economic reason for advising students against training for a career in Physics</u>.

It is not uncommon for students to be advised or sense the advice that physics is an overcrowded profession and it is unwise for economic reasons to enter it. This is, of course, a result of the well publicized underemployment problems for physicists. The employment problems that physicists have faced for the past several years were looming over the horizon well over a decade ago. The present situation could have been foreseen with reasonable assurance back then. And today we can anticipate what young physics students will face a decade from now. We will consider this future to see if there is justification for advising a student against a career in physics for economic reasons.

Let us first discuss the roots of our present situation and then in this light try to discern what the future holds. Basically, in addition to the unpredictable weak state of the economy, affecting everyone, the recent employment problems for physicists have two independent origins:

1. The Demographic Origins: The monotically and rapidly increasing college population of the sixties and early seventies is about to end. Some years ago, college faculty expansion stopped. Teaching jobs for physicists became scarce. At the same time, the number of physics B.A.'s and Ph.D.'s increased each year during the sixties at a very rapid rate. The annual number of physics Ph.D.'s granted <u>tripled</u>! This tripling was due to a larger fraction of young people going to college and a much greater interest in physics as a career. While for demographic reasons, academic physics jobs were disappearing, we were producing more and more physicists wanting such jobs.

2. The Technological Origins: Three "immature" technologies appeared after the war and grew rapidly in the fifties and early sixties. These were modern electronics, space and

ISSN:0094-243X/78/091/$1.50

nuclear energy. There were no appropriately skilled engineers in these areas. In those days, these new technologies needed a good deal of the basic research and development that physicists were well qualified and happy to do. As these technologies matured, their perceived need for basic research declined, and specialized engineers also became available. No new immature technologies with comparable demands for physics appeared. Physicists were seen as not being as well suited as the engineers for the mature technologies. Government research in many ways reflected the industrial situation. Thus in the nonacademic sector, jobs for physicists were also becoming scarce, but for technological reasons.

So what is the situation today? First of all we should realize that these changes (the vast increase in Ph.D. production, the slowing of university hiring and the maturing of the technologies) have already taken place. There is little reason to think that things will continue to get worse. We still, of course, suffer from these changes of the recent past. More physicists may still lose their jobs. But these factors have already had their impact on young people considering physics careers (whether they really understand them or not). They have all heard that physics Ph.D.'s drive taxicabs. (Actually, of course, most recent physics Ph.D.'s have good jobs they are happy with.)

Let us now consider the demographic and technological factors as they will eventually affect a young person <u>just now starting out on a possible career in physics</u>.

1. The Demographic Factors: The birthrate peaked in 1960. Today's freshmen are the most populous age-group in the country. From now on the number of seventeen-year-olds is going to decrease every year for the next decade and a half, at least. This means that each freshmen class is assured that each year as they graduate college there will be fewer and fewer college graduates. Furthermore, this will be at a time when the number of people in the twenty-five to forty-five year age-group, who most stimulate an economy, will be steadily increasing. It looks like the general job situation for people now entering college, and for those who follow them, will be much better than it has been for their older brothers and sisters. This is true for all fields, including physics.

   How many of these will be getting their Ph.D.'s in physics five years or so after graduation (about a decade from now) is harder to predict, but there is every reason to extrapolate that their number will be substantially less than that of the late sixties. If the proportion of students going into physics stays the same as it is now, the number of Ph.D.'s produced when today's freshmen receive them will steadily decrease year by year. Actually for the last five years, the number of Ph.D.'s given in physics has steadily and substantially declined (by about thirty percent) in spite of the increasing population in that age-group.

2. Technological Factors: No substantial new technologies analogous to those which grew two decades ago and which require a great deal of basic physics research are apparent. But there is also little expectation that the current level of physics research by industry and government will decrease. Actually, there are considerable technological developments at present and in the offing for which specific classes of engineers or other scientists are not well defined. Those that come most immediately to mind are related to our new energy economics and the rapidly growing realizations of the need for sophisticated adjustments in our technological behavior with respect to environmental modification. When new problems arise, the very fundamental training of physicists allows them to meet the requirements naturally. Furthermore, and at least as important, is that the attitudes of young physicists (and, as a result, the attitudes about young physicists) are changing. Their view of the type of job that is suitable for them is considerably less narrow than was held by their teachers when they were students. Slowly but inevitably the undergraduate and graduate education of physicists will also change to adapt them more appropriately to the career environment these young people will enter.

In summary, the demographic and technological factors which created the recent job shortage for physicists will no longer be operative when today's beginning physicists enter the job market. The situation is likely to improve with each succeeding class. And, of course, if the situation will be good for today's freshmen, it cannot be much worse for those only a few years ahead.

A comment about students who stop at the bachelor's degree: In slightly modified form, the demographic and technological factors discussed appear almost equivalent. The job situation for these beginners when they graduate should also improve each year from now on. Furthermore, an extremely wide range of non-physics graduate training is open to students with an undergraduate degree in physics.

A comment on "population control" and advising: It has been suggested that we should attempt to limit the number of physics students for the benefit of those already in the field. This technique is apparently practiced by some other respected professions. The moral aspects of such behavior is subject to debate. But, in any event, in advising one must give advice for the benefit of the advisee.

THE DYNAMICS OF FUNDING, ENROLLMENTS, CURRICULUM AND EMPLOYMENT

Harvey Brooks
Harvard University, Cambridge, Mass. 02138

ABSTRACT

During the 1960's synergism between academic research, expansion of undergraduate and graduate enrollments, and consequent expansion of faculty created an unusually favorable situation. There was a pronounced shift of job opportunities from non-academic to academic, especially in physics. Simultaneously the spectacular growth of the Ph.D. in engineering met a need in industry and government which had previously been filled by physics Ph.D.'s, a factor which was more or less unique to physics. The situation is unlikely to change soon.

END OF A GOLDEN AGE

The period from about 1955 to about 1967 will be looked back upon as the golden age of academic science in the United States. It was a period of unprecedented growth and prosperity, in which rapid increases in financial support were matched by remarkable advances in basic science. Today academic science is still benefiting intellectually from the dividends generated by that period of heavy investment. A recent study of the state of scientific research in the so-called research universities, conducted by Prof. Bruce Smith and associates through Brookings, concludes that U.S. academic science is still dynamic and productive, but that there are many symptoms of trouble and prospective decline on the horizon.

The relevant statistics are shown in the first three tables. Table I shows the total federal investment in academic science, measured in constant 1967 dollars. You will note how it grew rapidly in the early 60's and reached a peak in real terms in 1967. The drop off from the peak is 17%, and the apparent recovery in the last several fiscal years not shown has been almost entirely eaten up by inflation. A part of the loss is indicated in the precipitous drop in federal fellowships, shown in the lower half of the first table.

The second table breaks down federal research support by field. It indicates that the overall pattern is comprised of growth in the life sciences and social sciences balanced by shrinkage in the physical sciences and engineering. The total shrinkage appears less because this table does not include the loss of federal fellowships, which is taken into account in the totals of the first table.

The third table shows changes in the distribution of scientific and engineering manpower in academic institutions, classified by major activity. To be noted is the fall off in manpower whose primary activity is research, from 1969 on. This reflects a combination of the drop in research support with the rapid relative growth of purely teaching institutions, especially the community colleges. But of course it is also symptomatic of the academic market for new graduates.

ISSN:0094-243X/78/094/$1.50

Table I

Academic Science Constant (1967) Dollars	
1963	$1.445 B.
1965	1.912
1967	2.324
1969	2.186
1971	1.953
1972	2.091
1973	1.929
Graduate Students Supported by Federal Fellowships	
1961	11,591
1963	15,601
1965	26,425
1967	51,289
1968	51,446
1974	6,602

Table II Academic R. and D. in Constant 1967 Dollars, Various Fields

Year	Engineering	Phys. Sci.	Life Sci.	Psych. and Soc. Sci.
1964	0.136 B.	0.201 B.	0.488 B.	0.075 B.
1968	0.238	0.264	0.700	0.144
1972	0.209	0.218	0.727	0.134
1973	0.228	0.219	0.771	0.150

Table III Full Time Equivalent Scientists and Engineers in Academic Institutions According to Primary Activity (Thousands)

	Teaching	R. and D.	Other
1965	99.6	40.4	16.3
1967	119.0	47.5	19.8
1969	145.0	50.4	21.8
1971	170.8	49.8	22.1
1973	183.1	48.0	20.5

The great academic boom of the 60's was primarily a demographic boom. During the decade of the 60's the U.S. population in the 20-24 age group increased at the rate of 4.4% a year, compared with a decline of 0.5% a year in the preceding decade. The yearly output of Ph.D.'s in science and engineering increased by about 10.5% a year as compared with only 4% a year the preceding decade, but when the population of the relevant age cohort is considered the rapid growth of the 60's is not so remarkable. Nevertheless, the population growth created an educational demand which shifted scientists and engineers towards the academic system, and away from industry and government. By continually feeding the demand for new Ph.D.'s this phenomenon concealed the fact that the educational system was probably producing more Ph.D.'s than the economy could absorb in the long run. Derek Price, the Yale historian of science who likes numerology, has suggested that any departures from the three century long term growth of the scientific community at the rate of 6-7% a year is likely to be compensated rather promptly, and certainly there is evidence of a rapid drop off in graduate study in the sciences in the early 70's, with physics suffering the largest decline.

The character and extent of the academic boom is well illustrated in the fourth table, which shows the distribution of first employment of doctorates from U. S. universities. What is to be noted particularly is the drop off in initial industrial employment of physicists and chemists, with the rapid growth of initial university employment. It is true this gives a somewhat exaggerated picture because it includes postdoctoral appointments, whose holders often eventually move out of the academic pipeline. This table shows one other interesting phenomenon; engineering Ph.D.'s appear to be an exception to the rapid shift from industrial to academic employment. The percentage of engineers going to university faculties has actually declined modestly during the period 1958-1972. This is all the more remarkable when it is considered that engineering has been the most rapidly growing graduate field for the entire time period. The annual growth of output of Ph.D.'s in all fields of engineering reached 15% for a good part of the decade, and the annual number of engineering Ph.D.'s now exceeds 3,000, as much as physics and chemistry combined. Between 1973 and 1975, for example, the "stock" of engineering Ph.D.'s grew by 7,000 individuals. If one looks in more detail at what has happened, one is led to the conclusion that engineering graduate work has taken over much of the frontier training function that was provided by physics and chemistry during the 50's. Physics and chemistry Ph.D.'s were hired by industry and government during the 50's to do essentially engineering type work, because the training of engineers was too narrow and conservative to match the rapid change in technology of that period, especially the transition to solid state electronics. But what is happening is that much graduate work in engineering today is indistinguishable from what would have been called physics, chemistry, or applied mathematics 15 years ago. There has been a good deal of complaint about this fact from industry, but the figures I have shown on demand for Ph.D. engineers appear to belie these complaints to some extent.

Table IV First Employment of Doctorates from U.S. Universities (Percent)

	Univ.	Industry	Gov.	Non-Profit
Physics and Astronomy				
1958-60	47%	32%	10%	4%
1961-63	51	20	9	6
1964-66	55	18	9	4
1972	65	9	12	1
Chemistry				
1958-60	25	63	4	2
1961-63	38	45	5	3
1964-66	44	38	5	2
1972	69	14	7	1
Engineering				
1958-60	41	44	4	2
1961-63	40	40	3	4
1964-66	40	38	4	4
1972	38	35	15	2
Arts and Humanities				
1958-60	87	1	2	2
1961-63	87	1	1	2
1964-66	89	1	1	2
1972	84	1	2	1
Professional Fields				
1958-60	66	5	2	12
1961-63	70	4	2	10
1964-66	73	5	2	7
1972	75	5	5	7

The surprising mobility of doctorates is well illustrated by some figures from the National Register on the source of 1,894 doctorates employed in the general field of solid state physics and its applications in 1964. Of these only 2.5% received their original graduate training in solid state, while 19% were trained in chemistry and 73% were trained in fields of physics other than solid state, mostly nuclear. These statistics raise a question in my mind as to whether on the whole it is a good thing for universities to respond too closely to the currently perceived needs of industry and government in their training programs. In fact there is a certain paradox in the fact that the big shift of graduate study in physics towards solid state (now more than 40% of all Ph.D.'s in physics) took place after the big industrial advances in this field had been carried out mainly by people trained in nuclear and particle physics.

The prosperity of academic science is illustrated in another way in the fifth table, which shows patterns of publication of papers in the Physical Review in various subfields of physics. Note the degree to which university physicists became dominant in almost every subfield except condensed matter in the decade from 1959 to 1969. The sixth table also shows the same pattern in total employment of Ph.D. physicists, and compares it with publications. In general academic physics accounts for a larger fraction of *Physical Review* publications than it does of physics employment. Especially striking is the under representation of industrial physicists in the production of *Physical Review* articles in the field of condensed matter physics relative to their numbers. However, this is less surprising when one looks at the changing pattern of utilization of Ph.D. physicists in industry during the decade of the 60's. From 1960 to 1970 total industrial employment of Ph.D. physicists increased by 55%, from 2,450 to 3,800, but the number engaged in basic research declined absolutely and the fraction in basic research declined from 20% to only 10%. By 1970 nearly two thirds of the physics Ph.D.'s in industry were engaged in activities other than basic or applied research, mostly development or management. This parallels a similar shift which took place in federal laboratories, and the shift from research to teaching in the academic system, but seems more drastic. If you remember Table 5 it helps explain the drop in the percentage of publications in the subfields of physics coming from industry between 1959 and 1969.

Table V Institutional Source of Papers Published in *Physical Review*, 1969

Field		Univ.	Ind.	Gov.	Non-Profit
High Energy					
	1959	72.0%	0.0%	3.7%	24.1%
	1969	77.2	3.0	8.9	10.9
Nuclear Struct.					
	1959	47.7	4.6	7.7	40.0
	1969	67.8	1.6	4.8	25.8
Plasma, Fluids					
	1959	20.0	40.0	20.0	20.0
	1969	92.4	0.0	0.0	7.7
Atomic, Molecul., Electron					
	1959	56.3	18.8	6.3	18.7
	1969	73.3	2.4	14.6	9.8
Cond. Matter					
	1959	51.6	34.7	7.4	6.3
	1969	65.6	18.9	12.6	9.4

Table VI Institutional Employment Pattern of Ph.D. Physicists In Various Subfields

Field		Univ.	Ind.	Gov.	Non-Profit
High Energy					
	1964	54	2	5	24
	1968	75	2	3	19
	1970	76	2	3	17
Papers --	1969	77.2	3.0	8.9	10.9
Nuclear					
	1964	41	8	7	39
	1968	50	10	8	27
	1970	52	10	6	25
Papers --	1969	67.8	1.6	4.8	25.8
Plasma, Fluids					
	1964	31	22	8	35
	1968	44	23	8	21
	1970	48	20	9	19
Papers --	1969	92.4	0.0	0.0	7.7
Condensed Matter					
	1964	36	38	8	14
	1968	43	33	9	11
	1970	43	35	9	9
Papers --	1969	65.6	18.9	12.6	9.4
Physics and Astron.					
	1964	43	24	9	19
	1968	50	23	9	13
	1970	51	23	9	12
New Hires --	1972	64.6	8.9	12.2	1.0
	1973	55.6	21.5	13.6	
	1975	61.0	21.3	10.9	

During the last half of the 50's the prosperity of academic science owed a good deal to the rising demand for Ph.D. scientists outside the universities, principally in the industries which benefited heavily from the space and defense effort. During the period from about 1957 to 1964 more than 75% of the increase in S. and E. employment in industry was accounted for by the aerospace and electrical industries, chiefly electronics. At the same time biomedical research, by far the single largest segment of academic research, was stimulated by the take-off in the budgets of the National Institutes of Health which occurred after 1956, and actually continued through the 60's. Thus during the 50's, despite the fact that the age cohort between 20 and 24 actually shrank, organized research grew from 11% to 13% of total national expenditures for higher education. By contrast, during the 60's, the prosperity of academic research was of another sort. It was based on the rapid growth of student enrollments, especially in the public universities. This in turn made possible an expansion of faculty to meet increased undergraduate teaching needs, and the larger faculty meant a greater capability for research and the coverage of more scientific specialties in a single department or institution. Rapid expansion also provided unusual opportunities for younger scientists, and thus helped to impart an unusual measure of intellectual vigor and innovativeness, combined with a certain amount of fragmentation and disorderliness to the academic research effort. Academia was confirmed as the primary home for basic research in the physical sciences, engineering, and the social sciences. Between the 50's and 60's the percentage of total national basic research performance accounted for by universities rose from about 35% to 53%, although it is hard to be sure how much of this might be explained by changing definitions. At the same time the universities, through their medical schools and agricultural experiment stations, became increasingly important as well in applied research as in the life sciences.

The success of academic research was indubitable, and the American collegial graduate department became the model which the rest of the world looked to, displacing the European research institute dominated by a single professor as the prototype for the conduct of research and advanced study.

Moreover, academic research attracted graduate students and postdoctoral students from all over the world. Perhaps no other statistic as well illustrates the pattern setting character of the enterprise. Of course, money helped, but it is interesting to note that the pattern continued even after the money growth began to slow down. The situation is illustrated in the seventh table, which shows the percentage of postdoctoral fellows and research associates working in U.S. academic laboratories. Chemistry was the field in which the total number of postdoctoral students was largest, and it also had the highest foreign population. The table also shows the percentage of foreign born individuals among the 1972 doctorates. These percentages are actually larger than in 1966, indicating that foreign students continue to come to the U.S. for graduate work even with the rising scientific prosperity of Europe and the lower available support in the U.S. The bottom of the table also shows the country distribution of the more than 3,000 postdoctrals of 1969. I have not collected up-to-date data, but my impression is that this situation has not changed in a major way in the 70's, although there has certainly been some decline in foreign postdocs. and graduate students.

Table VII

Percent Foreign Postdoctoral Fellows and Percent Foreign Born Ph.D.'s In Various Fields

Field	Postdocs. 1969	1972 Ph.D.'s
Physics	49.6%	20.2%
Math	39.7	18.2
Chemistry	63.6	18.4
Earth Sci.	54.5	19.7
Engineering	63.7	32.7
Biosciences	44.1	19.9

Country of Origin for Postdocs. in Physical Sciences, 1969
Total Number in Sample 3,084

U.S.	49.0%
U.K.	12.9
India	9.2
W. Germany	6.3
Japan	6.2
Taiwan	3.3
France	1.6

THE PROBLEMS OF STAGNATION

As I have already mentioned, the development of science, especially academic science, has been based on continuous growth. As Derek Price has emphasized, all the measures of the intensity and output of science have been growing with a doubling time of about 10 years since the middle of the seventeenth century. Even during the depth of the great depression the funding and the number of people in academic science grew at an average rate of about 7% a year for the decade 1930-1940. A reversal from 1932 to 1934 recovered much more quickly than the general economy. Suddenly in 1967 the whole growth seemed to level off, and a few signs of some renewed growth are just beginning to reappear. Undoubtedly, given the problems that face the world during the next two decades, there will be some resumption of the growth of R. and D. For FY75 the energy crisis has already created such a turn-around, although much of it may be offset by inflation. The degree to which academic research will participate in this new growth is less certain. The growth of faculties in the most research-oriented universities has essentially stopped, and seems unlikely to resume, in the light of the projected decline in enrollments during the 1980's. As long as university size is basically determined by the student-teacher ratio, universities will not grow much. What are the implications of this slow growth?

First is the decline in the number of career opportunities for younger scientists on university faculties. This situation is aggravated by past growth, which has left many universities with a faculty age distribution skewed in such a way that the number of retirements will be abnormally low during the next decade. Faculty is heavily peaked in the 30-34 age group, about 28% in the case of physics. The eighth table shows age distributions in 1969 and 1972. In only three years the percentage of faculty over 40 increased from 50 to 61%, and the under 30 group dropped by more than half. There was a big increase in the proportion of faculty on tenure. In addition to the decline in the number of younger faculty there is likely to be a decline in the number of graduate students available for participation in research.

Table VIII Percentage of Faculty in Various Ages

Age	1969	1972
less than 30	16.0	7.0
30-40	34.9	31.0
41-50	26.7	32.5
greater than 51	23.4	28.2
tenured	46.7	64.7
teach 1-5 hr.	15.4	11.8
5-8	25.0	21.8
More than 13	22.5	31.4

The significance of the change in age distribution is not easy to assess. There exists a general folk wisdom to the effect that scientific productivity peaks at an early age, especially in the more mathematically oriented subjects. This is probably true, but the evidence is not as conclusive as usually thought because science has been growing exponentially, and this automatically means that at any one time the proportion of young scientists is high and always has been. Robert Merton has studied the question of age vs. scientific productivity, but was unable to reach definitive conclusions. One fact is certainly true. Scientists on the average spend a much higher proportion of their time in research when they are young. A study of academic Ph.D. physicists, for example, showed that those between 25 and 30 spent 65% of their time on basic research, while those between 55 and 65 spent only 10% of their time on basic research, and the decline was fairly uniform with age. Certainly the pull of non-research activities on older scientists is likely to increase, not decrease. Some work has been done on the publications of scientists as a function of age. It indicates that the most productive and highly recognized scientists tend to publish to a much later age than the average. Thus the statistics on work patterns alone may exaggerate the decline in the effective scientific productivity of groups, since other studies show that about 85% of the important scientific contributions are made by less than 15% of the active scientists.

To some extent the numbers problem has been accommodated by the classic market mechanism, namely decline in price accompanying increase in supply. Table 9 shows what happened to starting salaries for Ph.D.'s in various fields during two periods, 1964-69 and 1969-73. Note how the academic boom of the earlier period raised the salaries of professors relative to average labor force earnings and relative to starting salaries in industry. Note the drastic decline of all salaries of Ph.D. in the later period compared with industrial workers, but with professors suffering relatively less. The median salary of all Ph.D. scientists declined by 10% from 1973 to 1975 relative to the consumer price index, the decline varying from nearly 15% for computer specialists and atmospheric scientists to 6 1/2% for oceanographers.

Table IX Percentage Changes in Average Starting Salaries of Graduates Measured Relative to Annual Earnings of All Workers in Industry

Field		1964-69	1969-73
Ph.D. in	Chem. Eng.	+2.7%	-21.2%
	Elec. Eng.	-5.8	-19.3
	Mech. Eng.	-0.1	-18.2
	Civ. Eng.		-19.1
	Math.	-6.6	-24.4
	Physics	+1.0	-28.0
All Professors		+7.8	- 7.6

The tenth table is also of interest. It shows the percentage of time spent by Ph.D. physicists and all scientists in various activities. I also have figures for 1975 which confirm the fact that declines in research activities have continued, especially basic research. The figures are shown in Table XI.

Table X Percentage of Ph.D.'s in Various Activities - 1968

	Physics	All Science
In R. and D.	54%	38%
In academic R. and D.	28	19
In basic research	38	24
Some federal support	62	43
Defense Dept. support	17	11

Table XI Percentage of Ph.D.'s in Various Activities - 1975

	Physics	All Science
In R. and D.	45%	32%
In academic R. and D.	20	14
In basic research	24	15
Some federal support	57	40
Defense Dept. support	19	8

The tenure system in universities probably aggravates the problem of aging. In industry there are far more alternative activities for scientists who have lost their zest for basic research. The frontier basic science of today often becomes the ingredient of technology tomorrow, so that in an institution where the full spectrum from basic research to development and manufacturing is maintained, the basic researcher can find a rewarding career in gradually moving into development or management. It is interesting to note that in non-academic R. and D. organizations, involvement in basic research, at least for Ph.D. physicists, declines only from 50% to 15% with rising age. However, the most serious problem with aging is career blocking for the younger people. Even when older researchers remain productive the system as a whole, as Derek Price has remarked, depends on the injection of "new doctorates trained in new fields whose significance lies in the future and cannot be realized by manpower already trained in an earlier phase." Furthermore, the student, and especially the very brightest students, stand intellectually on the shoulders of several teachers with different specialties. The continual process of compression and codification which takes place as an integral part of the research process enables the able neophyte to assimilate a much broader area of knowledge than his teacher was able to master in the process of learning his specialty for the first time. Thus this process of cumulative compression of science as it progresses makes youth a very integral part of scientific progress.

THE CRITICAL MASS PROBLEM

Although much basic research in the universities is still highly individualistic, there has been a definite trend towards team research. Even mainly individualistic research depends to an increasing degree on occasional collaborators or on occasionally used special facilities too expensive to be justified for any single research group. Increasingly academic scientists are looking for potential collaborators in the institutions to which they go, and complain that they cannot do good work without the ready accessibility of a group of individuals in related fields. This is a problem not only of research but of teaching. A department feels it has to be "well rounded," and as knowledge in a discipline expands, the number of subdisciplines and people required for well-roundedness expands with it. However, the trend towards increase in the number of multiauthored papers, at least in physics, is still modest. For all Physical Review papers it was 1.75 authors per paper in 1936, and rose only to 2.25 by 1971. But in some fields, such as nuclear and elementary particle physics, virtually all papers are multiauthored, and very large groups are required to do research at all.

Academic research has adapted quite well to the growing size of frontier facilities in nuclear physics, particle physics, and radio and optical astronomy. Through the formation of "user groups" in the universities, academic scientists have remained the primary users of national facilities, such as those at Brookhaven, Batavia, and Green Bank, even after the major capital and operating cost investments have shifted away from campus locations. Thus, for example, in elementary particle physics in 1972 total federal support for operations, equipment, and research (other than construction) was about $150 million, of which 25% was in direct support of university groups. However, university groups comprised 76% of Ph.D. manpower, and accounted for an even larger fraction of the publications.

But the users mode of operation poses problems, especially during periods of transition from the older period of on-campus facilities, such as is now being faced in nuclear structure physics. Professors and students have to spend extended periods away from the campus to do experiments when they are scheduled, regardless of their own teaching commitments. With such off-campus activity the universities may require additional teaching staff to cover courses. Physicists with young families may not enjoy such a peripatetic life, and must weigh the excitement of the field against its logistic problems. Nevertheless, the pattern of users groups has served to keep the intellectual frontier on campus, and to permit a relatively wide diffusion of research activity among many universities while concentrating major facilities at a much smaller number of locations. It seems to me almost inevitable that this trend will continue and accelerate and will extend to an increasing number of fields. It presents problems in that it probably produces fewer opportunities for personal and individualistic participation in research. It is only a partial "holding action" in the seemingly inevitable trend towards the "rationalization" or "industrialization" of a growing number of areas of basic research.

The "critical size" problem is also arising in an entirely different context. With the change in national priorities, and the advent of such programs as the NSF "Research Applied to National Needs" (RANN), groups are forming on campus to participate in multidisciplinary coordinated applied research. Although the RANN program has met with mixed success, one of its difficulties has not been in finding groups to step forward with proposals. There is hardly a major campus today without its own center for energy, environmental, or urban research. It has been difficult to mount coordinated programmed efforts cutting across many different parts of the university, and to reconcile these efforts responsibly with the ongoing teaching and research responsibilities of disciplinary departments, but as in the case of the user groups in "big science", it has been done, and here and there one finds some success stories. The problem is a serious one, however, in a time of stagnation in growth, since interdisciplinary activities can often be undertaken only at the expense of the disciplines if they are to be dependent primarily on the leadership of regular faculty. Furthermore, the young faculty member competing for tenure faces a painful ambiguity as to what is expected of him, and what criteria will be used in his ultimate consideration for a dwindling number of tenure slots in the faculty. Where faculty promotion is determined by majority vote of disciplinary departments, will the young scientist who commits his or her career to a multidisciplinary team activity in the university have any long term career progress to look forward to?

The suggestion has been made that if this kind of research is to be undertaken in universities, in the long run, the volume of academic research will have to become more decoupled from the output of Ph.D.'s. Accompanying this may be the development of fully respectable career lines within the university outside the normal faculty ladder. A few universities created such career lines during the 50's and 60's to undertake development work in connection with space and defense activities. Among the best examples are the Draper Laboratory at M.I.T., the Jet Propulsion Laboratory at Caltech, the Lawrence Berkeley Laboratory, the Atomic Energy Laboratory at Iowa State University, and the Center for Astrophysics at Harvard. But these activities have tended to become gradually more divorced from campus activities, and debate still goes on as to the merits and demerits of their close association with the university. The employees of such laboratories are in varying degrees treated as second class citizens on campus.

An alternative possibility is the creation of what I have called "buffer institutions", research and application organizations closely allied to universities, and geographically close to clusters of universities, but administratively autonomous. Such organizations could encourage participation of faculty and students in their activities, while their own professional staff might serve as adjunct professors at nearby universities. The purpose would be to provide a kind of clinical millieu for faculty and students, analogous to the affiliated teaching hospitals associated with university medical schools. Such organizations could serve as intermediaries between the academic community and the external society, keeping the university institutionally at arms length from the more politically controversial aspects of the activities of applying knowledge to the implementation of social programs. Institutions of this sort may be especially appropriate for the application of the social sciences, because industry and current national research centers are quite weak in the social sciences.

MISSION-ORIENTED RESEARCH

As the size of university faculties stagnates, and graduate student bodies fail to grow, universities will more and more be faced with a policy decision as to the degree to which and the terms on which they are prepared to participate in the mission oriented research programs which will be supported by government and perhaps to an increasing degree also by industry associations such as EPRI and GRI. Will preoccupation with the difficult problems of administering such research erode the quality of education and more traditional basic research? Is there a fundamental cultural incompatibility between the conditions for the highest quality basic research, and success and effectiveness in the performance of applied or policy research? Most industrial organizations that have been successful in maintaining high quality basic programs have found it necessary to provide a measure of isolation for this part of their program, while providing incentives and opportunities for career changes from basic to mission oriented programs. Can universities with their much more collegial and less hierarchical structure ever hope to provide such a dual career track? Is the necessary financial stability possible, which could provide long term career prospects for people in universities doing mission-oriented or programmatic work? Even in organizations like those cited earlier, where there may be _de facto_ tenure, careers are _perceived_ as less secure and more subject to the vagaries of federal appropriations.

On the whole American universities have shown a remarkable ability to adapt to changing environments in the past, and I believe they will in the future. As I have indicated, they have succeeded in inventing new forms of organization and funding that have enabled them to participate effectively in "big science" and to retain the intellectual leadership and initiative in fields where logistic requirements far transcend the capabilities of traditional university management. As the government moves towards greater interest in long range problem solving in such areas as energy, environment, urban managment, social welfare, or international development one already sees a good deal of experimentation in universities with new organizational forms related to the new national priorities. In my view, it is essential that universities continue to be able to attract and hold some of the best intellectual leadership of each generation. In the long run effective interdisciplinary and problem-solving research depends on a constant infusion of new perspectives and new techniques from the basic disciplines. It would be dangerous if longer range mission-oriented research either became completely separated from the universities, or if interdisciplinary research became itself a new discipline, recruiting its leaders from its own ranks rather than from the related disciplines. But I think that universities will not be able to retain their intellectual leadership role if their mission is restricted by the requirements set by teaching needs alone. We must find ways in which the research role of the universities can continue to grow with research generally, more decoupled than in the past from the quantitative limits set by teaching needs, and hence by changing demography.

On the other hand, we must also be realistic about the limitations of academic research. Universities cannot and should not try to do everything. Close responsiveness to a demanding client is not their best stock-in-trade, nor is meeting deadlines and milestones. Nor should it be. Most university people have a refreshing but disabling naïveté about the difficulties of applying knowledge and understanding in the real world. In their enthusiasm for mission-oriented research, universities should not try to compete with other institutions better designed for such activities, lest they do an ineffective job, while in the meantime losing their unique capacity for developing fundamental conceptual insights.

At the same time, much experience has demonstrated that new and significant areas of basic research are opened up in the course of attack on applied problems, whether in technology or in efforts at social change. In my opinion it is this that should be the primary criterion of university involvement in social and technological problem solving. The "feedback" from problem solving into new research questions will vary from case to case; the universities should choose to be involved only where this feedback from applied into basic research and teaching is a major element.

HOW THE DEPARTMENT OF DEFENSE SHAPED ACADEMIC RESEARCH AND GRADUATE EDUCATION

Stanton A. Glantz*
University of California, San Francisco, California 94143

ABSTRACT

Although the military began after World War II with a liberal policy of supporting science more or less on its own terms, pressures from the Korean War, the Cold War, the Indochina War, and, later, shifting National priorities away from defense expenditures, acted in parallel with normal budgetary pressures to force the development of a hierarchial system for stimulating university research in areas of concern to the military. This process occurred slowly, with adequate time for the university scientists' interests to develop in parallel. Problems developed when the exponential growth in funds available from the military ended.

INTRODUCTION

A scientist's employment opportunities depend on his specialized knowledge. By funding scientific and engineering projects in universities, the Department of Defense has stimulated research and training in the skills it needed. This knowledge is often not central to solving non-military problems, so scientists trained in this system have difficulty finding work as scientists in the civilian sector. The situation did not develop overnight -- it evolved during the last 30 years.

After World War II, the Office of Naval Research was established to sponsor basic research in physics, electronics, and other sciences to "increase the general fund of scientific knowledge."[1] Its broad mission followed from the belief that this investment would pay off in the long run, just as untargeted research in nuclear physics and electronics had during the War. This attitude assuaged academic scientists' fears of heavy-handed military intervention in their research. The Office of Naval Research essentially permitted these scientists and engineers to resume, on a larger scale, projects started before the War. Students trained under these conditions were probably not oriented toward scientific problems of particular importance to the military. This situation began to change in 1950. The Korean War and the establishment of the National Science Foundation put pressure on the Office of Naval Research to add applied research projects to its traditional basic research program. (The other military research agencies, formed after the Office of Naval Research, had a more applied orientation from the beginning.) This policy change began the shift toward concern about the potential utility of research that has accelerated ever

*Dr. Glantz holds a Research Career Development Award from the National Institutes of Health.

ISSN:0094-243X/78/109/$1.50

since. In 1957, Sputnik catalyzed, among other things, a reorganization and tightening of the Department of Defense's organization for administering research. It also led to the establishment of the Advanced Research Projects Agency to stimulate new academic programs in areas including materials science and computer science. The belief in careful management that characterized McNamara's Defense Department during the 1960's continued the movement toward more careful selection of areas of science and research topics for funding. By 1970, the Defense Department had evolved a rational system for identifying and stimulating scientific research necessary to support its goals. The general budget squeeze that accompanied the Indochina War increased pressure on DOD to support proposals that seemed most related to its projected needs.

The all-volunteer army, begun in 1973, severely strained the discretionary portion of the defense budget and not only forced the Defense Department to continue tightening its standards for what research it will fund, but also led to an actual decline in constant dollars available for academic science. In addition, generations of graduate students had matured working on projects sponsored by the Department of Defense, so their native scientific curiosity had been channelled toward problems with military relevance. Thus, because Defense Department money formed the base for research in many physical science and engineering departments (Figure 1), the overall funding situation for these departments and for people seeking employment in them suffered as the nation's priorities shifted away from military expenditures.

THE EARLY YEARS: 1946 - 1950

During World War II, the American scientific community played a dramatic role in the American victory through such physics-based innovations as radar, the Norton bombsight, and the atomic bomb. In contrast to World War I, in which scientists were commissioned into military service, civilians managed the World War II scientific effort. This system permitted the scientists to collaborate with military personnel while minimizing military rigidities in the actual conduct of their work. The fear of military interference in the content of science, dating back to World War I, not only determined the structure of the World War II scientific effort but also spawned the fear of military control of science that permeated the American scientific community during the early post-War years. These fears motivated the scientific community to seek civilian control of atomic energy and a civilian-run Federal agency to sponsor basic research, including military research. Despite wide support in principle for such an agency, debates over federal patent policy delayed passage of the bill creating the National Science Foundation, which President Truman then vetoed on the grounds that the Foundation was too independent of the President.

Meanwhile, Naval officers who believed in the ultimate value of untargeted research moved to establish the Office of Naval Research inside the Department of the Navy.[2] Capt. R. Conrad, Director of the Office of Naval Research's Planning Division, captured the spirit of the day in a speech to the Commonwealth Club of San Francisco in 1946:

> Scientists during the war years were engaged in developing new weapons and devices in industrial, university and government laboratories, both under contract to the armed services and in collaboration with them in the remarkable civilian organization known as the Office of Scientific Research and Development.
>
> The knowledge stored up by research before the war was converted into the tools needed for victory. Very little actual research was done.
>
> The price we paid was the loss of knowledge, which research would have created if the war had not taken scientists from research and students from their studies.
>
> This is a far more serious loss for the national welfare than the depletion of any stockpile of critical material.[3]

After outlining the exciting areas of fundamental science that were then emerging - electromagnetic radiation, nuclear physics, relativity, statistical mechanics, genetics, computing machines, social sciences - he added:

> It will be a long time before the National Science Foundation can be enacted into law, staffed, supplied with funds and opened for business.
>
> In this critical interval, the Armed Services are providing the support so essential to science.
>
> ...
>
> By its activity since May, 1945, this Office has brought active financial support to scientific research workers in all fields of science -- including medicine -- in all parts of the country. Our contracts emphasize the fundamental nature of research, and are carefully designed to preserve the freedom of inquiry and action so essential to the spirit and methods of research work.
>
> ...
>
> I believe that the services are acting with wisdom and judgment; that this support will not degenerate into military control of scientists; and that a firm base is being laid for the National Science Foundation of the future.[3]

Conrad's speech accurately reflects the beliefs widely held at the time, that science held the key to solving the Nation's problems and that science was best left to the scientists. In fact, most officials believed that any attempt to manage fundamental research would ultimately destroy the product itself. For example, in the hearings to establish the Office of Naval Research, Secretary of the Navy Kennedy answered a Congressman's question about the level of control that the proposed Office would exercise over academic research by saying, "...there is one thing we want to be careful of with research, that we don't channelize research too much in one line. Research is a different kind of animal from production. In research, we want to get the benefit of all different kinds of people and different thoughts."[4] During the same hearings, Rear Admiral Harold Bowen, who was to become the first Chief of Naval Research, outlined a goal for the Office of Naval Research beyond supporting existing scientists: to develop a pool of skilled scientific personnell larger than the one that existed before World War II, in case the Nation needed to mobilize for war again. He pointed out that "most of the contracts are with universities...and the work done in many cases may be accomplished by graduate students who become acquainted with naval problems and may form a future scientific group to assist the Navy."[4]

This initial period was critical in the development of military-academic relations and, indeed, government-academic relations generally. Immediately after World War II, most academics expected to return to their prewar status, though perhaps retaining equipment that the government had purchased for them during the War. They feared military intervention into the content of science. Had the Office of Naval Research not adopted such liberal policies for funding scientific research, the universities might well have told the government to keep its money so they could maintain their independence. The Navy, however, provided money for good scientists to do good work with minimal administrative interference. The contracts were simple; proposals were funded on scientific merit alone; the research was untargetted; and none of the results were classified.

The early post-War years produced most of the rhetoric faculty and administrators used to justify the propriety of universities performing military research during the Indochina War 25 years later. By then, most of the graduate students Admiral Bowen had sought to interest in the Navy's problems comprised the mature leadership of academic society. And their concept of the military's role in academic research and development followed directly from their graduate student experience.

THE KOREAN EMERGENCY AND THE COLD WAR: 1950 - 1957

When fighting broke out in Korea in 1950, the Nation rearmed and mobilized its scientific resources. Part of this mobilization required a major policy change within the Office of Naval Research, reversing its previous position that applied research belonged in the Navy bureaus. As Admiral Solberg, Chief of Naval Research, told the House Appropriations Committee when testifying on behalf of the Office of Naval Research's 1952 appropriation,

> the Navy has been able to make an "investment" in fundamental research. That this "investment" is paying a high return during the current crisis is proven by the concrete scientific

> accomplishments and new developments already achieved, and by the fact that scientific manpower and facilities were available when this Office was required to expand its programs to include areas of applied research. Prior to the Korean emergency, the program of basic research of the Office of Naval Research was conducted to increase the general fund of scientific knowledge necessary for eventual solution of long range technical and scientific problems of the Navy. This program of continuing effort in the search for basic scientific knowledge is now being combined with the program of expanded applied research aimed at providing specific scientific and technical knowledge necessary for the solution of immediate Naval problems.[1]

The Office of Naval Research devoted its entire 1952 budget increment to applied research. Admiral Solberg added that "scientists who have been working with or for the Office of Naval Research on basic research projects during the past 5 years have themselves exhibited an extreme willingness to work on applied research projects of a military and classified nature."[1] Fearful that many of their best faculty would move to central government laboratories as they had been during World War II, many universities decided to introduce classified research and development to their campuses. When the Korean War ended, the fraction of the Department of Defense's research and development budget devoted to basic research increased, but the change in emphasis of the military research agencies never returned to its pre-Korean War liberality.

In addition to the direct pressures brought about by the fighting in Korea, the establishment of the civilian National Science Foundation in 1950 increased pressure from inside the military for the Defense Department to support basic research only in areas where it was likely that the knowledge would ultimately benefit the military. In addition, Congress began to express concern that there was a duplication of effort between the National Science Foundation and the military research agencies. As a result, in fiscal 1954, the Defense Department reviewed its general-purpose basic research projects and eliminated some areas with the understanding that the National Science Foundation would support similar projects. In fact, during hearings for the 1956 Department of Defense appropriation, Assistant Secretary of Defense for Research and Development, Donald A. Quarles stated, "...the Department of Defense Program now includes fundamental research only in areas where there is a high probability of future military application."[5]

Academic sources confirm this trend. James Killian, President of the Massachusetts Institute of Technology, told a 1952 American Society for Engineering Education symposium on academic research that

> the Department of Defense...has steadily supported the concept of basic research in those areas where the advance of knowledge is important to the military effort. The Department has only recently reaffirmed this policy, which provides for the support

> of basic research performed as an integral part of programmed research committed to specific military aims and for the support of academic research that promises ultimate military application.[6]

Similarly, in 1954 the American Council of Education Committee report, _Sponsored Research Policy of Colleges and Universities_, observed that, in contrast to the Office of Naval Research's position in the early postwar period, "...Government defense agencies have consistently taken the position that they are buying research which will strengthen national defense and not making contributions to higher education."[7]

The Committee reflected the universities' concern that the influx of defense money combined with the government's position that it was purchasing research to meet its own goals rather than supporting universities would have deleterious effects on the universities in the long run. But consistent with the general tone of the United States during the Cold War, the Committee concluded that

> institutions of higher learning and their faculties have the difficult, dual role of bearing their proper share of responsibility in meeting defense and other pressing needs of the Nation, while at the same time preserving, as fully as possible, their basic responsibilities in education and research.[7]

The general tone of the country during the Cold War probably facilitated the convergence of the DOD's progressively more directed and highly structured research program and the academic community's research interests. As Harvey Brooks, then Dean of Engineering and Applied Physics at Harvard, observed, the channelling forces were subtle.

> Scientific work involved a multiplicity of choices of direction, many of which depend on very small influences in the mind of the investigator. Even in a system of complete scientific freedom, the cumulative effect of the small biases placed in the mind of the investigator by a sponsor can have a profound effect on the direction and impact of his research. The mere need to defend what he is doing to a particular sponsor may be the factor which will trigger an important application. It seems to me no accident that both versions of the maser and the laser were conceived in university laboratories devoted to the broad advancement of electronic communications, and sponsored by the military services.[8]

Academic scientists, like other good citizens, wanted to contribute to America's strength and help fight off the communist threat. Because the university scientific community had already developed close rapport with many research administrators and scientific officers within the Defense Department, the shift toward targeted research must have seemed quite natural.

THE DEVELOPMENT OF A MATURE MANAGEMENT SYSTEM: 1957-1970

Before Sputnick in 1957, management of military research and development was decentralized in the various military services. As a result, the different services were competing rather than cooperating in the new U.S. space effort. In addition, the Secretary of Defense felt that the services were using research in areas such as missile technology to expand their traditional roles without his or Congress's explicit approval.[9] The competition between the services, while probably good for the universities because it provided a multiplicity of potential funding sources, was considered a management problem by the top civilians in the Pentagon. As a result, in 1958, the position of Director of Defense Research and Engineering was created in the Office of the Secretary of Defense to centralize the authority over and to manage military research and development.

The Advanced Research Projects Agency was created directly under the new Director of Defense Research and Engineering; it was given specific responsibility for developing, among other things, ballistic missile, antiballistic missile and satellite technologies.[9,10] Within a few years, this agency provided the money to stimulate universities to hire faculty and staff, recruit graduate students, and purchase equipment to establish "centers for materials research." These centers produced much of the fundamental solid state physics necessary for rapid development of heat shields and electronic devices for communication, night vision and computers. (The Advanced Research Projects Agency also stimulated rapid growth of computer science as a new discipline.)[11] These centers which enjoyed such spectacular growth in the early 1960's were to suffer disproportionately in the early 1970's when the Agency deemphasized materials science and transferred the centers to the National Science Foundation, where the competition for relatively scarce research dollars was much keener.

When he became Secretary of Defense, Robert McNamara worked to strengthen the Office of Secretary of Defense further. His implementation of the Planning-Programming-Budgeting System,[10,12,13] which was to provide management,direction and control of military systems from research through production and deployment, was a key element in his efforts to increase civilian control over the military. Whatever else it did, this system speeded the evolution of a sophisticated management structure to translate military needs recognized in the field or imagined by military planners into detailed scientific objectives to guide the research offices in selecting unsolicited proposals for funding. In contrast to the early postwar era, when unsolicited proposals were judged simply on scientific merit, proposals now had both to pass a scientific test and to fit into the military's research plan. However, this did not necessarily mean that the research that the Department of Defense decided to support was not fundamental in the sense that traditional academic research investigates long-range problems rather than develops products.

The result of this administrative structure was evident in a project-by-project study of all the research and development projects sponsored by the Defense Department at Stanford University that my coworkers and I worked on in 1971.[14-16] Originally, we expected that a few development projects would have clear military relevance, but that most of the research projects would have no particular military significance. Consistent with the perspective of the science and engineering faculty (many of whom were early Office of Naval Research graduate students), we did find that virtually all the work could legitimately be called basic research in that it was directed at understanding fundamental properties of natural or man-made systems, as opposed to contributing explicitly to a particular weapon. However, as we shifted our focus from the individual project to groups of contracts at Stanford, overall weapons-related programs emerged: one set of contracts, as a group, could be expected to provide knowledge to develop laser weapons, laser-and television-guided bombs, night vision devices, super-accurate intercontinental missiles, antiballistic missiles, advanced radar systems, and advanced helicopters. After we had essentially pieced together the Defense research and development program at Stanford, we obtained documents from the Department of Defense which permitted us to fit each Stanford contract into the Department's overall research plan and to outline how its research administration system converted problems perceived in the field or by military planners into research objectives to guide the research offices in screening unsolicited proposals.

The introduction to the Office of Naval Research's planning document, "Naval Research Trends," captures the flavor of research administration by the Department of Defense in 1971:

> Support for Nuclear Physics and Astronomy will be reduced in the next few years. Nuclear Physics will receive its main support from the Atomic Energy Commission and the National Science Foundation. The Navy will reduce its research in this area not only because it will be supported from other places, but also because the return on the investment no longer appears to be enough for us to invest the required large sums. Astronomy, too, particularly optical astronomy, seems unlikely to contribute much to our needs. We will decrease emphasis here considerably.
>
> There should be modest increases in General Physics, Oceanography, Terrestrial Sciences, Electronics, and Biological and Medical Sciences. In each of these fields, there are specific military requirements which are not likely to be funded by non-mission oriented agencies. In General Physics, much more will be done in the laser field. Amorphous semiconductors have potentials in military application. Superconducting technology and acoustic surface wave research appear promising and efforts in those fields will be increased

> modestly. The rate of expansion in oceanography over the next few years is expected to be somewhat less than it has been over the past seven or eight years. With the growth of oceanography programs sponsored by nonmilitary agencies, we must review and assess our efforts to give added strength to these programs of highest priority into military problems of the future. Our support for arctic research will increase in the next few years. Electronics is of primary significance to the military. Accordingly, our electronics research will increase with emphasis upon integration, miniaturization and reliability. Medical problems within the Navy and Marine Corps differ from those of the general public. We will, therefore, invest more money in this area because other agencies, particularly the National Institutes of Health, do not cover certain requirements found in military training centers and potential operational areas.[17]

Contrast these statements with Captain Conrad's praise for science and learning in general in 1946.

While each investigator was given a maximum of personal independence in the pursuit of his individual project, the Department of Defense had developed a highly rational structure for selecting those projects for funding that held the most reasonable promise for fitting into an overall research program oriented at developing the basic knowledge necessary for the Pentagon to fulfill its mission. Indeed, the Department's research management structure had evolved to provide a buffer of one or two administrative layers to shelter the academic community from the military motivation for supporting each project. This structure dealt effectively with academic researchers who, like creative people generally, react better to indirect control achieved through manipulation of their environment than they do to direct control achieved by management directives. For example, professors resist a Federal agency's attempts to tell them what or how to research, yet they stoically accept the simple fact that certain types of research are or are not funded.

Thus, during 4 to 6 generations of graduate students, the military's involvement with academic science grew from general diffuse support for good scientific work to a hierarchal system for stimulating and supporting scientific development in certain areas that could intelligently be judged of highest priority to the military. Although other agencies, especially the Department of Health, Education and Welfare, dramatically increased their expenditures for academic scientific research, these expenditures were rarely in the physical sciences or engineering, where the Department of Defense continued to play the dominant role (Figure 1). Graduate students supported by the Defense Department tended either to take academic posts, where they continued working in an area funded by the Department of Defense, or went to work for the aerospace or electronics industries.[15] The job outlook continued bright as long as military expenditures were increasing and the system was growing.

THE INDOCHINA WAR AND THE MANSFIELD AMENDMENT: 1970-1975.

This happy symbiosis between the Department of Defense and academia, which began in 1946 and continued through the late 1960's, ended abruptly when military funding for academic research and development, corrected for inflation, peaked and began to decline. (Figure 1 shows that this decline began at Stanford in 1968). The reason was that Presidents Johnson and Nixon were attempting to hold down the total Defense budget while escalating the Indochina War. The money available for academic research and development continued to decline as the air war escalated; research budgets failed to recover when the war ended because salary requirements for the new all-volunteer army continued to put severe demands on the Pentagon's total budget.

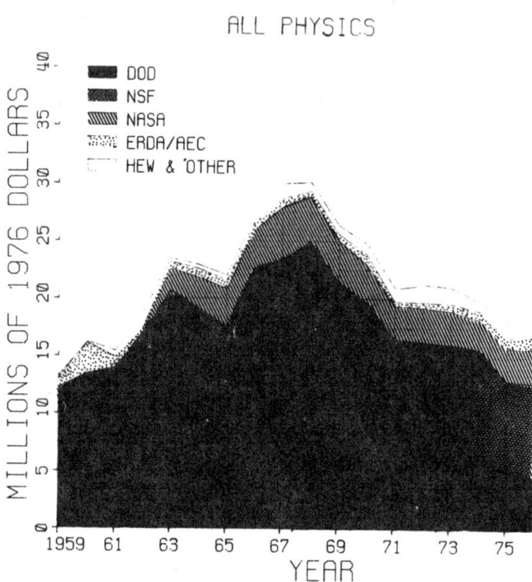

Fig. 1. Even though the amount of Federal money, corrected for inflation, coming into Stanford University for physics-related research and development (physics, applied physics, materials science and electrical engineering) from civilian agencies has been increasing, the large historic base of military money has fallen so far that there has been a large net decline in the constant dollars available. Data for Stanford were presented because, to obtain a meaningful picture, one must consider both the source of funds and the department receiving them. Aggregate national statistics of this nature are not available. Anecdotal experience suggests, however, that the trends at Stanford are typical.

Meanwhile, in the late 1960's, Senators William Fulbright and Mike Mansfield became concerned that the military's substantial resources made it too influential. They believed the military presence on campus should be lessened. In 1969, a Federal Contract Research Center, the Hudson Institute, published a book entitled Why ABM? which argued for deploying the antiballistic missile.

Senator Fulbright and other opponents of the antiballistic missile were incensed that such a large recipient of funds from the Department of Defense should enter the public debate over the ABM antiballistic missile. Senator Fulbright also objected to military social science research conducted abroad because he thought it harmed the United States' foreign relations; he felt such research was not in the domain of the Defense Department. Similar sentiments were expressed by other liberal senators and some conservatives supported tightening restrictions on what research the Defense Department could support on fiscal grounds. As a result, Fulbright's proposed amendment to the fiscal 1970 DOD appropriation was adopted. It required that

> none of the funds authorized to be appropriated by this act may be used to carry out any research project or study unless such project or study has a direct and apparent relationship to a specific military function or operation.[18]

Had Fulbright's amendment failed, Mansfield was prepared to reintroduce it alone, so it became known as the Mansfield Amendment.

Ironically, by the time Congress enacted the Mansfield Amendment, natural bureaucratic evolution and budgetary pressures had already brought the Pentagon into general compliance with its requirements. The amendment, with its requirement that all research relate to a specific military function or operation, had very little effect on the research supported by the Department of Defense. After a detailed review of all the academic research it sponsored, the Department had to cancel only about $8 million worth of planned research projects. In contrast, fiscal constraints required an overall $64 million cut in the research program.[18,19] Our investigation of Stanford's research projects agreed with the national picture; only a few projects could not reasonably be claimed to meet the Mansfield Amendment's standard. In fact, most of the contracts and grants we studied dated back into the 1960's and would have satisfied the Mansfield Amendment since their inception.

The Mansfield Amendment's major impact did not follow from its effect on research funding, but from its effect on researchers' psyches. Many academic scientists opposed the War while continuing to take military money for their research. To justify this behavior, these scientists generally resorted to the rhetoric of the early post-war period, preferring to believe that the military was supporting science in general in order to strengthen America or to express gratitude for science's role in winning World War II. Ironically, this rhetoric may have helped convince Congress of the need for the Mansfield Amendment. The amendment placed Defense officials, who by and large had already been meeting its standards, in an awkward position. They had to defend their diligence as managers of the public purse to an increasingly hostile Congress while continuing to shelter the academic community in order to preserve its supply of high quality research. In response to a question by Senator Pastore about the effect of the changing mood of the country on weapons researchers, Secretary of Defense Melvin Laird responded:

> If the interpretation of (the Mansfield Amendment) is that every researcher must certify in advance even in the basic research areas that there is some military or defense application for his research work, it will tend to discourage talented researchers from defense-related areas.
> ...
> I am going to recommend that we don't make the university scientists certify that any DOD-supported university research has a defense-related outcome.[19]

So the Defense Department sheltered its investigators from its own management structure. The Mansfield Amendment did, however, serve the important symbolic function of signaling the end of the era of post-World War II rhetoric.[19,20]

CONCLUSION

An intimate relationship has evolved during the last 30 years between parts of the academic scientific community, especially the physical science and engineering, and the research agencies of the Department of Defense. At first, the military was seeking to maintain the interest and cooperation of the scientific community and to expand the Nation's pool of trained scientists and engineers. Its support was diffuse and was based on the assumption that scientific research, in general, held the keys to solving our national problems. The initial policies of the Office of Naval Research, the first post-World War II agency to fund academic research and development, were explictly designed to foster untargeted research in universities. Since then, the Korean War, the Cold War, and the Indochina War, along with natural budgetary pressures have forced the Department of Defense to develop a progressively more hierarchal administrative structure to stimulate research proposals that mesh with the military's needs. At the same time, university scientists were interacting with their contracting officers, and their communication slowly focussed academic research efforts along the lines that the Department of Defense could justify funding. Since the late 1960's, however, budgetary pressures have forced the military to cut back its academic research and development budget, and shifts in the country's priorities away from large defense and aerospace projects, which had provided employment opportunities both inside and outside academia for physicists and other scientists, began to strain the long, comfortable relationship between academia and the military.

The new areas of concern to the public---energy, the environment, housing, and health care-- require a much smaller total fraction of their cost for research and development than do defense and aerospace projects.[11] In addition, many of the scientific questions whose answers are central to successful completion of military projects differ substantially from questions that are important in the new areas. Compared to the Department of Defense, the new agencies charged with addressing these problems appeared overnight, without the benefit of 30 years to evolve a comfortable symbiosis with the academic community. As a result, these agencies seem to have stringent requirements for relevance in the research and development they support. The part of the scientific community that has grown and matured under military sponsorship is having a difficult time adapting to these new social priorities.

ACKNOWLEDGEMENTS

I thank Bruce Rosenblum and Mike Casper for critiquing this paper, Mimi Zeiger for detailed editorial advice, Mary Helen Stull for assistance in prepairing the illustration, the reference librarians in the Government Documents Department at the San Francisco Public Library for research assistance, Earl Cilley and Mary Rerat for providing data on government projects at Stanford, Phillip Miller for providing background materials, and Marilyn Baram and Sylvia Smith for typing the manuscript.

REFERENCES

1. U.S. Congress, House, Committee on Appropriations Department of Defense Appropriations for 1952, 86th Cong., 1st Sess., 1951, pt. 3, p. 1086, 1089.

2. The Bird Dogs, Physics Today, 14, 30 (1971).

3. R. Conrad, The Commonwealth (Official Journal of the Commonwealth Club of California, San Francisco), 22, 240 (1946).

4. U.S. Congress, Senate, Committee on Naval Affairs, Miscellaneous Bills (S. 1547, S. 2133, S. 2178, H.R. 5911, S. 2246), 79th Cong., 2 d Sess., 1946, p. 11, 21.

5. U.S. Congress, House, Committee on Appropriations, Department of Defense Appropriations for 1956, 1955, p. 260.

6. J.R. Killian, Jr., J. Eng. Educ. 43, 13 (1952).

7. Committee on Institutional Research Policy, Sponsored Research Policy of Colleges and Universities (American Council on Education, Washington, D.C., 1954), p. 20, 71.

8. H. Brooks, The Government of Science (MIT Press, Cambridge, Ma., 1968), p. 112-113.

9. U.S. Congress, House, Committee on Appropriations, 86th Cong., 1st Sess., Department of Defense Appropriations for 1960, 1959, pt. 6, p. 13-14.

10. U.S. Military R & D Management (Center for Strategic and International Studies, Georgetown University, Washington, D.C., 1973), p. 15 - 28.

11. U.S. Congress, House, Committee on Science and Aeronautics, 91st Cong., 2d Sess., National Science Policy, 1970, p. 138, 944.

12. U.S. Congress, Joint Economic Committee, 90th Cong., 1st Sess., Planning - Programming - Budgeting System: Progress and Potentials, 1967, p. 1.

13. I.R. Hoos, Systems Analysis in Public Policy: A Critique (University of California Press, Berkeley, Ca., 1972), p. 64 - 71.

14. S.A. Glantz, C.A. Farlow, R.A. Simpson, N.V. Albers, D.E. Pocekay, W.E. Holley, M.V. Becker, S.S. Ashley, M.R. Headrick, D.O.D. Sponsored Research at Stanford, Volume I. Two Perceptions: The Investigator's and the Sponsor's (Stanford Workshops on Political and Social Issues, Stanford, Ca., 1971).

15. N.V. Albers, S.S. Ashley, M.F. Becker, C.A. Farlow, S.A. Glantz, R.A. Simpson, D.O.D. Sponsored Research at Stanford, Volume II: Its Impact on the University (Stanford Workshops on Political and Social Issues, Stanford, Ca., 1971).

16. S.A. Glantz and N.V. Albers, Science 186, 706 (1974).

17. Naval Research Trends: 1971 (Office of Naval Research, Arlington, Va., 1971) p. 1.

18. U.S. Congress, Senate, Committee on ARmed Services, 91st Cong., 1st Sess., Hearings on S. 3367 and H.R. 17123, 1970, p. 118 - 119, 159.

19. R.W. Nichols, Science 172, 29 (1971).

20. G. Caty, G. Drilhon, G. Ferne, N. Kaplan, S. Wald, The Research System: Comparative Survey of the Organization and Financing of Fundamental Research, Volume III: Canada, United States, General Conclusions (Organization for Economic Co-operation and Development, Paris, 1974), p. 62, 108-110.

DIRECTED AND RANDOM COMPONENTS IN THE EVOLUTION OF THE ACADEMIC PHYSICS DISCIPLINE

James R. Stevenson
School of Physics, Georgia Institute of Technology
Atlanta, Georgia 30332

ABSTRACT

Some industrial perceptions of the academic physics community are presented. Concerns are expressed over the suitability of the academic environment in physics to prepare industrial scientists. While the scientific content of the curriculum appears satisfactory, the discipline is criticized for its inability to shape appropriate attitudes in students. The academic response function of the physics discipline to changes in curriculum content is complex, but the response to a stimulus to change attitudes of students is an even more interesting aspect of the evolutionary process. A hypothetical model is proposed in which the present, "where we are," academic response is determined by the faculty assigning the highest personal priority to the attainment of both academic and personal security. Some possible changes in academic management and government policies, as well as student and faculty initiatives, could result in a desirable trend from an industrial perspective.

INTRODUCTION

This paper is part of a program entitled "Why Things Are The Way They Are." Before doing anything, I must define "things." In this discussion "things" refer to:

1. The industrial perception of academic physics as seen by an academician.
2. The response function of the academic physics discipline.

Before starting the formal discussion, a few acknowledgments must be made relative to the presence of this paper, and some perspective must be given to the bias of the author. For the last few years, I have been privileged to serve in a liaison capacity between the Committee on Applications of Physics and the Committee on Education of the American Physical Society. In addition, I have had the opportunity to participate in committee actions relative to the new APS Industrial Fellowship Program initiated by Joe Burton and Sidney Millman. Through these activities, meetings of the Corporate Associates of AIP, and our own attempts at Georgia Tech to initiate new curriculum and research activities in applied physics, some bias will develop in the course of the discussion.

Of particular interest to this discussion will be the results of a questionnaire[1] circulated to industry by a subcommittee of the Committee on Applications of Physics. This study is available as a report entitled "Industrial Impressions of Graduate Education

ISSN:0094-243X/78/123/$1.50

in Physics" from the American Physical Society.

Finally, the author admits to being both a positivist and an optimist. Filtering positive suggestions gives me much greater personal reward than responding to negative criticism. Although Voltaire satirized his character, Dr. Pangloss, in Candide for his optimism and positive approach to insurmountable problems, this author admits to a bias similar to Pangloss. Hopefully the author will come to a better end.

OBSERVATIONS

The product of the academic physics community--the graduate--is not as competitive in the industrial job market as anticipated. The initial reaction of those seeking the answer was that the subject matter content of the physics curriculum was not sufficiently relevant to the technology environment. Questions have been asked, and, in my opinion, the industrial response to the physics curriculum is a conditional satisfactory. Frills can be added to provide a more favorable first impression. The individual physicist is judged by industry as having a good comprehensive background. Let me illustrate this observation by a few excerpts from the report[1], "Industrial Impressions of Graduate Education in Physics."

Question I-d of the questionnaire asks, "We would like to know whether you believe the balance of laboratory and theoretical experience of recent physics Ph.D.'s is satisfactory for a physicist expecting to make worthwhile contributions to the technology of your company. Will you indicate below the extent to which you would like to see the balance change."

Table I - Response I-d

	Much more emphasis	Somewhat more emphasis	Present emphasis about right	Less emphasis	Much less emphasis
(i) Laboratory experience for experimentalists	7	11	11	1	0
(ii) Laboratory experience for theorists	8	13	7	0	0
(iii) Theoretical experience for experimentalists	2	4	19	4	0

To be complete, we should have included theoretical experience for theorists, but I doubt that the response would have been significantly different. The perception is that the theoretical aspects of the curriculum are about right, but that somewhat more emphasis should be given to laboratory experience.

Question I-b of the questionnaire asks, "We would like to know whether, in your opinion, a recent physics Ph.D. who has received a general and specialized physics education as outlined in (a) above (including your preference of specialization) has learned sufficient classical physics to enable him to make worthwhile contributions to the needs of your company. Will you indicate below the extent to which you would like to see changes made in the present standard undergraduate and/or graduate curriculum to include more, or less, classical physics. Use (U) for undergraduate, (G) for graduate curriculum, and (UG) for both. (The response is tabulated as (U, G).)"

Table II - Response I-b (U, G)

	Much more emphasis	Somewhat more emphasis	Present emphasis about right	Less emphasis	Much less emphasis
(i) Mechanics	(3,1)	(2,7)	(18,15)	(1,3)	(0,0)
(ii) Thermodynamics kinetic theory	(4,4)	(9,11)	(11,10)	(1,2)	(0,0)
(iii) Optics (including applications of lasers)	(3,1)	(9,17)	(10,6)	(1,1)	(0,0)
(iv) Acoustics	(3,2)	(4,8)	(15,16)	(2,1)	(0,0)
(v) Elasticity and Heat Transfer	(1,2)	(7,6)	(14,14)	(1,2)	(0,0)
(vi) Fluid Dynamics	(3,5)	(5,2)	(15,15)	(0,2)	(0,0)
(vii) Electricity and Magnetism	(2,2)	(5,7)	(15,18)	(0,0)	(0,0)

Again we find that the relative emphasis seems about right. Some added emphasis on optics at the graduate level and thermodynamics and kinetic theory are desirable additions. Most of the curriculum concerns can be addressed within the present framework of the academic physics discipline. The only problem is one of communication. Both faculty and, more importantly, students must be made aware of these industrial perceptions. A judicious choice of elective courses, as well as more attention to the minor requirement for the Ph.D., is needed. However, these subject matter content concerns are not the predominant problem facing the academic physics community in an effort to overcome an industrial bias towards graduates well qualified in an academic sense.

The critical perception by industry of the physics academic discipline is the attitude of the student. The most recurrent theme is the notion that the academic physics environment does not give positive reinforcement to desirable industrial attitudes and even imposes a negative bias to some desirable personality traits. Let me again refer to a few responses to the recent questionnaire.

Question II-a of the questionnaire asks, "There are now programs under way and planned which offer a M.S. degree in physics to students who complete an advanced program of study and laboratory work with emphasis on classical physics, instrumentation, and materials characterization. These students will typically have completed and reported on a number of short research projects, but will not have undertaken the specialized thesis research required for a Ph.D. degree. We would like to know if students trained in this way would have qualifications that are more desirable for employment in the technology activities at your company. Would you indicate how you expect them to compare with regular Ph.D. candidates engaged in work of similar scope and complexity in the three categories defined below."

Table III - Response II-a

	More desirable than Ph.D. student	Comparable to Ph.D. student	Less desirable than Ph.D. student
(i) Technical preparation for a career in industrial technology	6	8	12
(ii) Motivation for a career in industrial technology	14	9	3
(iii) Potential for important inventions and patents	1	17	8

Of particular interest is the response to the item on motivation for a career in industrial technology. Obviously the achievement of a Ph.D. is perceived as being destructive of this motivation.

Another series of questions asks the industrial scientist to compare the relative merits of physicists and engineers. The following responses were obtained:

Table IV - Response to Comparison of Engineers and Physicists

	Physicists		Neutral	Engineers	
(a) B.S. level					
(i) Originality	(4)	(3)	(13)	(1)	(1)
(ii) Willingness to do applied work	(0)	(0)	(9)	(5)	(8)
(iii) Ability to understand and solve practical problems	(0)	(1)	(8)	(8)	(5)
(iv) Ability and willingness to adjust rapidly to new assignments	(0)	(1)	(14)	(3)	(4)
(b) M.S. level					
(i) Originality	(5)	(6)	(9)	(1)	(1)
(ii) Willingness to do applied work	(0)	(0)	(7)	(9)	(6)
(iii) Ability to understand and solve practical problems	(0)	(1)	(9)	(10)	(3)
(iv) Ability and willingness to adjust rapidly to new assignments	(1)	(0)	(13)	(4)	(4)
(c) Ph.D. level					
(i) Originality	(10)	(5)	(7)	(1)	(1)
(ii) Willingness to do applied work	(0)	(0)	(3)	(9)	(12)
(iii) Ability to understand and solve practical problems	(1)	(0)	(7)	(10)	(6)
(iv) Ability and willingness to adjust rapidly to new assignments	(1)	(0)	(7)	(8)	(8)

Although the physicist rates high in originality, the perception of the willingness to do applied work steadily decreases in comparison to the engineer as their educational achievement level increases.

One does not need the results of a questionnaire to feel these "vibes" from industry. The meetings of the Corporate Associates of AIP have resounded with them in recent years. Recently Sidney Millman[2] sent me a copy of a talk presented by S. K. Kurtz of Philips Laboratories to an audience at Yale University. The title was "From Research to Successful Product: The Role of the Industrial Scientist." Dr. Kurtz summarized the characteristics of successful industrial scientists and engineers as:

1. Self-confidence.
2. Drive.
3. Leadership.
4. Broad scientific knowledge and technical skills.

A recent survey[3] reported in Engineering Education on 174 electrical engineering graduates (87% B.S.) shows that most of their industrial experience has seldom used any mathematics beyond algebra, and almost never do they use Maxwell's equations.

Although a strong technical background is a necessary component of a successful scientist in industry, the success weighting factors seem to be on attitudes and personal characteristics. These weighting factors are the important aspect of the talk by Dr. Kurtz and are probably the most misunderstood component in the industrial-academic dialogue. The academic community would like to think that a successful industrial career would be biased by about 80% weighting factor on achievement within the discipline, while industry seems to be telling us just the opposite.

Ten years ago our distinguished speaker, Professor Harvey Brooks, wrote in a National Academy of Sciences Report:[4] "The value of graduate education should lie partly in the confidence it instills in the student to solve new and challenging problems, and to assemble independently the information and the tools necessary to do it; yet too many students want to use their first work assignment as an opportunity to extend and improve upon their Ph.D. theses rather than to broaden their experience and skills." Maybe today the "partly" should be "primarily," but that is the "way things were and are." The industrial perception of the academic physics environment is one which is not appropriate for developing the personal characteristics for a successful career in industry. WHY?

SOME CONJECTURES

In asking a question, Why?, statistics can be given and case histories related, but basically the answer must be considered as a conjecture. My personal opinion is that one of the important components of the answer to the question lies in the relative priorities assigned to personal values between the population of physicists in the academic and industrial market place. In particular, I would single out the relative priorities assigned to self-confidence and security.

During the rapid growth of the physics discipline after the 2nd World War, most physicists had an opportunity to exercise an option between a career in industry or one in the academic community. A conjecture is that the exercise of this option resulted in a rather significant bias of the population. This bias resulted in the academic community assessing a higher priority to security than to self-confidence. In addition, the environment of the two populations reinforced the respective bias. Many academic physicists seemed to stay with minor extensions of their thesis problem until they lost the excitement of science and then seemingly lacked the self-confidence, as well as the resources, to use their background to challenge other problems. Most industrial physicists were not afforded that opportunity, and they seemed to develop even more self-confidence. Obviously the conjecture is statistical and many counter-examples are to be found.

In summary, the conjecture for basis of discussion and model building is that the academic community has a primary personal goal--the attainment of security--while the industrial community places a high priority on self-confidence. The reward structure in both systems tends to emphasize the difference.

ACADEMIC RESPONSE FUNCTION

Although the above conjecture delves into the area of psychology, and I am not a psychologist, the perception of the academic environment by industrial scientists also calls for attitude evaluations. Besides, nine years as an academic "mis-manager" qualifies me to take certain liberties. Before answering the question, Why?, to the industrial perception of the academic physics environment, some attention must be given to the academic response function and the "way it is."

Now we can spend an entire conference on the topic of the evolutionary process of the academic physics discipline and would probably not be any wiser. Much depends on the local environment, and most of us in academic careers have developed an intuition as to what response will be generated by a given input. The response function is somewhat time dependent. Previous papers have presented many of the components to the academic response function, such as funding, enrollments, employment opportunities, curriculum development, etc.; however, the actual response function is governed by a rather complex summation of the individual personalities of the faculty. If our conjecture is correct, a very substantial component of the academic response function is the security of the faculty. Curriculum revisions which would taint the purity of the discipline cannot be tolerated, as faculty feel more secure in an environment in which they have matured. It does not take an academic manager very long to realize that it is much easier to create a new department or discipline than to change the direction of an existing one. The security blanket reaches out to both the research problems we choose as well as the methods of instruction. We must choose those avenues which guarantee success with severe penalties to those that choose challenging problems and fail in front of our students and peers. Funding agencies dictate that to be a successful grant entrepreneur one must stay specialized, generate quantities of data, and be a prolific generator of publications.

The academic response function is geared to security, and the reward structure reinforces the attitude. That is the "way it is." The "why" I believe can be found in history of the European universities.

Why hasn't the academic community responded to the industrial stimulus? Maybe the academic physics community doesn't recognize the magnitude of the weighting factor which industry attaches to student attitudes. Maybe the academic community feels that the industrial perception of the academic community is not correct. Maybe the academic community feels a threat to both faculty and students.

FUTURE SHOCK

One way to develop the attitudes of self-confidence, drive, and leadership ability in students is to delegate to them significant responsibility in the conduct of their education. At the Ph.D. level this would mean the selection of new directions for research, participation in proposal and report writing, evaluation of research progress, and development of new techniques. The problem faced by the faculty member is that the judgment of his performance and his consequent security depends on his successful conduct of research. This delegation of responsibility places his future in jeopardy. Students are concerned with the amount of time they spend at an academic institution. If publishable work is necessary, and sometimes sufficient, to obtain a Ph.D., the obvious solution is to choose a very expedient path between well defined starting and ending points.

Can a new reward structure be created to recognize the desirable features of both academic achievement and attitude development?

Can self-confidence achieve a higher personal priority among the faculty than security?

If change is found desirable, many avenues exist. How many faculty positions are advertised for an elementary particle theorist to do research in theoretical acoustics. This is what we ask our students and industry to accomplish! Suppose tenure were only granted after a faculty member had demonstrated performance in two specializations? Suppose funding agencies were not allowed to support a scientist in one area of research for over five to eight years? Surprisingly many faculty would welcome the opportunity to change areas if the reward structure were altered. Non-tenured research faculty positions, which are permanent depending on continued high performance, can be created as an adjunct to the academic discipline.

Students with an eye to the future will demand educational opportunities which create a positive bias of industry to seek their employment. The positive efforts of the APS in the Industrial Fellowship Program is an important motivating force. More and more faculty are rebelling against being categorized for the life of their professional career in order to respond to preconceived ideas by government funding agencies. In the words of Dr. Pangloss, "everything is for the best."

1. A. M. Clogston, J. Ross Macdonald, James R. Stevenson, "Industrial Impressions of Graduate Education in Physics," A Report of the Subcommittee of the Committee on Applications of Physics of the American Physical Society (1976).
2. Sidney Millman, private communication (1977).
3. William S. Byers, Engineering Education 67, 758 (1977).
4. Harvey Brooks, Applied Science and Technological Progress - A Report to the Committee on Science and Astronautics, U.S. House of Representatives by the National Academy of Sciences 21, (1967).

PHYSICS AND POLITICS

Bernard V. Khoury
Association of American Universities

ABSTRACT

Federal policy, as most clearly defined by funding patterns, has been a very significant force in the tremendous surge in physics over the past thirty years. Funding has leveled in recent years and this has caused great stresses between static support and expectations reflecting earlier growth. In the current social and fiscal environment the progress of physics is becoming more and more inseparable from the compromises of politics. Physicists should seriously consider a more active and systematic lobbying role on behalf of our discipline.

INTRODUCTION

In my brief remarks this afternoon I would like to discuss the interplay between science and politics and especially between physics and politics. I believe that it is fair to say that most scientists know very little about politics and that most politicians know even less about science. In spite of this gap between the knowledge of scientists and that of politicians, there is little doubt of two items: 1) scientific knowledge has had an important impact on political decisions -- as it has had on almost every element of our lives, and 2) the political process has had a major influence on scientific programs.

FUTURE INTERPLAY

In addition to these two points -- that have been well-documented in other conferences -- I wish to make two additional assertions about the future interplay between science and politics: 1) politics will play an increasing role in determining the direction and the rate of scientific progress, and 2) science will play a diminishing role in political decisions.

This asymmetric interplay between science and politics will be the natural consequence of several facts having to do with the costs, the technological impact, and the social implications of research in physics. As technology has advanced, science has become more and more expensive, and only the Federal government has the resource potential to support much of the science now being done in the U. S. This is particularly true in physics which receives a large percentage of its total research support from the Federal government, as is discussed in other papers in this conference.

The public more clearly perceives the significant impact which technology has had on society and therefore will insist that science is too important to be left to the scientists. There are an increasing number of issues on which the broad public has insisted

ISSN:0094-243X/78/132/$1.50

that scientific priorities must defer to societal concerns and needs.

Scientific issues now under intense public scrutiny -- environmental, nuclear energy, reactor safety -- are so inextricably woven with social values that reputable scientists have diametric views. Thus, political decisions are likely to be made after largely discounting conflicting scientific views. The scientific reaction to such conflicting views is, of course, to study the issue further and to delay a final decision. This call for further study may not be acceptable to the broader society which is trying to address a real and immediate problem. (Parenthetically, I might add that use of a "science court" to address such contentious issues will likely further remove scientists from affecting public policy by demonstrating that most issues brought to such a "court" are so confused and confusing that there is little that is black or white and a great deal that is grey; political judgments will prosper in such an environment.)

Before digressing too far into speculating about the future interface between science and politics, let me return to my primary topic which is the importance of current government policy to the progress of physics, as well as the role which physicists play in formulating that policy.

FUNDING AND POLITICS

First, I shall define government policy as essentially identical to government funding (and any regulations which are imposed under threat of withholding or withdrawing those funds). Government funds have been extremely important to the progress of physics over the last three decades. The crucial role which Federal funds have played in the progress of physics is much more documented and much better understood than any other input into the recent advancement of physics. The earlier speakers in this afternoon's session and at numerous other meetings have each dealt with some aspect of this dependence of physics on Federal funds.

As we all know, Federal funds for physics have leveled and indeed declined by some measures over the past decade. One measure, documented in the National Science Board's <u>Science Indicators 1974</u>, shows that university basic research per physicist has dropped by 40% over the past decade. While funds have leveled or fallen, often our expectations have reflected the euphoria of an earlier era of exponential growth in funding, enrollments, and other forms of support. This gap between reality and expectation is especially severe for many who entered physics graduate study in the mid-60's and who subsequently entered the greatly constricted job market of the early 70's. In such an environment of social and fiscal pressures, the funding and thus the progress of physics are becoming more and more inseparable from the compromises of politics.

I use the word politics not in a pejorative sense. On the contrary, I cannot imagine a more desirable and realistic arena in which to make decisions about public policy including decisions about the broad directions of physics research. Politics will be important to the progress of physics whether or not physicists are active in the political process. My contention is that physicists should indeed become more active in the world of politics if they hope to influence decisions that are important to the progress of physics. Such decisions, which will be made increasingly in the public and therefore the political arena, will largely determine both the direction and the rate of progress in physics.

Physicists, of course, are not foreigners to the world of politics. A number of the invited speakers at this conference are physicists who by interest, abilities and occasional necessity spend more time politicking than they do in the physics laboratory. It is interesting to note that President Carter specifically sought a non-physicist as his science advisor and the director of the Office of Science and Technology Policy. His eventual nominee, Frank Press, a geophysicist, is in fact more a physicist than geologist. Harold Brown also brings the perspective of a physicist to the highest levels of the executive branch. The Congressional Science Fellows are another recent and increasingly effective input by physicists and other scientists into the political process.

In fact, most successful research physicists are effective "grantsmen," and "grantsmanship" is clearly a form of politics where the beneficiary is a single investigator or research group and the spoils of the victory are relatively limited (i. e., usually less than a million dollars). In addition to the difference in scale, there is another far more important difference between grantmanship and politics. The grantsman is competing with other physicists for a slice of the physics pie -- the politicians have long before decided how big the physics pie would be, and they have even largely determined how it would be apportioned among the specialties within physics. It is this larger political arena in which I believe physicists should become more active.

POLITICAL PROCESSES

Let me share with you some observations about the political process from the jaundiced perspective of someone trained as a physicist but for whom physics is now an avocation rather than a vocation and a hobby more than a form of employment. My comments will deal primarily with the congressional process where funds are authorized and appropriated -- except for aberrations such as impoundment, recission and deferrals these funds will actually be spent. I shall limit my comments to three items: 1) Politics is very slow, 2) Politics is very fast, and 3) Staff are the key to success of the political process.

Politics is very slow. The process of politics which is largely visible to the public is very, very slow. It consists of hearings before hundreds of committees and subcommittees and testimony by hundreds of witnesses. Many such hearings are held before only 1 or 2 Congressmen, usually the Chairman, and occasionally, the ranking minority member. Their purpose is largely to build a public record, occasionally to educate the Chairman and the Committee staff, and more frequently to provide a release valve for special interest groups.

Politics is very fast. Once the public record is established, the final decisions especially in the appropriations process are extremely fast. For example, the NSF appropriation of over $800 million may be passed with less than two minutes of discussion in the full appropriations committees. Because it is buried in a multi-billion dollar appropriations bill (including the Department of Housing and Urban Development and numerous independent agencies), it seldom gets noticed on the House or Senate floors. The conference committee, which resolves differences between the House and Senate versions, will usually do little more than split the difference.

As another example, the current discussions about an Office for Energy Research in the new Department of Energy consumed about one minute in the Conference Committee, but that minute had crucial impact on high energy physics which found its budget taken from this Office and placed in one of the operating divisions of the DOE which promises to be dominated by high technology, "quick fix" solutions to the Nation's energy needs.

Staff are the key to the process. Anyone who hopes to influence the legislative process must establish a continuing relationship of trust with key Congressional staff. The staff members themselves are the key to the political process precisely because they have such a relationship with their Congressmen and because the Congressmen, like most administrators of complex programs, have limited time and energy and therefore depend almost totally on staff decisions. Anyone including a physicist who hopes to influence this political process must become almost as close to congressional staff as those staff are to the Congressmen. Needless to say, this is almost impossible to accomplish on a part-time basis.

CONCLUSION

To summarize my remarks, I shall pose and respond to three rhetorical questions:

1) Does politics affect science? An unequivocal yes, and this will increasingly be true.
2) Should science affect politics? Another unequivocal yes.
3) Does science affect politics? Sometimes and to some extent.

I believe that physicists should seriously consider a more active lobbying role on behalf of our discipline; if we don't watch out for ourselves, it is clear to me that no one else will.

Thank you.

Author's Address: Association of American Universities
One Dupont Circle
Washington, D. C. 20036

CONCERN ABOUT EMPLOYABILITY AND THE SUBFIELD CHOICES OF TODAY'S GRADUATE STUDENTS

Deborah Van Vechten
University of Maryland, College Park, MD 20742

ABSTRACT

Twenty six American male, post Ph.D. qualifying exam students in the UMCP physics program were interviewed this June in order to probe why they had chosen their research subfield. The results were analyzed in terms of the relative weights given to, and the degree of overlap between, the student's inherent interests and the economic realities of the job market. Some conclusions are drawn and suggestions made. (Preconference versions of the paper are available from the author.)

MOTIVATION AND SAMPLE SELECTION

In thinking how I as a graduate student could make a contribution to this conference, I realized that few of the faculty members in attendance would have a clear sense of how heavily, relative to other concerns, today's graduate students had weighted their perceptions of the job market in choosing their specialty subfields. I thus interviewed individuals representative of the UMCP physics program in terms of both when they made their decision and which group they finally chose. Each interview took approximately 75 minutes and attempted to clarify the relative weights the individual had given to such factors as the inherent beauty and conceptual importance of the project, the societal significance of the project, the advisor's professional reputation and personality, the availability of an RA, and the time required to complete the degree, in addition to the employability of the area and their own career goals.

The sample was chosen from a departmentally supplied list of 129 individuals who had passed the qualifier, but not yet received a Ph.D. I excluded the 35 foreign students and the 12 to whom I could find no reference in the research group listings. Additionally, 17 were excluded who work at nearby government labs in positions that probably would not exist could permanent staff be hired. This left a reduced pool of 65 individuals. I actually interviewed 26 people -- 40% of the reduced pool and 1 of every 5 on the original list. Four points should be made about the sample:

1) The bigger pool contained no blacks or other low concentration minorities. The reduced pool contained only 2 women other than myself and the one I tried to interview left town 2 days before her mutually agreed upon appointment. Thus my results are derived strictly from white American men.

2) Table I displays the subfield distribution within the sample. With the exclusion of the cosmic ray and space physics (Goddard) group, this distribution is representative of the physics program. (Astronomy is a disjoint program within the department.)

3) The sample slightly overrepresents theorists. This may have arisen from my tendency to talk to people I already knew at least by name and the fact I am a theorist.

ISSN:0094-243X/78/136/$1.50

Table I: Sample Subfield Distribution

10 theorists	16 experimentalists
3 general relativity	4 quantum optics
2 high energy particle & QFT	3 plasma
2 nuclear	3 solid state
2 solid state	2 nuclear, cyclotron
1 plasma	1 e^- (ion) ring accelerator (plasma)
	1 lasers & plasma
	1 high energy
	1 exper. general relativity

Table II: Time of Subfield Choice Distribution

Year Passed	69	79	71	72	73	74	75	76	77	total
# in original pool	1	6	6	11	21	17	30	28	9	129
# in reduced pool	0	3	4	8	14	7	19	7	3	65
# in sample	0	1	2		4	3	8	4	2	26
Group 1	-	1	2	2	-	1	-	-	-	
Group 2	-	-	-	-	-	-	2	1	-	
Group 3	-	-	-	-	3	1	1	-	2	
Group 4	-	-	-	-	-	1	1	2	-	
Group 5	-	-	-	-	1	-	4	1	-	

4) Table II shows that the goal of making the sample representative of the times subfield choices were made was achieved.

DIRECT FINDINGS

On the basis of the weight given the subfield's employability and the extent to which the dissertation subfield mirrors the students historical maximal interests within physics, the sample divided into 5 groups. The first contains 6 individuals who chose their subfield as I imagine it was routinely done before the job market became a major concern: 5 simply maximized the overlap between their own sharply peaked interests and the interests of the faculty, while the last felt he could enjoy any branch of physics and so accepted the first RA that came to his attention. (Notice from Table II that only one of these 6 passed the qualifier after 1972. That one began his study of general relativity as a junior in 1971.) None gave much weight to the question of future employability when they made their choice, although all are aware of it now. Indeed, the two theorists, both in general relativity, say that few days go by without someone in their group making a joke or other comment about how poor their job prospects are.

The second group consists of three individuals, one of whom is on temporary leave from a teaching job and the other two of whom have standing job offers arising from a period of employment prior to graduate school. The first chose his subfield on the basis of a guaranteed quick dissertation project and an already established good personal relationship with his potential advisor. A second chose to stay in the area of his industrial experience because it guaranteed a much faster degree, because he could be an RA doing so, and because he finds all subfields of physics equally interesting. In contrast, the theorist in this group chose a dissertation topic for himself on the basis of an intense, long term interest in the problem area. However, his job offer is in electrical engineering, a field he left after college because it was "so easy it felt sinful". He is now reconsidering E.E. on the basis of its greater potential contributions to society and the moralistic feeling that physics and art are equivalently important and, as such, physics is over-populated and oversupported.

The third group consists of 7 individuals all of whom chose their subfield because of its bright employment outlook in the industrial or governmental labs context. Additionally, none experienced conflict between their choice and an earlier image of what they wanted to work on, i.e. they are comfortable working on their projects and look forward to continuing to do similar research later. They tend to emphasize the potential practical utility of their projects. They generally seem quite confident of their own abilities and can imagine themselves being happy in a broad range of contexts. Being supported as an RA was important to them all, as was getting out reasonably quickly and working for a person with a strong professional reputation. Additionally, it was important to them to get along with their advisors on a personal basis and, indeed, two had changed advisors, but not subfield, to achieve a better relationship. It is interesting to note that of the 7, the one theorist is the least optimistic. He notes that in the past 4 years the number of members in the APS plasma division has increased 500% and that it no longer seems clear fusion will ever be commercially feasible. Thus he is beginning to worry his choice of theory rather than experiment may have cost him the job security and sense of societal utility he chose plasma for. The experimentalists are still smiling and cheery.

The fourth group consists of 4 unusually confident individuals. Each has a clear idea of what he wants to do and sees his graduate school experience as helping him achieve his goal. For example, one is a solid state experimentalist who wants to work on international development projects, quite possibly in the area of intermediate technologies. Another wants to teach at a small college and has devoted 30 or more hours a week to the TA required by his choice of high energy theory as a dissertation area to developing his teaching talents and to establishing outstanding teaching credentials.

The final group are the 6 individuals who experienced conflict between the desire to work in the subfield they were most interested in and the need for the security of not believing their choice precludes their employment. That finding a workable compromise is not always easy is illustrated by the fact that all 4 of the students in the sample who changed subfield, as well as advisors, 1 or more times are in this group. Of the 2 current experimentalists, 1 started out in astrophysics, tried plasma experimental, and settled on high energy <u>experimental</u> because he found particle <u>theory</u> interesting. However, this student plans to shift again once he finishes his Ph.D. because he wants to work in one place & is distressed by the traveling and lack of permanent jobs. The second had been working in the theoretical general relativity group for about 2 years when he found himself stalling out -- he lost his sense of direction, couldn't find a good thesis topic and lost confidence in his own ability to do physics. Moreover, his desire to "eat, drink and dream" relativity, the norm in the group, was low. Thus he switched to experimental solid state where the prospect of being employed later is much better, his confidence has returned, and he is again making progress. The remaining 4 individuals are the 2 nuclear and 2 solid state theorists in the sample. Two of these 4 had spent between a semester and a year working in a relatively employable experimental area and quit because they were unhappy with the paucity of "physics" in the work. Both considered plasma next but rejected it as being too classical and phenomenological. The other 2 theorists seem very tentative in formulating and acting on their desires -- one had spent 18 months deciding who to ask to be his advisor and, although he has strongly considered public interest science, now feels tempted to hitch a ride on the currents his dynamo advisor is generating toward the traditional postdoc-assistant prof. pattern. The other is trying hard to "trust statistics and relax", to stay flexible, and to develop the ability to be content with whatever life has in store for him.

SUMMARY COMMENTS AND SUGGESTIONS

Several summary statements may be made. First, it is the theoretically inclined students who are having the hardest time finding something they perceive as employable which they also find sufficiently interesting. This is illustrated by their high concentration in group 5 and low concentration in group 3. One reason may be that the theorists seem to have a more sharply spiked interest spectrum -- they tend to spend longer investigating the various research groups and advisors before making a choice, are more willing to forego the better salary and fewer distractions of an RA to work in a poorly funded group, and are much more likely to demand a decisive role in the selection of their detailed thesis topic. The theorists appear to pay for this greater need for autonomy and control with a sense of their own reduced marketability. At least half of the experimentalists but only 1 theorist felt confident he could apply the skills he had learned doing a doctorate to 1 or more other subfields. The theoretical students' operating assumption seems to be that "x"-theory is only a little less employable than "x"-experimental. Lee Grodzin comments[1] 1) that while univeristy faculties are about 33% theorists, in all other contexts theorists constitute less than 15% and 2) that he could foresee no crossing of the supply and demand curves for theorists for at least the next 15 years suggests that these theoretical students are, if anything, overly optimistic about their employment prospects!

Second, teaching was mentioned as a desirable element in their future by only 3 individuals. (None expressed interest in management or administration.) In contrast, 25 of the 26 emphasized their desire to do research and seemed to desire a position in a well funded, low distraction, research lab. I suspect that this strong desire and expectation to continue doing basic research has characterized emerging physics Ph.D.'s for some time. For example, Beverly Porter[2] reports that the least happy group among the people denied tenure at the 18 "best" institutions since 1962 are those who found employment in other academic institutions where the quality of graduate students and research facilities were not as high. (My own experience with such individuals shows them to tend to be arrogant and bitter, to take their frustation and disappointment out on the students in their classes, and to contribute as little to their department as their colleagues will allow.) Moreover, note that a departments' research output is the prime determiner of its reputation. This has encouraged increasing numbers of institutions with teaching loads of 10-12 contact hours a week to hire and promote faculty on the basis of their research productivity.

Third, the attitudes of the graduate students toward their situation has changed. When the bottom fell out of the job market about 1970, many people near the output end of the pipeline -e.g. Bob Yaes[3] became angry, railed against the injustice of the situation, and vehemently complained they had been misled and deceived. By now, most of the anger has died out -- it was too debilitating to maintain. Today's students know the realities of the job market and take a self-preservationalist "I'll make due as best I can" attitude.

Each of these observations relate to a suggestion. Most important, the faculty at Ph.D. granting institutions need to make a conscious and conscientious response to the fact that, despite the improved job situtation for physics in general, the situation for theoretically inclined students is still quite bad. Most of the theorists being produced are trained and attitudinally suited only for traditional academic jobs and there are very few of these to be had. As I see it, either the number of theorists being produced who hope to continue in the field should be reduced still further or the sort of dissertations being produced should be drastically altered to make the new Ph.D. more saleable in nontraditional settings. Clearly, the latter course of action requires the faculty to demonstrate the sort of self-confidence James Stevenson[4] asserted they all too often lack. The former might be implemented by refusing to allow a faculty member to accept a new Ph.D. student if two or more of his present or former students do not yet have non-temporary jobs they, the students, are satisfied with. Such a ruling might have the additional virtue of motivating the advisor to be more concerned with the attitudes he is transmitting to the student.

A less drastic proposal is to try to shift the active awareness spectrum of at least the emerging students in the experimental direction. The attitude that theory is superior to, more beautiful and valuable than, experiment, needs to be replaced by the realization that progress in theory depends on progress in experiment and that neither facet is inherently better than the other. One method for accomplishing this substitution of attitude is to improve the undergraduate labs and make them more important gradewise. Additionally, in order to clarify the processes by which theoretical assertions are tested, lecturers can be strongly encouraged to include examples of how crucial experiments were designed. Questions asking the student to design and justify an experiment testing a specific hypothesis could be included on exams. Hopefully this would raise the status of experimental work and cause students undecided about whether to do a theoretical or experimental dissertation to opt for the latter. This plan might marginally reduce the amount of material covered in any given course, but it would also give students a more realistic image of what experimental research is all about and of the dependence of theoretical progress on the existence of experimental data. Moreover, it would reduce the sharpness and difficulty of the transition between learning what is already known in a neat and orderly fashion while taking courses and the massive uncertainties, frequent frustration and slow pace of actually doing research.

The teaching/research dichotomy is the second focus of my suggestions. In "Publish or Perish" debates of yore, doing research was presented as a means of staying alive intellectually in order to be a better teacher. I submit that the current heavy emphasis on research productivity in academic hiring and tenure decisions threatens to so down play the importance of quality teaching that the argument will soon read "I begrudgingly agree to teach in order to be able to devote most of my time to what I really love, my own research". Indeed, I suspect many big departments already have one or more tenured members who purposely do a poor job on committees and in low level courses in order to be given less burdensome assignments. Recall that almost all of the students in my sample want to do research, not teach. This suggests that many of them can be expected to do little to combat the general population's vision of physics as highly abstract, abstruse, & irrevelant. I strongly urge academic institutions to give more explicit consideration to the attitudes of job candidates toward students and teaching.

My last suggestions should be the least controversial. It is just that each graduate program should seek to insure that its students have available as much information as possible before making their career choices. For example, at least 2 faculty should offer to help students calrify exactly what it is that characterizes their interest areas and locate all the subfields wherein these elements exist. (For example, note that plasma, as well as general relativity, is classical.) Also, prequalifier research experience -- especially junior year summers programs, Senior theses, and first year graduate school jobs or RA's rather than TA's -- seems to be very helpful in allowing people to test out how well they really like a given subfield. Such experience should be encouraged. Postgraduate placement assistance is also desirable.

[1]Lee Grodzins, talk A5 and after banquet remarks this conference.

[2]Beverly F. Porter, talk A4 this conference.

[3]Robert Yaes, talk F10 this conference & "Physics From Another Perspective, a Cynical Overview", Newsletter of the Forum on Physics & Society, Vol 4, #1, p 34-35.

[4]James R. Stevenson, talk B5 this conference.

PHYSICS CAREERS AT WESTINGHOUSE RESEARCH
Experiences of the Past Decade and Recent Trends

J. K. Hulm
Westinghouse R&D Center, Pittsburgh, Pa. 15235

INTRODUCTION

I joined the staff of the Westinghouse Research Laboratories in 1954 and I have been with Westinghouse ever since, except for a recent two-year stint as the Science Attache at the American Embassy in London. In retrospect, the industrial research environment has happened to suit my particular life goals extremely well. For this Conference, I was asked to comment on the problems, challenges and opportunities confronting a physicist attempting to develop a career in a large industrial company. I believe that what I have to say is fairly generally applicable for high technology corporations in the United States, but of course some of it will be specific to Westinghouse.

My talk consists of essentially three parts, first, some historical background on Westinghouse and its Research Laboratories, second, some facts on the employment of physicists and other technical personnel at the Westinghouse R&D Center and in the Company as a whole and third, some personal views on what it takes for a physicist to survive and prosper in the large industrial environment.

RESEARCH AT WESTINGHOUSE

George Westinghouse founded the Westinghouse Electric Corporation in 1885, to construct a.c. power systems. George was a very prolific inventor, with over 300 issued patents to his name. He gave the new company a technological bias which it has retained to the present day.

Starting from a base of a.c. power stations, the company ultimately diversified into most phases of the generation, transmission, distribution and utilization of electrical energy. The product lines include not only electrical equipment, but a wide variety of special materials and components which are vital to the efficiency and reliability of electrical systems. It may surprise you to learn that Westinghouse operated the first commercial broadcasting station in the United States, just after the first World War, and also pioneered in the development of television through the work of Vladimir Zworykin, who worked for Westinghouse before joining the RCA Laboratories.

Westinghouse established its first separate Research Laboratory in 1910. The Company began to employ appreciable numbers of physicists in the 1930's and this trend accelerated during World War II, when the Company participated in the development of microwave radar and also in the Manhattan Project. In the 1940's, Edward Condon served as an Associate Director of the Central Laboratories and brought in many talented physicists under an Industrial Fellowship

ISSN:0094-243X/78/142/$1.50

Program. Basic nuclear physics research began at the Laboratories in 1937 under William Shoupp, and the presence of knowledgeable scientists in this field enabled Westinghouse to make a fast start in reactor development in the wake of the Manhattan Project. This is generally believed to have been an important contributing factor to the pre-eminent position in nuclear technology which Westinghouse holds today.

Following World War II, the Westinghouse Research Laboratories expanded rapidly in the physical sciences. The Laboratory acquired Collins Helium Liquifier #7 and superconductivity research started under Aaron Wexler. Daniel Alpert built up a fine group of low pressure gas physics specialists, including Fred Biondi and Art Phelps. Clarence Zener joined the Laboratories in 1951 and hired a lot of new people in solid state physics, materials science and metallurgy. I had known Zener at the University of Chicago and at his and Wexler's suggestion, I joined the Low Temperature group in 1954.

The present Research & Development Center of the Company is located 12 miles east of Downtown Pittsburgh in the suburban community of Churchill. This site, shown in Figure 1, was first occupied in 1956 and presently houses a staff of approximately 2,000 persons, including about 800 people with technical degrees. The Laboratory qualifies as one of the largest industrial research centers in the United States.

Westinghouse R&D Center, Pittsburgh, Pa.

The growth of the Westinghouse R&D Center over the past 20 years is illustrated by the uppermost line of Figure 2. At points A (1960) and B (1976), two existing Westinghouse development groups were consolidated with the R&D organization. Apart from these two discontinuities, in which the staff additions were mainly engineers, the Center has experienced a more or less uniform growth over the 20-year period.

PROFESSIONAL STAFF, WESTINGHOUSE R & D CENTER

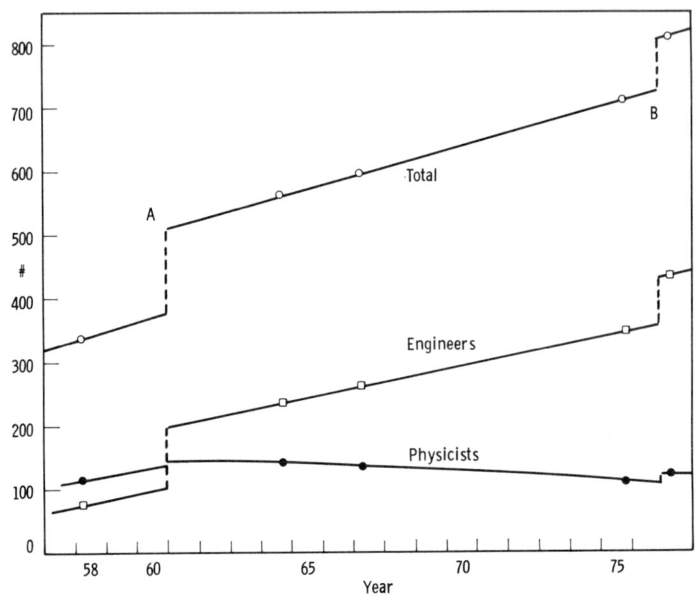

Figure 2 indicates that the number of engineers at the Center increased from about 75 to 440 between 1958 to 1977, whereas the number of physicists stayed more or less constant at around 120 in this same period. The consolidations at A and B contributed part of the engineer growth, but even if these are subtracted out, the engineers total still increased by a factor of 4. These personnel changes suggest a gradual shift towards greater emphasis on development and engineering activity at the R&D Center during the 20-year period under consideration. In this respect, Westinghouse is not greatly different from the U.S. technical community as a whole. In recent years, there has been a strong commitment of funding for R&D directed towards the solution of national problems, e.g., space, cancer, energy, etc., whereas basic research funding has been steadily drying up.

At the present time, a major portion of the funding of the Westinghouse R&D Center is supplied directly by operating units of the Company, which also control the goals and approaches of the programs at the Center. Additional funding is obtained under a

Corporate research program and by contracts with outside agencies such as DOD, ERDA and EPRI.

Figure 3 compares the 20-year variation of the physics population at Westinghouse R&D with that for other physical sciences. There is a little uncertainty regarding the two consolidations previously mentioned, in the sense that perhaps all the curves ought to exhibit slight step functions in 1960 and 1976. However, the data as shown seem to adequately represent the general trends in this period. Essentially, the number of physicists and chemists remained more or less steady for 20 years, the number of mathematicians, which includes operations research and computer scientists, increased by about 40% and the number of metallurgists and materials scientists, including ceramic specialists, quadrupled. The chemistry situation has not been quite as static as is suggested by Figure 3, however, since the chemical engineering staff of the Center increased by 60 people in this same interval.

TRENDS IN PHYSICAL SCIENCE STAFF, WESTINGHOUSE R & D CENTER

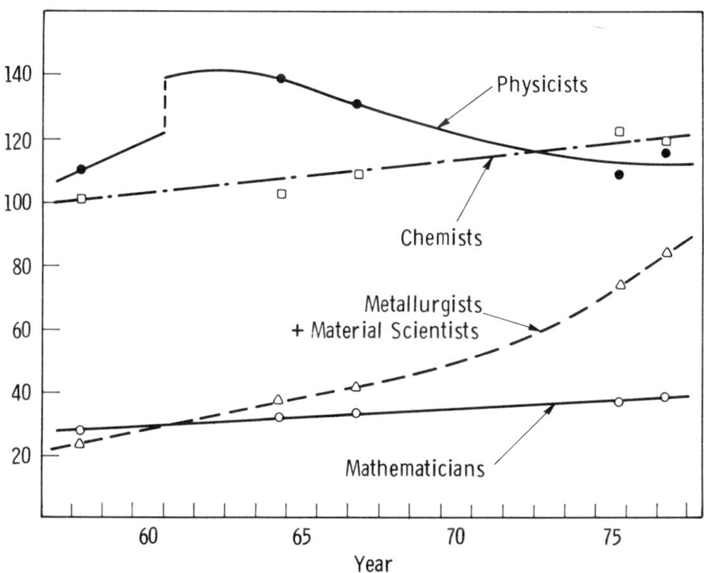

The basis for these trends in the physical sciences seems to be that both materials development and chemical process technology are more relevant to shorter range applied work than is basic physics. Physics has a lot to say about the front end of new technologies and impacts some of the general principles as to whether concepts are viable, but when it comes to constructing actual devices, the performance of materials immediately becomes crucial. In energy conversion, which is of prime importance to Westinghouse, endless examples can be given of performance and economic limitations imposed by available materials. Similarly, in conversion between various forms of fossil fuel, chemical process technology has a primary role to play and chemical engineering is the primary discipline.

A snapshot of the distribution of current technical activities of the physicists presently working at the Westinghouse R&D Center is shown in Figure 4. It should be noted that other disciplines are involved in each of the technological areas shown, so that the distribution of effort in the pie diagram would not be correct for the Center as a whole. Similarly, many other activities at the Center not involving physicists are omitted from this Figure. The Management group shown here includes only full time administrators. Many group leaders and section managers whose activities are mainly technical were counted in the technological categories. If all of the physicists classified by Westinghouse as managers had been included in the management sector of Figure 4, this sector would have constituted about 30% of the pie.

TECHNOLOGICAL ACTIVITIES BY PHYSICISTS AT WESTINGHOUSE
RESEARCH & DEVELOPMENT CENTER

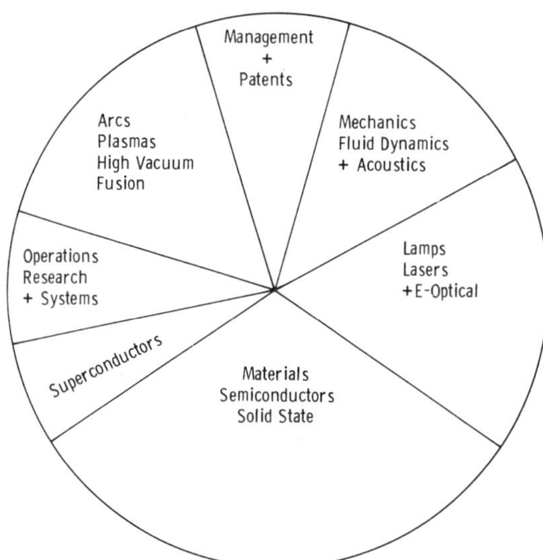

The technological areas of Figure 4 correspond to five out of the ten technical divisions of the American Physical Society, implying that as far as specialization is concerned, perhaps half of the physics graduate population could step directly into familiar disciplines at Westinghouse R&D. For persons in the non-related APS divisions, Biological, Cosmic, High Polymer, Nuclear and Particle & Fields, a change of field would be necessary. However, this might well be a painless transition; for example, a polymer physicist would find much familiar polymer materials work at the R&D Center.

Similarly, a nuclear physicist could relate very well to many of the reactor activities in the Nuclear Energy part of Westinghouse.

PHYSICISTS IN THE WESTINGHOUSE CORPORATION

The technological intensity of much of its business causes Westinghouse to maintain several major development and engineering laboratories in addition to the R&D Center. These laboratories are devoted to the specific needs of certain business activities such as nuclear power, avionics and underseas technology. In some cases, the technical staff of these business units is much larger than that of the R&D Center, and many physicists are employed. Whereas there are just over 100 physicists at the Center, there are in excess of 1,000 in the entire Westinghouse Corporation.

The Westinghouse Personnel Data System reveals that there are 1,121 employes in the Corporation with at least one degree in physics or engineering physics. Of these, 1,039 have a B.S. in physics, 918 have their highest degree in physics and 220 have a physics doctorate. In the following discussion, the larger sample, 1,121, will be used as the physicist population of the Company.

Figure 5 compares the age distribution of physicists in Westinghouse by five year intervals to that for the Company's electrical engineers. In terms of technical job requirements, the EE's appear to offer the greatest direct competition to physicists. There are about five times as many EE's as physicists, but the age distributions are rather similar and also rather flat. An exception to this

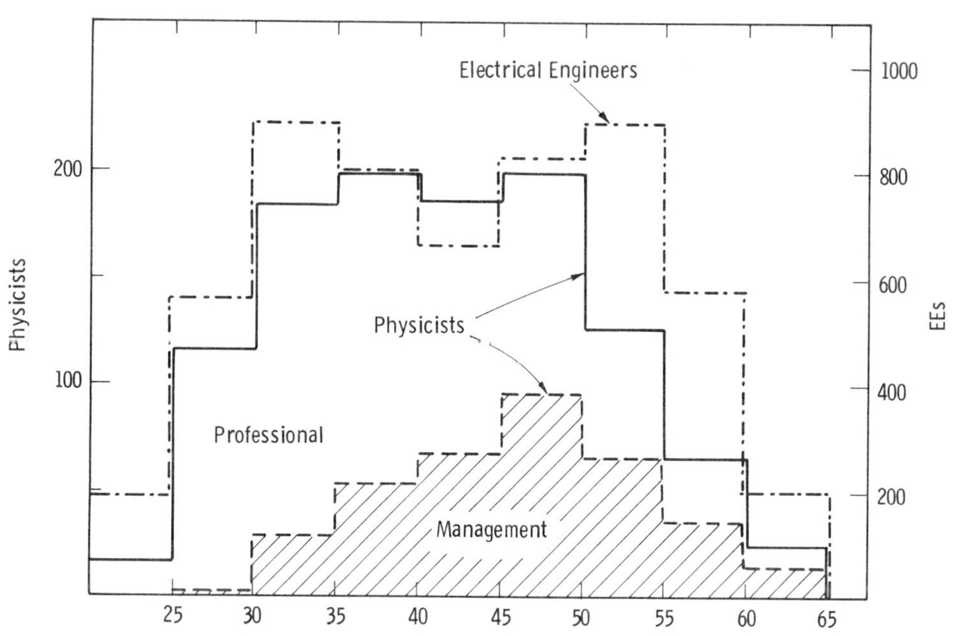

is the anomalously low physics population in the 50 to 60 age region. Assuming a continuation of recent trends, Westinghouse could expect to hire approximately 40 physicists per year due to advancement of the age block in Figure 5. Resignations and deaths would probably double this number.

Figure 5 also indicates that about half of the physicists in the Corporation attain management positions by age 45. Some of the senior executives of the Company belong to the physics population, for example, Tom Murrin, President of the Public Systems Company, and George Mechlin, Vice President of Research & Development. Several Business Unit General Managers are also physicists. Evidently, physicists can and do succeed in the business arena.

The Personnel Data System also contains a classification of employees by functional activity chosen by the individuals from the following categories: Administration, Business Systems, Controller, Distribution, Engineering, Field Sales, General Management, Corporate Services, Personnel Multi-function, Law, Manufacturing, Marketing, Purchasing, Quality Control, Research, Field Service and Support Services. It is interesting that the top six dominant categories are the same for both physicists and EE's, as shown in Table I. Evidently, physicists have a stronger preference for research than engineers do, whereas the reverse is true as regards Marketing, Sales and Field Service.

TABLE I

COMPARISON OF FUNCTIONAL ACTIVITIES OF
WESTINGHOUSE PHYSICISTS & ELECTRICAL ENGINEERS

FIELD / FUNCTION	PHYSICS	ELECTRICAL ENGINEERS
ENGINEERING	62%	58%
RESEARCH	14	3
MARKETING & SALES	7	17
MANUFACTURING	4	4
QUALITY CONTROL	3	4
FIELD SERVICE	2	7

Figure 6 shows the location of physicists within Westinghouse, including the level of doctorate degrees at each location. Nuclear technology and defense electronics surpass R&D in the employment of physicists. In this connection, it is clear that physicists have a major stake in the high technology sector of the U.S. economy and whether we like it or not, the health of our profession is highly dependent upon the U.S. maintaining its role as a world leader in technological innovation. In my view, this leadership is vital not only to physics, but also the entire U.S. economy and to our future as a world power.

PHYSICISTS AT WESTINGHOUSE, TECHNOLOGICAL ACTIVITIES

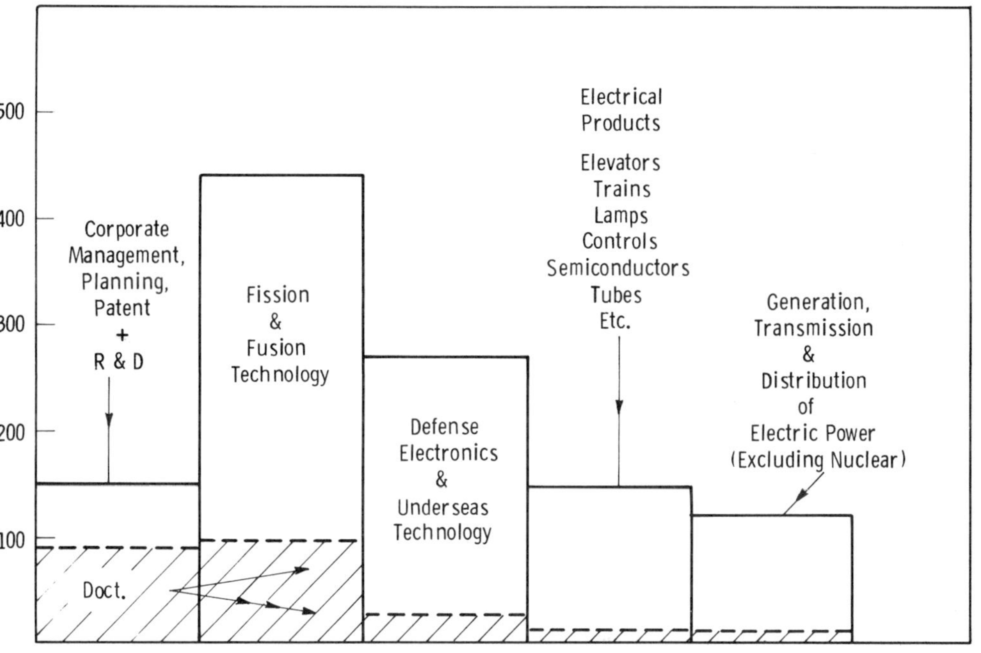

PHYSICS IN INDUSTRY, A PERSONAL VIEW

Hopefully, the data presented thus far has given the reader some insight into the kinds of careers that physicists get involved in at a large, technically oriented company. These activities are, indeed, so diverse that it is difficult to offer advice to the student preparing to enter industry as to what kind of specialized training would be most appropriate to this end. The skills that are needed depend upon whether the individual stays in technical work or whether he or she enters a business field which requires other disciplines such as business administration or economics in addition to technical knowledge. Even if the physicist chooses to remain in a primarily technical environment such as R&D, or an engineering department, there is a good chance that management opportunities will present themselves, requiring skills in handling people, sometimes in quite large groups. Scientists sometimes dismiss these non-science related skills as trivial in comparison with scientific problem solving ability; the fact is that people who show organizational ability are in greater demand in the modern world than many technical specialists.

In the remainder of this paper, I would like to offer some observations on what I perceive to be the "facts of life" for a physicist entering industry. I admit that these are purely personal views based upon my own experiences at Westinghouse. No doubt other physicists in other parts of the company might have quite different views of the industrial scene. However, I hope that my opinions are at least roughly valid for the environment which I know best, i.e., central R&D

First of all, I think it is obvious to most people that it is pretty hard to pursue frontier physics in an industrial laboratory. For one thing, a lot of the present day frontiers such as cosmology and particle physics are simply not worked on in Industry, either because it is too costly to get programs of critical size or there is no obvious connection with business goals.

Occasionally, important discoveries have been made in industrial laboratories, leading in some cases to the highest accolades of science, but these are the exception rather than the rule. It seems to me that such anomalies are even less likely to occur in the future, as industrial R&D becomes more application oriented. Thus, I would advise the young physicist who seeks the exotic frontier to stay away from industry - but no doubt he would anyway.

I can almost hear the howls of anger from some of my industrial colleagues who will insist that good basic research is done in industry and that it requires first class people to do it. I do not deny this - indeed I believe it to be true. However, I think it would be a confidence trick to tell a young physicist that he could expect a lifetime career of basic research in an industrial laboratory. A few years freedom he may well get, but sooner or later he will be asked to relate his work to the business goals of the company.

Perhaps I can illustrate the above point with reference to my own career. I started work at Westinghouse in superconductivity research at a time when this field was a basic research area, of no immediate use. Over the past 20 years, the field has moved steadily towards applications. Although there is still a lot of development work to be done, there now seems little doubt that important new technologies will be built upon the use of superconductors. Of course, this has been very exciting for me and I wouldn't have missed it for the world. However, creating a new technology is not the same thing as focussing one's life on scientific discoveries, even if some of the latter may be an essential component of the former.

Not every physicist can be as fortunate as I have been in participating in the birth of a new technology, but I know quite a few who have so participated and many of them are located in Industrial laboratories. I do not claim that this is the only possible motivation for industrial physicists, but it does seem to me to be a very important one.

One characteristic of the building of new technologies is that it requires a lot of team-work. It is this mechanism which frequently leads industrial scientists into management. The leadership of an interdisciplinary team of widely diverse backgrounds towards a major project goal has been one of the most exciting experiences of my life. Special "people management" skills are required in such a project and I know of no physics department in the U.S. that offers training in this area.

One of the reasons I like working in Industry is that it is a place where new technology receives the final acid test, the economic test of the market place. It seems to me that a lot of so-called development work carried out in academic and government laboratories tends to drag on interminably due to lack of this acid test. Industry runs on profit, the so called "bottom line." Some people describe this as a pretty base motive, but with respect to the development of new technology it has a quality similar to that attributed by Samuel Johnson to the threat of hanging - it tends to clear the mind.

The organizers asked me to discuss possible changes in physics training which would make physicists more suitable for employment in Industry. First, I would like to comment on the question of physicists versus engineers in job competition.

It seems to me that companies like Westinghouse will always need a lot more engineers than physicists. However, I think that physicists will continue to merit a place in the Company because of the unique training and thought process that they bring to bear. The essential difference is that the physicist is taught to be curious about the underlying mechanisms behind every phenomenon, whereas the engineer primarily needs to use the phenomenon to get a desired end use.

I have been asked if physicists should attempt to take business or economic courses before entering Industry. Of course, such knowledge is always useful, but in my view I would prefer to hire a well trained physicist rather than a person with half physics training and half business training. The determined scientist can always acquire an MBA later on, while working in Industry.

A more important aspect of training is the question of oral and written reports. I find many University graduates, even at the Ph.D. level, woefully inadequate in skills of presentation of their work to others. This is a great handicap in Industry, where a scientist will frequently have to explain his work to engineers and business managers. A modicum of salesmanship is absolutely essential here. I would like to see physics departments pay more attention to developing such capabilities in their students.

What does it really take to survive in the Industrial venue? There is no such thing as industrial job tenure, but as we have seen in recent years, tenure is itself a fragile concept where institutions do not have unlimited economic power. To my mind, the most healthy basis for job security in our society is continuous self development. This means developing oneself as a whole person as fully as possible, professional competence, value to a particular company in a particular industry, general skills and knowledge of the outside world.

Few individuals are good at everything, but there is a range of skills which are essentially personal. I have already emphasized communication by speech and writing. Other areas include meeting participation, collecting, storing and retrieving information, organizing people, things and events, presenting a good appearance and keeping in good health. With a modest effort, most people can achieve a reasonable standard in these areas.

One danger confronting the industrial scientist is that of losing touch with his profession in the outside world. The solution to this is outside contact through meeting attendance, presentation and publication of papers and professional society committee work. These have to be worked at, there is no substitute for continuous effort. The objective is to be known and respected in professional circles.

To my mind, the most secure industrial employee is one who maintains his negotiability outside the company. The curious dichotomy is that a person who is greatly desired by other employers will have the greatest attractiveness to his existing employer. I suppose this is true in the academic world as well, it is somewhat analogous to the star system in sports.

In conclusion, I wish to thank Ms. Carol Carcione for assistance in access to the Westinghouse Personnel Data System and Mr. William Prentice of the "New Scientist" for some clear thoughts on job security.

Dr. Paul Horwitz
Avco Everett Research Laboratory, Inc. Everett, Ma. 02149

Unconventional Jobs in Unconventional Companies

As I prepared this talk, I have been uncomfortably aware of a rather delicate dilemma. In speaking to you about unconventional job opportunities for physicists, I feel rather like the captain of the Titanic, extolling, in a farewell speech to the passengers, the benefits of a brisk swim in the North Atlantic. I am made doubly uneasy by the fact that I am addressing you from the relative comfort and safety of one of the few remaining lifeboats.

I am not going to pretend to you that the damage done to the good ship Physics isn't serious, or that rescue is on the way. On the contrary, under the circumstances, the best advice I can offer is to look around you and grab anything that floats.

The facts are too obvious and too well known to require elaboration: the number of physics Ph.D's. is increasing faster than the traditional job market can absorb them. The conclusion is inescapable: physicists are going to wind up seeking employment in places where no physicist has ever been employed before. In business terms, the physics community, in order to expand at projected rates, is going to have to penetrate new markets. In case that sounds a little ominous, let me be quite specific about what I have in mind.

As a member of the Selection Committee for the APS Postdoctoral Industrial Fellowship, I had the opportunity, recently, to perform what amounted to a market survey of unconventional jobs - jobs in companies which at present employ no physicists. The results were quite encouraging. Through one press release, one brief oral presentation, and a small number of personal contacts, I was able, in the space of a few weeks, to come up with half a dozen relatively little known, innovative, technology based companies that, although they employ no physicists at present, expressed an interest in interviewing qualified applicants from our profession. (The APS and AIP, working mainly through mailings, have identified more than 50 such companies.)

What kinds of firms were these, and what opportunities do they offer to what kinds of physicists? In particular, are they interested only in certain narrow, "relevant" specialists in physics, or is there hope for even the most academically oriented researchers? I can best answer both questions by citing a specific example.

ISSN:0094-243X/78/153/$1.50

Consider the plight of an astrophysicist, four years out of school, just finishing up a second postdoctoral research appointment in stellar structure and dynamics. If he (and for the purists, "he" is meant, here and elsewhere, to include "she" as well) is not lucky enough to be appointed to a tenured faculty position at some university (a likely assumption), how can he possibly find gainful employment doing research at all related to his specialty? Well, it so happens that one of the companies which came to my attention would be just about made to order for such a person, assuming he were flexible enough to make the switch from academia to the "real world" in the first place. The main product of this company at present is vacuum seals.

Lest you boggle at the notion of a scientist with his head literally "in the stars" happily working at turning out vacuum seals, let me hasten to add that the seals in question are based on the properties of a new set of materials known as ferrofluids. These are ferromagnetic fluids and they are rather fascinating things. They behave in all respects like an ordinary liquid, except that they have a high magnetic permeability and are therefore subject to magnetic forces.

In case you think that the motion of a ferrofluid in a changing magnetic field is simple and straightforward, let me point out that ferrofluids are also dielectrics, and they may be conductors. As such, their behaviour is governed by the full set of Maxwell's equations, as well as the Navier-Stokes equation. In fact, ferrofludic phenomena are quite poorly understood, since ferrofluids themselves are quite new, and there is plenty of interesting work for our friend the astrophysicist to do. He must, of course, be willing to concentrate his efforts on the invention, design, and improvement of useful devices <u>using</u> ferrofluids, rather than restricting himself to pure physics research. It is the devices, after all, that are going to pay his salary - something no number of the Physical Review articles can do. But along the way there are interesting physics problems to be solved, and if he is flexible enough and approaches his job with an open mind, who knows - he may even <u>enjoy</u> thinking up new devices and trying them out. He might even someday become interested in their manufacture, promotion, and sale - stranger things have happened!

I have gone over this talk before with my friends, and at this point there are usually a lot of objections raised. Let me discuss some of these here.

First of all, there is a sneaking suspicion on the part of some people, that I have pulled the standard scientific "fast one" of presenting my best data as though it were typical. I can only assure you that this is not so. In order to make my point I had to pick a particular company, but I could have picked one that deionizes water, one with a material that changes its opacity and reflectivity when a potential is placed across it, or still another that does statistical analyses of foreign exchange rates. And I have lists of literally hundreds of technology based companies, all in the Greater Boston area, which I have not investigated, but many of which are probably as promising as the ones I have mentioned.

A more serious objection is the one that goes: "no employer is going to hire a physicist for one of these so-called 'unconventional' jobs - he'll hire an engineer with a degree in ferrofluidics and three years of experience in vacuum seal technology first". Well, maybe so - if there were such a field as "ferrofluidics". But there isn't, of course, and even if there were it is not obvious that a good generalist with an inventive streak might not be a better buy for the company than a specialist who requires no on the job training, but who brings no new ideas with him either.

There is a common misconception which needs to be cleared up, by the way. In seeking employment at a profit making institution, you need not confine yourself to those companies that have publicly expressed a desire to hire someone. In contrast to universities and government agencies, companies do not, as a rule, have job openings which must be filled by a certain date. Rather they are seeking primarily to maximize profits, and if this can best be done by hiring a particular individual at a particular time, they are frequently, though not always, in a position to hire him on the spot.

This does not imply, however, that it is going to be easy for an unknown, untested physicist, straight from some university laboratory, to convince an industrial research manager to take a chance and hire him. In fact, it may be almost impossible -- and particularly so for the unconventional jobs which are the subject of this talk. This is a serious problem, of course, and I have a suggestion for overcoming it, but let me first address another concern which I have heard expressed.

A number of people have commented to me along the following lines: "Even if I were able to convince an employer to take a chance on me, I'm not at all sure I could hack it. I don't know anything about ferrofluids (or water deionizers, or money markets, or whatever). My training just isn't appropriate".

Without wishing to deny the importance of this concern, I would like to point out that to be ruled by it is to treat one's Ph.D. not so much as an opportunity for a satisfying career, but as a severe constraint on the form that career can take. Consciously or not, we have come to judge ourselves and others largely by our academic degrees. This is why, faced with the shortage of "appropriate" jobs for people with physics Ph.D's., so many of us have taken the course of going back to school to receive yet another degree, in medicine or in law perhaps, hoping thereby to qualify for one of the multitude of "inappropriate" jobs which were previously closed to us.

There is nothing wrong with this approach, of course, except for the obvious fact that it costs a lot both in money and in time. But it is a rather conventional solution to the job problem, a solution born out of the conviction that "What I am, and what I may become, are strictly defined by my academic training". While this is true for certain professions, it is certainly not true for most, and among these latter are the unconventional jobs we have been speaking about.

Let us return, then, to the problem of the prospective employer who says, in effect: "It may well be that as the only physicist working here, you would bring a unique set of skills to bear on our problems, once you understood what they were. This would be of great value to the company. The problem is that you don't have any of the specialized knowledge that we need right now, and we have no way of knowing how fast you would be able to pick it up. We just can't take the chance on you".

Everything he has said is doubtless correct -- hiring you represents very possibly an unacceptable risk. The situation is one in which both parties stand to gain something if only one of them (the employer) is prepared to take a certain risk. That is not very equitable, and I would suggest that the risk be shared.

It takes about a year to retrain someone to take on a new job. By the end of that time it has usually become pretty obvious to all concerned whether or not he has succeeded in adapting. An equitable arrangement, it seems to be, would be for the physicist seeking an unconventional job to accept it at half pay (or some other fraction) for a period of one year, at the end of which time he either gets the appropriate full salary (agreed upon in advance), or he quits. This may sound somewhat demeaning, but I submit that it is not. It simply recognizes the riskiness of the venture and shares the risk between the two potential beneficiaries. It may also appear to be an act of desperation and of "scraping the bottom of the barrel", but in fact it will most likely allow the applicant to pick and choose among a variety of interesting jobs, rather than forcing him to take the first one that comes along. Furthermore, the likelihood of any responsible employer viewing such a proposed arrangement as an invitation to acquire cheap labor for one year is, I think, minimal, primarily because it will take the better part of that year for the labor to become useful to him.

What I have been saying here is not meant to be taken as advice to any particular individual. This is not a group counseling session, assuming one were possible, and what I have suggested will probably appeal only to a small minority of my listeners. The underlying basis for my thoughts may have a more universal significance, however, and perhaps deserves some more explicit discussion.

As you are no doubt sick of hearing by now, things are tough all over. In a tough, competitive situation it is by and large true that the most difficult road to success is to play the game by the conventional rules. It is self evident that if you simply keep your nose to the grindstone, do the best job of research and/or teaching you possibly can, and don't try to be unconventional, you have a certain finite, though possibly small, chance of replicating your thesis advisor and pursuing a conventional academic career. If you have defined your goals sufficiently narrowly this may be the only career you are willing to accept for yourself.

It is possible, however, and I think under the circumstances preferable, to widen one's horizons, and to accept the possibility of a variety of physics-related careers. In this sense, a physics degree becomes rather like a degree in law -- it offers the opportunity to "practice physics", but does not constrain one to do so in a particular milieu.

Once one has accepted the notion of not "playing by the rules" in terms of career choice, it is a logical step to avoid the pitfall of evaluating oneself purely in terms of one's degree. What any of us has to offer is much more than the training and discipline symbolized by a physics Ph.D. Perhaps you enjoy writing -- you might consider a career in scientific journalism or technical writing. Do you enjoy meeting new people? As a physicist with research experience you could be an excellent salesman of lab equipment. Are you good with kids? How about designing educational toys? And so on.

"But", you may be thinking, "I trained long and hard to be able to do independent research, and now he's telling me to give that all up". Not at all! If you want to do basic research in your specialty, hunt around and find yourself a postdoctoral position or two. All I am saying is: "don't necessarily expect to do basic research for the rest of your life". I think that a few years of postdoctoral work would be very appropriate preparation for any of the unconventional careers I have mentioned -- not necessarily because the *work* will be directly relevant, but because the *experience* is what really makes you a working scientist. That scientific background is what you will bring to the job, and it is very important.

To sum it up, let me return to my "Titanic" analogy. If you look around you for something interesting that floats, you may find that having a deck chair all to yourself is preferable to sharing a lifeboat with a crowd.

LIFE IN A MULTIDISCIPLINARY GOVERNMENT LABORATORY*

Maurice M. Shapiro
Laboratory for Cosmic Physics, N.R.L., Washington, D.C. 20375

ABSTRACT

That a large government laboratory can also be a great research center is well substantiated. Both applied and fundamental research can flourish in such a center notwithstanding its mission orientation. Just as in the non-governmental labs, the applied research is often challenging and intellectually stimulating. Sometimes it is pedestrian—a trouble due in part to a civil service system that confers tenure rather prematurely. On the other hand, job security boosts morale and attracts some talented young scientists disenchanted with indefinite postponement of tenure elsewhere. In a highly diversified laboratory, complex scientific problems requiring an interdisciplinary approach can be tackled more efficiently than in a specialized institute. There are concomitant opportunities for professional advancement, especially for those having broad training and interests. (Unfortunately, most advertisements for vacant research positions demand a high degree of specialization.) Opportunistic hustling for grants and contracts—a syndrome not unknown to academia and industry—is prevalent; it takes the time not only of managerial "operators", but also of research workers. Historically, a substantial proportion of pure (i.e., non-programmatic) research has been encouraged in some government labs. This has been an invaluable stimulus and a source of strength. Lately, social and political pressures have been eroding the vitality of fundamental research. Science, as well as technology, should certainly respond to societal needs. But the pendulum has swung too far. Should the obsession with "relevance" not be moderated, then the climate and scientific stature of the laboratories would suffer, and they would find it difficult to attract the ablest scientists. Inevitably, the "D" component of their R-and-D mission would suffer too.

My assignment is to talk about life in a big government laboratory. Although I believe I am a physicist rather than a bureaucrat, the title of my talk might raise suspicions to the contrary. I have used a seven-syllable word—"multidisciplinary" instead of a one-syllable word—"big". Actually, there is a reason for my choice. Quite a few big laboratories are supported by the federal government, but not many of these are as multidisciplinary as the two centers that I have in mind as I speak to you--the Naval Research

*An invited paper presented to the Conference on Changing Career Opportunities for Physicists at the Pennsylvania State University 1-3 August 1977.

ISSN:0094-243X/78/158/$1.50

Laboratory and the National Bureau of Standards. Still, much of what I shall say is probably valid for other government research agencies as well.

The two centers I have mentioned have fulfilled their primary mission well enough to earn the support they have been getting for many decades. In addition, the fruits of their secondary mission—contributing to fundamental science—are well documented in the literature. Among the impressive examples are the pioneering achievements at NRL in space research and astrophysics, and the experimental verification of the non-conservation of parity at the Bureau of Standards.

By their very nature, government laboratories are devoted mainly to applied science. Now, as physicists, we know that the progress of our discipline has come about from the sustained interaction between theory and experiment. What we sometimes overlook is the symbiosis between pure and applied research (I use the term "pure" in the sense of non-programmatic). Instrumental innovations—such as those in microelectronics—make possible new or better fundamental experiments, and this exemplifies the feed-back from applied to pure science. Not only is this true of pure and applied research, but also of science and technology. Far from being orthogonal, they constitute a two-way street. So it is natural in an environment where fundamental exploration coexists with programmatic research, that each can enrich the other.

In a laboratory, as in other institutions, bigness is not an unmixed blessing. Yet, a large center is more likely to support a diversity of disciplines, and this has some advantages.

Let me touch upon a current example at NRL. A few of us have become interested in a new astrophysical enterprise having the acronym "DUMAND", which stands for "Deep Underwater Muon and Neutrino Detector". The idea is to set up a deep underwater observatory for the detection of cosmic neutrinos—especially those of high energy—that are believed to be impinging upon the earth, and indeed passing right through it, with occasional interactions. Originally, the detection was to be optical—using the Čerenkov light generated by the secondaries of neutrino interactions. Owing to the slippery character of neutrinos, hence the large detector volume needed to detect phenomena of astrophysical interest, and also in view of the short attenuation length of light in water, the number of photomultipliers required for such a project is rather astronomical. By good luck it was realized that the charged progeny of a high energy neutrino interaction could be expected to produce an acoustic signal. This was soon verified with particle beams at Brookhaven and Harvard. Setting up a large observatory several kilometers deep in the ocean will obviously require some innovations in ocean technology. As you might expect, there are experienced oceanologists at NRL. Likewise, there is a strong acoustics division. It did not take long for the cosmic-ray physicists to interest some of the acoustics specialists in exploring the nature of the new phenomenon of sonic signals produced by a stream or a shower of charged particles. It seems likely that, before long, experts in electronics, in precise timing, and in signal processing, from various parts of the laboratory will be involved, at least as consultants. Clearly, the ease of interdisciplinary exchange and cooperation can contribute to efficiency and productivity. I must acknowledge that most of our scientists do not take enough advantage of the readily available help from resident experts in other specialties. But then this is often true in many academic departments and industrial laboratories as well.

An important question is, what is the quality of scientific staff in the large laboratories? I should like to dispel the myth that the level is inferior to that in academia. Actually, the productivity of scientists in the big government laboratories compares very favorably with that in most universities. If my assessment is valid, then it is true—paradoxically enough—both despite and because of the civil service system under which most federal employees work. One can argue pro and con regarding the effects of this system on the caliber of the scientific staff. The provision for a single probational year after which an employee acquires tenure, tends to inhibit the selectivity required to build up an elite staff. Nevertheless, many talented and highly motivated physicists have accepted positions in the better government laboratories owing to certain attractions, e.g., good facilities, a reasonable level of support, freedom from teaching and related responsibilities, opportunities for further education and advancement, and job security.

The last of these has lately increased in importance, with the freeze on the number of secure faculty posts in academia. Many able scientists, discouraged by poor prospects of tenure, have become available, and the selection by government labs has tended to become more discriminating. If the grim situation in the universities should continue over the next few years, then a growing number of young physicists—and some not so young—may very well seek their fortune in the government laboratories.

Some of the more gifted fresh Ph.D.'s or young post-docs will compete successfully for the National Academy of Sciences-National Research Council research associateships available in the government laboratories. These appointments are normally renewable for a second year, and they give both the scientist and the laboratory a chance to get acquainted. A fair number of these post-docs subsequently find a staff position (it is interesting that the two-year associateship, when followed by a year's probational civil service appointment, corresponds to the three-year trial period of an assistant professor in a university.)

You may be interested in the overall employment of physicists by some federal laboratories, and in the recent rates of hiring. Tables I to IV give some relevant figures. In presenting the distribution of physicists in a large government laboratory, I have found it reasonable to combine certain numbers for the Naval Research Laboratory and the National Bureau of Standards into a composite

Table I. Distribution of Physicists in a Large Government Laboratory*

Number of Physicists (Approx. 1/3 of the Sci. Staff)		~ 515†
No. of Ph.D.'s‡:	293	%: 57
M.S.	106	21
B.S.	116	22

picture that applies to either institution within one standard deviation.** Each laboratory has a professional staff of some 1500 scientists and engineers, of which approximately one-third are Ph.D.'s. Of the ~ 1500, roughly one-third are physicists. Their distribution according to academic degree is shown in Table I; more than half are Ph.D.'s.

Among newly hired physicists, on the other hand, the disproportion of Ph.D.'s is considerably greater, as seen in Table II.

Table II. Hiring of Physicists at NRL per year in 1974-76

	Av. per year
Ph.D.'s	16.3
Others	4.3

The foregoing two tables do <u>not</u> represent the situation in governmental or Department of Defense laboratories <u>generally</u>. Thus, Table III compares NRL with six other Navy laboratories with regard to the fraction of Ph.D.'s among scientists and engineers grouped

*Composite Picture, NRL-NBS

†Approx. 10 per cent are temporary or part-time

‡Total number of Ph.D.'s in science and engineering ≈ 550 ≈ 1/3 of the scientific staff (Courtesy of D. Blome and E. Conrad)

**In stressing the similarity, one should mention a considerable difference between the two laboratories in the grade-level distributions of their Ph.D. scientists and engineers. NBS is more top-heavy: the fraction of employees in grades GS-15 and higher is distinctly greater than that at NRL.

according to seniority. At the Civil Service level GS-13, NRL has nearly four times as great a proportion of Ph.D.'s as that of the other labs. At the more senior GS-15 level, the factor is smaller, but still close to 2.

Table III. Composition of Scientific and Engineering Staffs (vs. "Grade" Seniority) at NRL and 6 Other Navy Laboratories

	% of Ph.D.'s in Grade		
	GS-13	14	15
NRL	37	40	52
OTHERS	10	16	28

Finally, looking at the general employment picture for physicists in the Department of Defense (DoD) laboratories, I show in Table IV some rough estimates provided by Dr. Alan Berman which suggest that overall, there may currently be opportunities for some 180 physicists per annum in the DoD, and roughly 60 of these positions would go to Ph.D.'s.

Table IV. Employment of Physicists in Department of Defense Laboratories*

Total	~ 4000
Turnover	~ 6%/Ann.
Nominal Openings	~ 240/Ann.
Currently (3/4)	~ 180/Ann.
If 1/3 are Ph.D.'s	~ 60 Ph.D./Ann.

You may ask, what are the early foreseeable prospects for employment of physicists in a laboratory like NRL? Let me quote a colleague who is more authoritative than I on this subject: Dr. Alan Berman, Director of Research at NRL, told me, "Frankly, the outlook is somber. I believe that we are in for a period of diminishing support for in-house R&D activities." The number of openings at NRL for young physicists will probably decline in the years

*Estimated by Dr. Alan Berman

immediately ahead. "I do not know what this reduction will amount to, but I am afraid it will be more than ten per cent." However, this forecast applies if the national and international scene should remain reasonably stable. "Support for science comes in spurts." An event similar to Sputnik, a catastrophic crunch in the energy supply—and science might again acquire a high national priority.

If now, and in the near future, we are faced with a shortage of suitable positions for trained physicists and for other scholars, what does this imply about a wise policy for the training of scientists? This is one of the core problems to which our Conference is addressed, so I would like for a moment to discuss this larger issue.

Are we in fact producing too many scientists? One of the contributed papers at this meeting contends that we are training some two to five times as many Ph.D. physicists as are likely to find jobs within the profession. Although this is deeply distressing, does it follow that it is in society's best interest to discourage the able and interested student from a career in science? It could be argued that we sometimes train too many graduate students motivated to work in certain special fashionable areas of research. But as to the broader question, are we educating too many physicists for the world's needs, I am not so sure.

Of the awesome dilemmas confronting mankind, many deal with the interactions between man and a formerly bountiful nature. It seems to me that we need to put more—not less—good minds, well trained in analytic thinking to work on these problems. I am not suggesting that all of mankind's crises can be overcome by a technological fix. But when we contemplate some of our critical troubles—a scarcity of energy sources, the hazards of energy production, the shortages in vital resources, the dangers to our environment—it becomes apparent that science and technology can and should contribute to the solutions. The prospects of alleviating the poverty, hunger, disease, illiteracy that afflict a major portion of mankind—these prospects are linked to our success in coping with the other problems I have mentioned. Admittedly, all of these problems are largely social, political, or economic, but there is surely a significant technological component to their solutions. Hence I believe it would be sheer folly to pursue national policies that permit the erosion of our scientific strength.

Let me now return to my assigned subject. What kind of education, experience, temperament, and attitudes are conducive to a successful career in a large government laboratory? The broader the training in physics, the better; thus the experimenter who can handle mathematical physics is in a favorable position. If he is conversant with a variety of experimental techniques or has special expertise in the treatment of data, this will pay off. As to temperament and attitudes, the physicist who is so fiercely independent as to insist on free choice of his own research problem may get away with it, but only if his talents are truly exceptional and recognized as such. Flexibility is a great asset.

What are the opportunities for advancement, and on what do they depend? Naturally, these are commensurate with the capacity to help solve problems. Other factors influence the rate of advancement—the breadth of training and interests, originality, and the willingness, in due course, to be responsible for some technical management. As in other occupations, the personality of the individual, how well he interacts with others, plays a role. If he is articulate and persuasive, this is bound to help. Fortunately, the assumption of ever-increasing managerial responsibilities, which was once a precondition to promotion at the higher levels, is no longer absolutely essential. The scientist who has proved himself can enjoy appropriate status and concomitant benefits. For many physicists, a career in a diversified government laboratory can be as rewarding as that in any other research environment.

Having said this, I should cite some problems encountered by the physicist in a government laboratory. A growing nuisance—one that he shares with his colleagues in the universities—is the need to spend much effort huckstering for grants or contracts—an effort that steals a lot of time from scientific work per se. There was a time when the productive scientist in a government lab did not have to hustle quite so aggressively for research funds. Perhaps this gave him an unfair advantage over his academic brother. But if so, this compensated for other limitations. One of these is the degree of control exercised by management. This is certainly greater in governmental or industrial laboratories than in universities. We all know of academic departments that do not operate quite democratically, but in general the role of management as it affects the life and work of the scientist in government or industry is stronger than it is in academia. So if you believe that in research leadership, he directs best who directs least, then you must realize that this noble _laissez faire_ ideal is more readily praised than attained. Actually, it is doubtful that an upper-echelon manager in a government laboratory nowadays could long survive if he acted on this philosophy.

In recent years the national commitment to the support of basic research has been faltering. The pressures responsible for this change have been partly social and economic, but I suspect that they are largely political. There is a lot of competition for national priorities, and there are constituencies whose voice is heard in Washington more loudly and clearly than that of the scientific community. So the basic remedies may lie in the political arena.

Within the scientific community, we must adopt attitudes and devise strategies that will make us more responsive to the needs of society. But we are not being self-serving if we decry the dangerous erosion of the scientific enterprise. The obsession in recent years with "relevance" has, in my view, already affected the intellectual climate and the scientific stature of some of our best laboratories. The insistence on demonstrating an immediate connection with desired end products of research can, in the end, be self-defeating. Our top scientific managers in the nation must clearly work within the constraints imposed by legislative and executive policies. But in certain areas they are not themselves without influence in establishing science policy.

I should like, finally, to discuss the role of fundamental* research in the larger, mission-oriented laboratories. Traditionally, a significant proportion of frontier-type research has been fostered in the larger government science centers as well as in some prestigious industrial laboratories. The strength of these institutions has been due in no small part to this farsighted policy.

People often ask what is the rationale for supporting fundamental research in a government laboratory? In the last analysis, any research program should help accomplish the principal aims—the *raison d'etre* of the laboratory. One reason why it is important to pursue pure research along with applied research or development is this: excellence in a research center is hard to achieve without it. At the risk of saying what may be obvious to you, I shall spell out the rationale a bit further.

A good laboratory—no matter what its special purposes may be—needs gifted, imaginative investigators consumed with curiosity about nature. In striving for innovations, for break-throughs, one such person is worth at least ten well trained but less talented workers in the vineyard of science. In order to get and to keep first rate physicists, it is necessary to cultivate an intellectual climate in which a highly gifted, dedicated scientist can feel at home. The motivated physicist who is involved mainly in applied science is likely to be more stimulated and satisfied professionally if he is working in the same laboratory with others engaged in frontier research.

The new, practical uses to which science and technology can be put depend upon more effective control over the natural environment. The better to exploit nature for our human needs demands a deeper understanding of how nature works. This deeper grasp of physical phenomena which leads to discoveries and new applications, is not acquired just by reading the scientific literature. One has to participate, contribute, and interact with others at the forefront. The need for active research in frontier areas is as compelling in a government lab as it is in a university.

With your indulgence, I will close on a semi-personal note. You are well aware that the purest, most ivory-tower research leads, sooner or later, to practical applications. Nevertheless, a few examples from my experience may be revealing. Thirty years ago pions were discovered among the secondary cosmic-rays—a turning point in elementary-particle physics. A year later, energetic heavy nuclei—from helium to iron—were found among the cosmic rays impinging on the top of the atmosphere. This exciting discovery fired my imagination. Apparently samples of matter—in the form of relativistic nuclei—were reaching us from beyond the solar system.

* I remind you that I use the term "fundamental" or "basic", to describe non-programmatic research, rather than the type whose avowed purpose is restricted to gathering data—no matter how new—that is required to do a well defined practical job.

At the time I was doing neutron and fission research at the Oak Ridge National Laboratory. My first love in physics—cosmic radiation—was rekindled, and by good luck the late Franz Kurie invited me to join the Nucleonics Division at NRL, and to start a new program in high energy physics and cosmic rays. The offer was irresistible, and I did not have to be asked twice. (Incidentally, in my first year at NRL I took time off from organizing a cosmic-ray lab to design a novel type of fission reactor for submarines.)

If anyone had then suggested to me that laboratory beams of pions and of relativistic heavy nuclei would find a practical use within a couple of decades, I would have been most skeptical. And yet, in recent years the cosmic rays have, so to speak, been brought down to earth. The proton Linac, the "meson factory" at Los Alamos, has for several years been probing the efficacy of intense pion beams in the treatment of cancer. Also, using man-made "heavy" cosmic rays—the beams of GeV ions accelerated for a while at Princeton, and under a sustained program at Berkeley—many physicists have been measuring the modes of breakup of these heavy ions in experiments of vital interest to astrophysics, lunar research, planetary sciences, and radiation shielding. Biophysicists have been using these beams, and cancer specialists have started to explore their possibilities for tumor therapy. So much for "irrelevant" research.

Just one final remark. If anyone had told me three years ago that work in cosmic rays would lead to an interest in acoustics, I would have been puzzled and probably incredulous. Nevertheless, the recently discovered phenomenon of acoustic detection of energetic charged particles has certainly proved exciting. What is especially noteworthy, is that this novel method of detection, which may yet have far-reaching effects, was discovered during a workshop last year dealing with a truly "far-out" subject—cosmic neutrinos.

CHALLENGING CAREER OPPORTUNITIES FOR PHYSICISTS IN THE GOVERNMENT

Martin J. Cooper
Energy Research and Development Administration
Washington, D.C. 20545

ABSTRACT

Today, opportunities for the physicist lie largely off-campus. Less than one physicist in two is now employed by an educational institution; one in three is working in a "nontraditional" capacity. This migration of physicists into nonacademic positions is expected to increase in he future. This paper looks at the various options for physicists in the Federal Government--the Nation's single largest employer of scientists and engineers. Typical careers in the various types of Federal agencies are described. The increasing need for scientists with breadth of perspective in policy analysis and decision making is discussed. Opportunities and means of entry into such nontraditional careers are explored; strategies for individuals interested in non-academic careers are outlined.

INTRODUCTION

Today, opportunities for the physicist lie largely off-campus. Less than one physicist in two is employed at an educational institution; one in three is working in a "nontraditional physics" capacity.[1] This migration is growing and is expected to increase in the future. The largest percentage of those persons leaving physics assume some other technical profession--primarily engineering. But a growing number are taking what are "nontechnical" jobs--jobs which make use of their physics training and experience but which do not actively involve research. Statistically, these persons will enjoy greater salaries than their counterparts who have remained in traditional physics.[2] This professional diffusion provides a real chance for the physics community to contribute more directly in all levels of our society. To the individual physicist, the trend presents a challenge and an opportunity. To college educators and our professional societies, it represents a questioning of traditional values and roles and has led us to the purpose of this Conference.

The largest single employer of physicists is the Federal Government. In this paper, I have been asked to describe some of the unique opportunities for physicists in positions other than research within the Government...to discuss what the various jobs are, what typical careers look like, the "rules of the road", and finally, how one can get into this type of work?

ISSN:0094-243X/78/167/$1.50

First, let me define the world I wish to describe, the various places of employment and the demand for physicists. This demand--whether in the Government, industry, or academia--is what the economists term "derived demand". That is, an employer hires a physicist to provide a service for which there is some demand or need. Physicists must see themselves as being capable of providing such service. This service generally makes use of the technical knowledge and/or the intellectual and analytical abilities characteristic of a physicist. These qualities are valuable attributes in many occupations besides the pursuit of research. Unfortunately, many graduates are ill-prepared to consider these opportunities in Government.

The Federal Government is a large and very diverse set of organizations consisting of three separate branches--the Executive, the Legislative, and the Judicial. The Executive Branch conducts a wide range of research activities through its various administrative agencies. This research may be conducted in a variety of ways: (1) within an agency's own research facilities, (2) by contract with individual research performers, and (3) at Federally Funded Research and Development Centers (FFRDC's), government owned, contractor operated R&D laboratories.

Careers as research performers within the individual research laboratories--both agency labs and FFRDC's--are discussed in another paper. I will concentrate on opportunities within the contracting (headquarters) agencies, such as the National Science Foundation (NSF), the higher levels of the Executive Branch, Congressional offices, and the Judicial Branch of the Federal Government.

Opportunities generally can be classified into one of three major types:

(1) direct technical program administration demanding specific knowledge of a scientific or technical area;

(2) staff-support requiring a general technical knowledge and familiarity with the conduct of research and development; and

(3) indirect opportunities.

First, we shall look at each type separately and then consider career mobility between them.

TECHNICAL PROGRAM MANAGEMENT

Agencies and departments whose mission depends upon a strong technical component represent the largest job market for the physicist interested in direct program administration. Individuals with bachelor, master, and doctorate degrees are hired to administer and direct a variety of scientific and technical programs, from high-energy physics research to the conduct of regional environmental assessments, from means for reducing hazards to the public to the development of new energy sources. Positions are competitive--candidates being graded on their technical credentials and relevant experience.

Most physicists tend to associate career opportunities with energy (ERDA), space (NASA), health (NIH), defense (DOD) or the NSF. But there are also fundamental research efforts at other agencies, at the U.S. Geological Survey (Department of Interior) in the earth sciences, at National Ocean and Atmospheric Administration in Commerce on weather and ocean conditions, and Treasury's Bureau of Alcohol, Tobacco, and Firearms on the development of modern forensic techniques.

The past decade has seen the growth of legislation and agencies concerned with public health and safety: first, the environmental concerns, than occupational health and safety and now consumer protection. The Environmental Protection Agency and Nuclear Regulatory Commission have become major employers of physicists and chemists. The Bureau of Radiological Health within the Food and Drug Administration (HEW) employs physicists to develop means to detect and monitor radiation from lasers and other electronic products. The Consumer Product Safety Commission conducts research aimed at establishing mandatory safety standards for consumer goods. Oftimes, the physicist joins with a lawyer to develop technically sound and legally enforceable regulations. Those physicists who would believe such jobs dull stuff after Quantum Field theory or High Energy Physics should consider the challenge of devising an "idiot-proof" measurement of laser intensity for use on a factory floor.

Traditionally, program administration in the more basic research areas at NSF, ERDA, and DOD requires a doctorate. Several years of actual research experience are highly desirable. A bachelor or master degree physicist will find greater opportunities in the more applied areas. Responsibilities vary greatly. In certain agencies, program administration depends heavily upon peer input and the program manager is little more than a coordinator for the decision-making process; in others, the individual program manager has virtual life-and-death control over the direction of the research.

Entry level salaries vary slightly between agencies but generally begin at the GS-11 for a Ph.D ($17,056). Two or three years experience can increase the entrant's level by up to one full grade. (See Table I: Government Salary Scale.) Advancement in technical program management follows a well-defined path with each step bringing greater and broader responsibilities (a larger program budget). Progress is governed by one's ability to administer a responsive and relevant program tailored to agency needs. Recognition comes through an increasing ability to influence the direction of the decision-making process. Mobility between different program branches within an individual agency and between agencies tends to be good by academic standards. This is because unlike university departments which are discipline oriented, agency programs tend to be multidisciplinary and thus seek to capitalize on the interchangeability and occupational mobility of technical manpower. One manager in ERDA's Solar Energy Program is an experienced high-energy physicist; a laser chemist now has senior responsibilities for advanced nuclear reactors; a liquids theorist advises on environmental research policies.

As one might expect, opportunities in technical program management are directly proportional to the individual agencies' R&D funds. More monies require more program administrators and hence present greater opportunities and mobility. The GS-18 (currently $47,500) is the highest level attainable within the Civil Service. Appointment from the GS-18 level to the (political) Executive Schedule in technical program management is not uncommon. Many of the directors of the National Institutes of Health and the National Bureau of Standards and Assistant Administrators at ERDA have come up through the ranks of Career Civil Service to take on Executive Schedule Appointments.

Many agencies offer special limited (term) appointments for individuals from the academic community under the Intergovernmental Personnel Act (IGPA). These new employees provide the agency with the fresh look gained from active participation in research. The university professor is afforded greatly enhanced appreciation of the internal workings of the bureaucracy. NSF has traditionally sought to use IGPA's in their physics, chemistry, mathematics, and engineering sciences programs.

STAFF OPPORTUNITIES

The next largest opportunity for the physicist lies in a staff support role-staff being an individual or entire organization which serves to assist some office of authority. Just as lawyers are retained by corporations to provide legal advice, persons with technical experience are required in today's Government as planners, analysts, and advisors. Estimates are that over one-half of the total Federal budget ($450 billion) now require decisions based upon fairly sophisticated technologies.

In my former position as program analyst with the National Bureau of Standards, my duties were to "understand, analyze, and evaluate scientific programs in the context of Bureau and Administration policies and to recommend courses of action to the Director of the NBS." My particular responsibilities covered the basic physical measurements mission of NBS involving everything from accurate time dissemination via satellites to laser metrology and precision radiation measurements.

One can easily go through the manual of Administrative and Executive agencies in Washington identifying similiar opportunities for the individual with scientific training: the Department of State's Bureau of Oceans and International Environmental and Scientific Affairs has a staff of 120, approximately one-quarter with scientific or technical degrees; the Federal Energy Administration has direct responsibilities for policies affecting energy conservation, utility-load management, and near-term solar heating and cooling technology. For the physicist with a bent towards accounting and business, there is the Security and Exchange Commission and the Bureau of East-West Trade in Commerce which administers the export licensing of technical products--electronic goods, computers, and scientific instrumentation; the President's Office of Telecommunications Policy which is responsible for the Nation's management of the electromagnetic spectrum; and of course, the Central Intelligence Agency which has for years monitored the state of science and technology overseas vis-a-vis U.S. capabilities. There is also the newly established Office of Science and Technology which advises the President on all aspects of science and technology.

Within the Judicial Branch, only the U.S. Court of Customs and Patent Appeals maintains a cadre of technical advisors--physicists, chemists, and engineers who are also law school graduates. These advisors function as law clerks and have the scientific training which enables them to "explain" complex technical issues and to use the literature effectively to understand the scientific terms found in that court's cases. A Congressional Commission on Revision of the Federal Court Appellate System[3] noted in their report that the courts "are increasingly being asked to adjudicate cases in which scientific and technical knowledge is a prerequisite to informed decision making...that the courts do not have access to a scientifically knowledgeable staff...(and that) the subject matter ranges far beyond the normal ken of judges."

In recent years, physicists, chemists, and engineers have been joining the legions of lawyers and political scientists in Congressional Staff Offices to assist in the construction of public policy. A Congressional Scientists Fellows Program now permits individuals from industry and the academic community to serve for a year in the Offices of Senators, Representatives, or Congressional Committees. Paul Horwitz, our speaker on Physics Careers In Business spent a year with Senator Kennedy as a technical advisor and legislative aide.

The growing importance of science and technology is also causing Congress to expand the technical support capabilities of its various staff organizations. The Office of Technology Assessment was created in 1972 to provide Congress with in-depth studies of the impact of science and technology on our lives. The Science Policy Research and Environmental Policy Divisions of the Congressional Research at the Library of Congress have been expanded and now employ over 100 persons, many with degrees in physics, chemistry, and biology.[4] And recently, the General Accounting Office, once the exclusive domain of accountants, has begun hiring physicists to review and evaluate the conduct of Federal research and development efforts.[5]

Physics Today[6,7] has been running a series of articles recounting the rewarding but hectic lifestyle of physicists on the "Hill". The remarks of Ben Cooper and Dick Werthamer,[6] the first two APS Congressional Fellows, are especially good in describing the demands "for clear and concise writing; for a generalist's approach to issues, with the ability to shift quickly into an intensive analysis or a particular point as it enters the center of political attention; for a feeling of the importance of the interaction between often conflicting personalities, outlooks, and goals, and for the severe discipline to accomplish one's tasks in the face of a hectic and overcrowded professional life." In other words--clarity, timeliness, and perspective. A good staff person must also possess the ability to work without the public or peer recognition most of us have come to expect.

Some agencies restrict staff positions to individuals already familiar with the agency mission or else reserve staff assignments for training purposes. Others use entry-level staff jobs to introduce newcomers to the agency before giving them permanent assignments. Advancement in a staff position can proceed in one of several ways: (a) upwards, with the individual assuming greater responsibilities and wider latitude or (b) into a direct management position with line authority. Many agencies use staff assignments to expose promising junior people to the everyday workings of the management hierarchy before giving them additional line responsibilities. Some individuals consider staff positions to be temporary, as places to look over an organization, and to learn. Others prefer the rapidly changing environment and anonymity associated with staff work. Mobility and flexibility are basic attributes to staff persons; continuity and security remain but secondary concerns. For those who wish to continue in a staff position, a change of scene every 2 years or so is almost mandatory. Anyone entering into such a staff assignment should consider carefully the relationship between himself and his boss. Clear understandings as to the limits of authority and mutual trust must exist if a staff person is to function effectively. Effectively done, staff work can be extremely rewarding with an individual making very real contributions to the Nation's scientific efforts. I have seen multimillion dollar R&D efforts initiated on the basis of an individual staff recommendation.

Career mobility between staff and line positions is good at the lower and higher levels in an organization but difficult at the mid-levels. The individual who has served in a staff position for any length of time loses the detailed knowledge and skills required in a mid-level technical position. The mid-level staff person usually lacks the management experience required to assume a comparable line assignment. Many staffers having seen an organization from above and knowing all too well the constraints on the system are reluctant to take on lower level management responsibilities. I know of one former OMB budget examiner who states he will never go to work in a program agency.

ADDITIONAL OPPORTUNITIES

In addition to the more direct opportunities I have been discussing up to this point, the Federal Government also offers several other careers for the interested physicist. The U.S. Patent Office is always in search of qualified technical professionals and will train new recruits to become patent examiners at the Patent Examiner Academy. Each year, most agencies conduct a Management Intern Program to assure themselves of highly qualified future managers. New recruits and promising young employees are given special introductory training, rotated through a series of edcational assignments, and then placed in selected positions with exceptional career mobility. Competition for the program is keen but technically trained persons usually do quite well. I know of one B.S. physicist who was recruited to ERDA (then the AEC) through the MIP following 2 years with the Peace Corps. He is now an R&D budget officer responsible for handling $1.5 billion annually. One young lady, a former laboratory technician at NIH, has just finished her MIP training and has accepted a position in the Office of the Director of NIH to work on policies affecting research on recombinant DNA. The Department of State conducts an annual Foreign Service Program Examination to gain new recruits for both domestic and international positions. I am told physicists do extremely well in the competition.

For those persons still in school, there is a Summer Intern Program which permits selected college students to work at an agency during the summer months and to experience Government employment. Unfortunately, this program is no longer used as widely as it once was. Information about any of these opportunities can be obtained from any agency or Civil Service Office.

FEDERAL SERVICE

Employment in the Federal Service is probably no better or no worse than work in any other large diverse organization. There are of course certain unique positions that can only be had by working in the Government--like, for example, helping to establish national policies and priorities for R&D. The one virtue usually attributed to a Government job is security and stability. Certainly there are no layoffs due to bad business conditions. But people do get released and technical positions eliminated as needs and budgets change. The world of the Government employee is one of divided responsibilities and limited power. Events move slowly, incrementally, and without completeness. It is a world orchestrated by large staffs, and governed by definite (many unwritten) rules. Like most large organizations it is dominated by a strict management hierarchy. Compromise and shared responsibilities tend to avoid risk and suppress innovation.[8] (It is ironic that these same organizations and people have the responsibility for fostering R&D which the private sector finds too risky.)

Salaries in the Government service are generally competitive with those paid technical persons in private industry, and more than those paid by most universities. The National Research Council reports the median salary for Ph.D. physicists during 1975 in Government was $25.5K, in industry $26K, and at educational institutions $22K.[9] Table II shows the distribution of grade level versus age for physical scientists in ERDA. For beginning and mid-level positions, Government scientists tend to make about the same as those in large companies. However, for individuals in senior positions with major responsibility, Federal salaries are well below those paid in industry. Challenge and power replace money as compensation to top management; dedication to public service replaces profits on the balance sheet.

Most agencies conduct formal career development programs for their employees. But they are poor in comparison to those at major corporations such as General Electric or IBM which pride themselves on their training of young executives. There is reimbursement for job-related college courses and legions of Federal employees have gained advanced degrees at Government expense. Special programs also permit selected career employees to be paid to go to college for a year. Many technically trained individuals have used the opportunity to obtain a master's degree in business administration. But generally, the majority of Federal supervisors regard training as a reward for a past job well done and an intrusion upon a valuable employee's time.

Civil Service employees enjoy excellent benefits (insurance and pension) and time-in-service credits which are transferable between agencies. This vesting of benefits is of real advantage to anyone considering moving from one Federal agency to another.[10] Congressional staffers serve at the pleasure of their congressman but do accumulate time-in-service benefits convertable to Civil Service credits.

The portability of Government experience into the private and academic sectors is a subject of constant debate. The prevailing attitude is that Government experience is but of limited value. Maybe so, but my own experience and that of others say that people are hired in any sector because they can get things done. Individuals with a record of demonstrated accomplishments and recognized effectiveness will find jobs seeking them out!

SUGGESTIONS

In closing, let me congratulate the American Physical Society for estabishing the Panel on Physics Manpower and for providing this forum further discussion of the challenges facing physicists and physics educators.[11] Almost 8 years ago, Drs. Koch and Crane[12] writing in Physics Today noted that physics was changing. How right they were! I noticed that the University of Michigan School or Graduate Studies has recently opened an Office of Nonacademic Career Counseling because "students often haven't had opportunities to become familiar with nonacademic career possibilities...there is a need to make graduate students more informed of possibilities outside the teaching profession."[13] For those of us in physics permit me to propose several ways to improve the effectiveness of our Society and university departments in helping younger physicists meet these challenges:

(1) APS Survey on Career Mobility

APS should conduct a survey to determine the career paths and mobility of physicists over the longer term to document what physicists actually can do 5, 10, and 20 years after graduation.[14]

(2) Market Structure of Academic Research

APS should consider funding a business school study on "the academic scientist as a small business man" to determine the impact of Federal policies and actions on researchers. In many respects, the university researcher hustling for research monies represents one of the last examples of a truly open, competitive "Adam Smith" market. We should determine what must be done to preserve this structure and to prepare students to more effectively compete for research funds.

(3) Course on Economics of Science and Technology

All science majors, especially doctoral candidates should be required to take a 1-year course on the economics and politics of science and technology with specific work on the economics of technology transfer. APS might consider development of such a course.

- REFERENCES -

1. I define "nontraditional physics" positions as those in which the individual is not directly responsible for the conduct of research. A degree in physics may or may not be a requirement for the job. R&D managers in a laboratory are "physicists"; whereas program managers such as those at ERDA or NSF are in the "nontraditional" category.

   The 1974 Survey of U.S. Scientists and Engineers (NSF 76-329) reports that of a total of 34,000 physicists/astronomers, 41% were employed at educational institutions, 16% in business and industry, and 16% in the Federal Government. The National Research Council 1975 Profile of Doctoral Scientists and Engineers estimates there are 20,700 Ph.D. physicists in the United States, 8% of the nation's total doctorate scientific/engineering manpower. Of this number, only 48% were employed in teaching and/or R&D at educational institutions.
2. Field Mobility of Doctoral Scientists and Engineers, National Academy of Sciences, Washington, D.C. December, 1975. A Report by the Commission on Human Resources of the National Research Council based on results of the 1973 Survey of Doctoral Scientists and Engineers.
3. Report of the Commission on Revision of the Federal Court Appellate Systems - Structure and Internal Procedures: Recommendations for Change, Preliminary Report dated April, 1975. See pgs. 82-85, Section on Technical Assistance.

4. See Physics Today, _28_, 77 (1975).
5. See Chemical and Engineering News _55-47_, 14 (1976)
6. Benjamin S. Cooper and N. Richard Werthamer, Physics Today, _28-1_, 63 (1975).
7. Paul Horwitz, Physics Today, _29-12_, 28 (1976).
8. See Willis Shapley, _Research and Development in the Federal Budget_, AAAS, Washington, D.C. 1976. Mr. Shapley describes the complex and often conflicting goals of R&D in the Federal budget, and documents some 123 steps over 5 years time involved in the request, appropriation, and expenditure of R&D funds.
9. National Research Council, 1975 Profile of Doctorate Scientists and Engineers.
10. There are various types of career appointments and tenure groups within the Federal Service
    (1) Competitive-Career Positions filled by direct competition from the general public with new Civil Service employees being given career (tenured) status following three-years probationary (career-conditional) service.
    (2) Exempted Positions made exempt from the usual Civil Service Commission competition but with career tenure.
    (3) Temporary appointments for some limited unit of time (usually under two years) which do not confer Civil Service Career status.

    For further information regarding the various types of career appointments and tenure groups, contact any Federal agency personnel office or a local Civil Service Commission office.
11. H. William Koch, Physics Today, _23-1_, 27, (1970).
12. H. Richard Crane, Physics Today, _23-4_, 26, (1970).
13. University of Michigan, Rackham Report, Winter, 1977.
14. Martin J. Cooper, Applied Optics, _15-4_, 845, (1976).

TABLE I

GOVERNMENT SALARY SCALE - COMPETITIVE SERVICE

Grade	Dollars
GS-5	$ 9,303
GS-6	10,370
GS-7	11,523
GS-8	12,763
GS-9	14,097
GS-10	15,524
GS-11	17,056
GS-12	20,442
GS-13	24,308
GS-14	28,725
GS-15	33,789
GS-16	39,629
GS-17	46,423
GS-18	54,410*

*Pay rates are limited to the new $47,500 ceiling.

TABLE II

AGE DISTRIBUTION BY GRADE* OF PHYSICAL SCIENCE SERIES IN ERDA (HEADQUARTERS) AS OF DECEMBER 31, 1976

Grade	%	Age Range	Median Age
GS-5	3	21-53	25
GS-6	1	23-61	31
GS-7	4	24-61	31
GS-8	1	28-62	51
GS-9	6	24-67	37
GS-10	1	28-64	55
GS-11	8	25-62	37
GS-12	13	25-75	44
GS-13	16	29-70	46
GS-14	17	29-76	47
GS-15	20	30-72	49
GS-16	6	34-70	48
GS-17	3	37-64	51
GS-18	2	39-63	50

*Physical Science Series does not include Administrator or Management Series positions. Distribution integrates all levels of education (high school through doctorate).

BIOENGINEERING AS A CAREER ALTERNATIVE FOR PHYSICS GRADUATES

D. B. Geselowitz and D. W. Arnett
The Pennsylvania State University, University Park, Pa. 16802

ABSTRACT

Bioengineering offers a career opportunity often overlooked by physics students. Many graduate programs in bioengineering will accept students with a baccalaureate degree in Physics. Our experience with such students is limited but quite good. At the Ph.D. level bioengineers generally are involved in research in medicine or physiology, and are concerned with development of instrumentation, prosthetic devices and sensory aids; application of mathematical-physical principles to the analysis of physiological systems; and determination of physical properties of biological materials. Examples include pressure-flow relations in the cardiovascular system, gas exchange in the pulmonary system, electric and magnetic fields of the heart and brain, biomechanics, effects of non-ionizing radiation and ultrasound. An area of considerable interest is that of imaging, which utilizes ultrasound, x-rays, non-ionizing radiation, electric currents, light, heat, etc. to provide information concerning the spatial organization of the interior of the body.

Career opportunities involving biomedical applications of physics should be given careful consideration by graduates of physics programs. Physics students and their professors are probably acquainted with the fields of radiological physics and biophysics. The field of bioengineering, however, is one which is somewhat less familiar.

For many years departments of radiology have had a physicist as a key member of their staff. The radiological physicist is concerned with maintenance and calibration of x-ray equipment, with determination of dose rates for therapy, and with a range of activities related to the use of isotopes in nuclear medicine. Radiology departments seem to be moving more and more into the general area of medical imaging. These departments, as well as other clinical departments, will probably soon require a staff member who is more concerned with the broader aspects of imaging than is the radiological physicist of today. It is not clear where such a person will receive his or her training, but a likely place would appear to be in bioengineering departments.

Biophysics involves the application of physics to medicine and biology. As the field has emerged in the past two decades, it has been concerned largely with biology at the cellular and subcellular levels. There are other applications of physics to biology which might be properly termed *biophysics*, but which are being undertaken by people who are more often identified with "bioengineering" than with "biophysics". To a large extent, bioengineers are concerned with biology at the organ systems level and are often involved in research which attempts to apply the laws of physics to particular

ISSN:0094-243X/78/179/$1.50

physiological systems, e.g. the cardiovascular system, the pulmonary system, the blood system, the renal system, etc. A major thrust is towards the development of appropriate mathematical models. Physiological systems tend to be non-linear and time varying.

What is bioengineering? Activity of bioengineers may be divided into the following areas:

(1) Design, development, calibration, and maintenance of medical instrumentation, including diagnostic and therapeutic devices.
(2) Development of prosthetic devices and sensory aids.
(3) Applications of the engineering sciences and technology to basic studies in biology, especially physiology.
(4) Study of physical properties of biomatter.
(5) Application of engineering concepts methodology and technology to health service delivery system.

Many, if not most, bioengineers, are primarily doing engineering in the sense of equipment design and maintenance and systems studies. These activities may be of less interest to physics students. On the other hand many aspects of research in bioengineering, examples of which will be described, should be of interest. Bioengineers who are working in research are generally people trained at the Ph.D. level.

Admission requirements for graduate programs in bioengineering vary. Surveys conducted several years ago indicated that roughly half the programs require a degree in engineering or physics while the other half would also accept students with a life science degree. Students entering with a life science degree generally require about an extra year of preparatory courses in mathematics, physics, and engineering. Such students have not done dramatically well in our experience. Physics majors, on the other hand, can fit into the graduate program with little or no loss in time. Our experience with physics majors, while limited, has been quite good.

Following are brief illustrations of some areas of current interest in bioengineering which may be of interest to physicists.

Studies in hemodynamics are directed toward understanding the flow of blood through the cardiovascular system and toward developing instrumentation for providing the physician with data to enable him to evaluate the clinical condition of the patient. Blood is a non-newtonian fluid. There is considerable interest in characterizing the rheological properties of blood. Blood flows in vessels whose walls are distensible. Furthermore, the flow is pulsatile. There is strong evidence to indicate that hemodynamic parameters may play a role in atherogenesis. The problem of developing a theory for the flow of blood in, for example, a branching, tapering, tethered, viscoelastic tube is a challenging one indeed. Just as challenging is the problem of measuring blood flow, especially non-invasively.

Closely related to studies of blood flow in arteries and veins is the problem of characterizing the heart as a pump. To this end, one must understand the mechanical properties of heart muscle. A fascinating aspect of the physics of muscle is that muscle actively generates force. Therefore, a mechanical model of muscle must clearly go beyond characterization of stress-strain relations to

include an active force generating element.

Another area of interest is that of electrocardiography and magnetocardiography. Understanding the relationship between the electrical activity in the heart and the electric potentials which are observed at the skin requires formulation and solution of a volume conductor problem. Once again, one is dealing with muscle as an active element, i.e. generator of electricity. Passive electrical properties of body tissues determine the pattern of thoracic currents which have their source in electromotive forces in the heart.

About a half dozen laboratories throughout the world are currently engaged in measuring the magnetic field of the heart. Parenthetically we might note that most of these laboratories are associated with physics departments. There is considerable interest in developing an appropriate theory for the magnetocardiogram and in learning how it might complement the electrocardiogram both theoretically and practically in the clinic. The inverse problem of determining cardiac sources from the electrocardiogram and/or magnetocardiogram remains to be solved.

Professor Nyborg in his abstract mentions the effects of physical agents on biological systems. We would like to emphasize a different aspect of the interaction of energy fields with tissues. We have already alluded to the development of suitable mechanical and electrical models for muscle as part of studies in hemodynamics and electrocardiography. Other fundamental studies might require knowledge of mechanical, optical, electrical, and thermal properties of a variety of tissues. Great interest exists today in the use of ultrasound for imaging internal structure of the body. In order to design an effective ultrasonic instrument, it is desirable to know the ultrasonic characteristics of tissues. For example, if the acoustic properties of malignant tissue differ significantly from those of normal tissue, then one might be able to design an ultrasonic system for detecting small cancerous lesions.

Imaging is a very important aspect of modern medicine and has attracted the attention of many bioengineers. Radiological physicists have traditionally been involved in x-ray imaging and in imaging based on ionizing radiation emitted by radioactive substances introduced into the body. Other forms of energy can be used for imaging. The use of ultrasound has greatly expanded within the past several years. Most current ultrasonic imaging systems are based on the detection of echoes resulting from partial reflection of incident ultrasonic energy at interfaces between tissues with different acoustic properties. Several laboratories are now working on transmitted ultrasound. Other laboratories have been interested in use of non-ionizing electromagnetic radiation for imaging. Equipment already exists for generating thermal images based on detection of heat emitted at the skin. The study of imaging involves the physics of the interaction of energy fields with matter, sensing of small fields, data processing of the detected signals, display, and finally pattern recognition. In the latter case, there is increasing interest in automating the analysis of the images which are generated.

These brief examples illustrate a number of challenging areas of research in bioengineering. They are not intended to be comprehensive, but rather to indicate topics which might well be of interest to students graduating with a degree in physics.

One should not conclude without some discussion of employment opportunities. To our knowledge comprehensive data are not available; most information tends to be anecdotal. It should be noted that bioengineering is a relatively small field, with a small number of graduates competing for a small number of positions. Remarks which have appeared in the literature generally state that schools report that their graduates are not having difficulty in finding positions. Possibilities for obtaining academic positions in bioengineering are much better at this time than for many other fields. Students matriculating now, however, will not be entering the job market for several years. All predictions are for a growing number of jobs in the field. It is also clear that the number of students in the pipeline is increasing. What is not clear is how to project the supply and demand curves.

BIBLIOGRAPHY

1. Engineering in Biology and Medicine Training Committee of the National Institutes of Health. The Future of Training in Biomedical Engineering. IEEE Trans. on BME, BME-19:148-155, 1972.
2. Committee on the Interplay of Engineering With Biology and Medicine. Study of Engineering in Medicine and Health Care, a Final Report to the National Institutes of Health, National Academy of Engineering, Washington, D.C., 1974.
3. Committee on the Interplay of Engineering With Biology and Medicine. An Assessment of Industrial Activity in the Field of Biomedical Engineering, Task Group on Industrial Activity, National Academy of Engineering, Washington, D.C., 1971.

NUCLEAR PHYSICS TO WELDING ENGINEERING*

S. S. GLICKSTEIN
Westinghouse-Bettis Atomic Power Laboratory, West Mifflin, Pa. 15122

ABSTRACT

The "art of welding" is rapidly giving way to what is now being described as the "science of welding." The welder is being replaced by highly sophisticated automatic machinery. For such a changeover to occur with high reliability and success, fundamental physics studies of various welding processes are needed. At a recent conference on "Welding R&D--Problems and Opportunities[1]" it was suggested that a central organization be designated to coordinate needed scientific research and development. It was emphasized that "more talented physicists are needed in the welding research and development field." Having recently been extracted from the world of nuclear physics and implanted within the welding community, I can attest with first hand experience that welding is a ripe and exciting field for the physicist to enter. Basic unsolved problems in welding that will challenge the most academic-oriented physicist are discussed.

INTRODUCTION

The connotation associated with the term "Welder" is to the layman, as well as to the scientifically disciplined physicist, that of a hard-hat, strong-armed individual sitting amidst flying sparks and surrounded by grease and grime. Since I have been labeled for more than a decade with a respectable title "Nuclear Physicist," it is easy to understand my skepticism at the thought of becoming associated with welding. In addition, I, and many of my colleagues, had found our niche in life. We had become experts in highly specialized technical areas and could not conceive of wasting years of study and experience by applying ourselves to an entirely new field of endeavor. The pros and cons of this kind of transition are not discussed. The real world has fortunately or unfortunately made that problem academic. Many specialized physicists in recent years have unexpectedly found themselves uprooted from their workplace and been required to enter areas of employment foreign to their basic physics training. But the change in job opportunity or field of study need not necessarily be thought of as catastrophic. Given the chance, one can find excitement and satisfaction in areas foreign to one's initial environment. The physicist can offer a refreshing new outlook to the variety of problems that exist. A few years ago, I found myself in this situation when I was asked to investigate

*This talk is an adaption of a detailed report by S. S. Glickstein, "The Physicist In the World of Welding" WAPD-T-2599, December 1974, available from NTIS, U.S. Dept. of Commerce, Springfield, Va. 22161

SSN:0094-243X/78/183/$1.50

certain problems which pertained to welding. As an experimental nuclear physicist engaged in measuring low-energy neutron cross sections, I was completely void of any association with welding. During the last few years I have learned to respect the formidable task that confronts the welder and welding engineer. By learning to appreciate the real-world problems, the physicist can contribute much to their solution. Association with the welding community has been a profitable experience for myself, and I believe the welding engineers at our laboratory have profited much from having an association with a physicist studying welding. The practical returns from these experiences are difficult to measure quantitatively, but the results are evident in the final product.

With this introduction let me now take the opportunity to open a door to a field that has been labeled by some, and rightfully so, as "black magic." I hope to reveal to you some of the formidable physics problems that pertain to welding and whose solutions lie dormant, waiting for resolution.

COMPUTER SIMULATION OF THE WELD PROCESS

Let us leave the welding world that we commonly associate with the auto repair shop and concern ourselves with the type of welding reserved for the space industry or the nuclear reactor field. Under these conditions there must exist an extremely high degree of confidence that the weld has been made properly. To successfully achieve this level of confidence, the welding technique is tested and retested, checked and rechecked. With considerable experience and experimental trial and error methods, a welding procedure is established; but only after expending much time, effort, and dollars.

To accomplish this task more efficiently, less expensively, and with improved reliability the physicist is needed. What can he do? As an example, he can help develop an analytical model that simulates on the computer the entire welding process. This process may be separated into the following areas: 1) energy transfer to the weldment, 2) energy transfer within the weldment, 3) metallurgical effects, and 4) mechanical effects. The achievement of such a modeling program will require each of these areas to be understood in much more depth than it is today. In addition, considerable experimental testing is necessary to elucidate some of the phenomena observed and to confirm the validity of the model developed.

INVESTIGATIVE AREAS OF WELDING ARC STUDIES

Now let us discuss some of the physics aspects associated with welding. Welding is defined as the joining of two metals by the application of heat. To illustrate the type of detailed physics programs that are required to successfully achieve this joining process, the discussion will be limited to electric arc welding and, in particular, to the commonly termed gas tungsten arc technique. This is only one of the more than thirty different welding processes in use today.

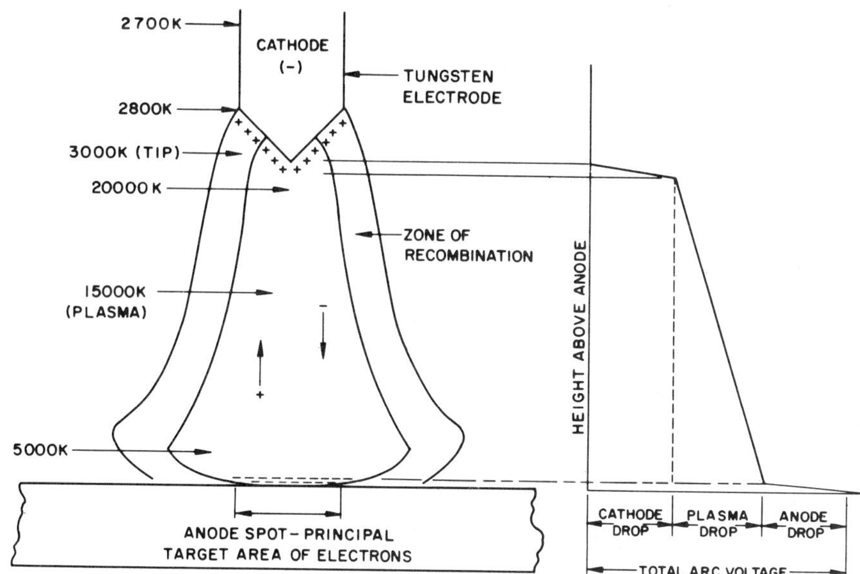

Figure 1. Typical Form of Gas Tungsten Arc
Direct Current - Straight Polarity

The electric arc employed in welding is a high pressure (~ 1 atm.) discharge of relatively large current (> 1 amp) and low voltage (10-30V). This is in contrast to a glow discharge of low current (10^{-3}A) and high voltage (1000V). The arc acts as a means of transferring energy to the surface of the weldment. A typical form of a gas tungsten arc is illustrated in Figure 1. In any model of the welding process, the first question that must be resolved is "What is the magnitude and distribution of the energy input to the weldment?" This opens the door to a multitude of problems that must be considered and other questions that need to be answered. Although arcs have long been the subject of physics investigations, many unsolved problems remain that are extremely pertinent to the welding application. Some of the arc physics studies that are needed include:

1. Effects of gaseous impurities on the arc discharge
2. Rate of vapor emission from the weld surface into the arc
3. Gaseous impurity effects on the anode and cathode drop regions of the arc
4. Determination of electric and magnetic fields within the arc for given welding conditions of current and voltage
5. Effects of electrode shape on the electric and magnetic

fields within the arc region

6. Measurement of arc jet flow incident on the weldment
7. Determination of the work function of the weldment surface.

These are just a few of the areas of physics involvement that are needed in order to accurately predict the magnitude and distribution of the input energy to the weldment. It is also important to understand how welding variables, such as current, arc gap, electrode type, welding speed, gas flow rate, etc. influence the arc and affect energy transfer to the weldment.

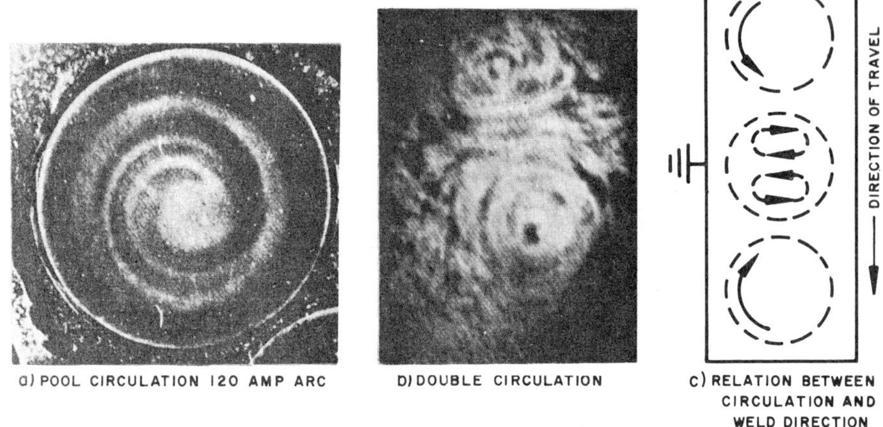

a) POOL CIRCULATION 120 AMP ARC

b) DOUBLE CIRCULATION

c) RELATION BETWEEN CIRCULATION AND WELD DIRECTION

Figure 2. Weld Puddle Circulation[2]

ENERGY TRANSFER WITHIN THE WELDMENT

If the energy input is known, the next question to be asked is, "How is the energy transferred within the weldment?" As a first approximation heat conduction theory may be used. But conduction is only one method of heat transfer. Upon close examination of the molten puddle during welding the liquid is observed to rotate[2]. Occasionally two weld pools are seen to circulate simultaneously as illustrated in Figure 2. This effect is very important and may be a prime mechanism of heat transfer in the workpiece. Very little has been studied or is known about weld pool circulation. There exists one school of thought that has treated the problem by considering electromagnetic stirring of the molten metal. Others have attributed the rotation to a change in surface tension along the liquid-solid interface which comes about because of temperature gradients within the molten weld pool. Both effects may be applicable. This particular phenomenon-weld pool circulation-has a profound effect on the shape and depth of the weld. It is a complex problem that requires considerably more study than is being afforded to it now.

CONSEQUENCE OF WELDING PROCESS

Once the energy transfer mechanisms are understood, the remaining task is to predict the metallurgical and mechanical properties of the welded material and the consequences of the welding process. These consequences may relate to problems associated with such effects as grain size, porosity, cracking, distortion, and residual stresses in the final weldment. While this admittedly is more appropriate for the metallurgist or mechanical engineer, it is extremely important for these people to interact with the physicist in the solution to these problems.

CONCLUSIONS

If the various areas of the welding process which include 1) physics of the welding arc, 2) energy transfer within the weldment, 3) metallurgical properties of the weld, and 4) mechanical response of the workpiece can be better understood, then the entire welding procedure can be successfully modeled for computer simulation. Having had some background in reactor physics, I like to think that the physics of welding is in the development stage where reactor physics was some 30 years ago. Yesterday's reactors were designed from back of the envelope calculations and trial and error experimentation. Now we have elaborate, highly sophisticated computer programs that can trace and calculate with extreme confidence every intricate step in the life of the neutron, from its birth to its death. Today we employ trial and error experimentation to produce a satisfactory weld. But today's black magic techniques need to give way to tomorrow's science. We have just begun to model the problem for computer analysis. The model has to be refined, enlarged, and tested. Successful computer simulation of welding can help alleviate expensive time-consuming experimental trial and error methods that are presently used for establishing welding procedures.

The Paton Welding Institute in the Soviet Union is already involved in some of the investigations that have been described. The Welding Institute in England and many of the universities of Japan and Europe have realized the potential and profit that can be gained through scientific physics studies in welding. Unfortunately similar efforts are being pursued on a very limited basis in the United States. By exposing some of you to these areas of investigations, this situation may be corrected. The problems in welding involve fundamental studies and the solutions can be of great benefit to the welding field. I invite the physics community to join in the effort to help solve these problems. The rewards can be extremely fruitful.

REFERENCES

1. Engineering Foundation Conference on Welding R&D -- Problems and Opportunities, held at New England College, Henniker, N.H., August 1-6, 1976
2. R. A. Woods and D. R. Milner, Weld. J. Research Supp., April, 1971

APPLIED MATHEMATICAL ANALYSIS IN BUSINESS

David W. Kraft
American Institute of Physics, New York, N.Y. 10017

and

Graduate School of Business Administration
New York University, New York, N.Y. 10006

ABSTRACT

The precedent for physicists to apply their analytical orientation and mathematical skills to areas beyond physics is well established. Opportunities to continue this tradition now exist in business, in such fields as economic, financial and investment analysis, mathematical and computer modeling, operations research, actuarial science, and related areas. The academic, corporate, and consulting settings for these activities, and their nature and character are described. The requisite background and methods of entry for physicists are discussed.

INTRODUCTION

Recent years have witnessed a marked increase in the mathematical sophistication of business. The formulation of concepts in mathematical terms, the mathematical modeling of business activities and processes, and the increased use of operations research ('management science'), econometrics, and statistics to form the basis for decision making has created a demand for individuals trained in the use of quantitative techniques. It is our thesis that physicists, already in possession of the necessary analytical orientation and mathematical skills, can, after some education in the language of business, be well suited to this work.

There is ample precedent for physicists to apply their talents outside the realm of science; perhaps the best known example is the work of Philip Morse in the development of operations research[1]. Other examples include contributions by physicists to economics[2], finance[3], and advertising[4]. Opportunities to continue in this tradition lie in economic, financial and investment analysis, mathetical and computer modeling, management science, actuarial science, and related areas.

There are three principal environments in which such work is performed: academic, corporate, and consulting. We will describe, briefly, the nature of each, the character of the work, and the possibility of physicists to gain entry.

ISSN:0094-243X/78/188/$1.50

ACADEMIC

The increased use of mathematics has led to the development, in graduate schools of business administration, of departments known variously as 'management science' or 'quantitative analysis'[5]. As may be expected, it is this setting that permits the widest latitude in the choice of work, and from which the more fundamental contributions emanate. Examples include the development of optimal strategies for the management of regenerative resources[6], and analyses of quota systems[7].

Since the field is not yet mature, one finds the faculty coming from a variety of sources, with statistics and engineering predominating; based on the writer's experience, there is no evidence to indicate that physicists would be unwelcome. Although many departments have attained a stable level, there is mobility between the academic and other sectors; such departing faculty need to be replaced. Also many institutions have yet to develop strong departments of this kind. These considerations, coupled with the growth in business school enrollments, suggest that suitably inclined physicists might do well to investigate opportunities in this area for an alternative academic career.

The credentials requisite for entrance are similar to those for departments of physics, with the graduate and stronger undergraduate institutions requiring a doctorate and evidence of scholarship. A physicist seeking to enter such a department cannot expect his specific physics background and publication record to be of much assistance except insofar as they call attention to his rigorous training and research ability. To be an attractive candidate he must be able to teach the "bread and butter" courses (calculus, probability, statistics and operations research), and to demonstrate that his research focus has shifted from physics to more appropriate areas. Obviously it would be advantageous to develop these new research interests before seeking a position; a convenient way of making this transition is to seek a collaboration with someone already working in the field of interest.

CORPORATE

Corporate opportunities exist principally in companies large enough to qualify for the Fortune '500'. The work is done either in staff groups bearing the names 'management science', 'operations analysis', 'corporate planning', 'market planning', etc., or it can take place in such functional areas as accounting, finance, or production. We list below some examples illustrative of the breadth of activity:

---The techniques of mathematical optimization are used to develop optimal inventory policies and optimal production and transporation schedules;

---Actuaries, trained in probability, statistics,and mathematics of finance are employed by insurance companies and pension funds to analyze risk and to determine premiums for insurance policies and annuities;
---In finance, regression analysis and the capital asset pricing model are used to forecast rates of return on a stock from rates of return in the market;
---In econometrics, regression and time series analyses are used to forecast levels of business activity from economic indices;
---In the securities industry, computer models have been developed for options valuation and trading;
---Statistical techniques are used in market research to obtain profiles of customer behavior.

The character of these activities can range from fundamental work of general interest, to applied work of chiefly local interest and intended solely for local consumption. Most of the work falls in the latter category. Thus, a physicist entering this setting should regard the opportunity to write a learned paper as an incidental matter, not as a goal, for he is likely to be involved more in the application of the well-known than in the discovery of the new.

The individuals engaged in this work have diverse educational backgrounds and are, by a large majority, at the bachelor's or master's level. The variations in their exposure to rigorous research methods, in their degree of professionalism, and in their sense of identification with some discipline are wide. Perhaps the most highly developed sense of professionalism belongs to actuaries where entry into the Society of Actuaries is by examination. Other societies which publish journals and provide means for professional identification include the Operations Research Society of America, The Institute of Management Sciences, the National Association of Business Economists, the American Economics Association, and the American Statistical Association.

Although there is much valuable and satisfying work to be done in this setting, the physicist seeking to become a business analyst should be aware of potential difficulties. He should realize that, as distinct from physics, most of the problems he will be addressing do not possess unique solutions, nor can these solutions always be judged as absolutely correct or totally wrong. The problem solver must understand the environment and highlight those elements of a solution that add understanding to the business management process. Further, there may be problems of communication with co-workers and supervisors who lack depth of mathematical training or exposure to research. These individuals are likely to be pragmatists, concerned more with the impact and implementation of a solution than with its derivation or form. Effective contributions to the enterprise can be made only if these viewpoints and concerns are taken into account.

Since the practitioners come from diverse backgrounds, a physicist need not to be at a disadvantage. However, many employers will require some exposure to or background in business. The above description of representative areas of activity suggests that necessary background is some mix of probability, statistics, mathematical optimization, operations research, computers, economics, and finance. Undergraduate physics majors might do well to take some elective work in these subjects. Physicists at the B.S. or M.S. level should consider graduate study, either at a school of business to obtain an M.B.A., or an M.S. in quantitative methods, or at an engineering school to pursue a graduate degree in operations research.

Physicists holding a doctorate, but without background in business face an uncertain reception. Although some employers appreciate the capabilities of such individuals to acquire the necessary background independently, others, not in a position to do so, will consider formal credentials in place of talent inventories. Also, in some quarters Ph.D,'s are considered impractical, "academic", overqualified, or threatening. To dispel these doubts one must, in some way, demonstrate a commitment to a career in business. Obtaining an M.B.A. is surely a solution, although one is reluctant to counsel a Ph.D. to pursue a lesser degree. Fortunately there are other paths. Some business schools have post-graduate programs wherein senior professionals take coursework tailored to their individual needs. A program might consist of a module of some half dozen courses designed to bring one up to date in a given field. At least one major institution awards upon completion, a certificate recognized by the state. For a physicist a module including work in economics, finance and advanced statistics might be an ideal way both to obtain the requisite background and to demonstrate the necessary commitment.

CONSULTING

Consulting is done independently or within the framework of a 'think-tank' or management consulting firm. Much of what was described for the corporate setting applies here, except that the work is of a project nature and is done on a contract basis. This suggests that the question of long-term career opportunities be approached with caution. Also some management consulting firms encourage frequent turnover of their junior personnel. Thus the principal benefit of working in this setting may lie in the exposure to the client firms.

CONCLUSION

Information concerning job opportunities can be obtained from the various learned and professional societies. Also, listings are published in the New York Times (Sundays, Sections 3 and 4), the Wall Street Journal (Tuesdays), and the Chronicle of Higher Education.

We should note that such institutions as foundations and hospitals as well as agencies of government also provide settings for work of the nature described herein.

ACKNOWLEDGMENTS

The writer is indebted to Drs. Aaron Tenenbein, Bertram Price and Lewis Slack for their helpful comments.

REFERENCES

1. P. M. Morse and G. E. Kimball, Methods of Operations Research (Technology Press and John Wiley & Sons, Inc., New York 1950).
2. P. Linhart, J. L. Lebowitz and F. W. Sinden, The Choice Between Capitalizing and Expensing Under Rate Regulation, Bell Journal of Economics, 5, 406 (1974).
3. M. F. M. Osborne, Brownian Motion in the Stock Market, Operations Research 7, 145 (1959).
4. A. G. Rao and P. Miller, Advertising/Sales Response Functions, Journal of Advertising Research 15, 7 (1975).
5. These correspond to departments called 'industrial engineering' or 'operations research' in an engineering school.
6. S. Chatterjee, A Mathematical Model for Pest Control, Biometrics 29, 727 (1973).
7. I. Kabak and D. W. Kraft, A Transient Analysis of Quota Systems, NYU/GBA Working Paper Series No. 77-72.

THE REFLECTIONS OF A FORMER HIGH ENERGY PHYSICIST DOING INDUSTRIAL APPLIED MATHEMATICS

R. A. Mercer
Bell Telephone Laboratories, Holmdel, NJ 07733

ABSTRACT

The author made the transition from an academic position in high energy physics to an industrial position in applied mathematics and analysis in June, 1973. This talk will compare several aspects of these positions, emphasizing the relative intellectual challenge and career satisfaction of the two. In the process, it will demonstrate a much closer similarity in the nature of day to day job activities associated with the positions than might intuitively be expected. The author's views on the strengths and weaknesses of a typical physics education as preparation for such an industrial position will also be presented.

TEXT

History has a way of repeating itself. When I entered the field of high energy physics in 1965, "bump hunting" - that is, looking for resonances above the expected smooth phase space background in the invariant mass distribution of particle combinations produced in high energy interactions - was in full swing. The well-known result of one such hunt, the ω^0, is shown in Figure 1. While I didn't participate in that experiment, I spent the next two or three years producing similar distributions in search of new resonances. Twelve years later, I have a "non-physics" position at Bell Laboratories. So, what am I doing now? Supervising a group which among other activities is fitting smooth curves to the distribution shown in Figure 2 to see how much of the distribution belongs in the peaks above the smooth background! Instead of invariant mass, the abscissa in this figure is now the elapsed time from when customers making long distance calls first hear ringing until they hang up because no one has answered (the peaks occur during or immediately after certain of the audible ring signals shown at the top of the figure). But if the name is different, the game's the same! Parenthetically I'll leave it to the high energy physicists in the audience to imagine the excitement that would be generated by the low mass enhancement in the figure!

ISSN:0094-243X/87/193/$1.50

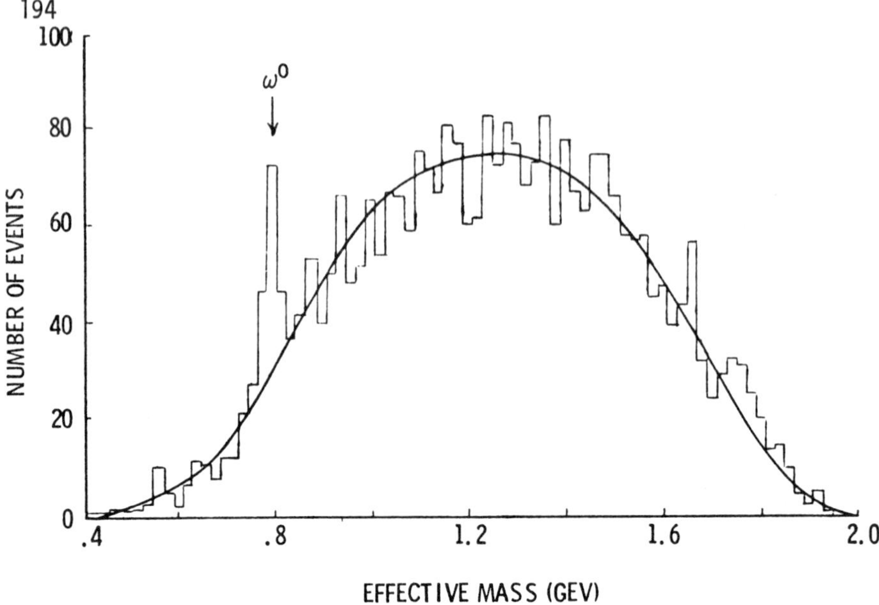

Figure 1. Curve fitting in high energy physics

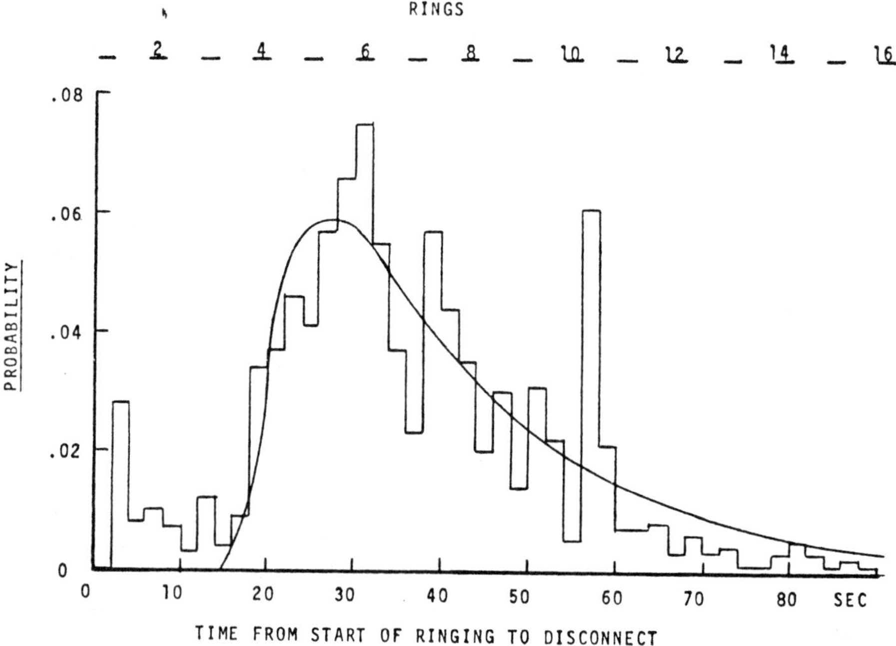

Figure 2. Curve fitting in "non-traditional" physics

This introduction leads me to the main point of my talk: that even in a job that falls well outside the traditional boundaries of physics - and in fact even near the limit of Grodzins "non-traditional" classification - one's day to day job activities may be very similar to those of a traditional physics position, even though the object of the work is quite different. To illustrate this similarity, let me describe the nature of my current job more fully. I work for a department at Bell Laboratories whose mission is to carry out large scale studies of Bell System network performance in meeting customers' telephone needs. Carrying out such a study involves the following steps:

1. Determination of the most important study to be done among many possibilities,
2. Development of a "system design" for the study - what type of data is needed, how it can be obtained and processed, scheduling, etc.,
3. The design and construction of appropriate experimental apparatus or procedures to obtain the data,
4. Data processing, involving large and often complex computer programs,
5. Data analysis, including appropriate statistical and modeling techniques to properly interpret the data, and
6. Administration - proposals to management, budgeting, overseeing clerical and technical help, etc.

Do these work activities look familiar? They should - especially to an experimental physicist - since I could have written an almost identical description when I was doing high energy physics.

But is it physics? Certainly not in name - in fact if I attached any label to the work it would be systems engineering (incidentally, that's a safe term to use. I've discovered no one, especially systems engineers, know what the name means, so no one will call you a pretender to the throne if you so label yourself!). Nor in subject matter - the object of the work is not to understand the physical phenomena of nature - like the social graces of quarks, or their taste, color, or (who knows, in the future) smell or feel. On the other hand, what I have found is that if I've given up a label (and thereby been removed from the endangered species list) and lost the one in a million chance that I might have pushed out a frontier of physics, I've gained the excitement of learning a new field and seeing how to apply my training to it, as well as experiencing a considerable improvement in some of the so called "bread and butter" aspects of my career.

Now, one might argue: why be trained in physics to do such a job, rather than in a more appropriate field. What field? My experience has been that people trained, for instance, in engineering, or statistics, or applied math usually suffer a serious defect: they have no hands-on experience with real data. They can write statistical formulae all day or perform modeling calculations, but faced with the prospect of actually obtaining and analyzing data, they do not acquit themselves well. In fact, I (modestly) claim that a standard physicists' training results in a fairly unique blend of mathematical ability, computer programming skills, often familarity with electronic and other experimental apparatus, and considerable data processing and analysis skills. Given our current employment problems, I think it is a shame we haven't done a better job of communicating this fact to industry - or, in fact, even realizing it ourselves. Incidentally, if a physics education has any weakness as preparation for a career in "systems engineering", it is that we don't learn enough statistics - I was quite surprised to discover that all of statistics is <u>not</u> summarized by the statement that the bin of a histogram containing n events has an uncertainty of size $\pm\sqrt{n}$!

In conclusion, then, let me say that the physicists' training provides a nearly ideal background for a position of the type I have described. That more physicists aren't found in such jobs I attribute to two factors: 1) we haven't realized our suitability for such work, and 2) we don't believe we would enjoy doing it. Concerning the first point, I'll simply say - you are! The main difficulty is in locating such jobs, which in different companies may be labeled systems engineering, applied statistics, or even operations research (although OR has a methodology and training of its own). My suggestion here is that if you are submitting a general application to a company, stress your background and interest in data analysis, programming, and (if applicable) building experimental apparatus. As for the second point, I encourage you to consider: Are you turned on by the object of your work or the challenge of solving problems - in other words, by what you <u>are</u> or what you <u>do</u>?

BIOMEDICINE AND THE PHYSICS POSTGRADUATE

Wesley L. Nyborg
University of Vermont, Burlington, Vt. 05401

ABSTRACT

Many contributions to pure and applied biology have been made by individuals through application of physical principles. These have led, for example, to an impressive array of instruments and techniques for viewing and characterizing bio-materials. Other contributions have led to better understanding of biological processes and structures, as in the use of statistical mechanics to treat phase transitions in bio-membranes. A broad area where the role of physics is obvious deals with effects of physical agents (e.g., light, X-radiation, microwaves, sound and ultrasound) on biological systems. This area increases in importance as we become more concerned with various aspects of manmade environment. Progress in these and other aspects of biology and the health sciences typically require the participation and/or leadership of individuals whose knowledge of physics extends beyond that of the usual B.S. graduate, and frequently beyond the Ph.D. Studies leading to the M.S. and/or Ph.D. in physics can provide excellent background for biomedical work, if they are suitably oriented.

INTRODUCTION

My purpose in this paper is to advocate, and comment on, an acitivity which seems important for this conference. In this activity, for which Helmholtz is a hero-figure from the 1800's, physical principles and techniques are developed for application to biology and medicine. (See Abstract.) Physicists play an important role here, and find rewards from a scientific viewpoint; the materials and phenomena of living systems are just as fascinating and challenging as those of nonliving substances. Besides scientific interests there are also humanitarian considerations. Since Archimedes, physicists have served the military in the defense of their various contries. Why should we not give, at least, as much emphasis to health needs, which transcend national boundaries?

The American Physical Society has a young and vigorous Division of Biological Physics. There are a number of physics departments in which research is carried out, with opportunities for graduate study, in biological physics. Ph.D.'s have been graduated in this subject, and they have found employment. However, the idea that physics departments should take this area seriously is rather new, and a number of questions arise. I shall attempt to take up a few of the concerns which have been voiced about biological physics by students, faculty and employers.

STUDENTS

1. Isn't biological physics a subject for biologists rather than

ISSN:0094-243X/78/197/$1.50

physicists?

Semantic discussions are of limited use but, as considered here, the topic should very likely be classified as physics, rather than biology. The problems to be solved and ideas to be generated call for mathematical prowess, experimental ability and physical insight typical of good physics graduate students. In terms suggested by some Russian scientists, we are speaking here of physicist-biophysicists (while recognizing the need also for biologist-biophysicists). In a graduate program, examinations and courses would appropriately be of the same level as for other physics students.

2. How does the physics student learn biology?

Background in biology can be obtained from a few well-chosen formal courses, by apprenticeship in research, by association with biologists and by reading of the literature. It should not be expected that the student who expends the time and effort required to be competent in physics would also become generally competent in biology. He may, however, become expert in a specific biological topic. Alternatively, or in addition, he may choose to carry out his work in cooperation with biologists; this can be a very fruitful arrangement in which the physicist and biologist each provides his own expertise. A requirement in such a team, besides personal compatibility, is that each know enough of the opposite field so that communication can take place.

3. Where can such graduate studies be carried out?

In earlier days there were very few opportunities, but now there are a number of departments in which biological physics is an available option. Consult the printed guides to physics graduate programs, search the recent literature for departments in which there is research activity, or ask someone in the field.

4. What are the employment prospects?

Sometimes very good; perhaps on the average not very different from those for other areas in applied physics. Examples can be cited of persons with recent Ph.D.'s in physics, or applied physics, or some closely related area, who are active in biological physics through teaching in university departments of physics and related fields, through research in university-associated institutes, and through research in government laboratories.

FACULTY

In physics departments it is often questioned whether "biological physics" is really "physics" and, related to this, whether biological physics should not be taught in a separate department from physics. It seems best to address these matters indirectly by treating somewhat simpler questions.

1. Are the usual graduate physics and mathematics courses, and Ph.D. comprehensive examinations, relevant for Ph.D. students in biological physics?

To a large extent, they are. However, biological physics is a very diverse field, and flexibility is usually advisable or necessary because of this. The schedule of required courses and examinations should ideally be such as to equip the student with specific knowledge for dealing with his immediate research and, in addition, with understanding in depth of physics generally. For example, three-fourths of his comprehensive examination(s) might be on "traditional" physics and the remaining one-fourth oriented toward his Ph.D. research.

2. Where are physics faculty to be found who can teach and advise M.S. and Ph.D. students in biological physics?

We have here a chicken-and-egg problem. An obvious source of such faculty is from Ph.D.'s in biological physics. Some of these are "coming down the pipeline" now, but not in large numbers. In addition there are "traditional" physics faculty (including distinguished examples) who have turned, or are turning, their attention to biological physics. By studying biology during summers and sabbatical leaves, and by associating with biologists some of these "converts" have become very productive and successful.

There is an obvious need nowadays for individuals with biological sympathies, for teaching service courses in basic physics to life scientists and health pre-professionals. For this reason alone, it is possible that most physics departments of medium or large size should now include biological physicists in their faculties. If these have research interests they will, of course, be available (in the usual pattern) as advisors to graduate students.

NONACADEMIC EMPLOYERS

We are now familiar with predictions that there will be more opportunities for physicists in nonacademic positions then in teaching. These forecasts may be just as valid for biological physicists as for others and make us realize the importance, to employment, of the attitude taken by administrators in government and industry. When positions become open in health-related private institutions or government agencies, the question may arise whether it should be filled by a biologist, a physicist, an engineer, or someone else. Arriving at a decision is not made easier by the fact that, especially outside of academia, "physicist", "engineer", and other vocational identifiers have variable meanings, and are often interchangeable. For example there is little difference between some "medical physicists" and some "biomedical engineers". A person identified as "engineer", "biologist" or otherwise often explains "I am really a physicist". On the other hand the "Chief Physicist" for a certain governmental health department obtained his Ph.D. in zoology.

In view of this confusion the decision maker should probably depend less on labels, than on an identification of the abilities and characteristics that are needed. If so, the question remains: What is to be expected of a person who has successfully carried out graduate studies in physics? More specifically, and relevant to the present topic, what are the expected attributes of a physics M.S. or Ph.D., whose specialty is biological physics? I shall not attempt to list these, but propose two broadly defined characteristics:

(A) Acquaintance with the basic principles of physics, especially those most relevant to biology, and some of their major consequences. Grasp of physical theory. Mathematical prowess and physical insight for dealing with advanced physical problems.

(B) Curiosity about new phenomena, particularly if they are reproducible and can be described quantitatively. The biological physicist, of course, will be especially fascinated by phenomena involving living systems and will want to find explanations for them.

In addition to the widely held qualities (A) and (B) are more special ones possessed by some individuals. These include general creativity, courage in attacking new problems, cleverness in the laboratory, facility with mathematics, and patience with difficulties in biological studies.

Of course, the possession of a Ph.D. in biological physics is neither necessary nor sufficient for possession of the above qualities. I believe physics departments are well suited for cultivating these characteristics, and that the physics M.S. and Ph.D. exemplify the level of physical background needed. However, as suggested before, the actual label on the field in which the person is educated or employed is not necessarily "physics" but may be "biophysics", engineering", "applied science", or some other identifier.

Health-related institutions, institutes, and government bureaus are increasingly in need of individuals with the kind of knowledge, abilities and attitudes described above. There is not space here for a catalogue of areas in which such persons can serve; a few of these areas are identified in the Abstract. For specialized fields additional training and/or experience may be desireable after an M.S. or Ph.D.. It is to be hoped, however, that employers will be able to hire scientists whose long-term potential is high, even if the experience does not exactly match immediate needs.

In conclusion: Biological physics is an option available to graduate students in some physics departments. Prospects for employment vary from average to very good and may improve as openings become available to fill needs in academic and non-academic institutions. At present employers might perhaps say, like the U.S. Marines advertise: "We need a few good men (women)".

OPPORTUNITIES TO APPLY PHYSICS TO ENERGY CONSERVATION PROBLEMS IN PROCESS INDUSTRIES. EXAMPLES FROM TEXTILES AND PAPERMAKING.

Thomas P. Sheahen
Office of Energy Conservation
National Bureau of Standards
Washington, D.C. 20234

ABSTRACT

The large mills that convert raw materials into finished products are often thought of as engineering wonders - elaborate large scale application of classical mechanics. However, there are many improvements possible through the application of new measurement concepts that are only now emerging from the research laboratories (laser optics is an obvious example). This paper suggests that there are many such applications, and illustrates the point with two specific cases, both of which deal with means of industrial energy conservation: (1) The process of making paper is predominantly a matter of water removal. Moisture gauges can easily be fooled by impurities in the input pulp, especially where paper is recycled; and thus substantial energy can be wasted by overdrying paper. Application of remarkably simple physical insight helps to overcome this problem. (2) Textiles must be held very straight while being heat-set in order to lead to good quality clothing, and either discarding or re-setting misaligned cloth wastes labor as well as energy. When combined with properly designed plates, the threads comprising the fabric generate Moire patterns that can be used to observe and regulate textile straightness.

INTRODUCTION

This paper is intended to demonstrate that there are some very interesting physics problems hidden away in factories. Physicists who are willing to seek applications of physics in unlikely places will find a variety of new career opportunities occurring in those industries that convert raw materials into basic process goods, such as steel, rubber, paper, textiles, glass and so forth. There is a growing class of companies that make instruments and/or control systems for use in such mills, and these companies have a permanent requirement for individuals who can utilize physical insight in either designing gauges to make new measurements or adapting existing gauges to unconventional applications. In most cases, the measurements must be made in real time, under factory conditions, on the process line. The data is fed into a computer which uses it to make decisions on how to run the machinery; this decision-making is normally accomplished by means of a mathematical model of the process. Therefore, there are both theoretical and experimental tasks to be done. Constrained by real time and the size of the minicomputer, the

ISSN:0094-243X/78/201/$1.50

theoretical model of the process must be able to handle unexpected inputs, without becoming unstable or making decisions that overreact to the data. The instruments must function with a very special type of reliability: planned, scheduled maintenance is permissible, but any failure of a gauge must be preceded by a warning signal that tells the computer to ignore the data. They must be inexpensive, durable, and tamper-proof.

Finding the solution to applied problems under this complex system of operating conditions is every bit as challenging as the problems one finds at a major accelerator facility. This paper cites two examples (one drawn from the paper industry and one from the textile industry) of how physics can be applied to industrial processes.

PAPER MOISTURE MEASUREMENTS

The pulp and paper industry is the fourth largest consumer of energy in America. The sheer size of the operations in a paper mill make them an impressive place to visit.

The pulping process begins with trees, removes the bark and reduces the logs to chips, which then enter a large chamber called the digester. Now a tree is predominantly cellulose fibres bound together by lignin. It is in the digester that the cellulose is separated from the lignin. The cellulose goes forward in the process leading to paper, while the lignin is separated out and burned, thus providing some of the fuel for the mill. (The optimum utilization of lignin and other waste products as fuel is a topic of much current interest among chemical engineers in the paper industry.) The cellulose is conditioned through bleaching, refining, and beating.

Once the pulp is prepared, paper is made by spraying a solution of 99% water and 1% pulp onto a high-speed moving screen (Fourdrinier Screen). Much of the water drips through the screen. Upon entering the dryer section, the sheet is typically 65% water. The drying process begins by squeezing the sheet between press rollers, then running the paper around the surface of a large number (≈ 50) of drying cylinders filled with steam. All this happens at a speed of about 6 m/sec = 1200 ft/min. An endless felt contacts the paper on the side opposite the surface of the steam cans, so that water is driven out of the paper as it passes down the line.

The rate at which water leaves the paper is controlled by the steam temperature. The paper contains about 7% water at the end of the line. Obviously, a lot of energy goes into drying paper. Indeed, a 1% increase in the water content of the final product corresponds to about an 8% decrease in the energy used in the drying section. Clearly it is important to know the water content of the paper rather accurately, especially since the modern paper mill is run under a computer-controlled feedback system. On-line, real-time measurements of several parameters of the paper (including moisture) are taken continuously and fed back into a minicomputer, where a mathematical model of the paper-making process acts upon this information and decides what settings of steam pressure, machine speed, and input flow rate will hold the paper weight and moisture content within acceptable limits. A faulty or erratic gauge is absolutely intolerable under these circumstances; if a measurement error were discovered only 1 minute after it began to occur, 1 acre of defective paper would have been produced, and this would have to be reprocessed at considerable cost of energy and dollars.

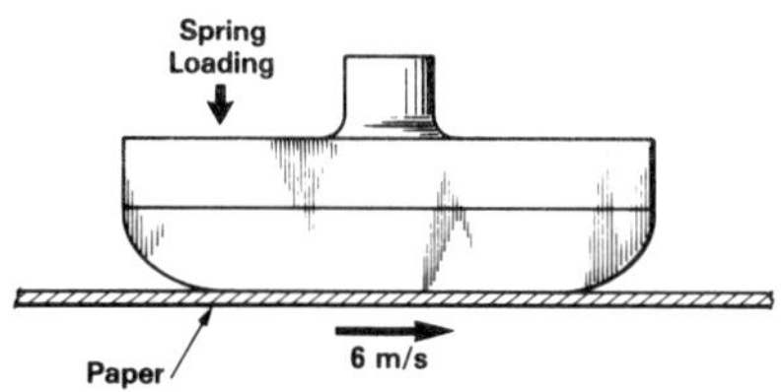

Figure 1. RF-conductivity gauge for measuring moisture, contacting the paper sheet. Side view.

One of the most common types of moisture-measuring gauges in use today is a type of RF-conductivity gauge, shown in Figure 1. The gauge is pressed against the paper as it slides by at a speed of about 6 m/sec. The contacting surface of the gauge is made up of a series of fingers, as shown in Figure 2. These are insulated from each other, and an electric field alternating at a typical RF frequency ($\approx$ 10 MHz) is applied to them. The energy absorbed from the driving oscillator depends on the dielectric constant of the medium connecting adjacent fingers. Thus when the gauge is in firm contact with the paper, the RF-conductivity is dominated by the water in the paper, and hence a measurement of energy absorption can be used, through proper calibration, to determine the water content of the paper.

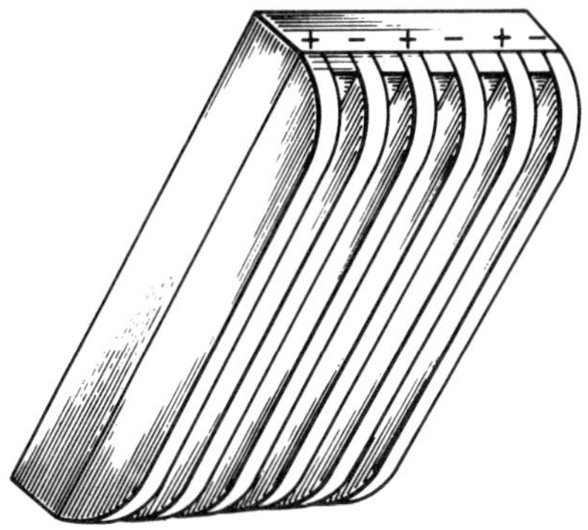

Figure 2. Underside of RF-conductivity gauge showing fingers through which RF signal is passed.

This principle works fine in practice as long as good contact is maintained between the fingers and the paper. But in recent years, a lot of paper products have been recycled, and recycling introduces foreign substances into the process. For example, cardboard boxes are generally held together with a tape containing asphalt, so that when they are recycled, the asphalt turns up all along the way throughout the paper-making process. One of the troubles it causes is shown in Figure 3. A thin veneer of asphalt collects on the fingers, lifting them off the paper a bit and thus destroying the accuracy of the moisture measurements.

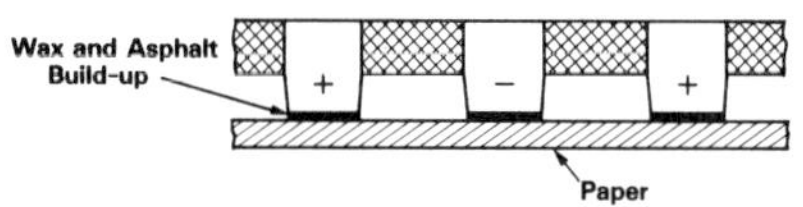

Figure 3. Fingers of moisture measuring gauge being lifted off paper by build-up of asphalt.

There are many ways to solve this problem, and most of them are expensive: For example, a chemical "dispersant" can be added to the pulp in order to spread the asphalt evenly throughout the paper. Again, a non-contacting gauge can be designed and built using an infrared measurement to determine water content; some instrument manufacturers have chosen this route. Third, a mechanism can be added to the apparatus to scrape or wipe off the contacting fingers every 30 seconds or so. Each of these offers a plausible solution to the problem.

The best solution is an application of the simple physical principle that viscosity generally decreases with increasing temperature. When the gauge is cooler than the paper, viscous liquids like asphalt tend to collect on the gauge. But by increasing the gauge temperature, the viscosity of the wax and asphalt coating diminishes, until it can no longer hold onto the metal fingers under the friction force of the sheet of paper going by. To carry out a test of this hypothesis, all we had to do was hook up a 115 volt line to a resistance heater on the gauge, bringing the contacting fingers up to about 100°C when the paper was at 95°C, and the problem disappeared. The fingers remained clean and shiny.

The program to correct this problem was budgeted for $65,000. The actual fix cost about $800, including overhead on our labor and travel to a paper mill. The whole purpose of this example is to show that remembering the very simplest principles of physics can often lead to the very simplest solution. The assertion made here is simple: Physics underlies every branch of engineering, and it can be used to penetrate through superficial symptoms to get at the underlying cause of measurement problems.

TEXTILE STRAIGHTNESS

There are many examples of ways to apply physics in the textile industry, especially in the application of high-polymer physics to the development of better synthetic fibres. The energy to be saved through greater efficiency in dying, washing, and finishing fabrics is possibly 40 to 50% of the total energy in some textile mills. However, I have chosen an example combining optics and mathematics, which is more in the mainstream of contemporary physics. This example is offered as a challenge for the future, not as a problem with a completed solution:

In a textile mill, hundreds of knitting machines turn out bolts of cloth about 5 meters wide and perhaps 200 meters long. These pieces are run through a long chamber known as a "heat-set tenter frame", in which the polyester fabric is conditioned so that permanent-press characteristics will remain in clothing despite several washings.

One of the most elusive problems associated with heat-setting arises because the cloth does not always remain perfectly straight as it enters the machine. This condition leads sooner or later to poor-quality clothing, which reflects back to the textile mill in the form of lower market prices for their goods, and hence smaller profits. The most common flaws are shown in figure 4: the fabric can bow or skew in the cross-machine direction, and the spacing between threads in the direction along the axis of the machine can vary irregularly. All these conditions could be prevented if the tightness and position of the mounting hooks on the tenter frames could be adjusted.

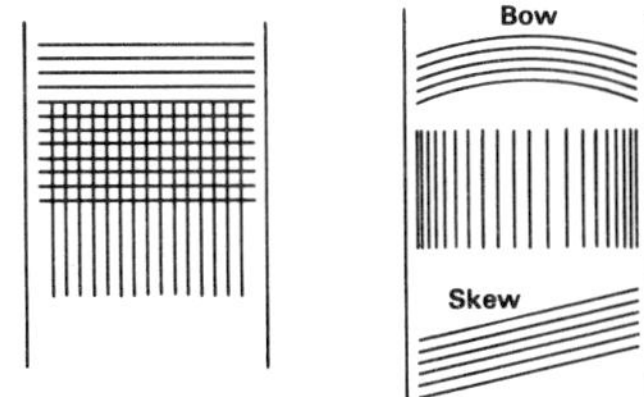

Figure 4. Deviation of threads from straightness during heat setting.

At the present time, control of straightness requires the manual intervention of a machine operator, who tries to tug a little harder on one side or the other of the fabric while it is unrolling and latching onto the hooks of the tenter frame. When he is unable to achieve straightness this way, or when the position of the cloth deviates after passing his post, then the cloth gets heat-set with a bow or skew in some part of it. That cloth must either be reprocessed correctly, at a substantial energy cost, or else must be sold as "second quality" for about half-price.

What is needed is a gauge that measures the spacing and direction of threads in real time, to provide information to the computer controlling the process; the computer would then send commands to adjusting mechanisms and thus maintain very straight cloth. One possible way of achieving such measurements may be based on the device shown in Figure 5: This is a photograph of a hand-held piece of plastic which is essentially just a Moire plate. The Moire pattern will be generated by superimposing this plate upon the cloth itself.

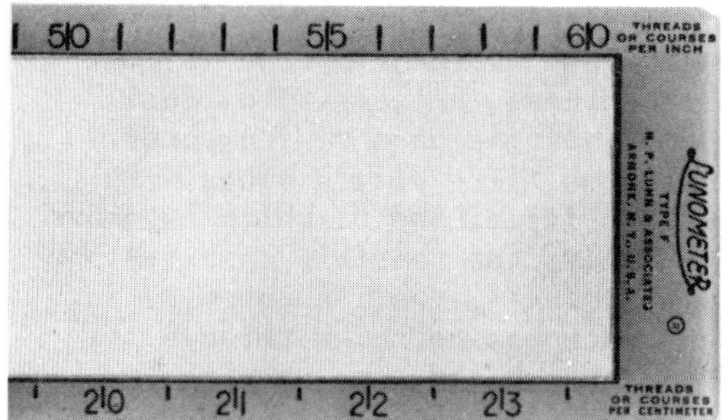

Figure 5. Close-up of one end of Moire plate used in conjunction with cloth to determine number of threads per centimeter.

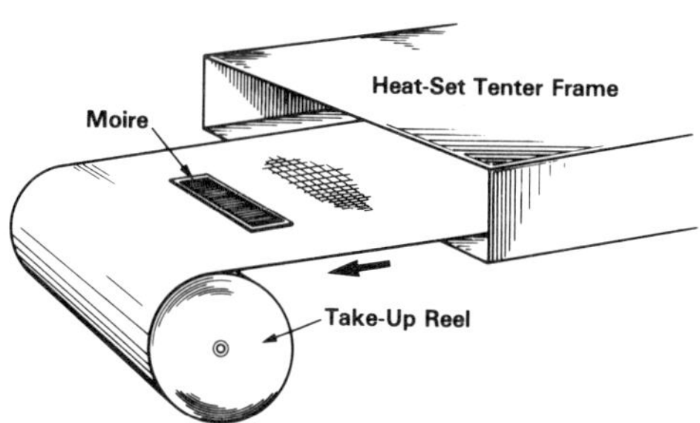

Figure 6. Schematic of exit end of heat-set tenter frame showing position of Moire plate.

Figure 6 shows that this Moire plate is place right over the threads just as the cloth comes out of the heat-set tenter frame. As a hand-held device, it offers only after-the-fact information about the finished cloth. To turn this into an automated measurement, interfacing with a computer, is a very challenging task for someone interested in optical image analysis.

Figure 7 shows the pattern that is produced when this Moire plate is held over some cloth having about 22 threads per cm. There are several points worth noting:

- First, it is hard to fix the center of the pattern within $\pm$ 1/2 thread/cm, but that doesn't matter, since that level of accuracy is

Figure 7. Photograph of Moire pattern generated when plate is held over cloth having about 22 threads per cm, with axis of plate lined up with cloth.

Figure 8. Photograph of pattern generated when cloth is at a skew angle relative to the Moire plate.

good enough for controlling textile manufacturing - so the gauge is suited to it's application.

° Second, the same kind of measurement is possible in the machine-axis direction by rolling the Moire plate up into a wheel and letting it rotate, and detecting the phase angle at which the center of the pattern appears.

° Third, any pattern-recognition scheme has to discriminate against the "harmonics" of the pattern at half the true value of threads/cm.

When the cloth is at an angle relative to the Moire plate, the pattern shown in Figure 8 appears. the thought of using this feature as a gauge to detect fabric straightness offers a real opportunity for cleverness in the application of optics to pattern recognition. Of course it is important to remember that if the computer is to use this data to control fabric straightness, any algorithm for such pattern recognition must run in real time on a minicomputer.

Finally, the superposition of two such Moire plates along with the fabric introduces unlimited possibilities, one of which is shown in Figure 9. It is fascinating to explore the possible combinations. However, the real need is for someone to think through the optics and come up with a practical gauge that gives a clear, sharp and unique determination of thread direction and spacing. There is obviously a financial payoff here, but the payoff in terms of overcoming a difficult problem through the clever and insightful use of physics is equally great.

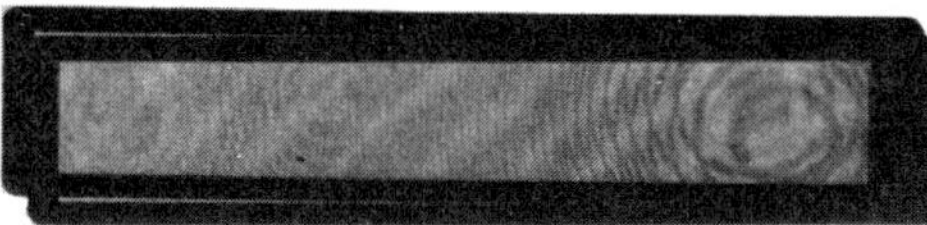

Figure 9. Superposition of 2 identical Moire plates, shifted slightly with respect to each other, upon the same cloth used to generate Figures 7 and 8. The "beat-frequency" pattern between the two plates is indicative of their angle and displacement.

SUMMARY

This paper has given two examples of the diversity of physics in its application to industry. It should be evident that these are mere surface scratches on a universe of potential applications. My contention is simply this: Physics is everywhere. It touches every corner of industry. Industry offers thousands of challenging and demanding career opportunities for physicists.

GETTING JOBS IN INDUSTRY*

James R. Wertz
Computer Sciences Corporation, 8728 Colesville Road
Silver Spring, MD 20910

ABSTRACT

Many students are unaware of how industrial hiring works in practice. This paper describes, for one major employer of recent Ph.D. graduates, (1) the nature of industrial employment; (2) how the hiring process works, including the major differences from academic hiring (immediate availability is important and may be critical, distance is important because companies pay moving expenses, hiring is less fraternal than the academic market -- more interest in what you have done than whom you worked for, etc.); (3) specific suggestions for resumes and job hunting (prepare a specific industrial resume, do not limit it to one page, phone (don't write) for information, accommodate your potential employer's time frame, etc.); and (4) suggestions for helping younger colleagues. Specifically, senior physicists may help recent graduates by (1) giving candid seminars on hiring practices in their areas, and (2) encouraging increased academic emphasis on technical communication, computer programming, and industrial research.

INTRODUCTION

Since relatively few professional physicists or astronomers have experience in industry, I will discuss three topics: the nature of industrial work, the hiring process, and writing resumes and finding jobs. Since receiving my own Ph.D. in theoretical astrophysics in 1970, I have spent three years in university teaching and three years in the Attitude Determination Department of Computer Sciences Corporation, doing analysis on orientation control of spacecraft as a contractor for NASA's Goddard Space Flight Center. My comments pertain specifically to my experience and to the department in which I work, but I believe much of this experience is representative of industrial work as a whole. My comments are directed specifically toward Ph.D. holders in physics or astronomy. The opinions expressed are entirely my own and do not reflect the views of the American Astronomical Society or Computer Sciences Corporation.

*This paper was originally prepared for the American Astronomical Society Committee on Manpower and Employment for publication in the AAS Bulletin and is repeated here with permission and modifications.

ISSN:0094-243X/78/207/$1.50

THE NATURE OF INDUSTRIAL EMPLOYMENT

In my experience the major disadvantage in going from academic to industrial employment is that you lose some freedom in the choice of research goals; however, you gain a challenging job and the opportunity to grow and progress both intellectually and professionally. As a specific example of an industrial research group, our department has a professional staff of about 120, including about 40 Ph.D.'s, most in physics and astronomy, some in mathematics and chemistry. The members work on closely related problems, and your technical ideas and ability to communicate them are regularly examined, debated, and improved. There is considerable opportunity for advancement--several Ph.D. holders with about five years experience are senior staff members or section managers, each of whom is responsible for the analytic work of about 20 people.

In the areas with which I am familiar, the salary is generally some what lower than in government work and higher than in academic work, but the differences are small. You may expect a somewhat higher salary if your graduate school experience is directly applicable to your job.

The major advantages of industrial work are:

(1) the opportunity to advance on your own merit and skill rather than by the availability of tenured positions;

(2) technically very challenging work, if you are aggressive in what you attempt;

(3) relatively little conflict over raises and promotions;

(4) good job security--"layoffs" are rare, even when contracts are lost;

(5) more interaction with others in your specialty. (This may be a function of the size of the group you work with.)

The major disadvantages are:

(1) you work on a subject selected by others (although you may have considerable influence in that);

(2) much less vacation and free time for your own projects than in the academic world;

(3) generally, less interaction with others in areas outside your speciality.

HOW THE HIRING PROCESS WORKS

The details of the hiring process vary considerably with the nature of the position, the time available for hiring, and the views of the responsible individuals. Nonetheless, many of the basic ingredients remain the same. The specific comments below are necessarily personal opinions with which others might disagree.

(1) Hiring is at least partly a random process over which you have no control. Don't get discouraged if you fail to get a particular job for which you felt you were qualified.

(2) There are three stages in the hiring process: Round 1--resumes are evaluated and most applicants are rejected for reasons mentioned below; Round 2--the remaining people are invited for interviews; Round 3-approximately 20% of those interviewed are hired.

(3) Because there are usually many resumes to evaluate, Round 1 is essentially a negative process--that is, the employer faced with a stack of resumes and somewhat uncertain as to how to choose the best potential colleague (as most of us would be), goes about it by eliminating people for one reason or another. Therefore, the key to success at this stage is avoiding negative factors. Specific factors considered:

(a) Distance: Companies pay interview and moving expenses; the further away you are, the better you have to be.

(b) Availability: Immediate availability is normally important and frequently critical; it's worth some sacrifice on your part to make yourself available when wanted.

(c) Salary: Recent graduates have an advantage here in that they are less expensive to the company. The company probably has a particular salary range in mind and you are unlikely to be able to change that much.

(d) Computer experience: Variety and depth are valued.

(e) General analytic skills: Largely evaluated on an individual basis.

(f) Time gaps in resume: These are extremely negative, except for summer school vacations. Specify clearly how you have spent all of your time since receiving your bachelor's degree.

(4) Round 2 (the interview) is a more positive process which serves to fill in gaps in the resume and permits the prospective employer to evaluate technical skills, experience relevant to the work at hand, ability to communicate, and motivation. The candidate should be as candid as possible.

(5) Companies want to hire what you want to sell--analytic skill, ability to think imaginatively, initiative, and the ability to solve problems and communicate your solutions; however, these are abstract qualities and difficult for either you or the employer to establish in concrete terms.

(6) From my (necessarily limited) experience, the major differences from academic hiring that you should be aware of are as follows:

(a) Money is important from the outset, whereas in academic hiring it is more important at a later, bargaining stage (probably with the dean).

(b) Your distance is important, because the company pays to move you.

(c) Availability is very important. Typically people are hired when they are needed and this is frequently not known in advance; thus, your chances of getting a job are better at times other than June.

(d) The type of person sought is largely the same in either area, although industry is less fancy--universities "appoint" and "fail to extend tenure," companies "hire" and "fire."

(e) The hiring process is much quicker in industry and the needs of a company can change in a period of months.

(f) Academic hiring is probably more "fraternal" than industrial hiring in that recommendations from well-established individuals in the profession play a more important role in academic hiring than industrial hiring; industrial employers are probably more interested in what you have done than whom you have worked for.

SUGGESTIONS FOR RESUMES AND JOB HUNTING

Getting a good industrial job is not easy and is governed largely by factors beyond your control. However, there are some steps you can take to improve your chances. My list of suggestions is as follows:

(1) Put real effort into writing your resume--it's important. Use an IBM Executive or other carbon-ribbon typewriter for the original--it cannot possibly hurt and it might help. Make sure the facts, spelling, and grammar are correct. Have someone else check your resume. An impartial, critical review of your resume would be useful, but these are very hard to come by.

(2) Prepare a separate industrial resume with a different emphasis. Omit discussion of future research you would like to carry out. Emphasize your analytic skills, computer experience, and initiative. Don't limit your resume to one page just because some resume guides suggest that. Any one interested in hiring a professional physicist or astronomer is more interested in the details of your experience than one page permits.

(3) Make your resume a general statement of qualifications and include in your cover letter skills specific to the position for which you are applying. Put the business part of the letter first and then the qualifications. Put yourself in the best light possible, but be honest and candid--it is refreshing and generally more impressive than being pretentious. In your cover letter, tell why you are leaving your present position. On your resume be sure to include both home and business address and phone (with area code), all of your experience (including being a shoe salesman to put yourself through graduate school), computer experience (including machine, operating system, and number of months), theses titles (M.S. and Ph.D.) and advisors, and a separate list of publications including the names of coauthors.

(4) Do not send a letter of inquiry--send your resume immediately. Phone for information. Don't be a pest, but one or two phone calls can't hurt. With phone calls, you will get more information and more help from professional employees than from personnel departments. Most professional physicists or astronomers are quite willing to answer questions or provide suggestions to potential colleagues over the phone. Letters are

much less likely to be answered (just because people are busy, particularly when they are so shorthanded that they need to hire others) and are less informative.

(5) Join the American Physical Society or the American Astronomical Society or both. Consider other professional organizations, such as the American Institute of Aeronautics and Astronautics, that might be closer to related fields toward which you are moving.

(6) Accommodate your potential employer's time frame. This is difficult because most academic work is on a one-year contract basis. Talk to your present supervisor and have him agree to let you go if the occasion demands. He can get another colleague a lot easier than you can get another good job opportunity. Tell employers that you can come at their convenience.

(7) Foreign students, particularly those with degrees from foreign universities should make a strong effort to demonstrate English proficiency since communication is important in industry. Try to publish some papers or reports in your name alone. Ask an American friend to check your letter or resume for possibly awkward usage or statements which are not clear.

(8) If an employer says that he has no openings at the moment, ask him when you should check back, and occasionally send an updated resume. It's a good opportunity to remind the employer of your interest. An interval of four to six months is probably about right, depending on the industry. Industrial hiring is often seasonal, depending on contract renewals and expansion plans. To improve your chances avoid the June rush.

(9) Remember that industrial physicists and astronomers are hiring colleagues and are looking for people they can work with effectively.

Good luck! Remember that there are people in industry who are eager to help you if they can. It is important for all of us to improve the employment status of our profession.

Helping Recent and Upcoming Graduates

Many graduate students are unaware of how the hiring process works in practice in government, industry, or academic areas. It would be extremely valuable to many graduate students (and younger faculty and staff) to hear short, candid seminars on how people are hired at various types of institutions. This hiring is largely controlled by senior faculty and staff, who are often the same people giving guest lectures and seminars on technical topics. Therefore, it would be relatively easy and a valuable service if those who are giving guest lectures would discuss the hiring process and potential openings in their institutions or in areas with which they are familiar. I would be happy to give such seminars and I think that many others would also. I believe that an exchange of information and open discussion of this topic could eliminate much confusion and frustration.

In addition to information on jobs and hiring, it would be valuable to make the educational process more responsive to the needs of post-graduate employment. This could include, for example, formal procedures to develop good scientific writing, increased emphasis on computer programming, and the offering of graduate courses taught by local industrial or government personnel on current non-academic applications.* The offering of "industrial" courses would give students a better idea of the nature of industrial work and valuable experience directly related to potential employment. The increased interaction between industrial and academic communities could be of benefit to both groups and could lead to new areas of research and new insights into current problems.

*I wish to thank Daniel Altschuler for this suggestion.

PUBLIC POLICY CAREERS FOR PHYSICISTS

Prepared by

Philip M. Smith, Assistant Director for Natural Resources and Commercial Services, Office of Science and Technology Policy, Executive Office of the President, Washington, D.C. 20500

I am pleased that Allan Hoffman has provided me with an invitation to speak to members of the American Physical Society on Public Policy Careers for Physicists. It gives me both the chance to get away from Washington for a day and an opportunity to talk to you about physicists in Washington. I am not a physicist. But over the 20 years that I have been in public service -- since the International Geophysical Year -- I have had the good fortune to know, work with, and support many physicists. I think I have been lucky. Martin Cooper in his paper this morning focused on some of the roles in government played by physicists -- with emphasis on program management, but non-research career opportunities in Federal agencies. I will focus on other aspects. I particularly want to trace the changing pattern of the involvement of scientists in public policy and then note five questions about future directions.

That physics and physicists have an impact in public policy can be seen in Washington in many ways. I recently saw a bumper sticker there -- it may have been planted by an APS member -- that proclaimed "Physics Makes The World Go Round." There is a great deal more truth in that than one finds on most bumper stickers. If one considers the virtual dependence of our day-to-day activities on communications and transportation systems rooted in solid state physics research, the degree our health technology is dependent on instrumentation that resulted from physical research, the physics base of our national security system, our financial and economic activities and other areas of modern life where we take the outpouring and reliability of our very new technologies for granted, it would be easy to see how a moratorium on the results of physics would be quite detrimental to our society.

That is physics. What about physicists? -- and particularly physicists in public policy, the subject of this session? Here is the view of Frank Press, President Carter's Science and Technology Adviser, in this month's Physics Today:

> "Physicists, both resident and visiting, play many roles in the Nation's capital. They have a direct and indirect influence on its thought and activities. And it is an influence that extends from the White House -- whose present occupant has more than a passing knowledge of physics -- through the Congress and Federal agencies and beyond to all those institutions, industries and individuals whose activities and lives are affected by the edicts, incentives and attitudes generated in Washington."

As hard examples of this influence and effect, I might mention the recent decisions on the B-1 bomber and the breeder reactor, both of which received major input from members of the physics community.

ISSN:0094-243X/78/213/$1.50

It might be worthwhile to trace briefly some history of the relationship of the physical scientist, and later the physicists, to the Federal government.

To do this, one could go back to Benjamin Franklin, an experimental physicist, and like Frank Press, a student of the earth and its processes. Franklin, and Jefferson, set the stage for the national embrace of science and technology.

But perhaps the first case of the Federal government turning to scientists in a formal fashion for their assistance was in the 1830s when an epidemic of steamboat boiler explosions threatened to undermine national confidence in this new and important technology. A group of scientists at the Franklin Institute in Philadelphia had started research on this problem. The government turned to them for help. A federally funded program of research was initiated. It culminated in the information and recommendations needed to set forth legislation on standards, inspection, operating procedures, personnel qualifications and penalties for non-compliance.

Deeper and closer relationships -- and especially the physicist-government relationship -- lay ahead. The National Academy of Sciences was chartered by the Congress in 1863 in response to the Federal Government's need for scientific support in solving military equipment problems of the Civil War. The establishing of the Academy was a major step in bringing science to the service of government.

But it was really as we got into the twentieth century that the relationship became strong. As you know, aeronautics and defense were a major stimulus. 1915 saw the establishment of a National Advisory Committee for Aeronautics (NACA), forerunner of today's National Aeronautics and Space Administration (NASA). In 1916, President Woodrow Wilson, at the Academy's suggestion, formed the National Research Council. Between World War I and 1933, the Council was the principal national organization for correlating and promoting scientific endeavors.

The 1940s, which witnessed the beginning of an unprecedented growth of scientific and technological development, was also the start of a new level of involvement of scientists in public policy. Physicists came into Washington and Washington-related policy activities in great numbers. They joined large government research efforts in even larger numbers. The Office of Scientific Research and Development (OSRD) was established by President Roosevelt and directed by Vannevar Bush. The Atomic Energy Commission and the Office of Naval Research followed, and then came the National Science Foundation and the National Institutes of Health. It was in the 1950s that science policy advising started to move closer to the White House and Congress. President Eisenhower initiated the idea of a Presidential science adviser. And scientists began parading in and out of Congressional hearing rooms on a regular basis, a new breed of expert witnesses foreshadowing others who would become concerned with the environment, health and other issues, and that would also represent other science disciplines in larger numbers.

Today, scientists, and particularly physicists, are in Washington in strength. In top-level positions, there are Harold Brown as

Secretary of Defense, Robert Frosch as Administrator of NASA, Hans Mark as Under Secretary of the Air Force, and John Martin as Assistant Secretary of the Air Force for R&D. Others in important policymaking positions include Joseph Nye at the State Department.

However, my own Office, which the Congress reestablished last year "to put science advice back in the White House," as the expression goes, mirrors the present situation best of all. A quite young group with physics backgrounds is entering public policy. Among our current OSTP Senior staff, we have a physicist-nuclear engineer who is now in environmental policy research by way of public interest activities, a mathematician and physicist who also holds a Ph.D. in political science and is working on energy and mineral policy for us, and an applied physicist who is dealing with university research policy as well as national security work. We soon expect to have on our staff a Ph.D. physicist who also has a law degree from Harvard and comes to us after serving as an assistant to a Supreme Court Justice. And I could cite other examples of consultants we have used and are using whose backgrounds have been in physics.

The question is often raised as to what makes a physicist -- or more broadly, a scientist -- effective in these kinds of jobs. Or stated in another way, what are the important attributes needed by people in public policy work? Mental attitude is most important. There is a myth taught to high school students about the scientific method which involves observation hypotheses, experimental design, and so forth. Any practicing physicist knows that actual basic research is a no-holds-barred struggle to understand by hook or crook what is going on, subject to the highest possible standards of intellectual rigor and quality of evidence. This is the best sort of training for public policy people.

What is needed for many policy posts is some combination of the following well-developed abilities: to be able to evaluate evidence, accept new inputs and points of view, make decisions on the basis of partial data, and deal with complex phenomena.

While these attributes are by no means unique to physicists, physicists do seem to be pretty well-trained in these skills. Further, physics tends to be pretty broad and multidisciplinary as it is practiced. Theoretical physicists have to know and appreciate some rather abstruse mathematics; experimentalists get to be good practicing engineers. Everyone gets to know how to put together proposals and to manage finances, at least in small quantities.

Beyond this, probably one of the most important attributes called for is the ability to write clearly and concisely. Those who can articulate their ideas in a manner understood by a wide range of people, who can communicate convincingly, will be greatly appreciated and much in demand. There are always a number of policy issues -- and that number seems to be growing -- that have a scientific or technological component that needs clear explanation in language that can be understood by political decision-makers and the public. Some of the most recent examples are: the cruise missile, the neutron bomb, the breeder reactor and nuclear fuel cycles, the fluorocarbon-ozone problem, and the recombinant DNA research matter. Others involving toxic chemicals, food and drugs, global climate and weather are surfacing and bound to become items of public interest and debate in the months ahead.

In spite of all that is written and said about such matters -- or perhaps because of it -- there is always a great deal of confusion and misinformation. If we are going to have decisions on these important issues that are in part based on informed public debate and intelligent government leadership, we badly need the input of scientists and engineers who can clarify and not confuse the major points that have to be understood and evaluated.

There is an increasing interest among scientists in the governmental function, and the relationships between science and society. Some public interest scientists are extremely effective. But one of the more disturbing occurrences is that some of them seem to vacate the professional habits of a lifetime when they reach policy questions. They take extreme positions of advocacy and disregard the standards of evidence and, in some cases, even the canons of intellectual consistency, let alone integrity. It is a curious phenomenon, and neither science nor society is well-served thereby.

Policy work needs people with broad background, for policy issues almost always involve tradeoffs among several communities. Thus, some practical knowledge of the dynamics of those communities is essential to the process, as is some practical experience in accomplishing something in one or more of those communities. The dangers of having policy development carried out by people who have never actually done anything is very real. The learning rate of young people who come to Washington in positions of power is very fast, but until they learn how the system works, the incidence of problems coming from some quarter unexpected by them is staggering.

Before concluding, let me raise a few questions related to what might lie ahead regarding the role of scientists in public policy.

First, there is the matter of turnover. As we move into the 1980s and 1990s, where will the new science policy leadership come from? A new generation will have to take over. What impact will demographic and institutional changes affecting our universities have on the flow of scientists in and out of academia and government? The last 25 years has seen a cycling and recycling of people between the universities and government. As some examples of this, I can think of Spurgeon Keeney, currently the Deputy Director of the Arms Control and Disarmament Agency (ACDA), and Eugene Skolnikoff, who was in the original Office of Science and Technology, returned to MIT, and is now a Senior Consultant in our Office of Science and Technology Policy. There are numerous such cases of a shuttling between academia and government.

Second, will women and minorities enter physics in increasing numbers and, if so, will their popularity for program management and public policy work be so overwhelming that few will become great scientists?

A third question that arises involves the relationship of industry and government. If more graduates continue to go into industry and if there is a further antipathy between industry and the government, how will this affect cooperation on public policy advice? Some of the best may be excluded because of corporate connections.

Fourth, State and local government have been the fastest growing sector of public service over the last decade. What challenges are there for physicists in those arenas? It is an area that I would suggest needs looking into. One of the panelists will be speaking to this later today.

Fifth, while we have a good number of scientists becoming involved in public policy through staff positions, why are there not more elected public officials from the ranks of scientists? Those few who are in the Congress, including an astronaut-geologist and nuclear chemist, are effective politicians and lawmakers. We could use many more. Will the spirit of activism that pervaded campuses in the 1960s bring more scientists into politics by the 1980s?

I think we should recognize that there is a finite number of line S&T jobs at the Federal policy level, although most of the major government organizations now have such positions. However, there will be a continuing need, particularly through the government's concern for energy, ecology, and our competitive industrial position (as evidenced by the growing interest in international technology transfer). And there will be turnover in the the 1980s that I mentioned.

The fact that I see some opportunities for physicists in public policy careers does not mean that I would like to see, or would encourage, a wholesale exodus from the halls of research to the halls of government -- or even to the town hall. We still need our best scientists doing science, and physics is an area of science where great contributions to society remain to be made, contributions on the frontiers of physics and relevant to our most urgent challenges. But for those of you who feel the need to seek other frontiers, your background in physics, and the intelligence, intellectual curiosity and training that brought you into physics will prove valuable to you if you move into the area of public policy. To all who contemplate such a move, I would say think twice, then once more -- and then good luck on whatever your decision.

MANPOWER NEEDS IN ENERGY RESEARCH AND DEVELOPMENT

Norman Seltzer
Energy Research and Development Administration
Washington, D. C. 20545

ABSTRACT

Under the Energy Reorganization Act of 1974, ERDA was mandated to help assure an adequate supply of manpower for the accomplishment of energy research and development programs by, among other things, assuring the collection, analysis, and dissemination of necessary manpower supply and demand data. To carry out this mandate, a Manpower Assessment Office was established in 1976 which set for itself a three-fold mission: (1) to implement ERDA's explicit manpower analysis mandate as specified in the 1974 legislation plus the Act's general mandate for near and long-term planning; (2) to provide a rational and credible basis for ERDA's education and training decisions through independent manpower assessment; and (3) to utilize the manpower assessment capability of other Federal agencies and private organizations both to avoid unnecessary duplication and to comply with the charge in the 1974 Act to build on the efforts of other public and private agencies. During the approximately one-year period since the Manpower Assessment Office came into existence an overall five-year plan has been devised which will: develop a comprehensive manpower information system to provide base line data on professional, technical, and skilled manpower; design a series of methodologies so that information can be converted to program intelligence; and undertake a program of recurring assessments to provide timely and relevant intelligence as a basis for energy program and policy decisions. By 1982, it is anticipated that near-, medium-, and long-term assessments of manpower requirements and supply will be available for each energy technology program area so that whatever appropriate actions are necessary can be taken to assure adequate numbers of qualified personnel to accomplish national research development and demonstration objectives.

PAPER

The American Institute of Physics has an obvious interest in future needs for scientific manpower, and scientific manpower certainly plays a vital role in the development of our energy technologies. Unfortunately, it is difficult at this time to be very specific regarding the extent of this role. There are many reasons for this. To begin with, as you know, manpower needs are derivative. That means, in our case, that before we can estimate the numbers and kinds of scientists needed to carry out the National Energy Plan, we must first know what that Plan is.

ISSN:0094-243X/78/218/$1.50

Federal energy matters are now in a period of transition. As you may be aware, however, the Energy Research and Development Administration (ERDA) was brought into being under the 1974 Energy Reorganization Act. Now, as you all know, the 1974 Act is being superceded and almost all energy activities are being reorganized under a new super agency--the Department of Energy. We do not know yet exactly what form the new agency is going to take or how it will alter energy administration, but we do have a definitive statement of national energy objectives. In summary, they are:

- Immediately: to reduce dependence on foreign oil

- In the medium-term: to contain U.S. oil imports within limitations of available foreign oil producing capabilities

- In the long-term: to develop renewable and essentially inexhaustible sources of energy for sustained economic growth.

Further, regardless of the ultimate form of the new Department of Energy, we do know that the Department is charged with following the Administration's National Energy Plan. The salient features of the plan involve:

- Conservation and fuel efficiency;

- Use of national pricing and production policies;

- Stable government policies;

- Substitution of abundant energy resources for those in short supply; and,

- Development of nonconventional technologies.

For the present, however, we are still under the current legislation, the 1974 Energy Reorganization Act. Under the 1974 Act, ERDA is charged with the responsibility for assuring that there will be an adequate supply of qualified manpower to carry out this plan and to meet national energy objectives with specific reference to energy research and development programs. The legislation is explicit: ERDA is directed to collect, analyze and disseminate energy manpower supply and demand data. We are also directed under the Act to do near- and long-term manpower planning. Finally, we are cautioned to build upon, not duplicate, the efforts of other public agencies and private organizations.

My office, the Manpower Assessment Office, functions under the above mandate. We have made some progress, but even if we did not have the burden of the forthcoming reorganization, we would still have numerous problems.

For one thing, the Manpower Assessment Office is young; age: 18 months, which puts us at about the toddler stage. Secondly, we didn't have to wait for the new concept of zero-based budgeting for Federal agencies; we started with a "zero" budget and little staff, and only the beginning of the current fiscal year was a very modest-sized budget allotted. When we started, we found that current energy manpower supply and demand data were not readily available. This placed constraints on our ability to do manpower planning, regardless of the Act's mandate. Further, the types of data collected by other agencies - which we are supposed to use and not duplicate - does not necessarily include the information we need for energy manpower assessment. To deal with these problems, we have underway a three-faceted program. First, we are developing a Comprehensive Energy Manpower Information System. Like other bureaucrats, we had to make sure we had an appropriate sounding acronym, i.e., CEMIS. Unfortunately, names and acronyms are not enough. In a mission agency (unlike the National Science Foundation, the Bureau of Labor Statistics or the Census Bureau), Administrators and managers want facts which provide a basis for policy and program decisions - not global data. For example, they may ask "How many nuclear engineers will be needed for waste management activities?"; "How many and what kinds of technicians are needed for commercializing solar heating and cooling?"; and "How many and what kind of scientists will be required if "X" amount of dollars are provided for R&D of synthetic fuels?"

CEMIS is intended to provide hard baseline data on the supply, employment, characteristics and utilization of all energy RD&D manpower as well as provision to update and maintain these data. This will give us much of the basic information we need. It is possible, of course, that with the establishment of DOE, our system will be expanded to include all energy-related functions.

Second, we will make both regularly recurring and special, as needed, in-depth assessments of manpower requirements to provide timely and relevant information as part of the input needed for energy program decisions.

Third, we will be supporting the development of a series of methodologies so that we can use the data to assess and analyze long-term manpower supply and demand.

We are pleased with the concept of CEMIS because it will enable us to integrate and to modify when necessary, but not duplicate, existing information. New data will be gathered only when needed to supplement what already exists or is being gathered by others.

When fully developed, CEMIS will provide much of the information needed for near- and mid-term assessments of manpower needs. These assessments will be available separately for each energy program such as: fossil fuels, nuclear, solar, geothermal, conservation, and will be modified to include additional programs as they evolve.

We have already launched a number of special efforts, two of which I will briefly describe. The first, although it deals with that part of the occupational spectrum usually far removed from your interests, is of great importance to the energy program. In consort with three other agencies, the Department of Labor, the Federal Energy Administration, and the Tennessee Valley Authority, we started last fall to develop a National Construction Manpower Demand System which will provide forecasts of requirements for some 28 different skilled craft occupations in all types of construction activity. ERDA's support (and that of FEA) is primarily concerned with developing an energy component so that national, regional, and even local area information will be available on manpower requirements for carrying out work on power plants, mining facilities, synthetic fuel demonstration plants, etc. We anticipate that within the next three to four months, data will be available on near- and mid-term requirements for several categories of the energy construction component.

Secondly, about two months ago, we contracted for the first national study of current employment and future requirements in the solar energy field. This effort will attempt to define the universe of organizations in all sectors of the economy involved in all segments of the solar field--from heating and cooling to photovoltaic to biomass conversion. Estimates will be provided on the numbers and types of scientists, engineers, technicians and skilled craftsmen involved in the different areas of the solar field and their characteristics. And finally, an assessment of future requirements over the next five to ten years will be provided.

As you will note, these projects will provide inputs for our data base in CEMIS and will also contribute to our planned cycle of in-depth manpower requirements assessment.

In the interim period, we must depend on recent or ongoing studies undertaken by others for any data that may be relevant to our needs. And, there have been a number of surveys conducted by other Federal agencies such as the National Science Foundation which have been useful to us.

These special studies provide the basis for our present manpower assessment capability. As indicated, we have a long way to go before we can carry out our Energy Reorganization Act mandate in the manner we think appropriate, but we can provide some information.

To illustrate our current limited capability, I am going to cite one special study we have recently completed. This also gives me the chance to do several other things:

- First of all, to demonstrate how we are attempting to carry out our mandate to build upon, without duplicating, manpower data developed by other public agencies;

- Next, it enables me to address in part my assigned topic and to discuss some findings relevant to assessing needs for manpower in Energy Research and Development; and,

- In addition, I can illustrate a continuing problem which plagues all manpower assessors: the fact that data collected for one purpose is only partially adequate for different types of assessments.

All of the foregoing excuses are made to prepare you for the fact that I have modified my assigned topic. My assignment is general: to assess energy manpower needs. And, although this conference is concerned with all educational levels, I am going to talk about one specific group, (Ph.D's), using information on those engaged in energy-related activities from a study primarily concerned with the occupational characteristics of all doctoral scientists and engineers.

The study illustrates how we intend to use, without duplicating, information developed by another agency. In this case, we have several organizations involved. The original data was collected for the 1975 Survey of Doctoral Scientists and Engineers. This survey was conducted by the National Research Council of the National Academy of Sciences. It is jointly sponsored by the National Science Foundation and the National Institutes of Health. Our study used these data to examine the characteristics of doctoral scientists and engineers who devoted a significant amount of time to energy-related activities. Just to compound the agency hash further, our study was carried out by the Oak Ridge Associated Universities and sponsored by ERDA through the Manpower Assessment Office.

Herewith, a few numbers to highlight our findings. In 1975 just about the time ERDA was established and Federal R&D funding for energy programs was running at about $1.1 Billion, about eight percent (21,000) of the more than 260 thousand doctoral scientists and engineers reported that they spent a significant amount of their time working in "energy and fuel" activities. As you might expect, this number was even higher for physicists. Fifteen (15) percent of all physicists with doctorates reported themselves as principally engaged in energy-related work. This compares with 11 percent of the Ph.D. chemists and 22 percent of those classified as earth, environmental and marine scientists. Incidentally, this probably understates the number engaged in energy-related projects since many faculty members reported themselves involved in education either in teaching or some other capacity. It may be assumed with some certainty that a number of the latter were to some extent involved in energy research. Also, some of those checking environment, health, and even defense might on closer inspection be considered energy-related.

Our data lends statistical dimension to the earlier discussion by Dr. Martin Cooper, also of ERDA. As you recall, he talked about the kinds of jobs physicists actually perform during the course of their government careers. The survey indicates that there is considerable mobility in both the Government and Non-Government sectors.

We found that one out of five Ph.Ds in both energy and non-energy jobs report that they were working in a discipline different than the one in which they received their degree. The data also show that a large number of energy-related Ph.D's were working in employment subfields different from their specific degree subspecialty. It is not possible, however, to estimate what proportion of this field switching was forced, e.g., lack of adequate jobs in the field, and what proportion was voluntary, i.e., more interesting work, better pay, and so forth. Parenthetically, about two-thirds (2,200 of 3,400) of the energy-related Ph.Ds with degrees in physics were working as physicists. When compared to the non-energy group, significantly more doctoral scientists and engineers working in the energy areas are in management and in research and development. Significantly fewer of the energy Ph.Ds are in teaching when compared to the total population of doctoral scientists and engineers.

Energy-related Ph.Ds are more heavily involved in R&D than the total group; and physicists even more so, with 66 percent of those in energy reporting an involvement in basic and applied research and another 14 percent in the management of R&D. Further, as you might expect, most jobs for those in energy-related work are in private industry. Nearly 60 percent of the energy-related doctorates worked in business and industry. This contrasts sharply with the total group, for nearly 60 percent of all scientists with doctorates worked in educational institutions, with relatively few in private business. Among physicists, 30 percent of the energy-related doctorates were in private industry. Unfortunately, this particular survey did not provide information in which specific industries these Ph.Ds were employed. (However, data developed through other earlier surveys reveal, not suprisingly, that Ph.D. physicists in industry are working in the nuclear industry, petroleum refining, chemicals, electronics, aerospace, and independent research laboratories.)

Where were the energy-related jobs located? Relatively, they are highly concentrated in the Southwest, Mountain and Pacific states. Two out of five in energy worked in those areas, compared to one out of four for the total group. For the energy-related physicists, two out of five were located in the Pacific and Mountain state regions, with the vast number in California and New Mexico. It may also interest you to know that doctorates in energy-related work earned 12 percent more than the total group in 1975. This is probably one indication of where the demand is. It is also likely that it reflects in large measure the usual salary differential between business and education.

Finally, a negative note. There are significantly fewer women and blacks in energy-related work than one might expect, given the distribution in the total population. One percent of all doctoral scientists and engineers are black. That is low, but only 0.2 of one percent of those in energy-related jobs are black.

There are far more women with doctorates: nearly nine percent of the total population. However, only 1.5 percent of those in energy-related work are female. This poses a problem of consequence in our current era of equal employment opportunity.

Now that some data have been revealed, the question is: what does it all mean? What does this kind of information tell us? Hopefully, it provides a few clues.

If you have a Ph.D. in science or engineering and want to get into energy related work, you can be fairly certain that most jobs in the near future are primarily in private industry. About 40 percent of the jobs are located in the west and southwest. Competency in, and affinity for research and development and for management are even more important if you want to follow an energy-related career than they are in non-energy jobs.

If you are black and qualified or if you are a woman and qualified, you might want to investigate carefully to find out why there are relatively fewer women and minorities in the energy-related sector than in the group as a whole.

A last item, energy jobs pay more. In addition to the obvious benefit, this could be an indication that there are relatively more energy jobs available than in the total universe. Higher salaries frequently mean that there are more jobs than qualified applicants.

As indicated earlier, this kind of study illustrates the limitations of the present state of the ERDA manpower assessment art.

The limitations are many. All the information is for a single year--1975; since there are no comparable energy-related data for other years, we cannot identify trends. We do have some equivalent data for scientists and engineers below the doctoral level for an earlier year, but it does not cover the entire population. Further, we are ultimately limited by the fact that the survey was designed for another purpose and contains limited information about the energy-related population.

Now, we can make some reasonable guesses about what is happening by drawing on this and other non-energy studies and using artistic interpretation--"artistic" for the want of a better term. The best estimate is that between 13 and 15 percent of all scientists and engineers are in energy-related work and that this will continue to increase by 1985--to what extent is, of course, uncertain at present since the Federal Government's supporting role for the various energy technologies is still undergoing changes and modifications; and the extent to which universities and colleges will play a role beyond that currently ongoing remains unanswered.

Under present Manpower Assessment Office plans, information from the doctoral study just cited will be plugged into CEMIS--the Comprehensive Energy Manpower Information System. Equivalent follow-up studies will be made for future years so that trends can be identified and used as the basis for forecasting. As a matter of fact, we are currently planning a special follow-up to the 1977 survey of doctoral scientists and engineers which will identify the specific energy areas in which these persons are involved. Data on non-doctoral scientists and engineers as well as other occupational groups working in energy programs will also be obtained and programs to assure comparability will be designed to assure comparability of all data.

If we are allowed to continue our work under the new Department of Energy for about three years, we will be able to talk to you about energy manpower needs using facts instead of artistic interpretation. By that time, too, we will have more specifics about manpower needed to accomplish the Administration's energy plan.

PHYSICS IS A TRANSFERABLE SKILL

Alan Bloch
333 East 30 Street, New York, N.Y., 10016

ABSTRACT

Examples will be drawn from a career as a technological problem-solver in the non-nuclear defense industry, and from a second career as an independent consultant in non-defense fields which have no obvious connection with physics. Training in physics seems to have provided a basis for skill in the art of successfully solving real-world problems.

Before I give you my ideas on what a non-academic physicist can do to make a living, let me tell you a little about my own life so that you can make some estimate of my competence as an oracle.

I came across an old copy of Kimball's College Physics sometime in the twenties. I was about ten, and the book may have been twice as old as I was. I'm not sure when I decided to be a physicist, but it was probably Kimball who put me on the true path to wisdom. I took my BA in '38 and my MA in '39. I dropped out for a year to make some money, and then went back to school and cleaned up everything but a thesis for my doctorate. I took the next year off again, for the same reason, and at some point I got angry enough to go to Canada where I took a commission in the Royal Canadian Air Force.

I spent the war working on problems connected with radar. I was lucky enough to get a crack at both technical and operational problems, and I learned a lot. After the war I went into what we then called the Defense Industry, where I stayed until I was washed out by the economy wave of 1969/70. Six months later it dawned on me that I wasn't going to get another job, so I tried going after free-lance work. I billed three thousand dollars that year. Things have improved since then and I now make a reasonable living. I run a one-man shop, I rarely have more than two or three clients active at the same time, I work like a horse, and I enjoy what I'm doing.

It seems to me that a good physicist approaches problems in a rather special way. I don't have time to talk about that now, but I'll give you a few examples of what I've been able to do.

During the war I dreamed up a trick of adjusting a radar display so that it operated in a mildly non-linear mode. With no changes in the equipment, we were able to pick up targets as much as 26 db below the noise level. Loosely speaking, we tripled our target-detection range.

ISSN:0094-243X/78/226/$1.50

When we introduced a new blind-approach system, also during the war, we had trouble convincing pilots that they could use it successfully, I solved that problem by demonstrating, in real airplanes, that even *I* could make it work.

A client of mine makes telephone switching equipment. We pass voice-band information through the switch as width-modulation on sub-microsecond pulses. We pipe these pulses around the system on ordinary wire, not coaxial cables, and we achieve a pulse-width resolution of about ten picoseconds. That's 10^{-11} seconds.

What do you do when three or more people are running for the same office? How do you find out who the voters *really* want? I thought I had an answer to this, and I got a small grant from the Ford Foundation. My hunch turned out to be wrong, but I finally came up with a good solution. One day soon I'll get around to publishing it.

I've figured out a way to handle the college admissions problem in a non-traumatic way — easy on the applications *and* on the admissions officers — but I don't know what to do with it.

What is the information content of speech? How many bits/second do you have to transmit so that you can recover a high-fidelity version of the original speech signal? The question came up in connection with manned missions to the neighborhood of the outer planets. If you digitize speech directly, you need about 200,000 bits/second. I figured out that this could be cut to something like 600 with optimum coding. How do you code it? I have some ideas but I never got to work on that side of the problem — NASA dropped the idea of manned missions to the neighborhood of Jupiter and Saturn.

If you'd like to compute the two-dimensional correlation between an image and a stored reference pattern, I can show you how to do it without a computer. All it takes is a lens.

I could go on like this for a long time, but I think you get the idea. I'm good at solving problems. Some of the tricks I learned on the job, and some I got from an old garage mechanic in my high-school days. Most of what I know about problem-solving, though, I learned as an undergraduate physics student. I had a great teacher.

Physics is a science, *doing* physics is a pretty esoteric art. To understand physics you need (at least) a broad understanding of science-in-general. To *do* physics you need something more — the ability to solve non-trivial problems. Solving a trivial problem is an exercise in applied logic, the solution is implied by the problem-statement. Solving a non-trivial problem is an exercise in applied intuition, whatever that may be. You use intuition to come up with a possible solution, and *then* you use logic to see whether you have a real answer or just another bad guess.

All of this may sound like nonsense to some of you. I promise, though, that it's a valid picture of the way things looked in the string-and-sealing-wax days before 1942. Any pre-war physicist is at least a competent scientific/technological generalist, and a good one is an intuitive problem-solving generalist. I don't know whether or not these things are true today, I haven't had very much contact with physicists for the last thirty-odd years. If they aren't true any more, maybe that's part of the problem we're here to talk about.

Let's take a look at the real world and see where a physicist can make himself useful. Not surprisingly, it turns out that the competent generalist — the physicist who's short on intuition — has a pretty rough time. He can give you some information about almost anything. He doesn't have the problem-solver's streak of curiousity thought, and there are always relevant data that never came to his attention. He'll tell you that there are problems associated with supersonic flight, and why there are problems, but he won't know that Mach-2 rifle bullets have been around for almost a hundred years. He'll tell you how to design structures that will survive a fifty-g acceleration, but it won't occur to him that parts of a high-speed camera shutter routinely live through something more than a thousand g's. You can spend ten minutes with a competent generalist and save yourself as much as a week of once-over-lightly literature searching. His usefulness as a generalist ends there though, which means that outside the physics community he can be used (as a scientific generalist) only in a large technical operation — and if he can't be used efficiently he won't be put on the payroll.

If a competent generalist is squeezed out of the physics community, he has nowhere to go unless he changes his working style. The number of industrial openings for a generalist — even a competent one — is infinitesimal. His only solution is to look for a job in some restricted area where his expertise gives him enough of an edge to let him compete successfully. He must turn himself into a specialist of some sort. Typical fields for an ex-generalist are applied mathematics, computer programming and electronics. If he has other skills he can move into areas like technical sales or technical editing — I know a couple of physicists who have done that. There is almost always a way out, but the prospect isn't a happy one. The change from generalist to specialist isn't simply a matter of shifting gears. It involves a basic alteration in the way one looks at life — and it isn't easy.

The other fellow, the intuitive problem-solver, is in a somewhat different position when he leaves the physics community. His game, after all, is the business of solving non-trivial problems and there are plenty of those around. The aerospace complex used to put out the welcome mat for an intuitive problem-solver at loose ends. A good physicist can enjoy himself there, the problems are interesting and many of them are non-trivial. Unfortunately, current management doctrine calls for using logical specialists to provide solutions — not intuititve generalists — and today our problem-solving physicist has a hard time finding anyone who will give him a chance to perform as a generalist. He can of course turn himself into a problem-solving specialist, typically in engineering or applied mathematics. The change isn't traumatic, he's still a problem-solver, but life as a specialist doesn't offer the continuing challenge he's used to.

The other things our intuitive problem-solver can do is broaden his area of operation and make a career of solving problems outside the field of physics. This means digging up people with exotic problems, usually multi-disciplinary and almost always beyond the current state-of-the-art, problems for which there aren't any specialists. It turns out that a good physicist is also good at solving exotic problems, even in such unexpected areas as market research and sociology. He is often effective, sometimes efficient, and outside the area of current practive he may be the only problem-solver around.

I could go on for a while and tell you something about the art of problem-solving and why physics training gives you some of the background you need. I could talk about the difference between managing people who solve problems and managing the <u>process</u> of problem-solving. I could talk about the morphology of problems and what we must do before we can attack the really important ones. I think, though, that it's time for me to stop.

WHAT DO PHYSICISTS DO IN A LARGE COMMUNITY COLLEGE ?

Sigmund P. Harris
Los Angeles Pierce College, Woodland Hills, Ca. 91371

ABSTRACT

The proliferation and growth of community colleges in the last few years has led to an increasing number of physicists both in teaching and other activities in these schools. Some of the career choices which faculty and students in our Physics/Engineering Dept. have made in the last few years will be summarized. The advancement of some of our physics faculty to administrative and counseling positions on campus will be included. A brief description of new socially-oriented courses offered by the Physics/Engineering Dept. will be given.

Los Angeles Pierce College is one of the nine community colleges operated by the Los Angeles Community College District. It has approximately 22,000 students and is located in Woodland Hills, which is a part of the city of Los Angeles located in the west San Fernando Valley.

First, I will review the career choices of two of our former students in the Physics/Engineering Dept. at Pierce. One of these spent two years in the Peace Corps in Peru after finishing at Pierce. He taught at a small school where there were just two in the Physics Dept. and he was the chairman. After he returned to the United States he received his master's degree at the University of Toledo and then continued working for a Ph.D. at the University of Illinois.

The second former student transferred from Pierce to the California State University at Northridge, where he received his bachelor's degree in Physics. After that he continued his studies at the University of Arizona at Tucson, majoring in Nuclear Engineering.

The Physics and Engineering faculty at Pierce now numbers seven. Two former Physics faculty members have become counselors and another has become Assistant Dean of Instruction. These are examples of upgrading, which has been mentioned by other speakers here.

In addition to the traditional lower division Physics courses for physicists and engineers, our department has recently added two socially-oriented courses, one on air pollution and one on energy. The Physics sequence now covers 3 semesters (Physics 37,38 and 39) instead of the former 4 semesters, in order to allow Physics and Engineering majors to have one semester of

ISSN:0094-243X/78/230/$1.50

Calculus before starting the Physics sequence.

I would like to give a brief description of the 3-unit air pollution course which I teach. It is listed in our catalog as both Environmental Studies 9 and Physical Science 5. The topics covered are:

1. Brief history of air pollution
2. Meteorology
3. Sources of air pollution
4. Elementary chemistry of air pollution
5. Effects of air pollution on man, animals, plants and materials
6. Instruments for measuring air pollution
7. Laws, regulations and enforcement
8. Engines
9. Control methods (including rapid transit)
10. Nuclear science
11. Fallout and nuclear power
12. Air pollution in foreign countries

There is no prerequisite for the above course and it has become quite popular. At the time I started teaching the course there was no elementary textbook available for this course. As a consequence I had to write my own textbook.

SOLAR ENERGY: RESEARCH AND APPLICATIONS CAREER OPPORTUNITIES FOR PHYSICISTS

Arthur C. Meyers III, Solar Energy Laboratory
University of Houston, Houston, TX 77004

ABSTRACT

The place and potential for physicists to work in the various career areas of solar energy are considered. The training, experience, and educational methods available for entering and working in solar energy are discussed.

INTRODUCTION

The field of solar energy, which has been historically dominated by certain engineering professions, offers many career opportunities for a unique, broad-based background that can be expected from a properly trained experimental physicist. This paper, because of space limitations, will outline some of the work done by the author in the area of the potential for application of physics to solving problems in energy and the environment. Here we will be specifically limiting our remarks to the application of the physics methodology to solar energy and the use of physicists in solar energy.

When considering the career potential for a physicist in a specific area, the critical criteria are always embodied in the words "properly trained." For a person working in solar energy physics, proper training beyond the minimum requirements of background, scientific knowledge and experience, should, for success, encompass the following concepts. One, the ability to apply broad based physics knowledge and principles to solving problems in the real world. Two, both an intuitive and a back of the envelope quantitative understanding of the physics behind observed phenomena. And three, the ability to model, scale and experimentally both design prototypes and systematically study a problem by progressively increasing the complexity of the aspects being considered.

RESEARCH ACTIVITIES

Solar energy research can be broken down into the following general areas; heating and cooling, solar thermal, wind energy, bioconversion, photovoltaic, and ocean thermal. The primary stumbling blocks to the advancement of solar energy are due to the lack, in many cases, of the proper experimental and theoretical information. Specific data exists; that in many cases, the experimental and theoretical determinations of the primary physical parameters have not been made in a systematic manner that would allow one to determine energy optimization. For each of the six areas of solar energy, possible research topics in which physicists

ISSN:0094-243X/78/232/$1.50

can be used and make highly significant contributions can be listed. The listing is for illustrative purposes and should not be considered all inclusive. There are obvious additional multiple applications in more than one area.

Research topics for each general area can be summed up as follows. Heating and Cooling: (1) Load Modification Techniques, (2) Energy Efficient Design, (3) Solar Collector Development, (4) Thermal Properties of Materials, (5) Surface Phenomena in Energy Conversion, (6) Physics of Materials, (7) Radiative Transfer and (8) Air Conditioning Systems.

Solar Thermal: (1) Physics of High Temperature Materials, (2) Selective Coatings, (3) Conversion Cycles, (4) Energy Storage, (5) Concentrator Optics, (6) Physics of Fluids and (7) Energy Transfer Mechanisms.

Wind Energy: (1) Atmospheric Physics, (2) Aerodynamics of Turbines, (3) Energy Conversion and Storage, (4) Atmospheric - Ocean Coupling, (5) Ocean Waves, (6) Land & Sea Breezes and (7) Wind Related Phenomena.

Bioconversion: (1) Biophysics of Photosynthesis, (2) Enhancement of Conversion Rates, (3) Aquafarming: Plant & Animal, (4) Microclimatology: Control and Modification, (5) Biomass Processing, (6) Solid Waste Recovery, (7) Geophysical Enhancement (8) Soil Physics and (9) Hydroscience.

Photovoltaic: (1) Solid State Physics, (2) Crystal Growth Mechanisms, (3) Development of New Materials, (4) Efficiency of Conversion, (5) Space Power Plants, (6) Organic Systems and (7) New Applications.

Ocean Thermal: (1) Oceanographic Studies, (2) Energy Extraction and Conversion Processes, (3) Physics of Materials, (4) Energy & Matter Transport and (5) Marine Fluid Dynamics.

TRAINING

Because of the Interdisciplinary characteristics of solar energy applications, as broad an education in physics as possible should be acquired. At the minimum, the Ph.D. research and/or the post doctoral work should be in the area of solar energy. The listing and outlines of specific applicable courses are beyond the scope of this paper. Necessary courses can be divided into two types. First, those courses most applicable to solar energy or where solar energy related material can be most logically introduced into the program, and secondly, specific courses of one or two semesters (1-3 quarter) in length on solar energy physics.[1,2]

CONCLUSIONS

Solar Energy offers a viable and challenging field as a career opportunity for the physicist. With proper training, a physicist has the potential to make needed and significant contributions because of the unique characteristics of the discipline. However, changes in programs and attitudes will be necessary if any proportionate number of physicists are going to enter the solar energy field. This is seen most readily in the lack of acknowledgement by the physics community of the complexity of solar energy physics and also its lack of recognition of solar energy as an interrelated physics discipline.

REFERENCES

1. A. C. Meyers III, "An Academic Program in Solar Energy Science Education," in Sharing the Sun, Solar Technology in the Seventies, 8, Storage, Water Heater, Data Communication, Education,(American Section of the International Solar Energy Society, Cape Canaveral, Florida, 1976), p. 273.
2. A. C. Meyers III, "A Solar Energy Program in Environmental Design," in Proceedings of the 1977 Annual Meeting American Section of the International Solar Energy Society, 1, 27-16, (1977).

A PHYSICIST IN TECHNOLOGY ASSESSMENT

Stephen N. Salomon, Ph.D.
Office of State Programs, U.S. Nuclear Regulatory Commission

ABSTRACT

From my own personal experience I describe my passage from physics to the technology assessment movement. This is especially for the benefit of you students majoring in physics that may be entertaining a change of career. First, I give a brief description of some of the factors that influenced my change of career. Then I describe a number of technology assessments in which I was involved in order to give you the flavor of the type of work that is done by a person actively involved in the field. Finally, I present some conclusions based on my own experience.

INTRODUCTION

Although surveys, statistical analyses and the like are valuable methods for revealing trends of physicists entering public policy careers, anecdotal information is often useful to supplement such studies. For this reason, I am relating my personal experience as a physicist who made the passage from physics into the technology assessment (TA) movement in 1971. In addition, I am sharing with you all, and especially you students of physics who may be contemplating a change of career, some of my highs in this evolving field since then.

TECHNOLOGY ASSESSMENT

But first what is technology assessment? Despite the fact that there are a number of definitions of TA, one developed by the Congressional Office of Technology Assessment (OTA) will be suitable here:

> Technology assessment encompasses a thorough and balanced analysis of all significant primary, secondary, indirect, and delayed consequences or impacts, present and foreseen, on society, the environment, or the economy that may occur when applications of a technology are introduced, extended, or modified.[1]

Elements of my interest in this kind of subject stem back to the 1950's and 1960's when I was a student at M.I.T. and the University of Paris and became concerned with the impact on society of technological and scientific innovations, especially in the area of communications and weapons. My first formal training came when I took a political science course from Professor Don Kash in 1965 while I was a physics doctoral candidate engaged in experimental semiconductor physics at Purdue University with H. Y. "Bill" Fan. My interest was further stimulated during a year's tour of the U.S.S.R. and Eastern and Western Europe as an exchange scientist. This program was sponsored by the National Academy of Sciences during academic year 1969-1970 which was after completing my Ph.D.

ISSN:0094-243X/78/235/$1.50

Actually, it was in Akademgorodok, the Soviet science city near Novosibirsk, Siberia that I learned from Soviet colleagues, such as Mikhail Lavrentev, of the problems that they too were experiencing in the TA field. In particular, the Soviets were concerned about the diffusion of science and technology establishments throughout the Soviet Union and how they could be used more effectively to meet the demands of society.[2,3]

Having returned from the Soviet Union to a depressed job market which had in my mind little excitement for semiconductor physicists with an experimental flair and with not much prospect for improvement, I decided that the time was ripe for me to exploit my closely held desire to go full tilt into TA. This decision was reinforced by previous conversations that I had with a small number of physicists who had moved into policy related fields of this kind.

Fortunately, within one year I was able to join an interdisciplinary team that Don Kash had assembled with a grant from the National Science Foundation. The objective was to do one of the first TAs. The subject was offshore oil and gas operations, a hot topic given the Santa Barbara oil spill of 1969 and the impending oil embargo. This activity was centered in the Science and Public Policy Program at the University of Oklahoma from 1971-1973 where I was a research fellow.

Simultaneously I was able to organize in the Physics department, where I was also visiting assistant professor of physics, an interdisciplinary course, "Electric Power and the Environment to the Year 2000." Here we systematically examined the fuel cycles of current and conceptual schemes of generating electric power with their associated, technological, economic, social, environmental, institutional, and political impacts. This course served to buttress the TA that was being carried out on offshore oil and gas. The latter resulted in a book, Energy Under the Oceans[4], that was released about a month before the 1973 Arab oil embargo. It was a timely study and became useful in helping to formulate National policy with regard to the development of oil and gas on the outer continental shelf. The major results of this study, which were primarily institutional in nature, I reported at the Energy Forum of the American Physical Society's Spring 1974 meeting.[5] Better government management of this technology was the central theme.

I should mention that during the one year interlude before joining the Science and Public Policy Program, I had the good fortune to beef up my background in economics, TA, systems analysis, social policy and oil policy at the JFK School of Government, Harvard University. I had the good fortune to work with people like Harvey Brooks and Don Price among others. Even though I was there for a short period of time, it was enough to explore the environmental and social impacts of two conceptual technologies, controlled thermonuclear fusion electric generating stations and oil supertankers. By investigating rather thoroughly a world electric economy of fusion reactors compared to liquid metal fast breeder reactors (LMFBRs), I was able to understand many of the difficulties that people get up tight over now with regard to LMFBRs, such as proliferation, and why there is so much enchantment with fusion reactors.[6] The megaton oil tanker study showed me clearly the trade offs of the economy of scale of tankers compared to the risk of considerable oil pollution. This background study proved very useful for me later in the Oklahoma TA when I helped to analyze principal alternatives such as the trans-Alaskan pipeline system and oil imports.

In August 1973 I joined the regulatory staff of the Atomic Energy Commission where I thought I could put some of my newly acquired TA skills to work. We had some interesting times trying to make the Environmental Impact Statements for siting nuclear generating stations into a meaningful decisionmaking management tool that it was meant to be. This was in response to the National Environmental Policy Act of 1969 and the Calvert Cliffs' court decision. I was particularly interested in developing cost-benefit methodologies for the selection of alternative energy sources and alternative cooling systems.[7]

Most of all I remember the stimulating and sometimes hectic involvement in the Nuclear Energy Center Site Survey-1975.[8] This siting policy study was congressionally mandated as part of the Energy Reorganization Act of 1974 which created the Nuclear Regulatory Commission (NRC). Congress asked us whether future nuclear facilities should be clustered or should the current dispersed policy be pursued. Our mandate was to investigate the economic, environmental, social, political, safeguard, and institutional impacts of the two concepts. My main involvement as a task force member concerned issues relevant to economics, socioeconomics, finance, and long-range forecasting of electrical demand and supply. The bottom line of the study was that centers most likely would evolve on their own.

While at NRC I have had the occasion to work with a number of other Federal agencies. One exciting experience dealt with the floating nuclear power plant concept. Such a technology is planned for commercial operation off the coast of Atlantic City in about 1985. The Congress wanted to know the social, environmental, economic, and institutional impacts associated with the deployment of such a technology - especially in conjunction with other potentially emerging offshore energy systems - offshore oil and gas operations and deep water ports.

On a six month detail from NRC, I assisted the staff at OTA in just such a TA. This work culminated in the Coastal Effects of Offshore Energy Systems.[9] My main concerns were policy analysis revolving around the safety, environmental, economic and institutional issues of these technologies. Results showed that there still remained a number of technical and administrative uncertainties to resolve before deployment of the technologies.

Currently, my TA experience has brought me into a policy analysis to appraise the current nuclear generating station planning and licensing process. Working in conjunction with the National Governors' Conference, we have sought ways for better government in our study, Improving Regulatory Effectiveness in Federal/State Siting Actions.[10] Special emphasis was placed on coordinated Federal/State regulatory activity with greater public involvement in the planning and approval stage of nuclear generating station siting. My specific role centered around environmental issues, public participation and financial issues in addition to being a principal author of the study. The results are principal input into the Carter administration's nuclear siting legislation that will be introduced into Congress shortly.

CONCLUSIONS

By my own experience, I am building what seems to me an interesting and varied career in the constantly evolving TA movement with a special focus on the energy arena. I believe that a background in physics provides a person with an excellent springboard into this interdisciplinary field. Some of the talents of a physicist that can be brought to bear on the subject that I have found especially relevant are: organization of team research; logical and methodical thinking; research skills, such as research design and cross correlation of facts; mathematical skills; modeling; ability to readily understand complex technologies; and technical paper writing.

As I see it, there is plenty of room for persons having these skills in government as well as in the private sector. Certainly, in commercial applications of nuclear energy, there still are opportunities for TA in the areas of waste management, reactor safety, alternative fuel cycle analysis, and safeguards.

REFERENCES

1. Office of Technology Assessment, U.S. Congress, Technology Assessment in Business and Government (GPO, Washington, D.C., 1977), p. 10.
2. S. N. Salomon, "A Year in Siberian Science," Technology Review, 10 (July/August 1971).
3. S. N. Salomon, "A Glimpse of Soviet Life," ChemTech, 32 (July 1974).
4. Don E. Kash, Irvin L. White, Karl H. Bergey, Michael A. Chartock, Michael D. Devine, R. Leon Leonard, Stephen N. Salomon and Harold W. Young, Energy Under the Oceans (University of Oklahoma Press, Norman, 1973), 378 pp.
5. S. N. Salomon, "Energy Under the Oceans," Bull. Am. Phys. Soc. 423 (April 1974).
6. S. N. Salomon, "Controlled Thermonuclear Fusion Reactors: Radioactive Pollution of the Environment," May 1971 (unpublished).
7. D. P. Cleary, S. N. Salomon, L. A. Pollnow and M. B. Spangler, "A Preliminary Matrix Model for Quantifying and Balancing the Socio-economic Impact of Alternative Cooling System Technologies for Nuclear Power Plants," Energy and the Environment--Cost-Benefit Analysis (Pergamon, N.Y., 1976), p. 531.
8. Office of Special Studies, U.S. Nuclear Regulatory Commission, Nuclear Energy Center Site Survey-1975, NUREG-0001 (NTIS, Virginia, 1976). Also, S. N. Salomon, "Some Considerations of Indirect Community Economic and Social Impacts of Power Nuclear Energy Centers," J. Int. Soc. Tech. Assess. 48 (Winter 1976-77).
9. Oceans Program, Office of Technology Assessment, U.S. Congress, Coastal Effects of Offshore Energy Systems, An Assessment of Oil and Gas Systems, Deepwater Ports, and Nuclear Powerplants Off the Coast of New Jersey and Delaware (GPO, Washington, D.C., 1976).
10. Office of State Programs, U.S. Nuclear Regulatory Commission, Improving Regulatory Effectiveness in Federal/State Siting Actions, NUREG-0195 (NTIS, Virginia, 1977).

A PHYSICIST IN COUNTY GOVERNMENT

Vernon J. Ehlers
Calvin College, Grand Rapids, Michigan 49506

INTRODUCTION

It is clear that science and technology have a great deal to do with the future course of our nation and its communities. It is equally clear that public policy makers and political decision makers need some means of evaluating the scientific and technological components of their actions and policies. Various means have been used to provide the scientific expertise for making those judgments, but most attempts have relied on the use of science advisors. A number of years ago I became convinced that a more effective route would be to have scientists serving as elected officials or as bureaucrats. Because I did not have the desire to become a scientist-bureaucrat, and because I wanted to remain in my chosen profession of physics and teaching, I chose to run for a part-time public office, that of county commissioner. This way I hoped to affect public policy in our local government, while at the same time maintaining my primary interest in physics as a career. This paper reports on some results of that decision.

HOW TO GET THE JOB

If one wishes to serve as an elected public official, one must first get elected. This is by no means simple, and is certainly far more difficult than landing a job in physics itself. Although there may be exceptions, in general there is more than one candidate for each position and it takes a very strenuous and hard-working campaign to get elected. Furthermore, one does not simply stand for election without any preliminary work. It is extremely important to be involved in community affairs for some time before running for office. This is true for two reasons: first, by being involved in community affairs one becomes knowledgeable about local problems and is able to develop effective solutions to those problems. Secondly, name recognition and public exposure are extremely important in the election process, and involvement in community affairs can provide the broad base of support which is necessary to run an effective campaign.

The campaign must seek to establish your credentials for the position, but also has to rely on traditional political techniques to win an election. One has to begin the campaign with the recognition that most people don't really care who their local elected representatives are. This appears to be a demeaning statement about the American public, but unfortunately is true. Even today, after several publicity-filled years on the county commission, less than 5% of the persons in my district are able to name their county

ISSN:0094-243X/78/239/$1.50

commissioner.

In my particular case I ran an issues-oriented campaign, and selected issues such as environmental problems, solid waste disposal, and our criminal justice system. I had identified these as being glaring problems in our community, and areas in which I could make a contribution. My campaign literature focused on these issues and proposed specific solutions.

However, more was needed than simply discussion of the issues. In order to establish name identification, I decided to distribute to each household in the district some small gift from me, a gift which would provide strong name identification. I further insisted that this gift be something useful, and not merely a trinket which would be thrown away after a short period of time. Our campaign team developed the idea of handing out small spruce seedlings, with a label attached urging the citizen to "Keep Kent County green--plant this tree and vote for Vern EHLERS'--with the "Ehlers" written in very large type. The note also gave instructions for caring for the seedling, including the suggestion that it be kept on the kitchen windowsill until Fall before being transplanted. (This meant that the householder would be looking at my name on that plant for a period of several weeks before the election.) Furthermore, it was a theme which fitted in well with my campaign. Most important, I felt it was an extremely useful item to distribute. We handed out 3,000 seedlings, and my best estimate is that at least 1,000 have survived and are growing well. I regularly receive comments from constituents about how well their tree is growing.

In order to get the job one must also have money, because campaigns cost money. I found this was not much of a problem. Even though most of my contributions were small ($5.00-$10.00), the $1200 needed seemed to roll in without too much difficulty. Furthermore, we were able to run a fairly inexpensive campaign by doing a great deal of work with volunteers. A professional politician once told me that volunteers are worth far more than money, and I certainly found that to be true. My opponent outspent me 3 to 1, but I had many more volunteers than he did. As a result, we could distribute our spruce seedlings at a net cost of only 4¢ each, because we had mammoth "pot-parties" at which volunteers took the bulk-purchased seedlings and potted them in small cups. If I had purchased potted seedlings commercially, they would have cost $1 each.

My campaign was successful, although the margin was excruciatingly close. I cannot take any credit for it; the strong support of my many friends, coupled with a good editorial endorsement in the local newspaper, played a greater role than anything I did as an individual.

HOW TO SUCCEED

Although getting elected is the most difficult part of the political process, one must not confuse the means with the end. The end, in my case, was to successfully influence public policy.

The key to doing so was to obtain positions on the appropriate committees, because our county government operates on the committee system, very much as the U.S. Congress does. Accordingly, I sought appointments on committees dealing with my areas of concern. I was immediately named chairman of the Solid-Waste Subcommittee, and also was placed on the Jail Committee. These were two issues I had addressed directly in my campaign. They also happened to be unpopular issues with my fellow commissioners, and thus it was not too difficult to get an appointment in those areas. After all, one can only make enemies, not friends, when handling solid waste.

In addition to those appointments I found myself appointed to key positions on other committees. I was made chairman of the Personnel Committee, the first time in the history of the Commission that a freshman had been appointed chairman of a major committee. Several other appointments came my way. These appointments did not just happen, they were arranged by consultation with key commissioners. Nevertheless, I was gratified to see that there was no built-in resentment against a new commissioner, against someone who had attacked some existing policies and organizations during the campaign, nor was there any anti-intellectual bias on the part of the commissioners.

Since that first year, I have received other appointments. I am currently serving on the Finance Committee, which is the most important committee in our county government. I have been elected vice-chairman of the County Commission and chairman of the Board of Public Works. I have been appointed to the Library Board. In fact, the major problem is to avoid getting too many appointments, simply because becoming too busy in too many areas dilutes effectiveness in the important ones.

I was very gratified to find that my fellow commissioners were very receptive to my ideas. The major lesson I had to learn was that one must not rock the political boat too much. One must work carefully with individual commissioners, convincing them that your position is correct, rather than simply firing broadsides in public. New and innovative ideas must be broached privately to the leadership, rather than released to the press.

All in all, I have been very pleased with the reception I have had. I have found it to be most enjoyable, very satisfying, and a positive experience in almost every regard. My scientific training has been very valuable in many areas, particularly those I have concentrated on. The biggest drawback: the work has made me incredibly busy, and has taken me away from my family much more than I would like.

THE FUTURE

A most amusing, and unexpected, development has been the frequency with which I am urged to run for higher political office. I initially had absolutely no thought of running for any other office, primarily because I wished to continue in my career as a physicist. However, it seems that once one gets in the political stream, one drifts almost inexorably towards other opportunities. I have been urged at various times to run for state representative, state senator, and U.S. Congress. Up to this point I believe my place is in local government, and I want to finish the projects I have begun there before I even consider any other political office. Furthermore, it would be an extremely difficult decision for me to run for any higher office, as it would involve a full-time commitment and would of necessity require that I give up my career as a physicist. In the meantime, I keep my options open and simply attempt to do the best job I can as a county commissioner.

SUMMARY

I have found serving as a local elected official to be an extremely rewarding and beneficial experience. I believe I have been able to make a contribution to local government, a contribution directly related to my skills and training as a physicist. My technical knowledge and background have proved invaluable in handling problems such as solid waste disposal. The analytical skills I have developed during my training as a physicist have been most helpful in analyzing matters such as the financial affairs of the county. I believe that any competent physicist can apply these same skills equally well, and I strongly encourage physicists to run for office in their local government.

ONE PHYSICIST'S PATH TO PERDITION OR WHAT'S A NICE PHYSICIST LIKE ME DOING IN A PLACE LIKE THIS?

R. A. Scribner
American Association for the Advancement of Science,
1776 Massachusetts Avenue, NW, Washington, D. C. 20036

ABSTRACT

This paper outlines the author's transition from research physicist to manager of public sector programs for the American Association for the Advancement of Science. The author's present career is varied, interesting, and satisfying. Drawing on this experience, younger physicists contemplating a move toward non-traditional physics careers in the public sector are urged to realize that there are many satisfying public sector career roles for physicists. Because more and more physicists will be moving to nontraditional careers, the APS is urged to find ways to provide organized, "physics community based" encouragement and other support and communication programs for those individuals within its ranks who are making such a transition. To further develop opportunities in the public sector, the APS is urged to undertake a program of "outreach" to other professional areas. Such efforts will result in new career opportunities. The Congressional Science Fellowship model is analyzed as an example of a mechanism to alter the conventional reward structure. Such a mechanism has obvious applicability to other areas: industrial physics, science writing, etc. Although such programs would be designed to achieve primary goals other than career change, they will aid in the development of new, nontraditional careers and lead to new ways of thinking about a physicist's career opportunities.

INTRODUCTION

When Allan Hoffman asked me to participate in this panel to discuss specific sector career experiences, he suggested that each panelist would be asked to describe: (1) How and why he did what he did; (2) What he has learned that is helpful to others; and (3) What he sees in the future for scientists interested in nontraditional careers. I will try to be responsive to Allan's charge.

CAREER CHANGE

I made the transition from a low-temperature physicist to manager of public sector programs in AAAS in 1971. I haven't regretted my decision although there was a period of uncertainty and anxiety just before and after the transition during which I felt relatively along in what I was then doing. In 1970 and 71, I was largely unaware of what other physicists had done in nontraditional careers, how they had fared, and how they felt about their new roles.

ISSN:0094-243X/78/243/$1.50

The major reason for making such a transition was my strong desire to find ways to use my knowledge and energies to help in some way to solve social problems. My interest in doing this began before I had completed my Ph.D. thesis in 1968. It matured during a brief post-doctoral stint and a three-year period as an instructor and research associate. I enjoyed my research, and found it and my teaching both stimulating and satisfying. But I wanted something more.

After two years of occasional volunteer work with a AAAS Committee, with the grandiose name of the Committee on Science in the Promotion of Human Welfare, I was offered a position at the AAAS to start up an Office of Science and Society Programs. I wrestled with making this kind of radical career departure (so it seemed at the time) and discussed the pros and cons with many friends and associates. I remember some of their responses quite vividly. One friend, a theoretical physicist with a European accent, gave me the advice: "Deek, you don't want to take dat job. Dat's politiks!"

While I have been with the AAAS I have been fortunate to work in the following areas:

- Developing and expanding the Congressional Science Fellow Program;
- Directing a AAAS annual meeting which included some 500 symposia, 30% of which were policy-related;
- Working with numerous advisory and working committees concerned with public sector programs;
- Assisting in developing linkages between scientists and state legislators and their staff;
- "Experimenting" with techniques, such as expositions, and various meeting techniques, to increase communication between scientists and lay people;
- Exploring ways for AAAS to become more involved in public education related to problems at the regional level;
- Generally getting involved in a spectrum of other science policy activities ranging from examining the need for a White House-level office of science and technology policy to assisting Congressional committee staffs in securing needed information regarding, for example, environmental legislation;
- Working with a group called the National Conference of Scientists and Lawyers; and
- Developing a component of the Congressional Fellow Program directed toward child and family policy.

In the context of the purpose of this conference a few of these activities are worth mentioning in somewhat more detail.

The Congressional Science Fellow Program.

Begun only four years ago, the Congressional Science and Engineering Fellow Program will have more than 65 alumni before the end of next year. A large fraction of these are physicists, and over 50% of the nearly 20 physicists have made decisions to redirect their efforts toward a public policy career. The program has

- demonstrated visibly and unequivocably that scientists can function in the legislative milleu and, because of their training and perspective, can make substantial contributions;
- allowed 30% of the Fellows to make a career shift into public policy;
- provided a model so that other scientists desiring to move into legislative public policy roles may find the transition easier than it was a few years ago;
- endowed the role with a high status and more appeal;
- indicated one way to effect change in the area of improving the interaction between science and legislative policy making; and
- pushed out the boundaries of what a physicist can do.

Personally, I derive a great deal of satisfaction from my role in helping to design, implement, and run this program. I derive even more satisfaction from working with the people - the Fellows - in the program.

As far as career opportunities for physicists within the Congress, there is no question in my mind that if a physicist wants to pursue such an option there is

(1) no substantial barrier to such a role, and

(2) every expectation that he or she could land such a position with enough exertion, provided of course that the person has the interest, ambition, self-confidence, and personal and communication traits appropriate to such a role

Media Fellowships

The AAAS is already involved in a mass media intern program and may soon develop something like a science broadcasting fellowship program. As mentioned I have had the privilege of working on several projects aimed at increasing public understanding of the role and limitations of scientific and technological matters in public problem resolution, as well as some projects aimed at exploring means to increase informed public participation. The relatively new "AAAS Mass Media Internship Program" promises to do for scientists interested in experiencing the media environment and exploring possible career roles what the Congressional Science Fellow Program has done for scientists interested in the Federal legislative process.

LESSONS AND FUTURE ROLES

What have I learned from my transition that might be of use to others possibly contemplating a similar change? I have two comments.

1. It's a big world out there with many, many good and interesting careers outside of physics. Yes, there is "junk" to be done in most of these jobs, just as academic research and teaching physics has its share of dull, boring tasks. But there are also some very substantial satisfactions which a person can derive from many nontraditional physics careers in the public sector.

2. There is need for a community to provide moral support to individuals making such transitions. For a period of time, 6 months to 2 years, a person may feel additional stress because of the lack of reinforcement from such a community. They should be able to meet, say, within the APS meeting, to be recognized for good work, and to not feel completely or suddenly estranged from the physics community.

What do I see in the future related to what I have described?

In government, scientists are carving bigger roles for themselves in the public policy process, and this is especially noticeable in the federal and state legislative branches. Perhaps it is wishful thinking, but I believe that I see today and for the future more and better use of multidisciplinary and interdisciplinary policy-oriented studies than has been the case in the past. Physicists have contributed to these and I believe there is a growing demand for many kinds of professionals to learn to work in these team efforts. Many physicists have been surprisingly good at not only mastering other fields, but also making transitions to "expert-generalists" working in multidisciplinary public policy areas. Many more can do the same in the future. The American Physical Society can aid in this by examining its own disciplinary outreach and interprofessional communication efforts and by finding better ways to "extend" the "comforts" of the physics community to those of its body who wish, or who _must_, find new career directions.

Circumstances often come full circle if we wait long enough. The "ex-physicists" who left physics for nontraditional careers are now finding greater interest on the part of at least some of the physics community in what they have been doing. Physics and society courses and programs are increasing in number and impact. Perhaps before too long the so-called nontraditional careers will be completely within the spectrum of what is acceptable for a physicist to do. (If the physics community doesn't reject them, as historically it has done.) Some former Congressional Science Fellows who gave up tenure and the academic life to seek a public sector career may ten years later find themselves back at the university possibly associated with a department of physics. And physicists who have every intention of continuing in what will then be regarded as a traditional career may think nothing of using a sabbatical term to serve as a visiting scientist in a state legislature. Farfetched? Not really, since things like it are happening now.

CHANGING THE REWARD STRUCTURE

There has been much talk, some of it at this conference, about changing the reward structure to affect the career models for physicists. Often people ask: "But how do you change this structure?"

The Congressional Science Fellow Program, mass media internships (which is a program also run by the AAAS), and the recently initiated APS Industrial Fellowship Program are all examples of programs which do change the reward structure. The APS Industrial Fellowship Program, if it continues and grows, will have a profound effect on attitudes toward careers for physicists in very applied research areas. The four years of experience with the Congressional Science Fellow Program illustrates this point rather dramatically.

A Second Observation

It seems clear that activities which are primarily aimed at bridging a gap between some other professional area, or area of endeavor, and science --physics-- also has the welcome secondary spin-off of pointing to nontraditional career opportunities for physicists, possibly even creating such opportunities. What about career retraining programs which have career change as a first purpose?

A recent report to the National Science Foundation entitled "A Survey of Institutional Practices and An Assessment of Possible Options Relating to Voluntary Mid- and Late-Career Changes and Early Retirement for University and College Faculty" contains the following statement:

> "(We failed) to turn up any formal (career) retraining programs (for academics) which spoke to the needs of this study: programs directed at the retraining, for different substantive areas of different work situations of tenured

> faculty in colleges and universities. Our search did, however, reveal the existence of two rather different types of programs which are relevant to our interests: (1) internship and fellowship programs which are manifestly intended to achieve goals other than career change, but which, as a by-product, lead to career change for some participants and (2) programs which retain academics for continued academic work in a different specialty or discipline."

A list of Fellowship programs for academics who can take leave of absence to experiment with new kinds of work in new settings can be found in "A Selected List of Major Fellowship Opportunities and Aids to Advanced Education for United States Citizens," prepared under contract with the National Science Foundation by the Fellowship Office, Commission on Human Resources, National Research Council, National Academy of Sciences, Washington, D.C.

The Professional Societies as Agents of Change and as Participants in the Public Policy Process

Later in the program George Pake will tell us about some of his ideas about the "Role of the APS Professional Society in Implementing Change." I am looking forward to George's remarks. However, I am sure that George and others in the leadership of the APS will be looking for additional ideas -- and suggestions of how to implement these ideas from participants of this conference.

As I have tried to suggest, programs which reach out to areas where physics has an interacting leading edge will have the by-product of facilitating career change. I think the professional physics community should be reaching out more helpfully and more aggressively

- to the federal policy-making community,
    - to the Congress,
    - to the Executive and the OSTP,
    - to the Agencies, and

  through not only the Congressional Science Fellow Program, but also through multidisciplinary and interdisciplinary policy-oriented studies, and policy setting papers;
- to the industrial, technological, applied physics community;
- to the legal and administrative communities;
- to state and local government, both at the legislative and executive branches; and
- to other professions and the general public.

The APS should reach out to these groups to collaboratively work on public sector problems.

All of these activities will enrich the physicists who participate, broaden the professional physics community they represent, help to break down the disciplinary barriers which inhibit cross-professional communication, and not so incidentally create new career opportunities for physicists.

SUMMARY OF PANELS DISCUSSING EDUCATIONAL CHANGE

V. L. Teplitz, presiding
(Virginia Polytechnic Institute & State University)

L. Sartori, secretary
(University of Nebraska)

Teplitz opened the session by citing a comment by a department chairman who, although he had heard many interesting talks over the past two days, felt he had picked up few concrete ideas for improving the preparation of his students, either graduate or undergraduate. Teplitz expressed the hope that this session would be action-oriented. He read the following list of questions (which he had sent in advance to the panelists) to serve as a basis for the discussion:

(1) What kinds of new graduate and undergraduate physics programs are needed to respond to the new, or newly perceived, needs of industry?

(2) What sorts of single courses, as opposed to whole new programs, are most useful?

(3) Are the needs of industry too diverse to be lumped together and discussed as a single entity? How do the needs of small companies differ from those of large?

(4) Is there a danger of over-reaction, too many new programs and new courses?

(5) How much do the new programs compete with traditional programs for fixed or shrinking resources? To what extent are they capable of generating new resources from Industry and Government?

(6) What comparisons are possible between new physics programs and programs in other natural sciences and engineering?

(7) How successful have the new programs of the past few years been?

(8) What is the potential, and what are the problems, for joint programs -- ones with M.S. and Ph.D. theses done in Industry rather than on campus?

(9) What is the future for Extension teaching -- graduate courses for those already working?

(10) How are industry oriented programs and courses received by other faculty members and students?

(11) Should graduate Birth Control be practiced? Should departments limit student numbers and should "marginal departments" be encouraged to discontinue their graduate programs?

(12) What steps are needed, in the face of increased emphasis on the applied and, even in the basic, on well-defined results, to keep an atmosphere that encourages (or at least does not discourage) genius?

ISSN:0094-243X/78/250/$1.50

F1. Non-academic panel

Panelists: F. E. Jamerson (General Motors)
S. Millman (AIP, formerly of Bell Labs)
E. Conwell (Xerox)
T. Sheahen (NBS)

Jamerson echoed the sentiments expressed by previous industrial speakers in stressing the importance of communication skills, both written and oral, in an industrial setting. In addition to conventional journal articles and research seminars, the industrial physicist must be adept at making presentations aimed at different audiences. He may, for example, be called on to make a three-minute report to corporation executives, who have no scientific training but are interested in the scientist's results and their implications for the goals of the corporation. The level and format of the presentation must be geared to the nature of the audience.

Millman's remarks were based on his long experience in recruiting Ph.D.'s for Bell Labs, as well as his recent role as co-ordinator of the visiting physicist program and of the APS industrial fellowship program. He stressed the distinction between the training of Ph.D.'s and that of bachelors and masters. He saw no need for change in the standard core curriculum for Ph.D. candidates. What is needed is a change in motivation. The student doing a Ph.D. should expect an exciting problem to work on; he should expect to learn useful techniques; but he should not expect necessarily to find a job in the area in which he does his thesis research.

On the B.S. and terminal M.S. level, Millman's criticism is that the courses are generally the same as those taken by Ph.D. candidates. The preparation for these students should contain much less theory, and emphasize laboratory work. As an example of a good program, Millman cited the applied physics program at Georgia Tech.

Sheahen spoke for small industry, having worked for several years in a small company before coming to NBS. Small industry is directly concerned with making its products competitive in the market place. The physicists' work must have immediate applications. Among the areas important to such industries, which do not receive sufficient emphasis in the modern university curriculum, are optics and dynamics. Increased emphasis on computer programs and microprocessors would also be useful.

Conwell also saw no need for new courses, but re-emphasized the importance of laboratory work and hands-on skills, for Ph.D. students as well as for lower level ones. Electronics, lasers, and programming are important skills. Some subjects which were commonly taught in the past but are now neglected ought to be restored. Semiconductor work, familiarity with materials science, and skill in crystal growing, are examples of attributes useful in an industrial setting.

Jamerson agreed with the remarks. We are marketing a product, he asserted: a highly skilled professional. There is competition: chemists, engineers and others are moving into areas formerly reserved for physicists. The physicist must be adaptable in order to compete.

Teplitz asked whether any change has been detected recently in the attitude toward industrial research on the part of university physicists.

Jamerson answered in the affirmative. He cited the interaction between universities and industry through the corporate associate program of AIP as evidence of changing attitudes. Conwell felt that university people are better informed, on the whole, than a few years ago, but there has been little change of attitude toward applied work--it is still regarded as second class, and carries less prestige. Perhaps there is the beginning of a change.

Sheahen cited the recent symposium on rubber organized by Professor Chandrasekhar of Case Western Reserve. Although the symposium was judged to be highly successful by the industrial participants, Sheahen questioned whether Chandrasekhar's academic colleagues really considered it an important contribution. Until faculty attitudes change, we cannot expect students to view industrial research with respect. Millman cited the role of the Committee on Applications of Physics, which specifically endorsed the rubber conference and encourages others of a similar nature. But moral support is not enough. Ultimately, someone has to take on the responsibility of actually organizing a conference.

B. Schwartz, from the floor, worried about whether "co-existence" between pure and applied physics is possible within a single department. He foresees a possible break-up into groups of departments in which applied work is emphasized (and in which the corresponding reward structure exists), and those which continue to emphasize basic research.

Jamerson stressed that the important things is not for universities to <u>do</u> applied research, but rather for them to train the people who will do it in industry.

L. Grodzins expressed the view that applied research is not necessarily considered second class by students, but it is generally third choice (the first two choices being teaching and basic research). Sheahen disagreed, saying that if something is third choice it automatically becomes second (or even third) class.

A. Bloch cited the problem of industrial secrecy as a barrier to communication between the two camps. The panel didn't consider this a serious problem for large companies; Sheahen felt that it might be one for very small companies. Industrial physicists disseminate the results of their work through publication, as well as patents. The delay sometimes caused by industrial secrecy considerations was not felt to be a major drawback.

S. Glantz claimed the distinction between pure and applied research is a phony one. Those who give you money to do research always have a reason for doing so; in that sense, no research is "pure", and people should not be ashamed of doing research which does someone some good.

A questioner pointed to a possible contradiction. Physicists are supposed to be generalists, broadly trained, and yet it has been suggested that universities concentrate on developing specific laboratory skills. Millman replied that the Ph.D.'s should be the generalists, while the bachelors and terminal masters should concentrate specific, directly applicable skills. Conwell added that it would be useful for a job seeker to have several such skills.

R. Yaes objected that although the panel has described what it takes to succeed in industry, it did not address the question of whether the industrial jobs are there. How many Ph.D.'s does industry expect to hire, and in what subfields? According to Conwell, the answer depends on the future state of the economy. If the economy does well, the jobs will be there. Millman agreed that the outlook at present is not bright. The visiting industrial fellowship program should be of help. There is a real interest in this program on the part of industry. Many companies which employ few or no physicists have expressed interest in the program. This will, it is hoped, lead to jobs in the future. Jamerson added that there are opportunities in many corporations. The challenge is to discover those opportunities, to get some feeling for what the marketplace is; the individual must do that for himself.

F2. Faculty and Student Panel

Panelists:
1. Pat Dreher, Graduate Student, Chicago (MBA, Rensselaer)
2. N. Greenberg, SUNY Binghamton
3. D. O'Shea, Georgia Tech.
4. B. Rosenblum, U.C. Santa Cruz (former chairman)
5. David Ladd, Graduate Student, Georgia Tech.

Teplitz remarked that at the 1974 conference, specific proposals were made by Rosenblum (broaden curriculum and shorten the time for Ph.D.) and by Greenberg (replace traditional thesis requirement by three shorter projects). We hope to learn the fate of those proposals during this morning's discussion.

First, O'Shea described the applied physics program at Georgia Tech. With 50% of bachelor's students terminal at that level, the faculty decided to create a curriculum designed for them, as well as for terminal masters.

TABLE 1. GEORGIA TECH APPLIED OPTICS PROGRAM

Course	Credits	Ancillary Skills
Geom. Optics	3-0-3	
Optical Inst. Lab.	1-3-2	
Physical Optics.	3-0-3	
Adv. Optics Lab.	1-3-2	...Lab. Notebook Format
Laser Physics*	3-0-3	
U V Spectroscopy	2-3-3	
Optical Design	3-3-4	
Optical Fabrication. . . .	2-6-1	...Procedure Writing
Seminar Cent. Op	1-0-1	...Oral & Written Presentations
Special Problems	0-3X-X	
Intro to Fourier Optics. .	3-0-3	...EE Grad Course
Electro Optics	3-0-3	...EE Grad Course

*Taught jointly with EE

GRADUATES

C.L.	MS	Martin Orlando	Electro - Optics
R.S.	BS	TRW	Chem. Lasers
H.H.	MS	Emory Univ.	Laser-Med Tech
L.D.	MS	Eglin AF Base	Project Initiation
L.G.D.	MS	United Tech.	Research - Pollution
J.S.	BS	Inst. of Optics (Rochester)	Grad Student

A brief description of courses in the applied optics program followed. Courses are 4000 level, open to undergraduates, but taken mostly by graduate students. The number of students enrolled in the program is small (2-3/year), although enrollments in some of the courses are greater (73 in laser physics, for example). Some students have come specially for this program. Some of the courses existed already in the Tech curriculum; the extra teaching load is not excessive. The program is judged to be quite successful, particularly for the kinds of students attracted to Tech. There are other tracks available, but applied optics is the most developed one.

Greenberg described the first few years' experience with Binghamton's alternative Ph.D. program. Most students have continued to choose the conventional program. Of those who have tried the alternative (three shorter research projects) several found they wanted to pursue a project farther, and thus in effect reverted to the standard program. Nonetheless, the faculty still feels the alternative plan has possibilities, perhaps for individuals who return from industry to do a Ph.D.

Rosenblum spoke of the experience at Santa Cruz. His concern is primarily with the students presently "in the pipeline". Eight or ten years from now, at least according to projections, the problem will no longer be severe. Rosenblum does not feel we should reduce the number of physics Ph.D.'s--society should be able to absorb the 1,000 or so a year we produce. But he conceded that little has been done at S.C. to implement the changes he suggested three years ago. The faculty did not respond enthusiastically. Rosenblum cited the tragedy of the commons--actions that benefit each individual are nonetheless harmful to the group as a whole. In the present case the action is producing students trained to follow in a faculty member's footsteps; this is ego-building for the faculty member. We have to adjust the reward structure if we are to bring about change.

Student comments. David Ladd gave Georgia Tech's program a grade of A. One reason is that Tech attracts a different type of student, one who anticipates an industrial career. Many of the things said at this conference about student attitudes don't apply to Tech students.

Pat Dreher has no quarrel with the core curriculum in graduate school. He feels, however, that his MBA will be very useful in pursuing an industrial career. Although he doesn't recommend that all students go out and get MBA's, he does feel that taking one or two courses in management, technical communications, and the like, would improve the coupling to industry. This is particularly valuable for a small industry. He also made the point that someone with strictly scientific training is likely to remain in technical work throughout his industrial career, whereas someone with broader skills is more likely to progress into a higher ranking management position.

QUESTION PERIOD

Teplitz asked O'Shea what is different about Georgia Tech that makes an applied physics program successful there. The reply was that the atmosphere at Tech is such that people don't look down on applied work. The contact with engineers on campus is helpful. Contrary to Schwartz's opinion, O'Shea feels that pure and applied work co-exist comfortably at Tech--there is no elitism one way or the other.

A questioner pointed out that physics at present is not a profession, and AIP does not concern itself with the professional needs of its members. He suggested that AIP has become a dinosaur and should be broken up into specific interest groups. Conwell replied that the AIP is already broken up into disciplines; she feels this is a bad thing. The professional concern committee of APS has recently become more active, but it is difficult to move the APS Council. Moreover, she sees no willingness within the community for the APS to assume a role similar to AMA--for example, in limiting the numbers in the profession. Even the Chemical Society and the IEEE have gone further along these lines than APS seems prepared to go.

Another questioner cited the evolution of U.S. professional societies, from the learned society (the Royal Society being the original prototype) toward a new role more concerned with the well-being of the Society's member. APS is farther back on this evolutionary road, but is being pushed inexorably along it by economic realities.

Someone pointed out that the APS leadership is made up primarily of academic physicists, products of the elite schools. They are therefore likely to be out of touch with the problems we've been discussing, which relate primarily to the industrial context.

Rosenblum amplified his earlier remarks and pointed out that, despite the lack of any substantial change in the Santa Cruz graduate program, all their graduates have jobs, several of them in non-traditional areas.

Wertz, in reply to an earlier question concerning numbers, stated that Computer Science Corporation had hired 30 Ph.D. physicists and 50-60 bachelors and masters during the past years. Most of these are recent graduates. The company is interested in analytical skills rather than specific fields. Wertz urges also that whatever communication training is given to students, it be done in a formal process, so that it can appear in the student's resume. (This need not be a course.)

F3. Chairmen and Students

Panelists: 1. Frank Bletzacker, Graduate Student, SUNY
2. P. Kahn, Chairman, SUNY
3. A. Liboff, Chairman, Oakland University
4. Rebecca Shields, Undergraduate, Auburn
5. C. Shugart, Chairman, N.E. Louisiana
6. R. Weinstein, Chairman, Northeastern University

Before the regular session, Chairman Teplitz asked for a poll of the audience on whether VPI & SU should abolish its physics graduate program. Since the best students go to places like MIT and the next rank to places like Maryland, VPI is left with marginal students in spite of its good faculty and the high caliber of research carried out. Perhaps VPI would do better by turning its 24 GTA lines into six assistant professorships. The suggestion met with only minority support; there was a substantial number of abstentions. There was a widespread fear that eliminating the graduate program would inevitably have harmful consequences for the department as well as the University.

Shugart discussed the problems of a less prestigious school, which are very different from those of, say, MIT. Last November, N.E. Louisiana organized a conference aimed at local industry. The conference was very successful--42 companies attended, and the result was greatly increased contact as well as some direct support (5 small grants, summer support for graduate students, some equipment donated, etc.). The industries now provide a valuable source of support in the state legislature, which had been casting doubtful glances at the small graduate program. The industrial people are pleased with the education the students are receiving, and the graduates (bachelors and masters) have little trouble finding good jobs.

Weinstein described the work-study Ph.D. program recently introduced at Northeastern. (The Chemistry Department has had an almost identical program operating for four years; Northeastern has a long-established cooperative work-study program with industry which involves 80% of the undergraduates.) The new graduate program works as follows: After passing all required courses and the qualifying exam, the student takes a one-year internship at a nearby company. The students have no previous industrial experience, and the program is competitive: only the students with the best grades can participate. This creates a reward structure. The student receives a regular salary paid by the company. The participating companies must employ Ph.D.'s, as well as enough M.S. physicists to permit them to add another one without causing a large perturbation. Furthermore, the company must be within commuting distance, since the student continues to take one course per quarter while participating. This feature restricts the program to urban universities. A faculty advisor follows the student through the year's experience. He visits the student at his company once a quarter, and talks to the student once a month. Beyond this, there are no commitments. When the student returns, he does a regular thesis in one of the conventional research areas.

Benefits to the company include the opportunity to look over a potential Ph.D. employee for a whole year with no commitment. The student benefits from the experience he gains. The faculty also gains from the ties established and from the knowledge that their students are earning a living with what they learned in the department.

Liboff next described the medical physics undergraduate program at Oakland. Job classifications at the interface between physics and the biomedical area include:

1. Biophysics--employment opportunities generally poor, except for specific areas such as theoretical biology and solid state biophysics.
2. Bioengineering
3. Straight medicine (or joint M.D.-Ph.D. program)
4. Medical physics. This includes "classical" areas such as radiology and nuclear medicine, as well as newer areas including imaging, use of linear accelerators and ultra sound. There is a job market in these fields, mostly at the MS rather than the bachelor level. At present, at least 33 institutions offer master's programs.

The Oakland program includes all the regular requirements for a physics major, plus considerable chemistry and biology, with the last year spent in a hospital environment. The students take no language, and fewer electives. But, in general, the program requires more of its students than does the conventional program. Despite this, about half of Oakland's 80 undergraduate physics majors are enrolled in the medical option, including a substantial fraction of females (about one-third). The students obviously like this program. In addition, the department has found local physicians and hospitals to be highly sympathetic and supportive.

Kahn next described some programs recently instituted at Stony Brook. One is a series of lunch meetings, at which speakers from other departments describe their problems and some of their research techniques. The purpose is to acquaint graduate students with the needs of other professions, the tools of other professions, and in general, how other professions go about making a living. Last year's seminar featured medical school faculty. There emerged from these talks a feeling that a lot of what the medical people do has a strong component from the physical sciences. However, the prototype examples they use are very different, as is their language. As a result, the inter-connection is not always apparent, and the physics graduate student may not be aware of the possible applicability of his knowledge and skills. A seminar this year will continue to explore the inter-connections. An allied effort focuses on instrumentation.

Interdisciplinary programs, e.g., in energy and in environmental studies, have not been successful. The graduate students are not attracted to these programs.

Another Stony Brook program is aimed at giving post docs some experience in areas outside their field of specialization. None of these programs create any jobs, but the increased awareness on the part of faculty, graduate students, and post docs is felt to be beneficial.

Rebecca Shields expressed the views of an undergraduate student. They are, nowadays, fully aware of the employment difficulties in the field. She feels that, on the whole, the smaller schools have responded more effectively to the problem than have the larger ones. The examples described this morning illustrate that point. Many of the large schools don't feel the need to participate in programs like SPS. In considering possible graduate schools, Shields places considerable emphasis on the opportunity to work on your own problem, i.e., not as a member of a large team.

Bletzacker has just finished his thesis in high energy theory at Stony Brook. He questioned whether the various programs described this morning really belong in physics departments. If he had wanted to go into medicine, he said, he would have gone to medical school. He essentially wants to see the status quo maintained. Some of the panelists tried to respond to this point of view, but the lateness of the hour brought the discussion to a close.

INDUSTRIAL INTERNSHIP OPTION IN A PH.D. PROGRAM

Roy Weinstein
Northeastern University, Boston, MA 02115

ABSTRACT

A Ph.D. option with a one-year Industrial Internship is being introduced to the Physics graduate program at Northeastern University. Except for the period of internship, the program requires that all usual course work and thesis research be done at the University. Selection criteria, which the students and the companies involved must meet, are reviewed. Although the program is new in the Physics Department, the Northeastern University Chemistry Department has, for four years, run a program differing from this one only in details. Anecdotal evidence is presented from the Chemistry program.

INTRODUCTION

At Northeastern University, we are introducing a new Ph.D. option which will be described below. The aims of this program are to improve the interface between industries and our department, provide students with experience in an industrial research environment, and improve student and faculty attitudes toward industrial research.

The program provides the student with a full year of experience in an industrial laboratory. This period of industrial work, referred to below as the Industrial Internship, occurs after the student has completed most of his required course work and passed his qualifying examinations, and before he has started his thesis research. Except for the period of Industrial Internship, the program requires the student to complete all the usual Ph.D. requirements, course work and thesis research at the University.

For the student, the program provides a year of experience in an industrial environment while maintaining his university contacts. The student gains industrial contacts and an ability to more realistically compare industrial and academic research.

Industry gains an employee at the master's level, but of Ph.D. potential. The industry is effectively provided a year-long interview,with a possible future applicant for a Ph.D. research position, in place of the usual brief and inadequate interview process. The industries may also be interested in a role which allows them to have effect on academic programs and contribute to societal needs at very low dollar cost. The industry does pay a penalty in that the Industrial Intern is imployed for a relatively short period and consequently training occupies a large part of the total employment period.

Industry and the Department gain from the interaction between industry and the graduate student's advisor. The Department also

ISSN:0094-243X/78/259/$1.50

gains industrial input via an industrial research seminar open to all faculty and students, and via the departmental committee which oversees this program and has two industrial physicists as members. It is hoped that more realistic attitudes toward industrial research will be developed on the part of both students and faculty as a result of this program.

Although the program is just being started in the Northeastern University Physics Department, a program differing only in details from this has been in operation for four years in the Northeastern Chemistry Department. At a later point, we will review some anecdotal evidence provided by the Chemistry program.

BOUNDARY CONDITIONS DESIRED BY FACULTY

When our department considered this plan, there was faculty consensus on the following points:

1) The student must meet all the usual Ph.D. requirements.
2) Course work is to be done at N.U.
3) Thesis work is to be done at N.U.
4) The student should have a one-year internship in industry.
5) During the internship, close relationships should be maintained with the Department.
6) The internship should start after the student passes the qualifying exam so that the student is, from his point of view, past the highest potential barrier to his Ph.D., and is very likely to return and complete his studies.
7) The industrial plants involved should be located within commuting distance of the University (a) so that the student can retain contact with the Department during his internship, and (b) so that close faculty-industry contacts are possible within the plan.

In essence the Department prefers a perturbation approach to this program rather than a dramatic restructuring of the Ph.D.program.

SELECTION OF STUDENTS

The program will intentionally be kept small. It is intended that there be competition among the graduate students for selection to this program. The following criteria will be used in the selection of students for the program:

1) Students will be selected from among those who pass the qualifying exam on their first try.
2) Only students who have had no significant previous industrial experience will be eligible.
3) Monetary need shall not be a criterion. The program is not intended to be a method of supplementing income during graduate school.

THE INVOLVED INDUSTRIES

The industrial experience the student gets should be at a

training level suitable to Ph.D. study. Therefore, the involved companies should generally employ Ph.D.'s in research, on projects of an advanced nature.

The graduate students in the program are, in essence, at the M.S. level. Also, it will be seen in the discussion below that it is a consequence of the details of the program that a company which opens a position in order to employ one of our graduate students on an Internship will often not have the position filled. For this reason the involved companies must employ a significant number of master's level scientists, so that a fluctuation of one will not be an insurmountable problem.

In addition, the Department desires to have the student remain closely associated with the University during his internship. For this reason, as well as to allow several other desired close contacts, described below, the companies involved in the work-study program are required to be within commuting distance of the University. However, the participating company may expect the same commitment to work by the intern as it expects of any full-time employee.

These requirements on the participating industries make this program suitable mainly for universities located in a highly industrialized urban area.

THE PROGRAM

The timing of the Industrial Internship is set by the Department's educational requirements. In our ongoing Ph.D. program, the student usually takes two years of classroom work. In September of the third year, a qualifying examination is taken. After passing this, the student may start research but usually takes special problems first to try out various research fields.

Under the Industrial Internship option, the first two years of graduate studies are the same as the standard program. The qualifying exams, taken in September of the third year, determine which students are selected for the program.

Year	Quarter			
	Fall	Winter	Spring	Summer
1st	Same As Standard Ph.D. Program.			
2nd	Same As Standard Ph.D. Program.			
3rd	Qualifying Exams; Courses.	Internship and One Course.	Internship and One Course.	Internship
4th	Internship and One Course	Return to NU for Thesis Research	Thesis Research at NU	Thesis Research at NU; Etc.

As noted above, the number of internships are limited and, among other requirements, a successful applicant must pass his qualifying exams on the first try. The Internship starts in January and lasts one year or 15 months. This timing is set primarily by the qualifying examination requirement.

During the academic year, while the student is on his internship, he is strongly encouraged to take one course per quarter. We believe this is very desirable in order to maintain student-faculty links. The course requirement may be waived by the Work-Study Committee described below.

DEPARTMENT PROCEDURES

When a student is selected for this program, a temporary faculty advisor is assigned to the student. During the Internship, the advisor visits the student and his industrial superior once per quarter. He also calls the student once a month, and reports quarterly to the Department Work-Study Committee. Although the student is <u>not</u> committed to undertake research with the advisor upon his return to the University, the student chooses a temporary advisor in his most probable research area. Since the Industrial Internship is also in the student's most probable research area, the temporary advisor provides expertise in the link between the University, the student, and the company. The need for the advisor to visit the company is another thing which requires that the company be within commuting distance of the University.

A Work-Study Committee receives job descriptions from the associated companies sometime in August. This committee, which includes two industrial members, interviews and selects students for the program. For the students selected, it arranges interviews with the participating laboratories, collects student reports at the end of the internship period, and receives advisors' reports each quarter. It arranges an annual dinner of industrial and academic personnel involved in the program. The Work-Study Committee also arranges, when possible, an industrial research seminar, available to all students and faculty.

The arrangements between students and companies are <u>laissez-faire</u>. The industry can accept or reject an applicant, and vice versa. Salary and working arrangements are determined by the student and the company.

The additional faculty time required by this program is significant. There is a large one-time effort required in order to contact the industries and set up the program. The Work-Study Committee expends about 150 faculty hours per year in the continuing effort needed to keep the program running. The effort of the temporary advisors is smaller but is not negligible.

ANECDOTAL EXPERIENCE

The Physics Department Work-Study Program is new. However, as noted above, the Chemistry Department at Northeastern has operated a similar plan for four years. Their program differs in detail from the Physics Department plan. For example, the Industrial Internship is taken in the second rather than the third year. However, much of their experience seems applicable to the Physics program. Fourteen students have taken part in the Chemistry program, two of whom now have received their Ph.D.'s. (One has taken a position with the company he worked with, the other took an academic position.)

One of the concerns voiced in our department was that students might drop their studies once they started to work. Two of the 14 Chemistry Interns did drop out. However, one case showed clearly that personal problems, having nothing to do with the work-study experience were responsible. In the other case, the student was indeed attracted by the rewards of the industrial job compared to the rigors of graduate school. The industry involved was later dropped from the program because of several difficulties in addition to the dropout of this student.

Faculty comments on students coming out of the program show certain common elements. The student is described as:

1) more mature.
2) highly motivated.
3) more efficient.
4) psychologically benefitted by a productive year after 18 years of educational experience.

On the negative side, faculty feel that return to classroom studies after the Internship comes as a shock to the student. This observation, as interpreted by the Physics Department faculty, makes even more desirable the retention of a one-course study load for the Interns. The Chemistry faculty also report that if the student returns to thesis research, rather than classroom work, there is less of a shock.

No student accepted by the Department Work-Study Committee, which includes two industrial researchers, has failed to be accepted by an industry as an Intern, although some have failed in one or two industrial interviews.

Typical salaries for the Interns have been about $12,000/year.

More students desire to enter the program than are approved by the Department.

The Department has had no success in trying early identification of those students who will apply for the program.

Lead time is a problem. Companies would like to interview candidates 6-7 months prior to the start of the Internship. The Department prefers three months. A compromise may be to judge likely students by grades, and work on the _probable_ results of the qualifying examination.

The Chemistry Department Work-Study plan involves 12 companies and, on the average, arranges an Internship with any one company once in three years. Some companies have exhibited annoyance at not getting an Intern, but this apparently has not been a serious problem.

PHYSICS OF ENERGY AND ENVIRONMENTAL TECHNOLOGY AN EXPERIMENTAL INTERDISCIPLINARY COURSE

W. F. Lankford

George Mason University, Fairfax, Va. 22030

ABSTRACT

A new graduate level course "Physics of Energy and Environmental Technology" was taught at George Mason University in the spring of 1977, for students with undergraduate science degrees. Its intent was to bring current issues of energy and environmental concern to the classroom at a level of sophistication to prepare the student for employment in energy related fields. To accomplish this an introduction to basic physics emphasizing thermodynamics, and a survey of applicable business and economic principles was provided at the beginning of the course. Subsequent study of the specific issues was then made within the boundary conditions imposed by these constraints. A case method was employed to illustrate actual techniques used in the field. Reference material was drawn from recent activity within the physics community addressing energy concerns.

INTRODUCTION

We have been told that the growth of the job market in the academic sector of the physics community is unlikely. However there do seem to be some paths to expansion available from within, and I would like to describe one of these that seems promising.

We have designed a graduate service course which offers students with diverse scientific backgrounds an introduction to the physics necessary to work in an energy related field. Our course presented a broad survey of energy and environmental topics developing the physics as necessary along the way, except for a brief background section on basic physics and thermodynamics. This course will be followed by a special topics continuation as described in the next talk.

COURSE APPROVAL

Nearly a year of interdepartmental discussions resulted in the approval of the course under the title Physics of Energy and Environmental Technology. The key factors which contributed to the approval by our graduate council were the following:

1. Written evidence of coordination with, and participation by other departments notably Business Administration, Biology and Chemistry.

ISSN:0094-243X/78/265/$1.50

2. The availability of published text materials.
3. The acceptance of the course for certification credit for earth science high school teachers by the state of Virginia.
4. The inclusion of the course in the NSF funded Women in Science Program.

Our experience in obtaining approval for this course suggests that careful attention be paid to possible resistance in such a non-traditional area by some key faculty members.

THE STUDENTS

When the course was offered the first time last spring, enrollment by those not in the Women in Science program was discouraged in order to keep the class size below 30. There was however considerable interest among area high school physics teachers as well as our own students in chemistry and biology. We hope to gear the course to their needs next spring. While all of the Women in Science program participants had B.A. or B.S. degrees in science or mathematics, the 2 to 15 year break since that education cast our course in a somewhat typical adult education category. When faced with this kind of background more extensive review and preparation seems advisable. Particular difficulty was experienced in the thermodynamics but this appears to be a more general problem we will mention later. One of the problems anticipated was that some of the students would be very knowledgeable in a few of the topics related to their own specific background, while other topics would require considerable study of basic concepts outside their area. It was hoped that in a graduate level course these demands would be acceptable and perhaps even expected by the students. Most of our students did accept these ideas in principle but few had the time available to put in the necessary work due to other courses and obligations.

TEXT MATERIALS

The texts selected for the course were:

Energy and Environment by Edward H. Thorndike, Addison Wesley, 1976.

Efficient Use of Energy by W. Carnahan et al. APS sponsored Summer Study on Technical Aspects of Efficient Energy Utilization, 1975.

The first book was nearly perfect in choice of topics for this course, however the treatment of many subjects was judged too sketchy by most of the students. A somewhat fuller treatment along these same lines would be welcome.

The much referenced APS study was not intended for use as a text although it claims to be "unabashedly tutorial in character." While its major thrust is the development and application of second law efficiency, it also contains an extensive study of energy use indoors that is beautifully developed. The second law efficiency concepts are based on what many physicists call engineering thermodynamics. Frankly, the engineering texts seem to do a more satisfactory job pedagogically of presenting these concepts. However the application of these ideas to current energy applications such as the home heat pump and solar heaters is valuable. I cannot urge too strongly that this material be rewritten in textbook format for use in such a course as this. Much improvement can be gained from adopting simpler and equivalent definitions and unambiguous notation.

THE COURSE

The course syllabus included the conventional range of topics in energy and the environment, however three sections were taught by professors outside the physics department. These became an essential part of the course. Particularly valuable were the two weeks of economic background on engineering economic decision making provided by a specialist in the field from the Business School. A model was developed along with the accounting calculations necessary to implement it. The students were asked to apply this process to the evaluation of several alternatives for home heating and air conditioning. The problem grew into a term project motivated by the interest of the students.

The section on biophysical energy systems was taught by an ecologist from the biology department and involved such topics as chipped wood fuel supplies and bio-waste utilization. The air pollution section was taught by a physical chemist from the chemistry department.

In Conclusion - The value of this kind of course to the employment picture seems to me to be at least twofold.

First - The generation of a new high enrollment graduate course expands the instructional need for physicists.

Second - The development of an employment opportunity for physics majors in energy fields will encourage more to enter the study of physics even though they don't intend to continue to the Ph.D. level.

And finally the value to the faculty members is that such a course can be fun and not overly competitive with conventional research activities.

SCIENCE CAREER FACILITATION PROJECT IN ENERGY-RELATED FIELDS*

Natalia Meshkov
George Mason University, Fairfax, Va. 22030

ABSTRACT

With the support of the National Science Foundation Women in Science Grant an experimental post-graduate program is being conducted at GMU to prepare women who have a background in natural sciences but who are not working in the field of their training, for employment or graduate study in energy-related fields. Among the 24 students in the program most have at least a BS or BA degree in physics, mathematics, chemistry, or other natural sciences. The interdisciplinary program includes one full year of training and is structured to bring students up to date on problems in energy-related fields and to update their knowledge of physics and related sciences. Specially designed courses and seminars are combined with regular offerings, individualized study, research participation, discussion groups and employment counseling.

INTRODUCTION

An experimental post-graduate program is being conducted at George Mason University. The program is supported by a Science Career Facilitation Project Grant awarded through the Women in Science Program of the National Science Foundation. It is one of the first 11 Science Career Facilitation Projects that received NSF support in 1976. Ten more such projects were funded in 1977. They are located at 21 different colleges and universities in 12 states and the District of Columbia.[1] These projects are aimed at women who received bachelor's or master's degrees in science between 2 and 15 years ago, but who are not currently working in the field of their training. Their purpose is to provide an educational program for these women to prepare them for immediate employment or for graduate study. No tuition is charged to the participants.

THE PROGRAM

At GMU the program is interdisciplinary and it is offered in cooperation with the physics department. It is designed to prepare students with backgrounds in natural sciences or mathematics for entry into energy-related fields. It combines regular university courses with special courses and seminars designed for the program, individualized study, research participation and internships, discussion groups and counseling.

The program started in August 1976 and is in three phases spanning two years. The first half year was devoted to preparation, publicity, recruitment and selection of participants. A full year,

*Supported by NSF Grant SMI 76-20568

ISSN:0094-243X/78/267/$1.50

starting in the spring term, 1977, is being devoted to the instructional phase of the program. The remaining time will be spent on placement of the participants, evaluation of the program and on plans to disseminate the results of the program.

Twenty-four students are currently participating in the program. Their backgrounds are mostly in physics, mathematics or chemistry; a few of the students had majored in other natural sciences. All students have at least a bachelor's degree, several hold advanced degrees, but none were employed in the field of their training when the program started.

The instructional part of the program is structured around two core full-year courses especially adapted to the program and offered by the physics department. One is an intensive physics review course, taught in a personalized system of instruction (Keller Plan). The other is a two-semester graduate level sequence on energy-related topics. The first course of the sequence, "The Physics of Energy and Environmental Technology" is a broad survey of energy and environmental topics and is discussed in the preceeding paper. The sequel to it is a special topics course, "Contemporary Problems in Energy Resources and Analysis", in which some of the topics covered in the spring semester will be selected for a more detailed study.

In addition, many participants are taking electives from regular university offerings in mathematics, physics, biology and economics. The choice of electives is based on their relevance to the program and on students' interests and backgrounds. The electives serve to review the fundamentals, such as calculus, or to complement the program. They include courses in computer science, electronics, ecology, computational physics, nuclear physics, and a course in economics with a special emphasis on resources. Some students will participate in research projects on energy-related topics.

As part of the program a series of bi-weekly seminars on energy has been scheduled. The seminars are presented by invited speakers who are active professionals in energy-related fields.

During the spring semester participants were meeting bi-weekly for two hour discussion groups organized and conducted by a faculty member who holds a joint appointment in physics and psychology. The discussion groups dealt with problems that women might face in re-entering the job market or graduate study and with improvement of job-hunting skills. The discussion groups will continue in the fall semester. The topics will emphasize employment opportunities and job-seeking skills.

For most of the participants the goal is immediate employment upon their completion of the program. Three students have definite plans to enter graduate school. Several students hope to combine employment with graduate study.

Early in the program about 100 organizations that employ scientists were contacted in the greater Washington, D.C. area, to inform them about the program and to invite their participation by providing internships for the program participants. A number of interested responses were received. As a result, four students are currently working in professional part-time positions, three of these on an internship basis. It is hoped that four more students will be placed in internships in the fall. Judging by the interest in the program among potential employers, the employment prospects for the program participants look good.

[1]A listing of other funded projects may be obtained from NSF Women in Science Program.

PROPOSAL FOR BROADENED UNDERGRADUATE SCIENCE MAJORS

J. D. Spangler
Department of Physics, Kansas State University
Manhattan, Kansas 66506

ABSTRACT

It is proposed that a well-organized undergraduate area major in physical science may have several advantages over a more narrow disciplinary major.

Four years ago the American Association of Physics Teachers conducted a survey to learn of careers followed by people who had received undergraduate degrees in physics. This was originally intended to be a preliminary survey, and the sample was relatively small. However, several results are of interest. Approximately half of the roughly 400 respondents perceived their primary career as not being in physics. These people listed a wealth of different career fields from divinity to agriculture, though engineering and computer science were the most popular areas. Of the people reporting a career in physics, slightly more than half had a Ph.D. degree and 7/8 had at least a masters degree. Of the people reporting a career not in physics, half had just a bachelors degree and only 1/8 had a Ph.D. degree (only one a physics Ph.D.); there were 13 possessing or working toward an M.D. degree.

One response to these data at a time of declining numbers of physics majors, especially when the number of majors is one important survival factor for an academic department, is to say that we need to broaden what we call physics and have more concern for the person who doesn't plan to attend graduate school. However, in the past year I have been led to consider another viewpoint about these survey results. I have watched my oldest daughter go through the exercise of choosing a field of study and a college at which to pursue those studies. Two things are apparent. First, she has seen enough of various fields in high school to know that she is interested in some areas and not in others, but not enough to want to make the relatively narrow commitment required by a "major". Second, she has been around the university enough to perceive that the parochialism of departments is something peculiar to the university - where there aren't many jobs anyway - much more than to "real life".

My daughter has dealt with this problem by selecting a program sponsored by a group of departments that emphasizes an area, physical science and applied mathematics, rather than a departmental major. As I have considered this, I have come to believe that for many schools this type of program that attempts to look at physical science in an integrated way could be a happy response to problems in attracting majors and in insuring that graduates have a choice of career possibilities that they perceive as relevant to their studies. Perhaps there are schools where successful programs of this sort quietly exist; if so, they need to make their experiences known. In

ISSN:0094-243X/78/270/$1.50

any event, the possibilities of this kind of program need to be discussed in the physics community.

My own school has had a physical science area major in the past, but it was generally looked on as a refuge for the weak or the dilettante. I do not propose a program that would be a second-rate alternative to a departmental major, but rather a first-rate replacement for the departmental major. The program should be respectable for the strongest students that the institution typically enrolls in the physical sciences. It must be planned and organized _de novo_. Although the framework can probably be built primarily from existing courses, they must be rethought in terms of the goals of the new program and the need for courses taught by different departments to be mutually supporting.

I shall speculate on how an integrated science program could be put together. The minimum participation for such a program would be the departments of chemistry, mathematics, and physics. Participation could also be obtained from geology, the more physical parts of biology, and perhaps other departments, depending on the local situation. There should be a Committee of Overseers composed of representatives from these departments who will be teaching in the program and a Director, with secretarial assistance, who spends at least half time for a term of about two years in the day-to-day process of keeping the program running and the participants enthused.

The initial need would be to clearly define program goals. There are the very practical goals of attracting a sufficient number of students to have a viable program and of having a program whose graduates can find relevant employment or enter graduate school in a particular field of interest. There are goals related to general characteristics, understandings, and skills that it is desired for graduates to possess. Some important goals of this type are: (1) Engendering the realization that all learning does not occur in organized, formal classes and developing the ability to study specialized and advanced texts independently. (2) Developing facility in independent problem solving. (3) Developing laboratory skills (relative to _modern_ techniques and equipment). (4) Creating an appreciation of the historical foundations of scientific knowledge.

On the basis of a clear understanding of goals, planning can turn to requirements and courses. I refrain from becoming entangled in specific questions of what courses should be offered and which ones required of all students, what texts should be used, and which courses should be taught by representatives of which disciplines. (I do have opinions on these points.) Numerous nontrivial decisions would be required, particularly since any broadened program requires that something be omitted. It would be essential that the Overseers make a much closer examination of course content and relation to other courses in the program than is usual for departmental curriculum decisions.

One difficulty that must be considered is how to make available specialized courses that may be desired by advanced students wishing to emphasize a particular area in their studies. Regardless of our goals, realism demands that we plan for competent students who nevertheless require more guidance than being told "Here is an excellent text; read it". At my own school a number of courses that might be desired would be offered in any event for beginning graduate students. Sometimes there would be a large enough number of students interested in a specialized subject to allow a regular course to be offered. More often, recourse would probably need to be made to schemes of individualized instruction. There are ongoing educational experiments in individualization, self-pacing, and modularization of upper-level college science instruction, and their experiences should provide guidance in this area.

On the level of politics and practicability there might be serious difficulties, many of which would be peculiar to the particular institution. This is not something every school could do. Certainly all departments involved must believe in the possibilities of the program and be committed to support it for at least several years. Although the impetus for any such curricular reorganization must come from the faculty, the dean of the college or other administrative unit must be favorably inclined toward the program and be willing to support a several year effort. This support must include proper recognition in the reward system. The need to achieve agreement and commitment among so many academics on a nontrivial matter would in many instances be fatal.

No one should be given cause to feel that any department is taking over the others. The Director must be respected by the faculty of all departments involved in the program. The Director must have an independent office and some operating funds. The surest way to arrange for these is to secure a grant. However, trying to shift a program from grant support to local funding is a difficult and painful experience. Working with local resources from the start might have some advantages in the long run. It is my belief and experience that deans and department heads can frequently make provision at the level needed here for things they really want.

Despite the practical problems involved in making any major changes in academic procedures, I think that a physical sciences area major has much to offer as an alternative to disciplinary majors, both with regard to having enough students to make the teaching program viable and with regard to giving graduates greater employment possibilities. A student who has not developed the habit of thinking of himself as a chemist or a mathematician of a physicist but who has a good foundation of knowledge in all these areas should find greatly increased career opportunities.

CHALLENGES AND REWARDS OF BEING A VOLUNTEER

James D. Reierson
Computer Sciences Corporation, Falls Church, Va. 22046

ABSTRACT

Volunteer work can provide the opportunity for a short-term career change. In 1973 the author quit his job and spent two years as a Peace Corps Volunteer Lecturer in Physics at the University of the South Pacific in Fiji. Challenges encountered as a volunteer included the isolation, new cultures and languages, the subsistence life-style, new teaching techniques, interaction with other faculty members, and difficulties in making long-term improvements. Rewards included travel, the cultural experience, the teaching experience, and playing "foreign expert." Challenges encountered upon return included job hunting, returning to a big pond as a small fish, and the culture shocks of affluence and inflation. The benefits of the experience, for the author, far outweighed the costs.

INTRODUCTION

My personal bias is that one's professional experience should be a progression of jobs rather than a single narrowly defined career. One vehicle for a short-term, no-strings-attached job change is to be a volunteer. On the basis of my own experience, I would like to present some generalizations about the challenges and rewards of being a Peace Corps Volunteer.

I received my PhD in Experimental Nuclear Physics from Iowa State University in 1969. I then worked for four years for Analytic Services, Inc., a small think-tank in the Washington, D.C. area. In June 1973, I quit my job and spent the next two years as a Peace Corps Volunteer Lecturer in Physics at the University of the South Pacific in Fiji. I returned to Washington in October 1975, spent three months looking for a job, and am now employed with Computer Sciences Corporation.

Fiji is an independent member of the British Commonwealth located on the International Date Line 17° south of the equator. The Fiji Island group consists of two main islands and several hundred smaller ones. The population of Fiji is 550,000: 43% native Fijians, 51% of Indian descent. Suva, the capital city, has a population of 60,000.

The University of the South Pacific (USP) was founded in Suva in 1968 on the site of a Royal New Zealand Air Force flying boat base. USP serves English-speaking island countries of the South Pacific with a combined population of 1.2 million spread over an ocean area roughly the size of the continental

ISSN:0094-243X/78/273/$1.50

U.S. In 1974, there were 981 full-time students at USP, 154 part-time and 135 taking correspondence courses. About 80% of the students were from Fiji. USP is patterned after New Zealand Universities. In 1974, there were 112 students working toward BS degrees -- a three-year general science degree composed of chemistry, biology, physics and mathematics courses.

My remarks on the rewards and challenges of being a volunteer are divided into three parts: the Peace Corps adventure, the teaching experience at USP, and the effects on my professional career upon return.

THE PEACE CORPS ADVENTURE

I found the Peace Corps adventure to be very rewarding. I thoroughly appreciated the travel experience and the exposure to Island, Indian and British cultures. There is a good feeling about being a volunteer -- of making new friends and doing something worthwhile.

Volunteer life in a developing country demands adjustments to the isolation of a small country, the loss of personal privacy, the climate, culture and language, and the subsistence life-style. Volunteer job assignments are a problem for many volunteers. A volunteer may be: a) given nothing to do; b) regarded as cheap help and treated as such; or c) placed in an overwhelming and impossible situation. Another challenge is the search for one's identity as a volunteer -- the problem of "where do we go after work?" When is the right time to play bridge with the white expatriots, or to play poker with the other volunteers, or to play vidi-vidi with the local people? In any of these situations it is possible to feel guilty and out of place.

THE TEACHING EXPERIENCE

One of the reasons I joined the Peace Corps was so that I could teach. I found the teaching experience at USP to be very rewarding. In addition I was exposed to most of the other aspects of academic life: I was acting Head of Physics for six months; I was on several faculty committees; I participated in the Fiji Government Alternative Fuel Technical Committee and the USP Satellite Communications Project.

The biggest challenge was trying to teach physics to students with diverse backgrounds and goals who had little previous exposure to science and for whom English was a second language. Interacting with the rest of the faculty can be a challenge because American degrees and teaching methods are sometimes suspect and the presence of a free volunteer can undercut faculty demands for localization, increased benefits and tenure. It is difficult to make long-term improvements when one is a short-term volunteer. Bureaucracy is not limited to large institutions and by the time a volunteer fully understands a problem and has formulated a potential solution, his tour may be up before the solution can be implemented. A small university in a developing country has most of the problems found in US colleges plus additional ones due to geographic isolation, lack of local support in areas where college graduates are suspect, a multi-cultural student population, lack of a permanent faculty, dependence on aid money from developed countries, the effects of a tropical climate on equipment and buildings and the conflict between the preservation of traditional values and the rising expectations of the students.

COMING BACK

The benefits of my Peace Corps experience to my post-Peace Corps career have been mainly philosophical and personal in nature. The Peace Corps adventure and the teaching experience increased my confidence in new situations, improved my interpersonal abilities and increased my sensitivity to other people. In addition, money and materialism are seen in a differenct perspective.

Although a volunteer experience can broaden one's career, it is not salary-enhancing. The most obvious cost is the loss of two years' salary, seniority and raises. New job opportunities are missed -- the energy bandwagon started up and left without me. There are also psychological let-downs upon returning. Some of my friends were not overly anxious to hear about my adventures. For the first time in my life, I was interviewed for jobs by people younger than I was. I had to adjust to life in a large corporation -- to being a small fish in a big pond.

CONCLUSIONS

In summary, a volunteer experience can provide an exciting and rewarding short-term career change, but costs and challenges should be considered in advance. In my case, the teaching and Peace Corps experience far outweighed the career costs I have experienced since returning.

The Peace Corps presently has around 6,000 volunteers and hopes to increase to 10,000 in the next two or three years. Science graduates are needed as volunteers for teaching (usually in high-schools) or to introduce intermediate technology, such as methane generating plants, to villages.

THE TIME HAS COME TO ABANDON THE PUMPS AND RUN FOR THE LIFEBOATS - REFLECTIONS ON LEAVING THE PHYSICS PROFESSION TO STUDY MEDICINE

Robert J. Yaes
Memorial U., St. John's, Nfld., Canada A1C 5S7 *

A decision to abandon a career that one has studied for eight years to prepare for and worked at for a further nine can only be made with the greatest reluctance. Nevertheless, such decisions are becoming more and more common as a matter less of choice than of necessity. The physics Ph.D. who will find a permanent position in physics has become the exception rather than the rule. While it is common knowledge that tenure - track academic positions have become as difficult to find as magnetic monopoles or charmed quarks, the myth persists that physicists can still find jobs in industry. However, a study recently released by the National Science Foundation[1] has found that "the total number of scientists and engineers employed by private industry in the United States dropped by 5% in the first half of the 1970's." Thus the phenomena, first noticed in the academic marketplace[2] of an excess of firings over hirings has been shown to hold in private industry as well.

While this situation is certainly alarming, what is even more alarming is that the decision makers who have the greatest influence on government science policy seem to view this situation with complete equanimity, taking notice of neither human cost nor its long-term implications for the future of basic research in the U.S. They continue to set their priorities as though we were still in the early '60's when research support was growing by 15% per year.

The unemployment problem can only be alleviated in two ways: decreasing the number of Ph.D.'s awarded (and also decreasing the number of visas granted to foreign Ph.D.'s to work in the U.S.) and in increasing the number of jobs available. For reasons of self-interest, neither of these options has been given serious consideration by those people who might have the power to implement them. A graduate program is a source of prestige to both the faculty members and institutions involved. It justifies a top-heavy department with twice the number of professors that the undergraduate program can use. Graduate students are a source of cheap, docile labor. They are paid about half as much as technicians, are better trained and usually more intelligent, will not join a union and will work long and odd hours (you can bet that it won't be a principal investigator watching the experiment during the midnight to 8:00 a.m. shift at Fermilab). As American students are not opting for careers in law or medicine where they will have a reasonable chance of making a decent living, more and more graduate students are being recruited from underdeveloped

*Dept. of Physics formerly; School of Medicine, presently

ISSN:0094-243X/78/276/$1.50

countries. Since the last thing these countries need is more gauge-field theorists, the employment prospects for these students back home will be even worse than in the U.S.

In an era of stagnant budgets, more jobs can be created only by diverting money from elsewhere: summer salaries, overhead, travel, equipment, "consulting fees" and major facilities. Since it is the policymakers who are the principal beneficiaries of these goodies, it is very unlikely that this will happen. If anything, the situation is getting worse. The fraction of the total government research budget going to the handful of "elite" institutions (and having arrived there being diverted to "summer salaries" and "overhead") is increasing. The cost of "major facilities" now being proposed has increased to the point of absurdity. The Large Space Telescope and the Very Big Accelerator would each cost at least several billion dollars over their operational lifetime. Graduating students are now told to lower their expectations which translated into everyday English presumably means "drive a cab or something and stop complaining". Needless to say, any suggestion that principal investigators at Harvard and Princeton lower their expectations in terms of research support, summer salaries, travel budgets, etc., is not thought to be worthy of serious consideration.

Ironically enough, it is the construction of these massive "major facilities" that presents us with the most compelling evidence of stagnation and decay. It is due to the almost total absence of new ideas in instrumentation that all we seem to be able to do is build the same thing over and over again...only larger. Years ago, higher energies were achieved by the development of totally different types of machines in rapid succession: Cockroft - Walton, Van de Graff, Cyclotron, Synchrocyclotron, Betatron, Synchrotron, Proton Synchrotron, Strong Focusing Proton Synchrotron, Intersecting Storage Rings. Today, Fermilab is nothing more than a scaled up version of the Brookhaven AGS, as PEP will be merely a scaled-up version of SPEAR. Fermilab's 15' bubble chamber is little different from Donald Glaser's original version except that the diameter has been multiplied by a factor of several hundred and the cost by a factor of about a million. Today "innovation" and "progress" means replacing a large array radio telescope with a Very Large Array Radio Telescope or a big accelerator with a Very Big Accelerator.

The same can be said for theory. Theoretical ideas that are now "HOT", non abelian gauge theories, renormalization group, quark models and charm are all ten to twenty-year old ideas that have been recycled, when it became clear that such concepts as double dispersion relations, dual resonance models, Meuller-Reggeology and whatnot were leading absolutely nowhere. Undoubtedly, if gauge theories prove less fruitful that current optimistic predictions would lead one to expect, dispersion relations and duality will themselves be resurrected a few years hence.

With much of research dependent on equipment that is incredibly expensive to both purchase and maintain and with many universities paying more than half of some faculty salaries from government grants the lifeblood of scientific research is no longer intelligence, ingenuity and creativity but cash flow and the principal task of principal investigator is to keep the cash from ERDA or the NSF flowing. Needless to say, this requires the talents more of a salesman than of a craftsman, of a P.T. Barnum, more than a Rutherford, a Fermi or an Einstein. Where large amounts of money are at stake, there is the tendency to stick with the safe, sure thing that has worked in the past. Just as the movie studios, having been taken over by the conglomerates, having given us Godfather II, Jaws II, Exorcist II, a remake of KING KONG, Airport, Airport '75, Airport '77 (and eventually no doubt Airport '84) so there is a tendency among experimentalists to repeat the same experiments over and over again, at higher energies with larger bubble chambers and large sodium iodide crystals. Theorists wait until the latest fad has received the official blessing from Harvard, Princeton and Cal-Tech before hopping aboard. Truly new departures could lead to major breakthroughs, but they might possibly not work out at all, and today few people are willing to take the risk.

Many individuals like myself were attracted to physics in the first place, by romantic stories about the golden age of discovery when modern physics was developed by Planck, Einstein, Rutherford, Bohr, Heisenberg, Fermi and their contemporaries. However, today, the individual creative genius has been replaced by the large research group, as surely as the mom and pop corner grocery has been replaced by A and P and Safeway, or the local blacksmith by General Motors. The single author experimental papers is as extinct as the Dodo and the single author theoretical paper is becoming as rare as the whooping crane. The style of work at Fermilab or SLAC is little different than that in a large corporation and the typical young high energy experimentalists could easily make the transition to an industrial research laboratory with little adjustment or loss of job satisfaction (assuming he had any to begin with).

There is, however, a more fundamental problem than individual job satisfaction. An industrial system ideally suited to producing tens of thousands of identical automobiles or color television sets, could not have produced the theory of relativity or quantum mechanics, or for that matter, Maxwell's equations, Newtonian mechanics, the theory of evaluation, penicillin, King Lear, the Moonlight Sonata or the Mona Lisa. In other words, as anyone who has ever worked on an industrial assembly line could tell you, efficiency is the antithesis of creativity. It is, therefore, not very surprising that "Big Science", for all the investment of money and manpower, has produced precious little that is really innovative and new. It would not be much of an exageration to say that the 3 papers published by Einstein in 1905 did more to change our view of the fundamental nature of the universe than all the work done at Fermilab to date. The Catch 22 of the situation is that even those few physics Ph.D.'s still able to find work will no longer find that work to be enjoyable, interesting, rewarding or even very productive.

The situation that I have described is apparent to anyone in the physics profession. It will eventually become known to the general public, which is footing the bill, despite a massive public relations apparatus geared up to tout each new resonance found in electron-positron scattering as the greatest advance in human civilization since the discovery of fire. When those in charge refuse to recognize a disaster as such, then each of us must decide for himself when the time has come to abandon the pumps and run for the lifeboats. I have made my decision and would advise anyone else who can to do the same.

1. See _Nature_ 267, 575(1977).
2. Lee Grodzins in _Proceedings of the 1974 Tradition and Change Conference at Penn State_.

HUMAN RESOURCES IN PHYSICS: FACTS

Robert R. Trumble and Joan M. Mernin
National Science Foundation

ABSTRACT

The National Science Foundation collects and compiles considerable amounts of data on scientific human resources. A summary of these data and projections is presented with emphasis on physicists and on overall factors that are affecting the employment and careers of physicists. In order to separate myth from reality, data from the NSF Manpower Studies Section are analyzed for the physical sciences and physics. These data, along with other information are used to reflect trends and clarify the present. With regard to changing career opportunities for physicists, trends and recent data for the following major factors are studied: (1) population and characteristics; (2) characteristics of the labor force; (3) employment of physicists by sector (university, industry, and Federal Government), primary work activity, and salary; and (4) educational attainment in terms of undergraduate degrees, and graduate enrollment and degrees.

DATA SOURCES

The bulk of the data used in this article comes from the Manpower Characteristics System which is comprised of the Roster of Doctoral Scientists and Engineers (S&E's), the National Sample of S&E's, and New Entrants Surveys. The Roster of Doctoral Scientists and Engineers consists of all known doctoral scientists and engineers in the United States starting with the year 1930. The Roster serves as a panel from which a sample of about 60,000 doctoral scientists and engineers were selected to provide data on the doctoral population of the Nation. The National Sample, consisting of about 50,000 individuals was drawn from those scientists and engineers who were in the employed labor force at the time of the 1970 decennial census. Information on this group of scientists and engineers was collected in 1972, 1974, and 1976 by the Bureau of the Census which maintains the National Sample. The New Entrants Surveys are designed to measure the magnitude and characteristics of scientists and engineers entering the S&E labor force since the 1970 decennial census.

ISSN:0094-243X/78/280/$1.50

POPULATION AND CHARACTERISTICS

About 42,000 individuals constituted the physicists* population of the United States in 1974. This was about 2.2 percent of the entire scientists' and engineers' (S&Es') population and has declined since 1972 as a percent of all S&E's. This is a result of a smaller rate of increase in the number of physicists contrasted to scientists and engineers generally. Minorities accounted for almost five percent of the physicists in 1974, a little more than the minority percentage of all scientsts and engineers. Asians constituted two-thirds of the minority physics population in 1974 compared to 42 percent of the minority S&E population. A small portion of the physicist minority population, fourteen percent, was Black.

The number of women in the field of physics was estimated to be about 2,500 in 1974. This was almost six percent of the entire physicist population. Women physicists reported a median age in 1974 of 28 years, eight years younger than their male counterparts. Male and female scientists and engineers reported similar age differences. This difference could be attributed to the fact that male physicists achieve a higher academic degree than female physicists and therefore enter the field of physics at a later age. In addition, the number of women entering the field of physics for the period from 1972 to 1974 was, in comparison to the number of women already in the field, proportionately higher than the number of men.

LABOR FORCE

The size of the physicist labor force in 1974 was estimated to be 35,100 individuals, giving an S&E labor force participation rate of 85 percent. The size of the overall S&E labor force yielded a similar labor force participation rate of 85 percent. Minority physicists have a higher S&E labor force participation rate, 93 percent vs. 82 percent. This is probably related to the higher educational levels of the Asians who comprise 67 percent of minority physicists.

For both the physicist labor force and the S&E labor force the unemployment rate was about one percent. Women experienced a slightly higher unemployment rate of almost two percent within the S&E labor force whereas there were too few cases of female

* The category of physicists encompasses astronomers also.

physicists unemployed to estimate an unemployment rate. The number of unemployed minority physicists also was too small to permit estimates of their unemployment rates. It should be remembered that at this time, unemployment for the entire economy was around 5.6 percent. In 1974, more than 34,700 physicists were employed yielding an employment rate of about 99 percent, comparable to the employment rate of all S&E's.

EMPLOYMENT OF PHYSICISTS

Type of Employer

Business and industry employed the largest number of scientists and engineers of any type of employer in 1974, as well as the largest number of physical scientists. However, unlike the other physical sciences, more than half of all physicists were employed by educational institutions. This comparison is expected since engineers comprise over half of all S&E's and are predominantly employed in industry while the highly educated physicists have prepared for academic employment. Physical scientists in turn do not have an educational level as high as that of physicists thus centering their employment in the area of business and industry. For physicists the second largest employer was business and industry. Educational institutions employed 41 percent of physicists, business and industry 18 percent, and the Federal Government more than 16 percent. As in other fields, physicists with a baccalaureate as the highest degree were mainly employed in business and industry. Physicists with a master's and especially a doctorate were more often employed by educational institutions than any other type of employer.

Primary Work Activity

Research and development was the primary work activity of about 40 percent of the Nation's scientists and engineers in 1974 and more than 58 percent of the physicists. Scientists and engineers were spread throughout most primary work activities, while physicists were more concentrated in the research and development area. More than 20 percent of the physicists were involved in an area of teaching; whereas less than eight percent of all scientists and engineers were involved in teaching.

Physicists tend to cluster in certain primary work activities depending on the number of years of professional experience. For instance, in 1975, 75 percent of the Ph.D. physicists with two to four years experience were involved in research and development compared to 41 percent with 10 to 14 years experience.

Salary

The median annual salary for all physicists in the National Sample in 1974 was $21,300 compared to $19,300 for scientists and engineers. Physicists tended to receive higher salaries partially as a result of their increased education and greater median age. Within the physics field median salaries varied considerably. Although there were too few cases of female physicists to estimate the median salary, in most other fields within S&E women received almost 20 percent less than men in the same field. Unlike most other areas of science and engineering, the Asian physicist received a higher median annual salary than either Black or White physicists, probably due to the high proportion of doctorates awarded to Asians. For all scientists and engineers, minorities received a smaller salary than did their White counterparts. The difference of about five percent is still less than the differential women encounter. Typically, the Federal Government pays the highest salaries of all S&E's with a median of $21,000 in 1974. However, physicists received their highest median salary from non-profit organizations and their next highest from the Federal Government, the amounts being $23,500 and $22,600 respectively.

Starting salaries for Ph.D. physicists do not seem to be related to standard market variables such as R&D expenditures in physics, and the number of Ph.D. degrees awarded, whereas in chemistry and other fields there is a discernible relationship. Initial analyses also indicate that graduate enrollment in the physical sciences, comprised principally of physics and chemistry, are positively related to several market factors including starting salaries for new Ph.D.'s and Federal Graduate Student Support. On the other hand, enrollments are negatively related to starting salaries for new physical scientists with a baccalaureate. Our preliminary finding is that graduate enrollments do respond to economic variables.

EDUCATIONAL ATTAINMENT

Undergraduate Degrees

The undergraduate degree was achieved by more than 987,000 individuals in 1974-75, a 66 percent increase over the 595,000 in 1966-67. The science and engineering field experienced an increase of 57 percent over the same period, while the number of degrees granted in physics declined by more than 20 percent. This decline was not new to the physics field since the number of undergraduate degrees granted has steadily decreased since 1968-69. The physical sciences in general have followed the same pattern, but not to as great an extent as the field of physics.

Graduate Enrollment

From 1966 to 1975 the number of students enrolled for advanced degrees in all fields increased 81 percent while enrollments for S&E fields increased by less than 26 percent. Although physics had a 34 percent decrease in enrollments during this period, the rest of the physical sciences had an increase of 9 percent mainly as a result of substantial increases in geology.

Graduate Degrees

The number of master's degrees granted in physics consistently decreased after the single year of increase in 1968-69 for an overall decrease of 25 percent from 1966-67 to 1974-75. By contrast, master's degrees granted in S&E during this period increased over 28 percent, and in all fields the number of degrees granted rose almost 86 percent. The total number of doctorate degrees granted for all fields increased by 65 percent from 1966-67 to 1974-75. The science and engineering fields had a 40 percent increase while the field of physics declined almost nine percent. Doctorates granted in physics increased about 25 percent from 1966-67 to 1970-71, but took a downward turn at this point and decreased by 27 percent from 1970-71 to 1974-75.

Highest Degree

Approximately one-third of the scientists and engineers held graduate degrees in 1974, whereas over 70 percent of physicists held graduate degrees. The Asian minority group achieved the highest level of education overall with 93 percent of Asian physicists holding graduate degrees. They are followed by 73 percent of White physicists with graduate degrees and 67 percent of Blacks.

CONCLUSION

Hopefully, the information provided on the preceding pages provide an overview of the labor force and education data of physicists. New information from the 1976 National Sample and New Entrants Surveys, and from the 1977 Roster of Doctoral Scientists are in various stages of tabulation and analyses in preparation for publication in the near future.

THE ROLE OF THE AMERICAN PHYSICAL SOCIETY IN IMPLEMENTING CHANGES IN CAREER OPPORTUNITIES FOR PHYSICISTS

George E. Pake
Xerox Palo Alto Research Center, Palo Alto, CA 94304

ABSTRACT

The recent measured participation of the American Physical Society in the public affairs arena is briefly reviewed in relation to the Society's stated purpose and financial resources. Notable programs bearing on career opportunities are the Congressional Fellowships and the new Industrial Fellowships. Some personal opinions are offered as to the proper balance of such programs for a scholarly professional society and the primary pitfall to be avoided.

INTRODUCTION

This conference, on the topic of Changing Career Opportunities in Physics, occurs almost precisely at the mid-point of my term as President of the American Physical Society. The period from the Annual Meeting, in late January or early February, through the 3-day or 4-day "retreat" of the APS Executive Committee in the summer, is in many respects the most intensive half of the presidential term, since it involves the Annual Meeting at which the President assumes office, then the large March meeting, followed by the late April Washington Meeting. The Executive Committee meets at each of these general meetings, as well as during its summer retreat. Council meets at the annual meeting at Washington, and at least one other time during the year. It is a busy life, and in fact I was on leave from my duties at Xerox for the five months of January through June.

The point of the foregoing recitation is not to emphasize the change in my own career opportunities occasioned by my election as President of APS. Presidencies of scholarly societies do not represent a very substantial class of job opportunities, and at least so far as APS is concerned, the job can involve long hours, pays no salary, and - thank God - offers no prospect whatsoever of tenure! The reason I have chronicled where I stand in the presidential term is to give you some sense of the perspective from which I am making my remarks today.

Interestingly enough, even the structure of the society's activities reflects a dominance of the academic viewpoint throughout APS history. We have traditionally held our large meetings after the end of the first quarter or semester of the academic year. The old pattern before World War II was often a vacation summer, perhaps some summer school teaching, maybe working on the manuscript for a paper or book, or, in rare instances, a summer job in industry. The colleges and universities reconvened in the autumn, and the professors and graduate students, who may even have taken the summer off in those days, rejoined each other in the laboratories. On the basis of research completed after the preceding summer and/or autumn, the several large APS meetings from January on through the end of the academic year afforded opportunities to present and hear these latest research results.

The post-war and then post-Sputnik stimulation of physics graduate study introduced almost universally the federal contracts and grants in support of university research - for a brief period of years readily available but now heavily sought after and hard-pressed to keep pace with research costs. Summer research

ISSN:0094-243X/78/285/$1.50

support from grants and contracts turned physics research into much more of a year-round activity, which in turn has had some effects on APS meeting patterns. But it is still true that colleges and universities are where most APS members are to be found, and that the university calendar in effect determines the APS calendar. It might be interesting to speculate whether the changing career patterns that are the topic of this conference will ever bring the day when academic physics does not dominate the APS calendar. In any event, at this point in APS history, the academic calendar quite properly does so.

There are more than a few signs of change in the air. Some are perhaps only suggestive. This is the first year in more than 30 years that the APS has a president from industry, and it will have another one the year after next. I read abstracts for this conference and I discover that TA can mean Technology Assessment rather then Teaching Assistant. But there are other very specific and hard data: examples are given throughout the meeting program of physicists in careers that would scarcely have been thought of 10 years ago, and certainly not 20 years ago; there are also the statistical and physics demographic studies that have been reported upon at this conference.

So: change is occurring. There is now and portends for quite some time a surplus of research-trained physicists for the available traditional kinds of physicist employment opportunities, and therefore it seems to most if not all of us that changes of one kind or another should be encouraged and accelerated. This brings us to the question that is my topic for today; What should be the role of the APS, as a professional scholarly society, in implementing change?

THE PURPOSE OF THE AMERICAN PHYSICAL SOCIETY

Although there have been revisions of the society's Constitution as the APS has grown, the statement of purpose has been the same for as long as I can remember:

The advancement and diffusion
of the knowledge of physics

Such a statement of purpose helps you to understand why I referred a few moments ago to the APS as a professional scholarly society: APS is dedicated to advancing and disseminating knowledge of a particular science or discipline, and I believe that qualifies as a scholarly activity. Advancing knowledge is, by my definition, research, within which I would certainly include reformulations of the existing body of DATA, measurements, and principles as WELL as, of course, the discovery of new information and principles.

The "diffusion of the knowledge of physics" might suggest teaching and the APS statement of purpose could well be interpreted to mean APS should operate university-like institutions for physics research and teaching. But colleges and universities in substantial numbers predated APS and we all know - or at least I presume - that the function of APS is to serve its purpose through the publication of research results and by organization of meetings at which physicists can convene to report upon research and to engage in discussions with each other about those "advances in the knowledge of physics."

Literally interpreted, then, it might well seem that the only change we are chartered to implement is that of the state of awareness of progress in the science of physics. I can tell you that APS is doing much more than that! My past 2 1/2 years on the Executive Committee and the Council (the APS governing body) have certainly educated me in the many activities of APS, a substantial fraction of which go well beyond the narrowest interpretation of the APS statement of purpose. On the other hand, I would not characterize APS as an activist organization advancing the cause of the profession in a socio-political sense. Our Constitution, as I read it, does not allow for such aggressive activism, and our tax-exempt status surely does not permit it. We are all aware that there is a spectrum of opinion within APS as to how narrowly to interpret the APS purpose, at one extreme, and, at the other, how far to push socio-political action.

COMMITTEES OF THE SOCIETY

If the APS is not activist, I observe that it surely is active! The number of hard-working committees of APS may even have doubled every decade since World War II. I didn't count them, but my file folder of committee rosters bulges mightily!

Of specific concern to this meeting are committees that bear rather directly on career opportunities. The first ones I should acknowledge are the sponsors of this conference:

The Forum on Physics and Society
Committee on Education
Committee on Professional Concerns

I should note that the Forum is a rather unique part of APS, being not a committee but analogous to a Division of the Society. These three groups that have sponsored this conference I believe have done a substantial service to physicists and to physics.

Other committees that bear on career opportunities are:

Committee on Minorities in Physics
Committee on Women in Physics
Committee on Applications of Physics
Physics Manpower Panel

I fear that I have overlooked one or two other relevant committees equally active and dedicated; please forgive any such oversight. There are also of course career related services, such as the Placement Service, which APS supports.

All of the foregoing groups develop studies, activities and programs that help to keep the community of physicists abreast of background information, trends, and opportunities. Often there are specific action items that may require approval by Council and appropriation of APS funds. You have heard in these sessions about the studies and surveys made, for example, by the Physics Manpower Panel and the Committee on Applications of Physics.

NEW CAREER OPPORTUNITIES THROUGH SPECIAL FELLOWSHIP PROGRAMS

Two programs of APS are especially noteworthy here. One is the Congressional Fellowship program, which I consider well established and a great success. As most of you know, applications are solicited by APS, and a very hard-working Committee, chaired by the APS Vice-President-elect and strongly assisted by the Deputy Executive Secretary, screens applications, interviews at least a half dozen of the most promising candidates, and selects two each year. The successful candidates are thus free to interview with various members of Congress to find a staff position, either with an individual Congressman or Senator of with a particular Committee of Sub-Committee.

The program is successful on several counts: (1) Congressional Fellows selected each year are quite impressive and are in great demand "on the Hill"; (2) runners-up to whom APS could not make awards are often interviewed for regular Congressional or other staff roles and take such positions. (APS supplies names of runners-up only if they consent); (3) Several scientific societies now have programs supporting one or more Congressional Fellows; (4) Many fellows stay on in Washington after their fellowship year in regular staff positions with Congress or with Federal agencies and departments.

The net effect of the Congressional Fellow program is that much higher quality staff help in relation to science - and technology-related issues has been placed in Washington and is continually being added to. Furthermore, the men and women so involved clearly enjoy the work, and in a very real sense a new career path has been opened up for physicists. Congress, the nation, and physicists all benefit.

The second APS fellowship program is just getting underway. It is the APS Industrial Postdoctoral Fellowship Program, the brain child of two people: Dr. Joe Burton, Treasurer of the APS, and Dr. Sidney Millman, Secretary of the American Institute of Physics.

The first three Industrial Fellowship awardees were just announced in late June. The new program was established to broaden the interaction between physics and industry and to open new opportunities for physicists in this country by demonstrating that their proficiencies are applicable to a wide variety of industrial programs. These new opportunities may be found in smaller companies that have hitherto employed few is any scientists or in larger companies that have employed few if any physicists. Each Fellowship stipend is shared equally by APS and the company at which the fellow will work, as are some funds for other expenses. The first three fellows will be working for Colgate-Palmolive, for W. R. Grace and Company, and for International Paper.

Paul Horwitz, a former APS Congressional Fellow, has already described in paper C2 some of the unique features of the task the Industrial Fellowship Selection Committee must perform. Not only must the quality ranking of candidates be made, but so also must a judgment of the potential of the industrial work opportunity be made, and then there must be an effective matching of candidates to opportunities. Considering that there are several dimensions of quality for both the candidates and the work opportunities, the selection process is a complicated optimization problem in an hyperspace!

Neither of these fellowship programs is large, but I believe they can do much as demonstration examples; indeed the Congressional program already has.

I am in fact quite proud of the APS for its innovativeness, its objectives, and its objectiveness thus far in these programs.

Perhaps there are still other imaginative ways for the APS to open additional dimensions of career opportunity for physicists. But before we get carried away with that idea, I want to examine some realities of the financial resources and of the purpose and nature of the American Physical Society.

THE FINANCIAL COST OF CAREER OPPORTUNITY-EXPANSION

Let us assume for purposes of discussion that the APS Industrial Fellowship Program will be equally as successful as the Congressional Fellowship Program. (That is by no means a foregone conclusion, because the complexity of the selection process for Industrial fellows and the important fact that Congressional Fellows all work in the same city and broad institute make important differences.) What I want to do now is rate the cost of our career-related programs to the size and resources of the APS.

There are 29,000 members of the APS. Without doing precise cost accounting, I examined the 1977 budget for expenditures of dues-related income, in order to obtain some feel for the cost per APS member of our several activities that relate to career opportunities. The relevant Committee activities, if one includes the Manpower Panel but excludes the Forum which has its own dues, amount to a little more than $2 per member. The Fellowship Programs and the Visiting Physicists Program, with proration of officer time, will in steady state consume about $3 per member. These combine to total about $5 per member per year for career-related activities although there are several further items that I believe should be prorated in addition. Your APS dues are $20 a year; I'd like to remind you that they are "the lowest in the scientific society business". So we are spending at least 1/4 and possibly 1/3 of dues-related income on career-related activities.

The remaining major dues-related expenditures are the for Bulletin, for AIP Service Charges, and for a proration of the New York APS office. In fact dues-related income by itself falls short, and our investment income is what enables us to get by with our present $20 dues. Looked at in this way, we don't have budgetary room for a great many activities to expand career opportunities.

There is another way to look at it, of course. APS publishes journals, organizes general meetings and topical conferences, has divisions by sub-field and sections by geography. Our annual budget is a few million dollars, so what is a $50,000 fellowship program here or there?

But by far the most important part of the APS budget is for journals, and the next most important activity is probably meetings. We try to make the journals are self-sustaining on their subscription income and the meetings self-sustaining on their registration fees. You have already heard how dues-related expenses exceed dues income, but the difference is essentially made up through investment income. It is of course impossible in a large budget such as APS's to guarantee previse detailed balancing of costs among the several activities. But that has been our general operating philosophy. Incidentially, I can assure you that I have found APS finances and the New York office to be exceedingly well managed.

But I think you can see the question to which I am building:

> To what extent will the membership, through Council, its representative governing body, support the use of society dues for programs aimed at expanding career opportunities in physics?

The answer to this question has both a financial and a philosophical dimension.

The financial expenditures have, thus far, received overwhelming approval of our constitutionally elected Council.

The philosophical question seems to me to be the one that I should address if I really speak to the topic suggested for this talk.

SCHOLARSHIP VERSUS SOCIAL ACTION

I am certainly not trying to open old wounds from a decade ago - nor to open any new wounds! I sense from the membership of APS only general pleasure with, and confidence in, the kinds of activities of APS that I have discussed thus far in this paper. The same general approbation holds for studies recently undertaken through our relatively new POPA (Panel on Public Affairs): the Light Water Reactor Safety Study of about two years ago and the Nuclear Fuel Cycle and Waste Management Study of this year.

But some members of the APS - individuals for whom I have high respect as scientists and as citizens - have told me that, in their view, "the APS should confine its activities to publishing research papers and holding scientific meetings, "Period". It is a tribute to the integrity of the process that APS has used in its public affairs activities of the past few years and its career-expansion projects that thus far no major controversy within the membership has been generated by these POPA-commissioned studies nor by our fellowship programs. There have been several essentially isolated instances of criticism, but nothing that has developed a large hue and cry.

In contrast, another technical professional society (not within the AIP) is currently in a state of serious polarization over activities in the public affairs or socio-political sphere.

I believe we have today, in APS, the situation of general approbation because of the extreme lengths to which the APS Council, the Executive Committee, and the officers over the years have gone to bring the integrity of the science of physics itself to these several activities in the public sphere. In my own view, because humans though made of atoms are less reliable and predictable than the atom, no human association can ever fully achieve that integrity. But is we ever fall seriously short of that goal, the integrity of even our science could become suspect in the eyes of the external world. Perhaps before that could happen, a severe break in consensus within the APS might well have forced the Society out of the public affairs arena. But the danger that a discredited public affairs activity could tar our science with the same brush, is in my opinion real.

CONCLUSION

My answer to the question of the role of the APS in implementing change is - somewhat unexcitingly, I fear - that we have got it just about right in the set of activities of APS Committees and in the programs of the APS as a whole which I have mentioned in this talk. There is nothing personally self-serving in my statement, since not one of those good things was my idea and all I have done, with a great deal of competent and dedicated help, is preside in a formal way over the machinery of the APS for about six months.

Those good things are good because they have been carefully planned, steered by well thought-out guidelines, attended by checks and balances, given thoughtful mid-course corrections, and carried out by dedicated and public-spirited physicists who have indeed brought the integrity of their science to those activities. I can testify from watching selection committees, study groups, review panels, and the whole set of APS governing processes at work that enormous amounts of time and energy are required. I believe, therefore, that the APS can continue to make the kinds of solid, if sometimes small, contributions to implementing change that I have described, provided APS meets three conditions:

1. It must be vigilant to maintain the standards of integrity it has thus far met.

2. It should be careful to avoid over-extending itself.

3. It must never lose sight of its primary purpose as stated in the APS Constitution and exemplified in the balance of current APS activities.

As I have already indicated, I am proud of the American Physical Society's accomplishments while indeed maintaining its full credibility in fulfilling its stated purpose.

A Perspective on the Conference

Martin L. Perl
Stanford Linear Accelerator Center
Stanford, California 94305

Contents

1. INTRODUCTION

At this conference the speakers and participants have drawn a full picture of the physics employment situation and of current career opportunities for physicists. I think we now have a better view than we have ever had before as to where we stand and as to where we are going in these areas. Each of the participants has certainly formed his or her summary as to where we stand and where we are going. My summary will be built around a central theme: the effect of the employment situation and career opportunities on the quality of life for physicists. First I will describe what I mean by quality of life and then I will explain why it is so important to physics.

A. The Quality of Life for Physicists. The quality of life for a physicist is made up of three components.

a. The Employment Situation. The employment situation for physicists is satisfactory if all B.S., M.S. and Ph.D. physicists who want to use physics in their careers can find permanent careers using physics. This simple criterion is sometimes ignored. Sometimes the concept is put forth that students should study physics for its own sake; and that getting a job using the physics they have learned is unimportant or of no concern to the

ISSN:0094-243X/78/292/$1.50

physics community. On the contrary, the vast majority of students who take graduate degrees in physics and many students who take undergraduate physics degrees would like to use physics in their careers.

b. The Work Environment. There are several components in a physicist's work environment which affect his or her quality of life. Is the employment full time or part time? For example, there is an increasing trend in junior and four-year colleges to hire part time instructors. A physicist so employed, who really wants full time employment, is not in a good work environment. A related component of the work environment is the question of tenure or other job security. Again junior and four-year colleges are increasing their temporary hiring to avoid carrying a large load of tenure faculty. Other work environment questions are: Does the physicist have mobility to improve his position in an institution, can he change the physics he works on, and can he grow as a physicist?

c. Living Standard. By living standard I simply mean how are physicists' salaries changing relative to the cost of living. The relevance of this question is fully demonstrated by Table I taken from H. Brook's talk at this conference. In 1969-1973

TABLE I

Percentage Changes in Average Starting Salaries of Graduates Measured Relative to Annual Earnings of All Workers in Industry.

Field		1964-69	1969-73
Ph.D. in	Chem. Eng.	+2.7%	-21.2%
	Elec. Eng.	-5.8	-19.3
	Mech. Eng.	-0.1	-18.2
	Civ. Eng.		-19.1
	Math.	-6.6	-24.4
	Physics	+1.0	-28.0
All Professors		+7.8	- 7.6

Ph.D.s lost ground relative to starting engineering Ph.D.'s, relative to all professors, and relative to industrial workers!

The quality of life for physicists is important for two reasons. First, as members of the physics community our feelings of comradeship in science require that we be concerned with all the members of the community, particularly the younger members. Second, the health and vitality of physics itself demands that its practitioners be reasonably secure and comfortable; and that young creative people see physics as a way to both do science and to make a decent living. I grew up in the Great Depression and I have heard most of the stories of how hard it was to do physics in those days. But I simply don't believe that a student can study as well as he can, or do as good research as he can, when he sees few jobs or poor salaries or poor working conditions after graduation. Not in this affluent society!

B. Who Are the Physicists and What Do They Do? As a basis for discussing the current employment and career situation it is useful to summarize the number of physicists in the United States, Table II, and what they do, Table III and IV. These tables are taken from T. Senator's talk at this conference. All the tables are based on the 1974 National Sample of Scientists and Engineers.

TABLE II

The number of physicists to the nearest thousand in the United State according to various criteria based on the 1974 National Sample of Scientists and Engineers.

Criteria	Highest Degree			
	B.S.	M.S.	Ph.D.	Total
Number who say they are employed as physicists	3,000	4,000	14,000	21,000
Number who meet STF criteria a)	5,000	6,000	17,000	28,000
Number with highest degree	19,000	11,000	20,000	50,000

a) The STF criteria are that a physicist must have at least two of the three characteristics (1) employment in physics or a related field, (2) a B.S. in physics or a related field, and (3) self-identification as a physicist.

TABLE III

Occupation of physics degree holders in per cent. (The entries do not total to 100% because of round-off errors.)

	Highest Degree		
	B.S.	M.S.	Ph.D.
Engineering	61	39	10
Physics and Astronomy	13	28	65
Other Natural Sciences	9	13	12
Managers or Administrators	13	13	11
Other	5	9	3

TABLE IV

Employment Sector of physics degree holders in per cent by highest degree (The entrees may not total to 100% because of round off errors

	Highest Degree		
	B.S.	M.S.	Ph.D.
4-year colleges and universities	3	11	45
Other academies	1	7	2
Research institutes	17	20	27
Business and industry	61	48	20
Government	14	10	4
Other	4	4	3

Before going on to the main body of this summary paper I must apologize to the many authors whose papers I have not cited here. These papers all appear in this Proceedings and so there was no need to attempt summaries which would be worse than inadequate. I have only cited those papers which contain data that I have used to illustrate the main points of my summary.

2. THE FIRST PENN STATE CONFERENCE AND THE EMPLOYMENT SITUATION IN 1974

The physics employment situation in 1974 was simply summarized as grim. In spite of the warnings of Cartter[1] and of Grodzins[2] the physics community had not yet faced as a community the realities of the employment situation. That reality is illustrated in Fig. 1, taken from the proceedings of the Conference on Tradition and Change in Physics Graduate Education held at the Pennsylvania State University in August, 1974. About 1400 physics Ph.D.s were graduating per year in the United States. Yet there were only about 500 openings per year into permanent traditional careers in academia, industry, and government.

The first Penn State Conference made no formal recommendations. Yet a consensus developed on the value of quite a few proposed partial solutions. Few of these proposals were new — some had appeared in the "Bromley Report".[4] None of these proposed measures provided a complete solution of the economic problems; indeed they came to be known as 5 and 10% solutions. The informal recommendations of that conference were:

a) Graduate Enrollment: There should be no increase in physics graduation enrollment in the foreseeable future. We have no present knowledge of the capacity of non-traditional fields to absorb physicists 5 or 10 years from now. And it is these fields which must already provide 500 new permanent careers each year. The American educational machine has a very quick response, and a sudden need for physicists, if it should develop, could be filled in 4 or 5 years.

b) Annual Manpower Reports: Physics manpower reports with projections of the type made in this article should be issued annually. Every physics department should have a faculty member expert in the manpower statistics and projections, so that the student has an immediate source of information.

c) Program Variations: Physics departments should continue to experiment with different variations on the traditional graduate program. Economic constraints prevent a single department from trying out too many different variations.

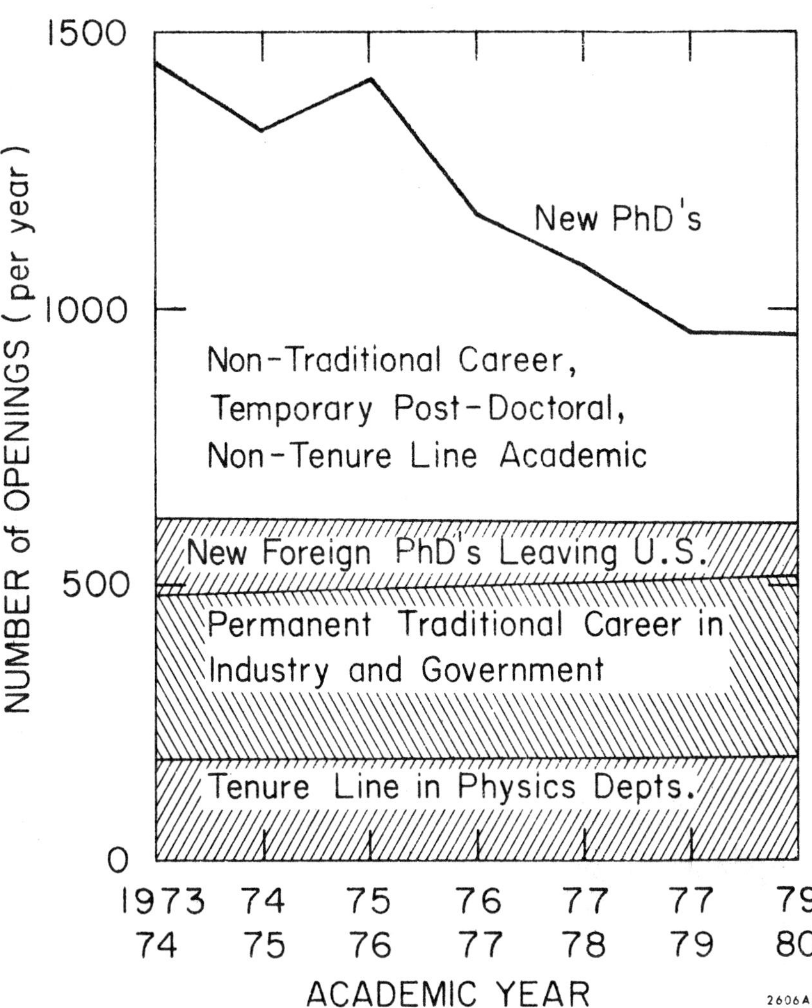

FIG. 1. Projected number of new physics Ph.D.'s awarded per year, and physics career openings per year for the United States from the 1974 Conference on Tradition and Change in Physics Graduate Education held at The Pennsylvania State Univ.

d) Faculty Attitude: The attitude of physics faculties toward careers in applied physics, engineering type physics, and public interest physics should change toward a greater acceptance of these careers. They should be accepted as equal to the traditional careers in the hierarchy of values of the physics community. A change in the reward structure of physics to reinforce the change in attitude should be considered.

e) Applied Physics: Physics departments should establish ties with applied research laboratories in industry, government and other institutions. These ties may influence the selection of research areas at the university departments, may lead to greater awareness by the faculty of emerging technologies, and bring about a greater involvement by faculty and students in cross-disciplinary contacts.

f) Non-traditional Fields: It should be made clear to each student early in graduate school that there is at least a 50% probability that he will have to build a permanent career in a non-traditional field of physics or in a field completely out of physics. The student should design his graduate program accordingly.

g) Career Mobility Among Older Physicists: For example: during his sabbatical a Professor might be required by his institution to work in an area outside his specialty. He might end up liking the new area, leave his old career, and make a job for a young physicist. Department policies might, through the offer of seed money or reduced course load, encourage faculty members to try non-traditional fields, thus producing openings for young physicists in a traditional field.

3. THE CHANGES THAT HAVE OCCURRED IN THE 1974-1977 PERIOD

A. Employment Changes During 1974-1977. No substantial quantitative changes have occurred in physics employment in the past three years. For example: total academic employment has decreased slightly; new areas such as research and development in enery have not produced large numbers of new positions; and the flow of Ph.D. physicists into non-traditional fields has continued. Some qualitative changes have occurred. As is discussed in many papers in the Proceedings, the movement of Ph.D. physicists into non-traditional field is being done with increasing ingenuity on the part of those making the move, and it is meeting with increased acceptance in the physics community. In particular, thru the APS Congressional Fellowship Program and thru individual institutions there have been an increasing number of physicists building careers in state and national government outside of the agencies which traditionally employed physicists.

B. Physics Education Changes During 1974-1977. To survey the physics education changes which have occurred in the 1974 to 1977 period I shall use the first Penn State Conference informal recommendations as a guide (Sec. 2.). I do not mean to imply that these recommendations were particularly influential. But they do provide a yardstick with which to measure progress.

a. Graduate Enrollment. Figure 2, taken from the report of S.D. Ellis,[5] shows that rate of granting Ph.D.s has flattened out and will be flat until at least 1981. Since we have seen in the previous section that employment opportunities for permanent careers using physics have not increased; this is a desirable trend, and the hope of the first Penn State Conference has been fulfilled. I say hope because as shown in Table III (Friedlaender et al.[6]) less than 10% of physics departments have deliberately limited the number of physics majors at any level. It is the prospective physics students themselves, having assessed the career opportunities in physics, who have entered physics in reduced numbers.

b. Annual Manpower Reports. Physics employment and manpower is now being carefully and fully studied by the American Institute of Physics and by the Physics Manpower Panel of the American Physical Society. I need only refer the reader to the papers of M.D. Fiske, B.F. Porter, and D. Harrison in the Proceedings. In addition we have the reports of the A.I.P. manpower statistics division written by S.D. Ellis.[5] And in addition to employment studies we have very useful studies of attitudes and job satisfaction. For example D. Harrison's paper at this conference shows that physicists formerly in academic employment report just as favorable work environments in non-academic employment. And B.F. Porter's paper also reports encouraging findings as to job satisfaction. Thus the AIP and APS rate very high marks with respect to phsyics manpower studies.

Academia does not rate so well. Only about half[6] of all four-year college and university physics departments have a faculty member specifically designated to keep students informed of the overall employment situation.

c. Program Variations. New courses and programs have been introduced to help physics students prepare for non-traditional careers by about half of all physics departments (see App. II of this Proceedings). I think the introduction of new courses and options will occur rather slowly in the future for several reasons. First, it is the consensus of the physics community that the traditional core physics curriculum should be preserved. Second, the non-traditional careers open to physicists are very fragmented in their non-physics subjects as is shown by many of the talks at this Conference. Therefore it is difficult to justify any particular deviation from the traditional curriculum. Third, the stagnation in the size of physics faculties has prevented the extensive hiring of new faculty members from non-traditional fields. Finally there is not a strong demand for more changes in Ph.D. physics programs by industry. This is shown by Table V taken from J.R. Stevenson's paper in these Proceedings.

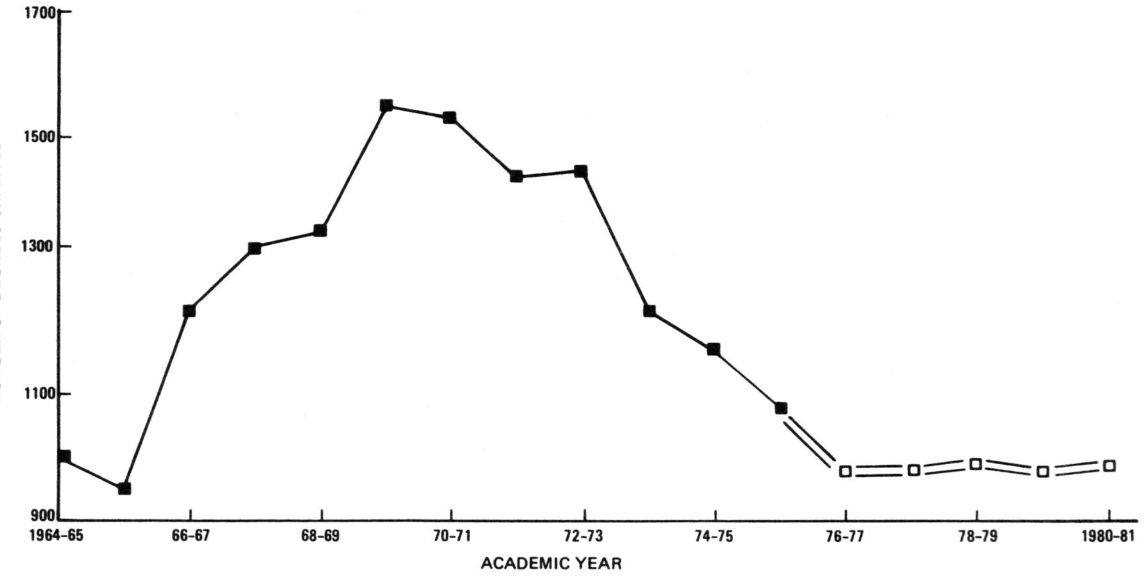

FIG. 2. Actual and projected number of physics doctorates granted 1964-1981 from Ref. 5.

TABLE V

The question leading to this table was, "We would like to know whether, in your opinion, a recent physics Ph.D. who has received a general and specialized physics education as outlined in (a) above (including your preference of specialization) has learned sufficient classical physics to enable him to make worthwhile contributions to the needs of your company. Will you indicate below the extent to which you would like to see changes made in the present standard undergraduate and/or graduate curriculum to include more, or less, classical physics. Use (U) for undergraduate, (G) for graduate curriculum, and (UG) for both. (The response is tabulated as (U,G).)"

	Much more emphasis	Somewhat more emphasis	Present emphasis about right	Less emphasis	Much less emphasis
i - Mechanics	(3,1)	(2,7)	(18,15)	(1,3)	(0,0)
ii - Thermodynamics kinetic theory	(4,4)	(9,11)	(11,10)	(1,2)	(0,0)
iii - Optics (Including applications of lasers)	(3,1)	(9,17)	(10,6)	(1,1)	(0,0)
iv - Acoustics	(3,2)	(4,8)	(15,16)	(2,1)	(0,0)
v - Elasticity & Heat Transfer	(1,2)	(7,6)	(14,14)	(1,2)	(0,0)
vi - Fluid Dynamics	(3,5)	(5,2)	(15,15)	(0,2)	(0,0)
vii - Electricity & Magnetism	(2,2)	(5,7)	(15,18)	(0,0)	(0,0)

Stevenson's comments on the table were: "Again we find that the relative emphasis seems about right. Some added emphasis on optics at the graduate level and thermodynamics and kinematic theory are desirable additions. Most of the curriculum concerns can be addressed within the present framework of the academic physics discipline."

d. Faculty Attitudes. The first Penn State Conference made a strong plea for a change in the attitudes which see a hierarchy of values in physics at the bottom. I don't know of any studies that have investigated whether such attitudes have changed in the physics community. However from this conference it is clear that physics faculties now know that the majority of their students must find careers in applied and non-traditional fields of physics.

e. Physics Departments Ties With Applied Research in Industry and Government. Tables VI and VII, taken from Friedlaender et al.,[6] shows that these ties have increased. In particular the APS Visiting Scientist Program directed by S. Millman continues to grow.

TABLE VI

The question addressed to Ph.D. institutions was, "Has your department taken any steps to increase the interaction of students with industry or governmental agencies, such as participation in the APS Visiting Scientists Program or allowing students to do doctoral research supervised in part by industrial physicists?" Some MS/BS institutions also answered

	MS/BS	Ph.D.	TOTAL
YES	12	37	49
NO	8	29	37
NO ANSWER	77	0	77
TOTAL	97	66	163

TABLE VII

Method of interaction with industry or government and comments.

Number of times item appeared	Method of interaction or comment
22	interact with industry, such as students doing thesis or internship in industry or grants from industry.
20	participate in APS Visiting Scientist program
11	interact with government agencies
5	already involved with industry or government -- nothing new

TABLE VII con't.

5	have a speakers program
2	have sponsored a conference on this topic
1	visits to industry
1	have set up industry committee to improve interaction with industrv

4. THE NEXT TEN YEARS

A. Employment. The statistics on present and future physics employment have been presented in several papers at this conference, and there is no need for me to repeat these statistics. I call your attention particularly to the very extensive and important work of Lee Grodzins which is described in his paper in these proceedings. However, I will summarize in Table VIII the consensus as to the expected changes in the absolute level of physics employment in various areas.

TABLE VIII

The expected change in the absolute level of physics employment in various areas in the next ten years.

AREA	PREDICTED CHANGE IN EMPLOYMENT	REASONS
Academia	slight decrease	enrollments are leveling off and institutions are increasing teaching loads or using more part-time instructors.
Federally funded research and development centers	constant or slight decrease	federal funding is constant for these centers or decreasing.
Traditional, high technology industry such as electronics & aerospace	slight decrease	their expenditures on research done by physicists is decreasing.
Traditional government employment such as NBS, NRL and DOD	slight decrease	budgets for research are constant or decreasing

TABLE VIII con't.

Engineering	will oscillate but no dramatic increase	this employment can only increase dramatically if U.S. economy improves.
Energy research and development	there seems to be more switches into this area or re-labeling of other research, than there is substantial growth in employment	much energy research does not use physicists, national energy policy is not fixed.
Public service and public interest science	the increase will be relatively large but the total numbers will still be small	
Biological and medical fields	substantial increase may occur	the use of high technology in health care is increasing rapidly, although using costs may limit growth.
Self-employment	some increase but probably not substantial in terms of total numbers	requires an entrenaural personality and a flourishing U.S. economy.

Table VIII is quantitative, but the conclusion is clear; no substantial increase in total physics employment can be expected in the next ten years. We also know that the rate of graduation of new physics Ph.D.'s is gradually coming into equilibrium with the rate of opening of employment opportunities in physics as the former rate decreases below 1000 per year. Therefore if that equilibrium is to be attained and mantained, the rate of graduation of new physics Ph.D.'s must stay below 1000 per year in the next ten years.

Grodzins in his paper presented at this conference is slightly more optimistic. He predicts, Fig. 3, the demand for new physicists might exceed the supply of new physicists in the mid 1980's. His conclusion is quantitatively not very different from mine, but it tends to sound more optimistic. One reason is that Grodzins expects a substantial rate of upgrading of positions now held by bachelor level physicists. Such upgrading is occurring in teaching and in government, but I believe the upgrading in teaching will cease because of economic pressures on all educational institutions.

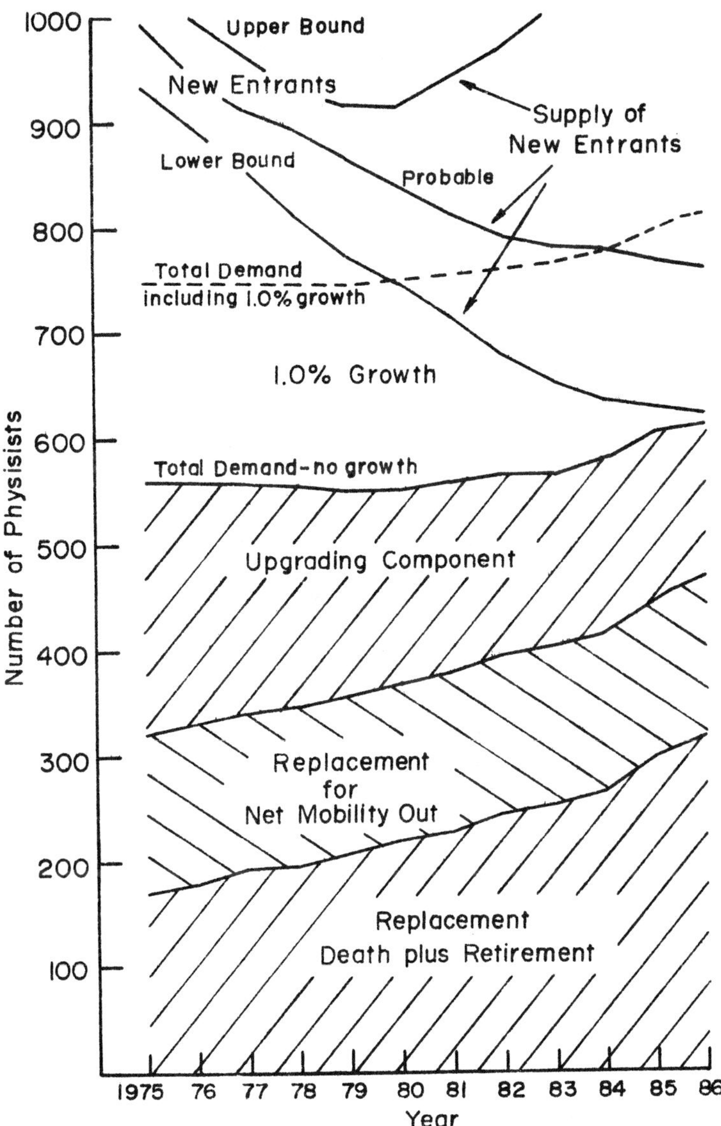

FIG. 3. Supply and demand for physics doctorates as predicted by L. Grodzins from his paper in these Proceedings.

Another reason for the difference between Grodzin's outlook and mine is that he reduces the number of new Ph.D.'s per year by 10% for those foreign students who immediately leave the U.S.; and then by 15% for those new Ph.D.'s who immediately seek employment outside of physics. I have some doubts as to whether this 15% actually wants to leave physics as soon as they get their Ph.D. or whether the poor employment prospects induce them to leave physics immediately. Therefore I am reluctant to reduce by this 15% the number of new physics Ph.D.'s per year who would like to have permanent careers in physics.

To summarize: _if_ physics graduate enrollments do not increase; _if_ the U.S. economy does not worsen; _if_ the trend of declining federal funds for basic research is halted; _if_ the trend of declining investment of private industry in physics related research is halted; then all U.S. physicists receiving Ph.D.'s in the next ten years will be able to find permanent careers using their physics training. There are four crucial _ifs_ here, so we certainly cannot be optimistic; and we certainly must not allow physics graduate enrollment to rise. That is the only _if_ the physics community can control.

There is yet another pessimistic factor of which I was not aware when I presented this talk at the conference. There is a nationwide trend to extend the mandatory retirement age or even to abolish a mandatory retirement age. It is now illegal in California for an employer to set a mandatory retirement age. And Congress is considering laws raising the minimum mandatory retirement age to age 70. Such laws could have a devastating effect on physics employment. For example, if the 10,000 academic physicists extend their "working age" by an average of three years each; then 1000 new academic jobs disappear (This assumes an average "working" life span of 30 years).

B. _Quality of Life for Physicists._ Whether or not we believe we will attain employment equilibrium in the next ten years, it is clear that the quality of life for physicists will worsen for the following reasons.

a) Average physicists' salaries in inflation corrected dollars are decreasing.

b) Average physicists' salaries relative to the total work force are declining.

c) Part-time and temporary employment is increasing in education.

d) In spite of the work of the APS Professional Concerns Committee their has been no substantial change in employee protection for physicists. (Other science professions are improving their employee protection.)

e) Federal funding for research and development in physics *per* physicist is decreasing.

Unfortunately just as the employment problem has hit the young physicist hardest, so will the burden of decreasing quality of life be borne by the young physicist disproportionately.

5. CONCLUSIONS

My conclusions are by this point obvious:

a) We should remain very cautious about the employment situation.

b) We must not let a false optimism increase graduate physics enrollments.

c) We must begin to discuss how to control or further reduce graduate physics enrollments in case physics employment decreases.

d) We must begin to pay attention to the quality of life for physicists, particularly for the young physicists.

REFERENCES

1. A.M. Cartter, Science *172* 132(1971); contains his earlier references.
2. L. Grodzins, Bull. Am. Phys. Soc. *16*, 737(1971). This is a Special Report of Economic Concerns Committee of the American Physical Society entitled *The Manpower Crisis in Physics*.
3. M.L. Perl and R.H. Good, Jr., Newsletter of the Forum on Physics and Society, Vol. 4, No. 1 (1975) page 15.
4. For a summary see D.A. Bromley, Physics Today, July (1972) page 23
5. S.D. Ellis, A.I.P. Pub. No. R-151.14(1977).
6. L.A. Friedlaender *et al.*, Appendix II of this proceedings.

ON TENURE AND POSTDOCTORAL APPOINTMENTS

Roger M. Herman
The Pennsylvania State University, University Park, PA 16802

ABSTRACT

Comments and recommendations are made concerning multiple postdoctoral appointments.

INTRODUCTION

One of the long-recognized benefits of the tenure system in U.S. colleges and universities is that if a person is not accepted for further promotion, or if a position simply doesn't exist within the institution, he may not be allowed to work for more than a specified period of time. The academic community has thereby seen that it is improper to retain professional staff beyond a specified length of time, without hopes of further advancement or job security.

It is precisely contrary to this intent that the present system of multiple postdoctoral appointments, which seems to be quite prevalent at the present time in the U.S.,[1] serves to retain hopeful young physicists within the physics community as a whole for long periods of time, without a firm guarantee of job security. Multi-institutional sequential appointments in nontenured positions certainly must have an effect upon a persons career quality similar to (or worse than) continued employment without tenure within a single institution. We are therefore perpetrating multi-insitutional employment practices which the individual institutions themselves have long ago deemed unethical.

To the author, to accept physicists into non-tenure-track positions after five (or certainly six) years of previous postdoctoral experience is unconscionable, regardless of which institutions have employed the person previously. The argument that it is indeed a satisfactory policy to do so because the prospective employee himself is dedicated to, and has a deep love of, his work is not acceptable. Indeed, every such person claims to so love his work; obviously everyone in his situation is bravely smiling on the outside, when applying for another position.

RECOMMENDATIONS

It is therefore the recommendation of this author that

1) Since, to the author's knowledge, no recent statistics on multiple postdoctoral appointments exist (the last such statistics,[1] acquired in 1973, showed that at least 10% of all postdocs had been employed in non-tenure-track positions for five or more years, with an increased percentage expected in the future), a new survey should be performed by the AIP, say, which would indicate the actual magnitude of the problem at the present time.

ISSN:0094-243X/78/308/$1.50

2) The AIP, together with its member institutions, should develop recommendations based on individual institutional tenure policies, as to a reasonable maximum length of time for a person to spend in multi-institutional postdoctoral experience, with the clear implication that to hold physicists in such employment beyond this point is deemed unethical.

REFERENCES

1. B. F. Porter, Post-Doctoral Positions in Physics and Astronomy, American Institute of Physics, New York, New York 1975.

So, for a composite of reasons, the undergraduate does not receive sufficient counseling in these occupational areas, and his course work often remains identical with his graduate school bound classmates. The assumption is often made that undergraduate preparation is sufficient to launch into industry; the company will train the new physicist to suit their own needs. This is fallacious. Employers find it more profitable to wait and select candidates who possess the specific knowledge they require.

The B.S. student now finds himself in a dilemma. He is caught between an educational world preparing him for one thing, and a working world that is going to expect knowledge from him that he does not possess. He wishes to remain in physics, but he is uncertain as to how he is going to appear employable at the same time. The most natural weapon for combating this communications obstacle is faculty understanding of the problem. With the change in employment trends, physics department responsibilities must shift to keep abreast of the times. Preparation for graduate work is necessary and important, but changing economic realities clearly show that other futures must be provided for. Students electing to terminate their studies at the B.S. level must of necessity curtail work in pure physics. Therefore, the emphasis should be shifted to providing supplemental knowledge that will make the graduate attractive to prospective employers. Awareness of the faculty advisor to the specialized needs of the B.S. physicist must be increased. If the advisor stays informed of industry problems and job opportunities, he is in a much better position to aid his students in properly investigating these new areas, by means of special courses or independent research. By so doing, he will insure that his B.S. students will possess the necessary entry skills that will make them salable to industry. In addition, the advisor can serve as a link between industry and the student, providing each with a better understanding of what the other has to offer. The student gains a good understanding of industry requirements through this, and the companies, as prospective employers, gain a better understanding of what a physicist can do for them.

Faculty awareness alone, though, is not sufficient. Physics departments must examine their curricula and work to implement changes which will plug this gap. The two program approach, offering pure <u>and</u> applied physics simultaneously, is not flexible enough and is too expensive for many small departments to operate. A program that is centered around the basic physics core, with available electives and supplementary courses to suit individual needs should prove to be ideal. It should be kept in mind, though, that the more flexible the program is, the stronger will be the guidance required to execute the program effectively. Every effort must be made to expose students to new areas of application for their physics training, no matter what the program. This will provide a direct relation of course work to the needs of industry.

Obviously, this is a rather difficult task for a department to pursue on its own. Information on physics-related fields is often unclear or hard to obtain concerning the necessary preparation to enter these areas. It is with this in mind that we ask the American Institute of Physics for help. The AIP must give increased attention to the educational and employment needs of the B.S. physicist. Because of the diversity of physics-related fields, we recommend that the AIP publish specific opportunities brochures aimed at the B.S. level. These brochures should contain manpower statistics on specific opportunities available to B.S. graduates, such as geophysics, microscopy, solid-state electronics, and computer science. These would be accompanied by a listing of the requisite skills necessary for employment in these specific jobs and the background course work required for each. These publications will greatly aid the development of curricula by physics departments to meet the current and future needs of the B.S. graduate.

Furthermore, AIP must reexamine its philosophy of what is physics and what is a physicist to increase the role of the B.S. graduate. In this manner, a better professional standing would be accorded the bachelor's degree, and the holder would be received into the scientific community as a useful, contributing member, rather than an appendage. AIP should also serve as a direct link between prospective employers and B.S. graduates by bringing them together more effectively through its Placement Service. College placement organizations often work well within the geographic vicinity of the institution, but they cannot offer the advantage of nationwide contacts that the AIP can supply. This will add official recognition to the B.S. status, and serve as a good source of feedback on industry needs. To further the understanding of manpower and training requirements, AIP should begin immediately to gather data on the degree of success that B.S. recipients have enjoyed in all fields during the past ten years, and compare this to the level of success that B.S. physicists working in specialized fields have attained. This will serve as an excellent indicator of the suitability of undergraduate preparation in physics to the actual demands of the working environment.

We hope that these comments have been favorably received, and that the points touched upon here will generate positive action for the benefit of the entire physics community.

Comments From Physics Students Concerning the Conference on Changing Career Opportuntiies for Physicists

Patrick A. Dreher, Univ. of Chicago, Chicago, Illinois 60637

On Tuesday evening at the Picnic at Stone Valley Pavillion, 17 graduate and undergraduate students gathered to discuss their reactions and observations concerning the conference itself, the material presented, and their own career plans. I have received the following written comments and observations submitted by some of these students of the Tuesday evening discussion group for inclusion in the conference proceedings. Hopefully their ideas and comments may also help other physics students in formulating their own career plans.

****

Comments by Deborah Van Vechten, Univ. of Maryland, College Park

I wish to comment on Martin Perl's suggestion[1] that the physics community place some formal limit on the number or cumulative duration of the postdocs an individual can take. Presumably, Perl's motivation is two fold: 1) He fears that the indentured servitude of being a postdoc is being transformed into a form of slave labor by the disappearance of permanent jobs for these people to progress into, 2) When he sees the pain and depression of postdocs at SLAC about to leave for a less desirable postdoc or job, he identifies with their plight and feels uncomfortable. Were the maximum duration of the postdoc phase limited by the entire physics community, individuals unable to find academic employment by the deadline would be forced to look elsewhere for a job. By virtue of being externally imposed, some individuals might find this easier to deal with than having to decide whether to give up trying on their own. The endpoint would be clear and inescapable, a reality everyone would know about in advance and presumably prepare to accept. This inevitability could be used by job-secure individuals such as Perl to protect their own feelings -- "He knew what he was getting into when he took the job. I'm not responsible for his being denied the benefits I enjoy."

While I appreciate Martin's concern, I oppose his suggestion on two grounds. First, the fact is that many people denied tenure at one school eventually receive it at another[2]. Thus Perl's time limit would, in fact, be much more absolute than the AAUP's 6 year up or out rule. Second, and more important, such a time limit constricts the individual's ability to make his own decisions about his own future, to be his own master. It reminds me of the practice of not offering a married female a job unless something can also be offered her husband. Presumably the individual is doing something productive or else he would be unable to keep securing successive postdocs. The transience, relatively low pay and lack of professional autonomy and respect of the typical postdoc is not inobvious to the holder of such a position. That some hang on so long -- hoping to luck out and get a tenure track position -- should give

ISSN:0094-243X/78/314/$1.50

some idea of how hard and painful it can be to let go of the image of oneself that has motivated and assuaged the discomforts and frustrations of the past 7 or more years of effort. Externally imposing a deadline doesn't circumvent this pain, just diffuses it onto the "society" at large and encourages "If only. . ." thoughts. A deadline diminishes the individual's ability to learn from his experience and to come away from it stronger. What the individual needs instead is compassionate counseling, beginning no later than the first postdoc, discussing what his realistic prospects for an academic job are and, if appropriate, how else he might productively use his talents. Indeed, as Bob Yaes' departure[3] from physics into medicine shows, even without such counseling most people in the perennial postdoc groove will eventually decide they have had enough. Is the reduction in guilt experienced by the professional gate keepers truly worth the extra deprivation of the people unfortunate enough to be affected by such a deadline?

1. Martin Perl, Session H this conference.

2. In his 1974 "Tradition & Change in Physics Graduate Education" conference talk, Lee Grodzins quoted the figures for the early 1970s as 1 in 6 overall, 1 in 4 for those denied tenure at the most prestigious schools.

3. Robert Yaes, talk F10 this conference.

****

Comments by Patrick A. Dreher, Univ of Chicago, Chicago, IL 60637

The information and observations presented to us in the Changing Careers Conference for Physicists at Penn State are of primary importance to both graduate and undergraduate students in physics. We are the people who will encounter the uncertain employment prospects after graduation and stand to lose the most, both in time and money, by continuing our studies in this field. However, when the students gathered together Tuesday evening, I don't recall anyone saying that this conference had convinced them to throw in the towel completely and abandon their studies in physics.

What did seem to emerge was a consensus that if a graduate student in physics expects to carve a professional career for himself after graduate school (based on his physics training that he has acquired), he must not only present his research credentials in the form of publications and a Ph.D. diploma, but must also convince his employer that he is a creative, flexible, and innovative person, capable of adapting himself and using the training he has acquired to tackle problems and concerns within the job that is being offered (regardless of how well this job compares to the traditional areas of physics). The graduate student who possesses these abilities will be far more likely to succeed than the student who does not and has no interest in cultivating these attributes while also obtaining his formal graduate physics education.

Comments by Ted. E. Senator, MIT, Physics Dept. Cambridge, MA 02139

The main point that I believe a student should take away from this Conference regarding the planning of his own career is to be flexible. Students should not feel that non-traditional careers are second-class and, more importantly, the physics community (which is currently comprised almost entirely of people in traditional careers) should not give the impression that a non-traditional career is followed only by those who can't "measure up" to the standards necessary for following a traditional career. That physics is a widely applicable training and that non-traditional careers are not second-rate are two general principles all physics students would do well to accept.

As the physics community widens its standards as to what constitutes an acceptable career for a physicist, it must convince those who are making employment decisions; i.e., corporate executives and government officials, to hire physicists. Pontificating that "of course the world needs physicists in order to solve all its increasingly complex technical problems" is of little use if the only people who believe that are themselves members of the physics community. No one should be encouraged to enter physics on the basis of such a statement. The only meaningful statement would have to be of the type, "Projections, according to a definite methodology, are for a certain number of positions to be available during the next 10 years."

****

Comments by Dennis S. Pritchard. P.O. Box 622, Aberdeen, MD 21001

Attending the conference on Changing Career Opportunities for Physicists was well worth my time and effort. It gave me some new insights into the problem of hirability in the physics field, and confirmed some of my existing ideas on the subject.

My main concern at this point in time is: What can I do to make myself more hirable? Clearly, it is not to my advantage to pursue a Ph.d. in physics as a goal of itself. Acquiring a Ph.d. simply for the sake of having one, then hoping to find a well paying job later is an outmoded concept. A specific employment goal must be in existence before the Ph.d. is taken. Also, more programs should be devised for the pursuit of a degree that is multidisciplinary and less specialized. Employment opportunities for many will be less and less optimum until this is accomplished. There is no light at the end of a long dark tunnel for most ultraspecialists in physics.

It is to me a deplorable state of affairs when such a highly skilled group of individuals as physics Ph.d.s has a difficult time earning a decent living. Physicists are a special interest group. I say it is time we started acting accordingly. As it was aptly stated at the conference: "If we do not start doing something about the situation ourselves, it will be handled for us in a manner not to our liking".

TWO RESPONSES TO THE CAREER CONFERENCE

Shaun P. Morrissey
Carnegie-Mellon University, Pittsburgh, Pa. 15213

Two particular themes presented themselves throughout the conference. The first, and most obvious, had to do with manpower statistics. The latter theme described what is required of the new Ph.D. physicist for economic survival or success. The first provides some motivation for change, the second appears to support maintaining certain elements of the status quo.

During the conference there was a strong effort to be quantitative about the manpower situation. It was a noble effort, but it was unsuccessful. The data was not available, or was open to challenge on grounds of timeliness or sampling bias. This highlighted two separate problems.

First, it was extremely difficult to define the terms "physics," and "physicist," for demographic purposes.[1] The elements of this problem are detailed in other papers in the proceedings.

Second, there was a lack of relevant raw data. The speakers who did manage to be quantitative all spoke of difficulties in getting data, and even greater difficulties in getting current data.[2] If future decisions by students, faculty, and government are to be vaguely reasonable, this information must be available. The problems noted at the conference show the need for a mechanism that keeps track of the demographics and the economics of the profession.[3]

The second theme revolves around the discussions and the anecdotal information provided by the conference. I will itemize these points, and suggest an interpretation.

Historically, physicists are employed during the immature stages of the development of new technologies. As fields mature, the employment of physicists declines.

The undergraduate degree in physics is widely accepted as good preparation for advanced work in other fields.

There is a crying need for people with broad scientific and technical understanding in local, state, and federal government, provided they can face political realities.

The feeling, articulated by representatives of large industrial laboratories, that physicists bring a special fundamental viewpoint to their problems(This was cited as a reason for <u>not</u> changing curricula).

The success of physicists in regulatory agencies, and in the Congressional Fellow programs, where a "generalist" attitude is required.

The willingness, and the ability, to change fields shown by those physicists in non-traditional careers.

The common element in all of the above is a need for a combination of analytical skill, imaginative problem solving, and, above all, flexibility. People who have the flexibility and creativity to respond to additional concerns, political, social, and scien-

ISSN:0094-243X/78/317/$1.50

tific, will be successful. My point is that the curriculum for the Ph.D. in Physics has little, or nothing, to do with the success of the new Ph.D. in the world today. The individual must be imaginative, capable, flexible, and willing to take a broad view. The curriculum seems largely irrelevant, except that it allows or encourages the development of such an individual without narrowing his or her perspective. Thus, maintaining the traditional structure of the degree program seems prudent.

Overall, the need for demographic work has been demonstrated. Also, the content of advanced work should remain unchanged. The concern must be with keeping the graduate environment sufficiently challenging.

---

1. Often, working in physics was part of the definition of being a physicist. Dr. R.J. Yaes rather colorfully pointed out that if physicists are defined as people employed in physics, there is no such thing as an unemployed physicist.
2. I feel the conference may be unique in this one respect. I do not ever expect to hear another group of physicists giving papers who were so willing to "poke holes" in their own data and results.
3. Lord, Forgive Me for this call to additional bureaucracy!

Questionnaire on the Conference

John P. Decker
Physics Department
Stephen F. Austin State University
Nacogdoches, Texas 75961

(The following was abstracted by the editor from a report of Professor John Decker to Professor Roland Good, Jr., the Conference co-chairman by permission of Professor Decker.) Twenty-two students who attended the Conference were polled and twelve responded. They were asked to answer the following questionnaire and to add additional comments. Professor Decker reported:

> "Only one student responding left the Conference more discouraged regarding job opportunities than when he arrived while six were more encouraged by the Conference."
>
> "Half of those responding will make some changes in their curriculum because of their attendance at the Conference. Only three of the twelve respondents are undergraduates and eight are studying toward the Ph.D."
>
> "The students indicated a strong confidence in the accuracy of the picture presented by the Conference."

RESPONSES

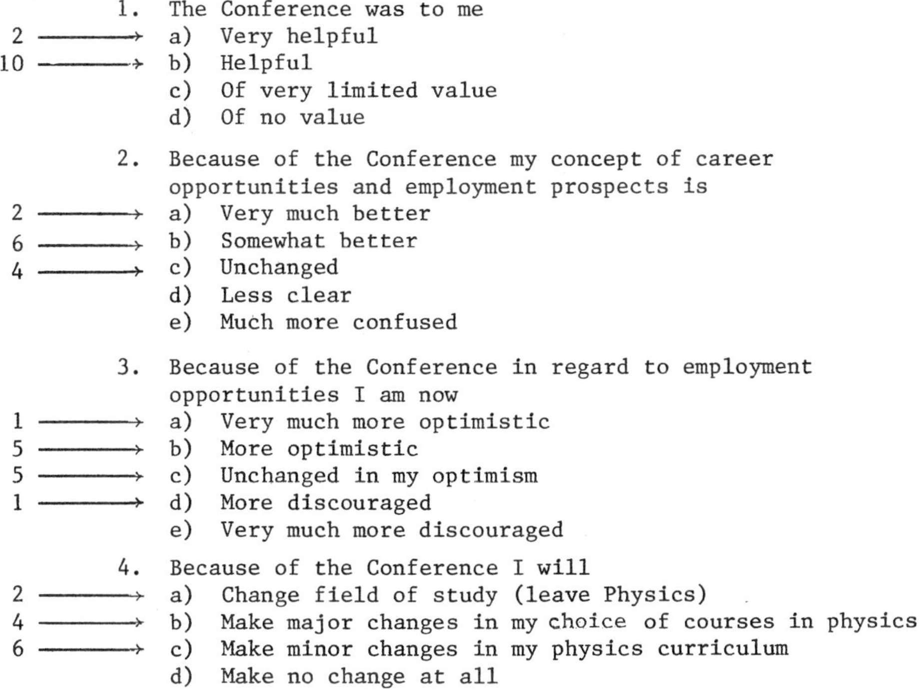

1. The Conference was to me
   - 2 → a) Very helpful
   - 10 → b) Helpful
   - c) Of very limited value
   - d) Of no value

2. Because of the Conference my concept of career opportunities and employment prospects is
   - 2 → a) Very much better
   - 6 → b) Somewhat better
   - 4 → c) Unchanged
   - d) Less clear
   - e) Much more confused

3. Because of the Conference in regard to employment opportunities I am now
   - 1 → a) Very much more optimistic
   - 5 → b) More optimistic
   - 5 → c) Unchanged in my optimism
   - 1 → d) More discouraged
   - e) Very much more discouraged

4. Because of the Conference I will
   - 2 → a) Change field of study (leave Physics)
   - 4 → b) Make major changes in my choice of courses in physics
   - 6 → c) Make minor changes in my physics curriculum
   - d) Make no change at all

ISSN:0094-243X/78/319/$1.50

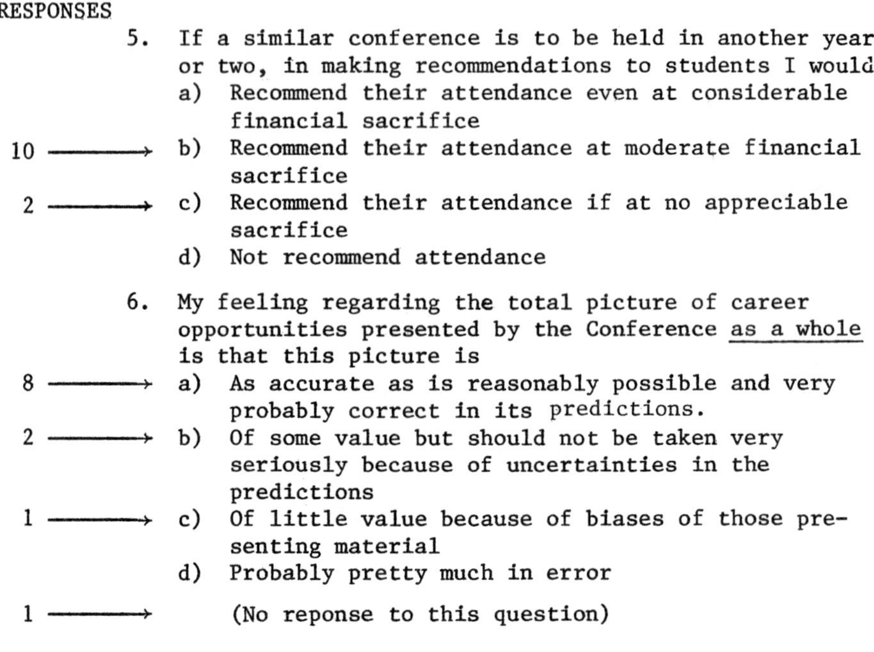

RESPONSES

5. If a similar conference is to be held in another year or two, in making recommendations to students I would
   a) Recommend their attendance even at considerable financial sacrifice

10 ⟶ b) Recommend their attendance at moderate financial sacrifice

2 ⟶ c) Recommend their attendance if at no appreciable sacrifice

   d) Not recommend attendance

6. My feeling regarding the total picture of career opportunities presented by the Conference as a whole is that this picture is

8 ⟶ a) As accurate as is reasonably possible and very probably correct in its predictions.

2 ⟶ b) Of some value but should not be taken very seriously because of uncertainties in the predictions

1 ⟶ c) Of little value because of biases of those presenting material

   d) Probably pretty much in error

1 ⟶ (No reponse to this question)

Classification of the level of study of those responding:

Ph.D. - 8; M.S. - 1; Sr. - 1; Jr. - 2.

Appendix I

REPORT ON A SURVEY OF RECENT CHANGES WHICH HAVE OCCURRED IN THE EDUCATION OF PHYSICISTS IN THE UNITED STATES

Lenore A. Friedlaender, Leslie B. Klein and Martin L. Perl

Stanford Linear Accelerator Center
Stanford, California 94305

I. Purpose

The information collected in this survey was presented at the 1977 conference on "Changing Career Opportunities for Physicists" held August 1-3, 1977 at the Pennsylvania State University. Since the early 1970's it had become increasingly difficult for young physicists to find permanent careers in the traditional areas of physics employment. In particular, the number of tenure line openings for physicists in colleges and universiites had decreased drastically. The 1974 Penn State Conference on "Tradition and Change in Physics Graduate Education" investigated and summarized the career situation at that time. The purpose of this survey was to discover what changes have occurred in the training of physicists since 1974. We were specifically interested in the training of students who intend to have careers in physics or who, if they are in interdisciplinary fields, intend to make substantial use of physics in their careers. This survey was not concerned with changes that have been made in physics service courses for engineers, other sciences, or non-science majors. The 1974 conference emphasized PhD level training. The 1977 conference went beyond the 1974 conference in that it also considered the training of physicists whose highest degree is at the bachelor or masters level. For this reason we asked for information at all three levels.

II. Sample Size

The survey questionnaire was sent to all departments of physics or applied physics in the United States who are listed in the 1976-77 AIP Directory of Physics and Astronomy Staff Members and who have more than five faculty members. Table I gives the sample size.

TABLE I

	J.C. Junior College	MS/BS Highest degree granted is bachelors or masters	Ph.D. Highest degree granted is doc-doctorate	TOTAL
number of questionnaires sent	40	196	163	399
number of questionnaires returned	4	97	66	167
per cent returned	10.0	49.5	44.9	41.9

With respect to doctoral level institutions, for the 25 listed in the AIP Directory of Physics and Astronomy Staff Members as granting the largest number of physics Ph.D.s, 44% responded.

ISSN:0094-243X/78/321/$1.50

III. Questions on Enrollment

Question 1A. Does your department have a faculty member who has the specific duty to keep students informed of the physics employment situation, career opportunities for physicists in other fields, the limited openings in some traditional areas of physics (such as university teaching) etc.?

TABLE II

Answers to question 1A.

	JC	MS/BS	Ph.D	TOTAL
YES	2	39	41	82
NO	2	58	25	85
TOTAL	4	97	66	167

Questions 1B. In view of the more limited physics employment opportunities of the 1970's compared to the 1960's, has your department limited the number of physics majors at any level?

TABLE III

Answers to question 1B.

	JC	MS/BS	Ph.D	TOTAL
YES	0	5	10	15
NO	4	92	55	151
NO ANSWER	0	0	1	1
TOTAL	4	97	66	166

A summary of comments associated with question 1B is given in TABLE IV. These numbers have no statistical significance they simply indicate the number of comments of each type made.

TABLE IV

Number and types of comments associated with question 1B.

	MS/BS	Ph.D.	TOTAL
There has been a natural decrease in enrollment or self-limitation by the students themselves has occurred	13	8	21
Limited financial aid has decreased enrollments	0	9	9
Students given discouraging advice about employment situation	4	1	5
Ph.D. program abolished	1	2	3
Enrollment increasing or would like it to increase	2	3	5
All students get jobs	0	3	3

IV. Doctoral Level Courses and Programs

Questions 2A and 2B concerned doctoral level physics courses and programs.

Question 2A. **In view of the changing career opportunities, has your department introduced any new courses since 1974? Please list such courses.**

TABLE V

Answers to question 2A.

	Ph.D
YES	28
NO	35
NO ANSWER	3
TOTAL	66

TABLE VI

Doctoral level courses listed in response to question 2A.

number of times items appeared	course type
8	lasers, holography and modern optics
6	plasma physics and magnetohydrodynamics
4	radiology and radiation biology
4	superconductivity and cryogenic technology
4	space physics
3	surface science
3	computer science
3	applied physics
3	energy and environment
3	fluid mechanics
2	medical physics
2	biophysics
2	materials science
2	digital electronics
2	solid state physics
1	oceanography
1	meteorology
1	mechanics of continuous media
1	advanced electricity and magnetism
1	mathematical physics
1	spectroscopy
1	phase transitions and critical phenomena
1	modern atomic physics
1	acoustics
1	nature of the universe

Questions 2B. **Has your department made any substantial changes in the requirements for a doctorate in physics, introduced any new doctoral level options or programs or made any other changes which would help students go into applied or interdisciplinary fields? Please briefly describe the changes.**

TABLE VII

Answers to question 2B.

YES	19
NO	45
NO ANSWER	2
TOTAL	66

TABLE VIII

Doctoral level options and programs and other comments in response to question 2B.

Number of times item appears	**Option, program, or comment**
3	medical physics option introduced
3	biophysics option introduced
3	mineralogy, geophysics and petroleum engineering options introduced
2	teaching physics through Ph.D. level
2	fewer courses required for Ph.D.
2	interdisciplinary studies encouraged
1	solid state program introduced
1	applied research program introduced
1	Ph.D. thesis in industry program introduced
1	Ph.D. program in interdisciplinary physics introduced
1	restructure of masters and Ph.D. programs into: 1) experimental and theoretical physics 2) medical physics, 3) computer physics, 4) teaching
1	summer program in electronics instrumentation, liquid crystal physics, and research methods
1	computer programming required for major
1	foreign language requirement removed
1	cooperation with plasma physics program in Engineering school
1	some Ph.D. thesis done in Medical school and in Radiology Dept
1	there has been a shift of emphasis from theory to experiment
1	federal funding allows energy research
1	planning Ph.D. program in medical physics and biophysics

Question 2C. Has your department taken any steps to increase the interaction of students with industry or governmental agencies, such as participation in the APS Visiting Scientists Program or allowing students to do doctoral research supervised in part by industrial physcisits?

TABLE IX

Answers to question 2C. Some MS/BS institutions also answered.

	MS/BS	Ph.D	TOTAL
YES	12	37	49
NO	8	29	37
NO ANSWER	77	0	77
TOTAL	97	66	163

TABLE X

Method of interaction with industry or government and comments.

Number of times item appears	Method of interaction or comment
22	interact with industry, such as students doing thesis or internship in industry or grants from industry
20	participate in APS Visiting Scientist program
11	interact with government agencies
5	already involved with industry or government -- nothing new
5	have a speakers program
2	have sponsored a conference on this topic
1	visits to industry
1	have set up industry committee to improve interaction with industry

V. Masters and Bachelor Level Courses and Programs

Questions 3A and 3B concern masters and bachelors level courses and programs. Note that MS/BS refers to institutions whose highest degree granted in physics is a masters or bachelors; Ph.D. refers to institutions which grant degrees through Ph.D. level.

Question 3A. Has your department introduced any new undergraduate level physics courses since 1974 which would help bachelor level physics majors move more easily into applied or interdisciplinary fields or into non-traditional physics careers? Please list such courses.

TABLE XI

Answers to question 3A.

	MS/BS	Ph.D.	TOTAL
YES	51	33	84
NO	36	33	69
TOTAL	87	66	153

TABLE XII

Courses listed in response to question 3A.

Number of times course mentioned	Courses
21	energy and environment
21	optics and lasers
20	electronics
15	biophysics
10	medical physics
8	astrophysics and astronomy
8	science and humanities courses
8	microprocessors and digital logic
7	fluid dynamics
7	computer programming, computer science
7	radiology
7	engineering (mechanical, electrical)
6	advanced laboratory
6	acoustics
6	geophysics
4	oceanography
3	thermodynamics
3	cooperative education and work experinece
2	plasma physics
1	meteorology
1	chemical physics
1	spectroscopy
1	planetarium management
1	surface physics
1	cryogenic technology
1	wave phenomena
1	mathematical physics
1	applications of elementary physics
1	hydrology
1	bioelectronics

Some comments in response to question 3A were: physics requirements have been reduced; the mechanics sequence has been lengthened; there is emphasis on inter-disciplinary studies; a curriculum in applied physics has been proposed; a number physics instrumentation course is being planned; a laser course is being planned; a 5 year physics-engineering program has been reintroduced; a biophysics course is being planned.

Questions 3B. Has your department initiated any new options or programs at the undergraduate or masters level for the purpose described in question 3A? Please briefly describe such options or programs.

TABLE XIII

Answers to question 3B.

	MS/BS	Ph.D.	TOTAL
YES	48	24	72
NO	47	41	88
NO ANSWER	2	1	3
TOTAL	97	66	163

TABLE XIV

Options or programs listed in response to question 3B.

number of times item was listed	options or program
13	engineering physics and joint programs with engineering
9	energy and environment
9	geophysics
8	computer science and digital systems
7	medical physics
6	teaching physics
5	electronics and instrumentation
5	applied physics
5	biophysics
4	chemistry and physics, and chemical physics
4	interdisciplinary programs
3	oceanography
3	cooperative education
3	mathematical physics
3	BA in physics
2	atmospheric physics and meteorology
2	radiology
2	acoustics
2	astrophysics and astronomy
2	materials science
1	nuclear science
1	program for industrial physicists to get MS
1	early research option
1	technician program
1	science, technology and society option

1	optics and lasers
1	plasma physics
1	5 year BA-BS program
1	physics and public policy
1	business option

VI. General Comments

Questions 4. Any remarks you care to make on any aspects of this problem would be very welcome.

TABLE XV

Comments made in response to question 4.

number of times comment was mentioned	comment
11	no difficulty placing graduates in jobs
6	more interdisciplinary courses or programs needed
6	courses and research are more applied now
3	this survey was a good idea
3	department doesn't have resources to specialize in research areas
2	our job is to educate physicists, not to train workers
2	needing more teaching aids in career selection
1	physics is not engineering and it is not a social science.
1	demand for physicists is high in surface science areas and in nuclear engineering
1	program changes always follow a crisis too late
1	more emphasis on teaching needed
1	general interest courses are successful
	an office of industrial cooperation was created and is successful
1	due to low budget and low enrollment there is lots of pressure to "popularize" (make easier) physics courses
1	internships very successful
1	require thesis for BS; machine shop, glass-blowing, research experience and skills very helpful
1	more emphasis on laboratory work now

Appendix II — List of Participants

ANDERSON, Charles H.
Fellow of the Staff
RCA Laboratories
Princeton, NJ 08540

BARTLETT, Albert A.
Professor
University of Colorado
Dept. of Physics
Boulder, CO 80309

BAUTZ, Laura P.
Senior Staff Associate
National Science Foundation
1800 G Street, NW
Washington, D.C. 20550

BLETZACKER, Frank
Graduate Student
SUNY at Stony Brook
Dept. of Physics
Stony Brook, NY 11794

BLEULER, Ernest
Professor
Penn State
University Park, PA 16802

BLOCH, Alan
Consultant
Alan Bloch
333 East 30th Street
New York, NY 10016

BREITENBERGER E.
Professor of Physics
Ohio University
Clippinger Labs
Athens, OH 45701

BRODY, Burton
Assoc. Professor of Physics
Bard College
Annandale-on-Hudson
New York, NY 12504

BURNS, Jay
Dept. of Physics & Space Science
Florida Institute of Technology
Country Club Road
Melbourne, FL 32901

CARR, Howard
Physics Dept. Professor
Auburn University
Physicist Department
Auburn, AL 36830

CASPER, B. M.
Chairman
Carleton College
Physics Department
Northfield, MN 55057

CHERRY, Leonard V.
Assoc. Professor of Physics
Franklin and Marshall College
Department of Physics
Lancaster, PA 17604

CONWELL, Esther M.
Principal Scientist
Xerox
Xerox Square, W114
Rochester, NY 14644

COOPER, Martin J.
Physicist/Advisor, ASGA
ERDA
Room 3238, 20 Mass. Ave., NW
Washington, D.C. 20545

CROW, Terry T.
Professor of Physics
Mississippi State University
Box 5167
Mississippi State, MS 39762

DANIELS, Theodore C.
Professor
Gettysburg College
Gettysburg, PA 17325

DARNELL, Frederick J.
Associate Director of Research
DuPont Company
Experimental Station
Wilmington, DE 19898

DAVIDSON, J. P.
Professor & Chairman
University of Kansas
Dept. of Physics & Astronomy
Lawrence, KS 66044

DECKER, John P.
Head of Physics Department
Stephen F. Austin State Univ.
Box 3044 SFA Station
Nacogdoches, TX 75961

DOBBINS, James T., III
Student
University of North Carolina
Chapel Hill, NC 27514

DONAHUE, Douglas J.
Professor
University of Arizona
Tuscon, AZ 87516

DREHER, Patrick A.
Grad Student
University of Chicago
403 Harper Hall
Chicago, IL 60637

FARRELL, David E.
Assoc. Professor
CASE-WRU
Physics Department
Cleveland, OH 44106

FEHRS, Mary H.
Assistant Professor of Physics
Lafayette College
Olin Hall
Easton, PA 18042

FISKE, Milan D.
Physicist
General Electric Corp. R&D
P. O. Box 8
Schenectady, NY 12301

FLEMING, Carolyn G.
Student
Virginia Commonwealth University
2416 Bryan Park Avenue
Richmond, VA 23228

FRAIME, Charles R.
Associate Professor
USAF Academy
Department of Physics
USAF Academy, CO 80840

FRANKEL, Richard
Physicist
MIT National Magnet Lab.
Cambridge, MA 02139

FRANZ, Judy R.
Associate Professor of Physics
Indiana University
Department of Physics
Bloomington, IN 47401

FRIEDLANDER, David
Scientific Programmer
Oceanroutes Inc.
3260 Hillview Avenue
Palo Alto, CA 94304

GALLAGHER, William J.
Graduate Student
MIT
Building NW14-3111
Cambridge, MA 02135

GESELOWITZ, David B.
Professor
Penn State
University Park, PA 16802

GILCHRIST, Jason
Professor
North Carolina A&T University
Greensboro, NC 27401

GINSBERG, D. M.
Professor of Physics
University of Illinois
265 Physics Building
Urbana, IL 61801

GLABERSON, William I.
Dir. of Grad. Program, Physics
Rutgers Uniersity
Department of Physics
New Brunswick, NJ 08903

GLANTZ, Stanton A.
Assistant Professor
Univ. of Calif. at SF
1186M
San Francisco, CA 94143

GLICKSTEIN, Stanley S.
Fellow Scientist
Westinghouse Bettis Atomic
Power Lab
P.O. Box 79
W. Mifflin, PA 15122

GOLDBERG, Joshua N.
Syracuse Univ.
Dept. of Physics
Syracuse, NY 13210

GRIESACKER, P. B.
Chairman Dept. of Physics
Gannon College
Perry Square
Erie, PA 16501

GRIFFIN, James J.
Professor
University of Maryland
Physics Department
College Park, Maryland 20903

GRODZINS, Lee
Professor
MIT
26-421
Cambridge, MA 02139

JACOBS, Don
Assistant Professor
The College of Wooster
Physics Department
Wooster, OH 44691

HAMELL, Dennis
Research Manager
3M Company
St. Paul, MN 55101

HANSEN, Uwe J.
Professor of Physics
Indiana State University
Physics Department
Terre Haute, IN 47809

HARRIS, Sigmund P.
Associate Professor of Physics
Los Angeles Pierce College
6201 Winnetka Avenue
Woodland Hills, CA 91371

HARRISON, Kent
Professor
Brigham Young University
Provo, Utah 84601

HARVEY, John
Grad Student
University of Rochester
Wilson Lab
Ithica, NY 14850

HERNDON, David
Student
College of William and Mary
510-A Brookhaven National Lab
Upton, NY 11973

HILLARD, G. Barry
Grad Student
University of Illinois
Department of Physics
Urbana, IL 61801

HILLS, Richard G.
Associate Professor
Weber State College
Physics Department
Ogden, UT 84408

HOUK, T. William
Associate Professor
Miami University
31 Cyller Hall
Oxford, OH 45056

HULM, John K.
Chemical Sciences Div.
Westinghouse Research Labs
Westinghouse R&D Center
Pittsburgh, PA 15235

JOHNSON, Fred T.
Professor of Physics
Eastern Michigan University
Physics & Astro. Department
Ypsilanti, MI 48197

JOHNSON, Robert A.
Assistant Professor
Bucknell University
Physics Department
Lewisburg, PA 17837

JONES, Charles E.
Professor
East Texas State University
Physics Department
Commerce, TX 75428

JONES, Lewis H.
Research Associate
University of Maryland
Dept. of Physics & Astronomy
College Park, MD 20742

JOSSEM, E. L.
Dept. of Physics
The Ohio State University
174 W. 18th Street
Columbus, OH 43210

JUDD, Floyd L.
Chair Person
California State University
Physics Dept.
Fresno, CA 93711

KAHN, Peter B.
Dept. of Physics
SUNY at Sony Brook
Stony Brook, NY 11794

KASDAN, Stuart H.
Instructor of Physics
Princeton University
Dept. of Physics, Jadwin Hall
Princeton, NJ 08540

KAST, James R.
Grad student
Johns Hopkins University
Charles & 34th Streets
Baltimore, MD 21218

KECK, Winfield
Dept. of Physics
Lafayette College
113 Olin Hall
Easton, PA 18042

KELLY, William H.
Professor and Chairman
Michigan State University
Department of Physics
E. Lansing, MI 48824

KERN, Sanford
Associate Professor
Colorado State University
Dept. of Physics
Fort Collins, CO 80523

KHOURY, Bernard V.
Assoc. of American Univ.
One Dupont Circle, Suite 730
Washington, D.C. 20036

KLEBAN, Peter
Research Associate
University of Minnesota
Dept. of Chem. Engineering
421 Washington Avenue
Minneapolis, MN 55455

KONIGSBERG, Alvin S.
Professor
State University of New York
at New Poltz
New Poltz, NY 12561

KRAFT, David W.
Professor/Placement Consultant
New York University
American Institute of Physics
335 East 45th Street
New York, NY 10017

KRASNER, Sol
Assistant to the Chairman
University of Chicago
kkk0 E. 58th Street
Chicago, IL 60637

KRIEGER, Joseph B.
Chairman Physics Department
Brooklyn College
Avenue H & Bedford Avenue
Brooklyn, NY 11210

KURCK, James Maxwell
Grad Student
Princeton University
Physics Department
Princeton, NJ 08540

LADD, David S.
Grad Student
Georgia Tech
Box 37121
Atlanta, GA 30332

LANHFORD, William F.
Associate Professor
George Mason University
Physics Department
Fairfax, VA 22030

LIBOFF, Abraham R.
Professor
Oakland University
Rochester, MI 48063

LOH, E. L.
Chairman
Towson State University
Department of Physics
York Road
Baltimore, MD 21204

LONG, Howard C.
Professor of Physics
Dickinson College
Dept. of Physics & Astronomy
Carlisle, PA 17013

LUBKIN, Gloria
Senior Editor, Physics Today
American Institute of Physics
335 E. 45th Street
New York, NY 10017

MAK, George
Research Associate
Carnegie-Mellon University
4400 Fifth Avenue
Pittsburgh, PA 15213

McDERMOTT, Mark
Professor of Physics
University of Washington
Dept. of Physics - FM 15
Seattle, WA 98115

McGINNIS, Eugene A.
Professor of Physics
University of Scranton
Monroe Avenue, Loyola Hall
Scranton, PA 18510

McIRVINE, E. C.
Manager Technology Assessment
Xerox Corporation
800 Phillips Road, Bldg. 102
Webster, NY 14580

MERCER, Robert A.
Supervisor
Bell Laboratories
Bell Labs, Room 2F-602
Holmdel, NJ 07733

MESHKOV, Natalia
Assoc. Prof/Project Director
George Mason University
Physics Department
4400 University Drive
Fairfax, VA 22030

MILLER, Walter
Chairman
University of Notre Dame
Department of Physics
Notre Dame, IN 46556

MILLMAN, Sidney
Secretary
American Institute of Physics
335 East 45th Street
New York, NY 10017

MILLS, Roger E.
Assistant Vice President of
Academic Affairs
University of Louisville
Louisville, KY 40208

MITCHELL, George R.
Assoc. Professor of Physics
Purdue University
Dept. of Physics
Hammond, IN 46323

MOFFA, Philip
Research Associate
University of Maryland
Physics Department
College Park, MD 20742

MOORE, T. W.
Professor Physics/Chairman
Mount holyoke College
S. Hadley, MA 01075

MORRISSEY, Shaun P.
Grad Student
Carnegie-Mellon University
Physics Department
Pittsburgh, PA 15213

NEWTON, Victor J.
Dept. of Physics
Fairfield University
Fairfield, CT 06430

NYBORG, Wesley L.
Professor of Physics
University of Vermont
Burlington, VT 05401

O'SHEA, Donald C.
Associate Professor
Georgia Tech
School of Physics
Atlanta, GA 30332

PAYTON, Warren H.
Physicist
Naval Air Development Center
AETD-Magnetics Code 2022
Warminster, PA 18974

PEERY, Benjamin F.
Professor of Astronomy
Howard University
Washington, D.C. 20059

PERL, Martin L.
Professor of Physics
Stanford University
SLAC
Stanford, CA 94305

POMERANTZ, Martin A.
Director
Bartol Research Foundation
Whittier Place
Swarthmore, PA 19081

PORTER, Beverly Fearn
Sociologist-Director Manpower
AIP
1335 E 45th Street
New York, NY 10017

PREGGER, Fred T.
Chairman, Physics Department
Trenton State College
P. O. Box 940 Hillwood Lakes
Trenton, NJ 08625

PRIEST, Joseph
Professor
Miami University
35 Culler
Oxford, OH 45056

PRITCHARD, Dennis S.
Junior Physicist
U.S. Army Ballistic Res. Lab.
Aberdeen Proving Ground
Aberdeen, MD 21005

RANEY, William T.
Sr. Policy Analyst
OSTP
5942 Wilton Road
Alexandria, VA 22300

REIERSON, James D.
Computer Scientist
Computer Sciences Corp.
400 Army-Navy Drive
Arlington, VA 22202

RENERO, Ignacio A.
Professor, Facultad de Ciencias
National University of Mexico
Mexico City, Mexico 20, DF
Ciudad Universitaria

RESNICK, Robert
Professor of Physics
Rensselaer Polytechnic Institute
Science Center, R.P.I.
Troy, NY 12181

ROBERTSHAW, J. E.
Chairman, Physics Department
Providence College
River and Eaton Streets
Providence, RI 02918

ROSENBLUM, Bruce
Professor of Physics
UC at Santa Cruz
Physics Department
Santa Cruz, CA 95064

SALOMON, Stephen Neal
Task Leader
Office of State Programs
US Nuclear Reg. Comm.
Washington, D.C. 20555

SANDS, Richard
Professor of Physics
University of Michigan
1049 Randall Lab
Ann Arbor, MI 48109

SARTORI, Leo
Dept. of Physics
University of Nebraska
Behlen Lab of Physics
Lincoln, NE 68588

SCHETZINA, J. F.
Assoc. Professor
NC State University
316 Cox Hall
Raleigh, NC 27607

SCHILLINGER, E.
Chair, Physics Department
DE Paul University
1215 Fullerton Avenue
Chicago, IL 60614

SCHNEIDER, James
Chairman-Physics Department
University of Dayton
Physics Department
Dayton, OH 45469

SCHWARTZ, Brian B.
Senior Scientist
MIT
Cambridge, MA 02139

SCRIBNER, Richard
Manager, Special Programs
American Association for the
Advancement of Science
1776 Massachusetts Avenue, NW
Washington, D.C. 20036

SEIDEL, George
Professor
Brown University
Physics Department
Providence, RI 02912

SELTZER, Norman
Manpower Analyst, ERDA
1094 Larkspur Terrace
Rockville, MD 20850

SENATOR, Ted E.
Undergraduate Student
MIT
Room 26-506
Cambridge, MA 02139

SHAFFER, John C.
Chairman, Dept. of Physics
Northern Illinois University
Faraday Hall 214
DeKalb, .IL 60115

SHAPIRO, Maurice M.
Lab. for Cosmic Physics
NAV - Res Lab CODE 7020
Washington, D.C. 20375

SHEA, Dion W. J.
Director, SPS-ETTE
American Institute of Physics
Grad Physics Building, SUNY
Stony Brook, NY 11794

SHEAHEN, Tom
General Physical Scientist
National Bureau of Standards
Tech. A129 NBS
Washington, D.C. 20234

SHEPHERD, Stanley
Associate Professor
The Pennsylvania State Univ.
104 Davey Lab
University Park, PA 16802

SHIELDS, Rebecca
Student
Physics Department
Auburn University
Auburn, AL 36830

SHOAF, Mary L.
Deputy Executive Secretary
American Physical Society
335 E 45th Street
New York, NY 10017

SHWE, Hla
Dean, Faculty of Science
East Stroudsburg State College
East Stroudsburg, PA 18301

SHUGART, Cecil G.
Professor and Head
Northeast Louisiana Univ.
Physics Department
Monroe, LA 71209

SIMMONS, R. O.
Head, Dept. of Physics
University of Illinois
209 Physics Building
Urbana, IL 61801

SLACK, Lewis
Assoc. Director for Gen. Activities
American Institute of Physics
335 East 45th Street
New York, NY 10017

SMITH, B. L. R.
Professor
Columbia University
410 Riverside Drive, Apt. 92
New York, NY 10025

SMITH, James H.
Professor of Physics
University of Illinois
Department of Physics
Urbana, IL 61801

SMITH, Ronald J.
Grad Student
University of Minnesota
148 Physics Building
Minneapolis, MN 55455

SNEDEGAR, William H.
Professor of Physics
Clarion State College
Physics Department
Clarion, PA 16214

SPANGLER, John D.
Associate Professor of Physics
Kansas State University
Department of Physics
Manhattan, KS 66506

STAIB, Jon A.
Associate Professor
James Madison University
Harrisonburg, VA 22801

STEVENSON, James R.
Director, School of Physics
Georgia Institute of Technology
Atlanta, GA 30332

SYBERT, J. R.
Chairman, Physics Dept.
North Texas State University
Physics Department
Denton, TX 76203

TAMRES, David H.
Student
University of Michigan
1016 Lincoln Avenue
Ann Arbor, MI 48104

TEPLITZ, V. L.
Professor and Head
VPI and SC
Physics Department
Blacksburg, VA 24061

TUFT, Richard A.
Associate Professor of Physics
Worcester Ploytechnic Institute
Olin Hall of Physics
Worcester, MA 01609

UM, Gregory
Student
SUNY at Stoney Brook
8B-15 Ava Place
New York, NY 11432

VanVECHTEN, Deborah
Graduate Student
University of Maryland
Dept. of Physics
College Park, MD 20740

VASSELL, William C.
Ford Motor Company
Scientific Research Labs
Room 3036
Dearborn, MI 48121

VEHSE, William E.
Chairman, Physics Department
West Virginia University
244 Hodges Hall
Morgantown, WV 26506

WALSH, Walter
APS Committee for
Profession Concerns
Bell Labs
Murray Hill, NJ 07974

WEITZ, James R.
Physicist
Computer Sciences Corp.
8728 Copesville Road
Silver Spring, MD 20910

WETSTONE, David
Scientist
158 N. Beacon Street
Hartford, CT 06105

WINBOW, Graham
Physicist
Rutgers University
Serin Lab
New Brunswick, NJ 08854

WINGET, Don
Graduate Student
University of Rochester
420 Space Science Center
Rochester, NY 14627

WINTER, Robert M.
Dept. of Physics
Shippensburg State College
Shippensburg, PA 17257

WOODRUFF, Eugene R.
Student Assoc. Councilor Ret.
Juniata College
1700 Moore Street, Box 1343
Huntingdon, PA 16652

YAES, Robert J.
Medical Student
Memorial Univ. of Newfoundland
Valleyview 4B-407
St. John's, Newfoundland
Canada

ZAPOLSKY, Harold
Professor & Chairman
Rutgers University
Physics Department
New Brunswick, NJ 08903

ZUCKER, Sister Licianne
Department Chairman
Notre Dame College
4545 College Road
Cleveland, OH 44121

SUPPLEMENT REGISTRATION LIST

BROOKS, Harvey
Professor
Harvard University
46 Breuster Street
Cambridge, MA 02138

GOOD, Roland H.
Professor
The Pennsylvania State Univ.
103 Davey Lab
University Park, PA 16802

HERMAN, Roger
Professor
Penn State
217 Osmond Lab
University Park, PA 16802

HORWITZ, Paul
Principal Research Scientist
Avco Everett Research Lab.
2385 Revere Beach Parkway
Everett, MA 02149

RENNEX, Brian
Student
University of Maryland
Physics Department
College Park, MD 20742

SMITH, Philip M.
Asnt. Dir., Natural Resources
Office of Science & Tech. Policy
Executive Office of the President
Washington, D.C. 20500

THOMPSON, Michael D.
Student
SUNY at Albany
1400 Washington Avenue
Albany, NY 12222

VAJED-SAMII, Mina
Student
State University of NY
484 Yates Street
Albany, NY 12222

AIP Conference Proceedings

No.	Title	L. C. Number	ISBN
No. 1	Feedback and Dynamic Control of Plasmas (Princeton) 1970	70-141596	0-88318-100-2
No. 2	Particles and Fields - 1971 (Rochester)	71-184662	0-88318-101-0
No. 3	Thermal Expansion - 1971 (Corning)	72-76970	0-88318-102-9
No. 4	Superconductivity in d- and f-Band Metals (Rochester 1971)	74-18879	0-88318-103-7
No. 5	Magnetism and Magnetic Materials - 1971 (2 parts) (Chicago)	59-2468	0-88318-104-5
No. 6	Particle Physics (Irvine 1971)	72-81239	0-88318-105-3
No. 7	Exploring the History of Nuclear Physics (Brookline, 1967, 1969)	72-81883	0-88318-106-1
No. 8	Experimental Meson Spectroscopy - 1972 (Philadelphia)	72-88226	0-88318-107-X
No. 9	Cyclotrons - 1972 (Vancouver)	72-92798	0-88318-108-8
No. 10	Magnetism and Magnetic Materials - 1972 (2 parts) (Denver)	72-623469	0-88318-109-6
No. 11	Transport Phenomena - 1973 (Brown University Conference)	73-80682	0-88318-110-X
No. 12	Experiments on High Energy Particle Collisions - 1973 (Vanderbilt Conference)	73-81705	0-88318-111-8
No. 13	π-π Scattering - 1973 (Tallahassee Conference)	73-81704	0-88318-112-6
No. 14	Particles and Fields - 1973 (APS/DPF Berkeley)	73-91923	0-88318-113-4
No. 15	High Energy Collisions - 1973 (Stony Brook)	73-92324	0-88318-114-2
No. 16	Causality and Physical Theories (Wayne State University, 1973)	73-93420	0-88318-115-0
No. 17	Thermal Expansion - 1973 (Lake of the Ozarks)	73-94415	0-88318-116-9
No. 18	Magnetism and Magnetic Materials - 1973 (2 parts) (Boston)	59-2468	0-88318-117-7
No. 19	Physics and the Energy Problem - 1974 (APS Chicago)	73-94416	0-88318-118-5
No. 20	Tetrahedrally Bonded Amorphous Semiconductors (Yorktown Heights, 1974)	74-80145	0-88318-119-3
No. 21	Experimental Meson Spectroscopy - 1974 (Boston)	74-82628	0-88318-120-7

No. 22	Neutrinos - 1974 (Philadelphia)	74-82413	0-88318-121-5
No. 23	Particles and Fields - 1974 (APS/DPF Williamsburg)	74-27575	0-88318-122-3
No. 24	Magnetism and Magnetic Materials - 1974 (20th Annual Conference San Francisco)	75-2647	0-88318-123-1
No. 25	Efficient Use of Energy (The APS Studies on the Technical Aspects of the More Efficient Use of Energy)	75-18227	0-88318-124-X
No. 26	High-Energy Physics and Nuclear Structure - 1975 (Santa Fe and Los Alamos)	75-26411	0-88318-125-8
No. 27	Topics in Statistical Mechanics and Biophysics: A Memorial to Julius L. Jackson (Wayne State University-1975)	75-36309	0-88318-126-6
No. 28	Physics and Our World: A Symposium in Honor of Victor F. Weisskopf (M.I.T. 1974)	76-7207	0-88318-127-4
No. 29	Magnetism and Magnetic Materials - 1975 (21st Annual Conference, Philadelphia)	76-10931	0-88318-128-2
No. 30	Particle Searches and Discoveries - 1976 (Vanderbilt Conference)	76-19949	0-88318-129-0
No. 31	Structure and Excitations of Amorphous Solids (Williamsburg, Va., 1976)	76-22279	0-88318-130-4
No. 32	Materials Technology - 1975 (APS New York Meeting)	76-27967	0-88318-131-2
No. 33	Meson-Nuclear Physics - 1976 (Carnegie-Mellon Conference)	76-26811	0-88318-132-0
No. 34	Magnetism and Magnetic Materials - 1976 (Joint MMM-Intermag Conference, Pittsburgh)	76-47106	0-88318-133-9
No. 35	High Energy Physics with Polarized Beams and Targets (Argonne, 1976)	76-50181	0-88318-134-7
No. 36	Momentum Wave Functions - 1976 (Indiana University)	77-82145	0-88318-135-5
No. 37	Weak Interaction Physics - 1977 (Indiana University)	77-83344	0-88318-136-3
No. 38	Workshop on New Directions in Mössbauer Spectroscopy (Argonne, 1977)	77-90635	0-88318-137-1
No. 39	Physics Careers, Employment and Education (Penn State, 1977)	77-94053	0-88318-138-X